W9-AQM-601

Pigs for the
Ancestors

Ritual in the Ecology
of a New Guinea People

Second Edition

ROY A. RAPPAPORT

WAVELAND
PRESS, INC.
Prospect Heights, Illinois

For information about this book, write or call:
　　　Waveland Press, Inc.
　　　P.O. Box 400
　　　Prospect Heights, Illinois 60070
　　　847/634-0081

ISBN 1-57766-101-X

Printed in the United States of America

7　6　5　4　3　2　1

For

my parents
my wife
my children

About the Author
ROY ABRAHAM "SKIP" RAPPAPORT, Walgreen Professor for
the Study of Human Understanding, University of Michigan, a major
figure in the theory and practice of anthropology, died October 9,
1997, after a long battle with cancer. Having joined the Department
of Anthropology in 1965, he became its chairman for five years in
1975. He served as President of the American Anthropological
Association (1987-89).

Rappaport's dissertation became the first edition of *Pigs for the
Ancestors*, a landmark in ecological anthropology for its scrupulous
empirical research, innovative use of systems theory and interpretive
and heuristically powerful arguments about the role of religious ritual
in the adaptation and ecological regulation of certain kinds of communities. The second edition, reprinted here, deals with the extensive
responses to the book and tries to develop epistemological issues
involved in his approach.

CONTENTS

v

Epilogue, 1984

FOREWORD, 1968

Roy Rappaport's study of the functions of ritual among a primitive farming people is one of the first to be published on the ethnography of New Guinea's highland fringe. Here at the time of Rappaport's fieldwork were found what A. P. Elkin, in his 1961 review of urgent research needs, described as some of the few remaining "untouched" peoples in Australian New Guinea.[1] Further, as Elkin predicted and Rappaport now shows, cultural adaptation has taken somewhat different forms in the fringe than in the central core of the highlands. The book helps to fill major gaps in New Guinea ethnography.

Yet this is a book not just for New Guinea specialists. It should be of interest to anybody concerned with problems in functional analysis, human ecology, and the study of religion. Some remarks on certain of these problems in relation to Rappaport's study are in order here.

Functional analysis in the social sciences has been widely criticized in a number of ways. Among the most common criticisms are three that are appropriate for our consideration: (1) that functional analysis is inadequate for the explanation of the presence or origins of cultural traits and institutions; (2) that functional analysis is one-sided and almost "panglossian" in its focus on utility, harmony, integration, coherence, etc. in the status quo; and (3) that there can be no objective testing of hypotheses in functional analysis because of the lack of clear empirical import for crucial terms and concepts.

1. A. P. Elkin, 1961, Urgent research in Australian New Guinea and Papua. *Bulletin of the International Committee on Urgent Anthropological and Ethnological Research* 4, 17–25.

The first criticism is based on the recognition that more than one trait or institution may fulfill a specified function. It follows from this that demonstrating functions of particular traits cannot explain why they, rather than some functional alternatives, should be present or should have developed in a particular place or time.

The criticism is logically sound but it is also irrelevant if the object of analysis is, as for Rappaport, a demonstration of how things work rather than an explanation of why they exist or how they have come to be. In Rappaport's study, the presence of certain rituals in the cultural repertoire of the Maring people is simply accepted as given, and the problem is to show how these rituals operate in relation to various environmental processes and in relation to land use, warfare, food distribution, and other Maring activities. More precisely, the problem is to show the operation of negative feedback systems, i.e. to show how the rituals function to maintain a number of variables or activities in certain appropriate or advantageous states despite the action of disturbances tending to remove the variables or activities from those states.

Is there something "panglossian" about the choice of such a problem or is the second of the previously noted criticisms of functional analysis inapplicable? In the crude version which attributes to functional analysis Dr. Pangloss' view that all is necessarily for the best in this best of all possible worlds, the criticism certainly is inapplicable, for a concern with how extant systems operate by no means commits the analyst to the proposition that no other systems could operate better.

It nevertheless remains true that the functional analyst looks for order, coherence, equilibration, and the like rather than for their opposites, but the procedure is a defensible one on heuristic grounds. As Philip Leis has said, "The objective of revealing pattern where there seems to be only chaos or irrationality, even when pursued as an article of faith, is assuredly the most provocative and stimulating perspective to maintain." [2] And we may assume that evolutionary selection is working continually to produce pattern or order and to reduce disorder and that, accordingly, there is much order to be found, even if there is disorder too as a result, for example, of change

2. Philip E. Leis, 1965, The nonfunctional attributes of twin infanticide in the Niger delta. *Anthropological Quarterly*, 38:97–111.

in environmental conditions without the emergence of new patterns to meet them.

The preceding remarks may seem sufficient justification for a program of looking for functions, but there remains the problem of how one can know when one has found them. If our hypotheses about functions include key terms without clear empirical import, then the third of the previously noted criticisms is pertinent and the presence of hypothesized functions cannot very well be empirically validated or objectively tested for. This is so in the case of some classic statements in the literature of functionalism—for example, about the functions of various rites in reinforcing group identity or maintaining a continuity of social structure or meeting some purported needs which are never defined in any operational way. The inadequacies of such formulations have been convincingly exposed by Carl Hempel [3] and other critics.

These inadequacies are, however, not inherent in functional analysis. As Paul Collins, for example, has noted, a feasible procedure is to specify systems of operationally defined variables which are hypothesized to be maintaining some particular variables within determinable limits.[4] Part of the interest of Rappaport's study is that it constitutes a sustained attempt to isolate such systems and to validate hypotheses about their operation through the use of extensive quantitative data on the systemic variables. A way is being shown here for using empirical procedures in functional analysis. Even when Rappaport's data are insufficient for firm conclusions, the implication is not that data cannot be employed for testing the hypotheses but rather that more data need to be collected.

The fact that the systems dealt with by the indicated procedures are sets of selected variables and not the "whole" societies, cultures, or communities of traditional functional analysis is likely to invite criticism on the grounds of incompleteness. There is an easy answer to this: simply to admit that things are indeed being left out and at the same time to insist that they have to be if analysis is to proceed and to be rewarding, for the investigator can never deal meaningfully with all of the infinite number of variables confronting him and must

3. Carl Hempel, 1959. The logic of functional analysis, *Symposium on Sociological Theory*, L. Gross, ed.

4. Paul Collins, 1965, Functional analyses in the symposium "Man, culture, and animals," *Man, Culture and Animals*, Anthony Leeds and Andrew P. Vayda, eds.

therefore make a selection among them. There is, however, a further answer to be made, and this consists of noting that the analysis can become progressively comprehensive as more and more systems are dealt with and as their articulation with one another also is investigated. Biologists, in their study of feedback systems, have found that they can begin with analyses of simple components and then eventually incorporate the results of these analyses in large and comprehensive flow diagrams without impairing the validity of the original partial schemes.[5] The possibility that the same will be the case in the anthropological study of feedback systems is additional encouragement for proceeding the way that Rappaport has. As a matter of fact, he does have some things to say about the articulation of systems in which the Tsembaga local group of Maring people is involved, and the reader may find himself impressed more by how much is systematically included in Rappaport's analysis than by what is left out.

The interest of the study for human ecologists lies in large part in the data reported, i.e. data on the production and expenditure of calories, on the management of scarce protein resources, on techniques of conserving forest land, and on many other aspects of a particular nonindustrial people's adaptation to their environment. But interest for those concerned with problems in human ecology lies also in a methodological feature of the study: the inclusion of certain noncultural variables in the systems analyzed. Although there have been numerous pleas for treating cultural, environmental, and human biological variables as parts of one system, these pleas have been but little heeded by most social scientists.[6] Even among the relatively few contemporary social scientists who are especially concerned with the relation between cultural and noncultural phenomena, the prevailing tendency has been to define the cultural variables

5. H. Kalmus, 1966, Control hierarchies, *Regulation and Control in Living Systems*, H. Kalmus, ed.

6. Some recent examples of such pleas are: O. D. Duncan, 1961, From social system to ecosystem, *Sociological Inquiry*, 31:140–49; Clifford Geertz, 1963, *Agricultural Involution: The Process of Ecological Change in Indonesia*, ch. 1, Berkeley, University of California Press; D. R. Stoddart, 1965, Geography and the ecological approach: the ecosystem as a geographic principle and method, *Geography*, 50:242–51; Andrew P. Vayda, 1965, Anthropologists and ecological problems, *Man, Culture, and Animals*, Anthony Leeds and Andrew P. Vayda, eds., Washington, D.C., American Association for the Advancement of Science 78; and A. P. Vayda and R. A. Rappaport, in press, Ecology, cultural and non-cultural, *Introduction to Cultural Anthropology: Essays in the Scope and Methods of the Science of Man*, James A. Clifton, ed.

and the other ones as belonging to separate systems and then to ask about the influence of the systems upon one another.[7] In the case of many social scientists, the procedure seems to be an almost automatic one, consonant with the ingrained habit of seeing the inorganic, organic, and sociocultural as separate realms or levels of phenomena.

The alternative procedure exemplified by Rappaport's work is to make the assignment of variables to different systems depend upon either a demonstration or a testable hypothesis to the effect that the components of each system operate, at least at times, independently of the components of other systems. In other words, the discrimination of systems by this method is based on the knowledge or the expectation that the traits or variables regarded as components of any particular system do, in some way and at some times, affect one another more than they affect or are affected by extra-systemic traits or variables. The procedure has considerable heuristic value in that, as Rappaport's study illustrates, it directs attention to investigable questions about just how and when and to what degree are different traits or variables, whether cultural or noncultural, affected by one another. The same heuristic value clearly cannot obtain if it is taken as axiomatic that cultural variables belong only to strictly cultural systems.

Finally, it must be noted that Rappaport's emphasis on certain rituals as variables in the systems analyzed makes his work pertinent in the study of religion. Seeing rituals as being without practical effects on the external world has been, as Rappaport notes, a dominant view in this field of study. By elucidating the role of Maring rituals as counteracting responses to factors disturbing the people's relations with their environment, Rappaport effectively challenges this dominant view and points the way for fresh approaches in the study of religion.

Andrew P. Vayda

New York City, July, 1967

7. See, for example, Thomas G. Harding, 1960, Adaptation and stability, *Evolution and Culture*, Marshall D. Sahlins and Elman R. Service, eds., Ann Arbor, University of Michigan Press; and Marshall D. Sahlins, 1964, Culture and environment: the study of cultural ecology, *Horizons of Anthropology*, Sol Tax, ed., Chicago, Aldine.

PREFACE, 1968

The fieldwork that forms the basis of this study took place between October 1962 and December 1963 under a grant from the National Science Foundation to Columbia University. I also received personal support from the National Institutes of Health in the form of a pre-doctoral fellowship.

Professor Andrew P. Vayda, of the Department of Anthropology, Columbia University, was principal investigator. In addition, the expedition consisted of Professor Vayda's wife, Cherry Vayda, Allison Jablonko, also of the Columbia University Department of Anthropology, and her husband, Marek Jablonko, and my wife, Ann, and myself. Research among the Maring people has been continued under related grants by the geographers William Clarke, of the University of California, and John Street, of the University of Hawaii, by the Vaydas, who made a second visit to New Guinea in 1966, and by Georgeda Bick, of the Department of Anthropology, Columbia University. I wish to thank all of these workers both for their suggestions concerning interpretation and for the factual contributions they have made to this study.

The list of those who have offered help and encouragement before, during, and after the period of field work is long. On the way to the field E. H. Hipsley, of the Commonwealth Department of Health, Ross Robbins, of the Australian National University, and Jacques Barrau, then of the South Pacific Commission, offered invaluable advice and suggestions. John Womersley, director of the Department of Forests Herbarium at Lae identified all plant specimens, and Joseph Szent-Ivany, government entomologist, Port Moresby, took

responsibility for the identification of insects. Hugh Popenoe, director
of the Department of Soils, University of Florida, analyzed the soil
specimens that survived the year-long trip to his laboratory. To these
specialists I wish to express not only for myself, but for the others
as well, our deepest appreciation.

Our life and work in the field were made easier and pleasanter
through the kindness of many residents of the Trust Territory of
New Guinea. R. McCormac, District Agricultural Officer, Madang,
was particularly generous in providing us with personnel and equipment and in assisting us with some of our logistic problems. The
personnel of both the Lutheran Mission Hospital at Yagaum and the
Government Hospital at Madang acquainted us with prevalent local
diseases and initiated us into such mysteries as the use of the hypo-
dermic needle, and the Government Hospital also provided us with
medical supplies.

To the staff of the Anglican Mission at Simbai we are deeply
grateful not only for their assistance in overseeing our supplies and
arranging for them and our mail to be sent out to us, but also for
their warm hospitality on our visits to Simbai. We also wish to
acknowledge with gratitude the cooperation and hospitality of Alan
Johnson and Gavin Carter, the officers in charge at the Simbai Patrol
Post during our stay in their area.

Several people, during visits to our field location, opened our eyes
to phenomena previously unnoticed or not assigned their proper significance. The visit of Douglas Yen was a turning point in my study
of horticulture, and Ralph Bulmer made tentative identifications of
a large part of the avifauna.

Many members of the Department of Anthropology of Columbia
University, both students and faculty, have listened to me patiently
while this study was being written and have offered valuable comments. I am particularly indebted to Morton Fried, Marvin Harris,
Margaret Mead, and Andrew P. Vayda.

Others who have offered valuable help and suggestions include
Alexander Alland, Jacques Barrau, Elizabeth Brown, Ralph Bulmer,
Marshall Childs, William Clarke, Paul Collins, Harold Conklin,
Gregory Dexter, Fred Dunn, C. G. King, W. V. Macfarland, M. J.
Meggitt, George Morren, Ernest Nagel, Jane Olson, David Osborne,
John Sabine, Marshall Sahlins, Harold Scheffler, John Street,

Marjorie Whiting, and Aram Yengoyan. It is to Collins that I owe many of the notions concerning functional systems that are explicit or implicit in this study. Barrau, Clarke, Street, and Whiting have been particularly generous with comments, assistance, and suggestions, all of which have been appreciated although not all accepted. I personally must accept full responsibility for the shortcomings of this study.

I would like finally to express my gratitude to many Maring and Narak friends and informants.

Roy A. Rappaport

PREFACE, 1984

This new edition of *Pigs for the Ancestors,* with its extensive epilogue, addresses the voluminous discussion that the original book has provoked. Regarding the often correct criticisms, I might have contented myself with the thought that books may sometimes be more valuable for their mistakes, for their limitations, and for the thoughtful disagreements that they excite than for their achievements. Yet, in reviewing the controversy, I have felt moved to address issues beyond this single book, for I have been struck by the wastefulness of our discipline. We are ever moving on to new approaches without having assimilated the lessons of older ones. We are, I think, inclined to claim too much for new "paradigms," to expect too much of them, and then, perhaps as a consequence of our disappointment, or, possibly, in antagonistic reaction to the excessive nature of the early claims of enthusiasts, to discard them before their possibilities have been adequately explored. We are inclined to dismiss rather than modify or correct for reasons that seem to me insufficient or even wrong. And so we continue to move without advancing, without having learned all we could, or should, or need to, from our experience, our knowledge, and our mistakes. Clarity of thought is discouraged, moreover, by the polemical nature of much of our criticism—simplifying, parodying, and even misrepresenting that which it opposes, exaggerating its weaknesses, ignoring its virtues.

In reading critiques of *Pigs for the Ancestors* with which I could not agree, I came to realize that, if full use were to be made of its shortcomings as well as its virtues some misunderstandings would have to be set straight. Moreover, criticism of the book had raised larger problems of anthropological theory and method, issues which warranted further discussion. I came to feel that my responsibility with respect to *Pigs for the Ancestors* had not been fully discharged by its original publication. Readers of this new edition will therefore find in my "Epilogue, 1984" a supplement of considerable length, in which my aim has been to write something more than a rejoinder to critics. I would like to express my deep thanks to Keith Hart, Emilio Moran, and Aram Yengoyan for reading this supplement and offering valuable suggestions for its improvement, and to Ellen Graham and Elizabeth Casey for shepherding it through production at Yale University Press.

R. A. R.

October 1983
Ann Arbor, Michigan

NOTE ON MARING ORTHOGRAPHY

Since it is assumed that the reader's primary interest is not linguistic, the orthography employed in this study is not phonemic. It is, rather, a "broad transcription" of Maring speech, and signs representing specific sounds have been selected as much for their familiarity to the English speaker as for their phonetic accuracy. The letters used in the Maring terms have English values with the following exceptions and limitations:

a as in f*a*ther
i as in m*i*ss or m*ee*t
e as in *e*rror or m*ay*
o as in b*o*ne
u as in B*u*ddha
oe as in French *oeu*f
ü as in German *ü*ber
ñ as in Spanish ma*ñ*ana
ŋ as in si*ng*
č as in *ch*urch
r is pronounced with a quick flap of the tongue tip similar to the Spanish r
initial b, d, and g have slight prenasalization (ᵐb, ⁿd, ᵤg)

Although the area occupied by the Maring speakers is not large, there are differences among the local groups in both the rendition of some phonemes and in some items of vocabulary. The pronunciation and terms included in this study should be understood to represent the speech of the people among whom we lived, principally the

Tsembaga, and not necessarily the speech of the entire Maring population.

It was only in the last few months of fieldwork that my command of Maring was sufficient to serve as an ethnographic tool, and in the earlier stages of fieldwork, especially, I relied upon pidgin English (hereafter referred to as "p.e."). The use of pidgin required interpreters, since no Tsembaga could speak that language. Two interpreters were used alternately, and, in matters in which ambiguity was present or error or misunderstanding suspected, the information obtained through one was checked with the other.

CHAPTER 1

Ritual, Ecology, and Systems

Many functional studies of religious behavior have had as an analytic goal the elucidation of events, processes, or relationships occurring *within* a social group of some sort. Works of Chapple and Coon (1942:507), Durkheim (1912), Gluckman (1952), Malinowski (1948), and Radcliffe-Brown (1952) may be cited as examples.

While the scope of the social unit is frequently not made explicit, it would seem that in some studies it is what Durkheim called a "church," that is, "a society whose members are united by the fact that they think in the same way in regard to the sacred world and its relations with the profane world, and by the fact that they translate these common ideas into common practices" (Durkheim, 1961: 59). Frequently, however, it is a smaller and more bounded group that provides the context within which the role of ritual in relation to other aspects of culture is studied. Such units, composed of aggregates of individuals who regard their collective well-being to be dependent upon a common body of ritual performances, might be called "congregations." In many small-scale societies the congregation is coterminous with the local group. Such is the case in this study of the Tsembaga, a group of shifting horticulturalists living in the Bismarck Mountains of New Guinea.

This study differs from those mentioned above, however, in that its main concern is not with the part ritual plays in relationships occurring within a congregation. It is concerned, rather, with how ritual affects relationships between a congregation and entities *external* to it.

Maring rituals are conventionalized acts directed toward the in-

1

volvement of nonempirical (supernatural) agencies in human affairs.[1] Although suggestions have been made by a number of writers
concerning the possible role of ritual in the adjustment of social
groups to their environments,[2] this problem has not engaged the attention of many students of either religion or human ecology. Some
writers, interpreting what appear to be economically wasteful practices, have taken the view that ritual frequently interferes with the
efficient exploitation of the environment.[3] Others have tacitly assumed that the empirical relations of the congregation to its environment remain unaffected by ritual performances.

Indeed, one of the important functionalist theories of religion is
based upon such an assumption of empirical independence between
ritual and the world external to the congregation. It asserts that
since men are unable to control many of the events and processes
in their environments that are of crucial importance to them, they
experience a feeling of helplessness. This helplessness produces anxiety, fear, and insecurity. The performance of rituals suppresses
anxiety, dispels fear, and provides a sense of security. A statement
by George Homans summarizes this line of thought nicely:

> Ritual actions do not produce a practical result on the ex-
> ternal world—that is one of the reasons why we call them
> ritual. But to make this statement is not to say that ritual
> has no function. Its function is not related to the world ex-
> ternal to the society, but to the internal constitution of the
> society. It gives the members confidence, it dispels their
> anxieties, it disciplines their social organization. [1941:172]

No arguments will be raised here against the psychological or sociological functions that Homans and others have imputed to ritual.

1.   This statement is merely descriptive. It does not purport to be a definition of
Maring ritual, much less ritual in general.
2.   Among those who have made such suggestions are Brown and Brookfield
(1958, 1963), Cook (1946), Firth (1929, 1950), Freeman (1955), Izikowitz (1951),
Moore (1957), Stott (1962), and Vayda, Leeds, and Smith (1961). Concern here
is with ritual, rather than taboo, which may be described as the supernaturally supported proscription of physically feasible behavior. It may be mentioned, however,
that a number of writers have noted the possible role of taboos in the conservation
of resources, and a recent paper by Harris (1965) has elucidated the critical role of
the taboo against the consumption of beef in the human ecology of India.
3.   See, for example, Luzbetak (1954:113) concerning waste at a New Guinea pig
festival.

But it will be argued that in some instances ritual actions *do* produce a "practical result on the external world." In some instances the "function" of ritual *is* related to the "world external to the society." Among the Tsembaga, ritual not only expresses symbolically the relationships of a congregation to components of its environment but also enters into these relationships in empirically measurable ways.

To state simply that a people's ritual actions may measurably affect components of their environment is of course to state the obvious, if not the trivial. If, to perform a ritual, a man cuts down a tree, the environment is affected. If ritual requires that large numbers of visitors be entertained at prolonged and lavish feasts, extra-large gardens will be planted, or more wild animals than usual will be killed, or particularly large quantities of wild vegetables will be collected. All of these are actions that by any definition of environment affect the environment.

But it is not the obvious effects of isolated ritual requirements that are the central concern here. The interest, rather, is in the ways in which ritual mediates critical relationships between a congregation and entities external to it. Among the Tsembaga, and other Maring-speaking groups in New Guinea, through ritual the following are effected:

1. Relationships between people, pigs, and gardens are regulated. This regulation operates directly to protect people from the possible parasitism and competition of their pigs and indirectly to protect the environment by helping to maintain extensive areas in virgin forest and assuring adequate cultivation-fallow ratios in secondary forest.
2. The slaughter, distribution, and consumption of pig is regulated and enhances the value of pork in the diet.
3. The consumption of nondomesticated animals is regulated in a way that tends to enhance their value to the population as a whole.
4. The marsupial fauna may be conserved.
5. The redispersal of people over land and the redistribution of land among territorial groups is accomplished.
6. The frequency of warfare is regulated.

7. The severity of intergroup fighting is mitigated.
8. The exchange of goods and personnel between local groups is facilitated.

Ritual will be regarded here as a mechanism, or set of mechanisms, that regulates some of the relationships of the Tsembaga with components of their environment. The terms *regulate* or *regulation* imply a system; a system is any set of specified variables in which a change in the value of one of the variables will result in a change in the value of at least one other variable. A regulating mechanism is one that maintains the values of one or more variables within a range or ranges that permit the continued existence of the system.

It should be emphasized that neither the Tsembaga nor any of the actual components of their environment are themselves variables. As Hagen (1962:506) has put it, "A variable is a single dimension of an entity, not the entity itself." The size of the Tsembaga population, for instance, but not the Tsembaga themselves might be regarded as a variable. The amount of land in cultivation, expressed in acres, might be designated a variable, but the gardens themselves could not be.

The systemic relationships described in this study are more than regulated; they are self-regulated. The term *self-regulation* may be applied to systems in which a change in the value of a variable itself initiates a process that either limits further change or returns the value to a former level. This process, sometimes referred to as "negative feedback," may involve special mechanisms that change the values of some variables in response to changes in the values of others. Thermostats, for instance, may be regarded as mechanical regulating mechanisms in systems in which measurable quantities of heat emanating intermittently from a controlled source and the temperature of a surrounding medium are variables. It will be argued here that Tsembaga ritual, particularly in the context of a ritual cycle, operates as a regulating mechanism in a system, or set of interlocking systems, in which such variables as the area of available land, necessary lengths of fallow periods, size and composition of both human and pig populations, trophic requirements of pigs and people, energy expended in various activities, and the frequency of misfortunes are included. There are numerous additional variables to be considered as well. While it has not been possible in all cases, numerical values have been assigned to most of the variables on the basis of measurements performed in the field.

As Collins (1965:281) has pointed out, "Functional analysis makes no prescription concerning the nature of the variables . . . constituting the system." The selection of variables is a product of hypotheses concerning possible interrelations among the phenomena under investigation, and these, in turn, flow from the interests and theoretical conceptions of the analyst. The hypotheses that have led to the selection of variables in this study have already been stated in the form of a number of propositions concerning the role of ritual in the adjustment of the Tsembaga to their environment. Underlying these hypotheses is the belief that much is to be gained by regarding culture, in some of its aspects, as part of the means by which animals of the human species maintain themselves in their environments. There should be no conceptual difficulty in treating culture much as one would the behavior of other animals. As the sociologist Hawley pointed out over twenty years ago:

> Culture is nothing more than a way of referring to the prevailing techniques by which a [human] population maintains itself in its habitat. The component parts of human culture are therefore identical in principle with the appetency of the bee for honey, the nest-building activities of birds, and the hunting habits of carnivora. To argue that the latter are instinctive while the former are not is to beg the question. Ecology is concerned less now with how habits are acquired, than with the functions they serve and the relationships they involve. [1944:404]

Hawley's statement has important methodological and theoretical implications for cultural anthropology, and Vayda and I (Vayda and Rappaport, in press) have noted some of these as follows:

> Consistent with usage in [general] ecology, the focus of anthropologists engaged in ecological studies can be upon human populations and upon ecosystems and biotic communities in which human populations are included. To have units fitting into the ecologists' frame of reference is a procedure with clear advantages. Human populations as units are commensurable with the other units with which

they interact to form food webs, biotic communities and ecosystems. Their capture of energy from and exchanges of material with these other units can be measured and then described in quantitative terms. No such advantage of commensurability obtains if cultures are made the units, for cultures, unlike human populations, are not fed upon by predators, limited by food supplies, or debilitated by disease.

The adoption of populations and ecosystems as units of analysis, it should be stressed, does not require any sacrifice of anthropology's primary goal of elucidating cultural phenomena. Quite to the contrary, such a procedure can make important contributions to the attainment of that goal. A population may be defined as an aggregate of organisms that have in common certain distinctive means for maintaining a set of material relations with the other components of the ecosystem in which they are included. The cultures of human populations, like the behavior characteristic of populations of other species, can be regarded, in some of their aspects, at least, as part of the "distinctive means" employed by the populations in their struggles for survival. It has been suggested by the biologist G. G. Simpson (1962:106) that the study of cultural phenomena within such a general ecological framework may provide additional insights into culture, "for instance, in its adaptive aspects and consequent interaction with natural selection."

The lead suggested by Hawley and Simpson has been followed in this study. The Tsembaga are regarded here as an ecological population in an ecosystem that also includes the other living organisms and the nonliving substances found within the boundaries of Tsembaga territory. The rituals upon which this study focuses are interpreted as part of the distinctive means by which a population, the Tsembaga, relates to the other components of its ecosystem and to other local human populations that occupy areas outside the boundaries of Tsembaga territory.

It should be made explicit perhaps that the operation of ritual as a regulating mechanism is not necessarily understood by the Tsembaga. In the language of sociology, regulation is a "latent function" (Merton, 1949:19ff) of Tsembaga ritual. The Tsembaga themselves see the purposes of the rituals as having to do, rather, with the relations of people to various spirits—for the most part, those of deceased ancestors. The rituals with which this study is concerned are conceived by the Tsembaga to maintain or transmute their relationships with these nonempirical entities. It would be possible to elucidate the regulatory functions of Tsembaga ritual without reference to Tsembaga conceptions, but it is reasonable to regard the conceptions of a people as part of the mechanism that induces their behavior. Native views of the rituals will therefore be included in this study. The inclusion of native views in a description of ecological relations, moreover, permits us to ask some important questions concerning ideology. We may, for example, ask whether or not actions undertaken in reference to understandings that are not empirically valid are, nevertheless, appropriate to the actual situation in which the actors find themselves.

CHAPTER 2

The Tsembaga

THE PEOPLE, THEIR LOCATION, AND THEIR LINGUISTIC RELATIONSHIPS

The Tsembaga are a group of about 200 Maring-speaking people living in the Madang District of the Australian-administered Territory of New Guinea. The name *Tsembaga* as a designation for this cluster of clans is recent, having been first used in this way by a government patrol officer in 1960. Previously Tsembaga had denominated only one of the constituent clans; the cluster as a whole was unnamed. Since 1960, however, the use of Tsembaga to designate the entire local group has not only become enshrined in the census book and on maps, but has been taken up by the people themselves.

The Tsembaga occupy an area of slightly more than three square miles at approximately 5° south latitude, 145° east longitude on the south wall of the Simbai Valley, which separates, in this region, the Bismarck Range to the south and a spur of the Schrader Range to the north. The land is very mountainous, rising within the confines of the small Tsembaga territory from 2,200' at the river to 7,200' at the top of the Bismarck ridge, and is, for the most part, heavily forested. Most of the area above 5,000' shows no signs of ever having been cut, while at lower altitudes, secondary forest prevails, although some small remnants of primary forest and a few patches of grassland are to be found.

The amount of contact with Europeans to which the Tsembaga had been exposed at the time of fieldwork (October 1962 to December 1963) was slight. The first patrol of the Australian government to enter the area crossed their territory in 1954, but a second did

8

not appear for several years. The Simbai Valley was pacified in 1958,[1] but the government did not officially regard the area as controlled until 1962. A *luluai* (headman) and a *tultul* (assistant headman) were appointed by the Australian government in 1959, and a second *tultul* was appointed in 1961. However, in 1963 the prerogatives of these government headmen generally remained restricted to dealings with the government. Both those who held the titles and the people at large regarded these offices as largely irrelevant to internal affairs.

At the time of fieldwork only two young Tsembaga men had gone out of the Maring area as indentured laborers, and they had not yet returned.[2] Although the Anglican mission had maintained stations with two other Simbai Valley groups for some years, the Tsembaga remained unmissionized and their religious beliefs and practices included no apparent European elements. No Tsembaga spoke pidgin English, and only a few of the younger men had ever visited the government patrol post, established in 1959 at the headwaters of the Simbai River about 25 miles away by trail, until our arrival.

Indirect contact began, of course, much earlier. The first steel tools came to the Tsembaga in the late 1940s, and by the early 1950s stone implements had been completely replaced. Epidemics, probably of European origin, also entered the area long before white men. A dysentery epidemic, bearing the pidgin name *sikman*, killed a large number of people in the early 1940s, and there is evidence of measles several years later.

Cargo cult also came to the Tsembaga long before white men. In the early 1940s, news of impending flood, earthquake, and ancestral return came to them from the north, along with accounts of unfamiliar treasures that they might receive. Although they followed instructions, building special houses and so on, the ancestors did not return bearing gifts amidst flood and earthquake, and the disillusioned Tsembaga have remained more or less impervious to cargo cult talk ever since.

In sum, while the arrival of Europeans and European commodities have produced important changes, particularly through the in-

1. Since our departure from the field in December 1963 some small-scale, short-lived armed altercations are reported to have occurred among Simbai Valley Maring.
2. Fifteen young Tsembaga men are reported to have been recruited on two-year labor contracts early in 1964.

troduction of steel tools and the suppression of warfare, the degree to which the adaptation of the Tsembaga to their immediate environment has been affected is limited. Steel tools and a few new crops, such as maize and certain varieties of sweet potatoes, have without doubt affected agricultural production, but the Tsembaga remain subsistence gardeners, making gardens in accordance with patterns that prevailed when there was no maize and when they had only stone tools with which to work.

The Tsembaga are one of more than twenty similar local groups of Maring-speaking people occupying territories in the middle Simbai and Jimi Valleys. The size of these groups ranges from a little over 100 to 900 persons, and in all there are about 7,000 Maring (or, as the language is occasionally and somewhat mysteriously labeled on linguistic maps, Yoadabe-Watoare) speakers. Wurm (1964:79) classifies Maring as a member of the Jimi subfamily of the Central Family of the East New Guinea Highlands Stock, which includes most of the languages of the East New Guinea Highlands (Micro) Phylum. The Maring area is the most northerly of those occupied by speakers of Central Family languages; the land to the north and west of the Maring is held by speakers of Karam and Gants, languages only distantly related to the East New Guinea Highland Stock.

The Central Family, which includes at least fourteen languages with a total of 286,000 speakers (Wurm, 1964:79), occupies a large area in the Eastern, Western, and Southern Highlands districts. This geographical distribution suggests that the ancestors of the Tsembaga and other Maring entered the general area that they presently occupy from the south. The presence of extensive tracts of unoccupied virgin forest to the north and east of the easternmost Maring groups supports this view. Tsembaga tradition, moreover, places the origins of four of its five constituent clans in the Jimi Valley in the third or fourth generation ascending from men who were middle-aged in 1962 and 1963. Tsembaga tradition is unreliable as history, but recent arrival in their present location is also suggested by such negative evidence as the lack of any clear signs that the environment has been degraded, and such positive evidence as the large size of the trees composing the secondary forest in which gardens are cut, and the reports of many older informants, who state that extensive tracts of primary forest existed in the lower altitudes until forty or fifty years prior to fieldwork.

Details of Tsembaga subsistence procedures will be discussed in the next chapter, and in later chapters the relationship of ritual to subsistence practices and other aspects of the Tsembaga adaptation will be analyzed. It may be helpful to mention here, however, that the Tsembaga and other Maring are bush-fallowing, or swidden, horticulturalists, planting their gardens in secondary forest. Their starch staples include taro, yam, sweet potato, manioc, and bananas, but they also enjoy a large number of other crops, including sugar cane, many greens, and the fruit of the *Pandanus conoideus* (p.e.: *marita*). Pig husbandry is also important. Hunting, trapping, and gathering also play a part in Tsembaga subsistence; feral pig, cassowary, and birds are the most important quarry taken in hunting, and marsupials are the animals most frequently caught in traps. The yields of gathering include not only some vegetable foods, notably edible ferns, but also timber, animal and vegetable fibers used for clothing, vines used as rope, and leaves, fruits, and earths used as dyes.

The technology of the Tsembaga is simple. Only the digging stick, the steel ax, and the bushknife are used in gardening. Bows and arrows are used in hunting, and also form, along with spears, axes, and wooden shields, the technology of warfare. Traps include snares, deadfalls, and pits. Gourds and bamboo tubes are used as containers, and bamboo tubes occasionally serve as cooking vessels also. Aside from these there are no others; most food is prepared directly on the fire or in an earth oven. Net bags, loin cloths, caps, and string aprons are woven from a variety of fibers; intricately woven waist and arm bands are made from orchid stems, and some bark cloth is made. Prior to the establishment of the patrol posts in the Jimi and Simbai Valleys in 1956 and 1959 respectively the Tsembaga manufactured salt by boiling water obtained from mineral springs. Much of their salt production in earlier times was traded south over the mountain in exchange for stone ax blades, which were quarried, shaped, and polished in the Jimi Valley.

Men and women live in separate houses. During 1962 and 1963 the men's houses, which accommodate males above the age of seven or eight, ranged in number of occupants from two to fourteen. Each

married woman and widow has a separate house, where she resides
with her unmarried daughters, small sons, and pigs. Most cooking
takes place at the women's houses. Although the interior arrangements of men's and women's houses are somewhat different, their
size and construction is similar. Both are framed in light timber,
with roofs and walls thatched with *pandanus* leaves. The dimensions
of men's houses range from 7'x20' to 10'x35', with a height at the
ridge pole of 4½' to 6'. Women's houses are of comparable length
and breadth, but on the average they are lower than the men's. A
portion of the interior of a woman's house, however, is devoted to
the shelter of pigs, each of which is accommodated in a separate
stall with its own entrance from the outside.

DEMOGRAPHY AND PHYSIQUE

Both the subsistence procedures and trophic requirements of the
Tsembaga will be assessed in the next chapter and an attempt will
be made to estimate the maximum number of people who may
pursue their subsistence activities on Tsembaga territory. Among the
biological characteristics of the Tsembaga population that are germane to these and other assessments and estimates to be made later
are: (1) the total number of individuals included in the population,
(2) the age and sex composition of the population, and (3) the
average body sizes of the constituent individuals. Information concerning Tsembaga demography and ontogeny can only be outlined
here. Discussions of underlying factors will be published elsewhere
by other workers.

Population Size

Between October 1962 and December 1963, the local population
of the Tsembaga territory varied from 196 to 204 persons (the larger
figure will be used in later computations).

There is considerable evidence to indicate that the population had
been considerably larger before the period of fieldwork. For one
thing, about twenty-five Tsembaga were living sororilocally, uxorilocally, or matrilocally with other local groups in 1963. These people,
or their parents, had lived on Tsembaga territory until military defeat in 1953 forced the Tsembaga to flee. Most Tsembaga had returned to their own territory by 1963, but these twenty-five still

remained elsewhere. Informants agree, further, that in earlier times there were many more people, and genealogies bear them out. They blame disease for much of the population decrease, although they admit that many were also killed in fighting. The early years of contact are especially dangerous to groups such as the Tsembaga, for they are exposed to new causes of death, particularly disease, before the old ones, especially warfare, are suppressed.

Considering the number of Tsembaga presently residing elsewhere, and considering the consensus among informants and the support given to such consensus by genealogies, a population size of 250 to 300 persons in the 1920s and 30s is not unlikely.

Population Structure

The age-sex composition of the Tsembaga population is presented in Table 1. Some of the characteristics of Tsembaga population structure, particularly the imbalance of males and females in the younger categories, and the change in the male-female ratio at estimated age twenty-five, require comment.

The Tsembaga, who are happy to admit that they kill one or both of twins, unanimously deny practicing female infanticide. They themselves point to the economic importance of women and suggest that the killing of female infants would be foolish. The reversal of the usual ratio in the estimated five- to ten-year-old category lends support to their protestations.

It is not possible to arrive at any explanation here. Data are insufficient to say with any certainty whether the disparity is a result of differential frequencies in male and female births, or differences in the rate of survival of males and females, or both. Data are sufficient to indicate, however, that a deficiency of females, although especially marked among the Tsembaga, is not peculiar to them. A. P. Vayda's census figures indicate totals of 3,722 males and 3,420 females among the Maring and only one local population where females outnumber males. Nor is such a disparity peculiar to the Maring. An excess of males exists among the people of the Tor District in West Irian. As is the case among the Tsembaga, the imbalance between the sexes is most marked in the younger categories, and Oosterwal (1961:37f) attributes it to a greater frequency of male births.

Table 1. The Structure of Tsembaga Population, November 1963 (total 204)

It must be noted that the sex imbalance exists despite the fact that among the Tsembaga, at least, males suffered heavier losses in warfare than females. The change in the Tsembaga male-female ratio at estimated age twenty-five is quite clearly an effect of differences in casualty rates.

Body Size

The Tsembaga are very small in stature. The average height of forty-nine adult females was 54.3″, the range being 51.75″ to 57.75″. Their average weight was 84.4 pounds, with a range of 75 to 100 pounds. The average weight of fifty-nine adult males was 102.6 pounds. Their weights ranged from 87 to 140 pounds.

Since many young men wear their hair in massive coiffures hardened with grease extracted from the fruit of the *Marita pandanus*, I could only guess at the location of the top of the skull. The average of the heights recorded for adult males, 58.1″, must therefore be regarded as an approximation. The extremes, however, 53.25″ and 62.5″, are represented by men whose hair was cut short. To what extent Tsembaga stature is an expression of genetic constitution, and to what extent it is a function of dietary deficiency, parasite infestation, and other pathology remains to be determined through future research.

POPULATION DISPERSION AND SOCIAL ORGANIZATION

Although a quantity of a necessary resource, such as arable land, sufficient to meet the trophic requirements of all the Tsembaga exists within the borders of their territory, this does not necessarily indicate that each Tsembaga has enough to meet his needs. Many societies are characterized by differentials in access to resources between individuals or between groups. In some societies this is a concomitant of social stratification. In others it may be the result of differences in the demographic fortunes of land-holding descent groups. It is therefore necessary to describe the social means by which the Tsembaga are dispersed over their territory in subsistence activities.

The Tsembaga form a single territorial unit as far as defense is concerned, and all Tsembaga may hunt, trap, and gather in any part of the territory. These rights in nondomesticated resources are exclusive. That is, members of other local groups do not enjoy rights in nondomesticated resources to be found on Tsembaga territory, and, conversely, the Tsembaga do not have such rights on the territories of other groups.

Although the entire territory is open to the hunting and gathering activities of all Tsembaga, it is divided into "subterritories," smaller areas claimed by less inclusive groups. Membership in these smaller groups is particularly important in reference to rights in garden land.

The Tsembaga are organized into five putatively patrilineal clans (*kai:* root; or *yu kai:* root of men): Merkai, Tomegai, Tsembaga, Kwibigai, and Kamuŋgagai, which ranged in resident membership from fifteen to seventy-eight persons, including in-married wives in 1963. These clans are the most inclusive units claiming a common ancestry, but such ancestry can be demonstrated only in the case of the small Kwibigai clan (twenty-one members), all of whose members are descended from an immigrant who arrived among the Tsembaga in the late nineteenth century.

The two smallest clans, Tomegai (fifteen members) and Kwibigai, are unsegmented, but the three largest clans, Kamuŋgagai, Tsembaga, and Merkai, are each divided into three smaller segments, or subclans, also termed *kai* or *yu kai*, ranging in resident membership from seven to thirty-seven persons. Subclan men claim descent from an ancestor less remote than the common clan ancestor, but this descent cannot be demonstrated in all cases. Subclans are also named, and in the cases of all three segmented clans the subclans bore the same names: *Wendekai, Amangai,* and *Atigai* (*Wend:* oldest; *Amang:* middle; *Ati:* youngest).

Ideally, it is a clan that should claim a subterritory, for the Tsembaga, like other Maring, associate territory with agnation. But although Tsembaga is composed of five clans, the subterritorial division of Tsembaga territory is only tripartite. The main portion of the territory is divided into three adjacent strips running from ridge top to the Simbai River, with the Kamuŋgagai claiming the western strip, the Merkai the eastern, and the Tsembaga, Kwibigai, and Tomegai clans jointly claiming the central subterritory.

Although marriage rules stipulate clan exogamy, exogamy in fact seems to correlate more closely with subterritoriality. The Tsembaga, Tomegai, and Kwibigai clans, which share a common subterritory, are antigamous in reference to each other, and in the past marriages between members of separate subclans within the Merkai clan were contracted. I believe that these intraclan marriages took place in conjunction with a process of clan fission and perhaps subterritorial separation, a process that was subsequently reversed (as will be discussed later).

While the three subterritorial groups seem to be exogamous, the Tsembaga as a whole are not. Indeed, there is an explicit and statistical preference for marriage to women of proximate origin. Of the fifty wives and widows residing on Tsembaga territory in 1963, 44% were Tsembaga in origin, and an additional 22% came from the Tuguma immediately to the east. The remaining 34% came from nine other local groups, in most cases occupying territories across the river or over the mountain.

Subterritoriality is expressed ritually. Claims to subterritories are ratified on certain occasions by planting on them small trees or bushes called *"yu miñ rumbim"* (*yu miñ:* men's "souls"; *rumbim: Cordyline fruticosa* (L.), A. Chev.; *Cordyline terminalis,* Kunth; p.e.: *tanket*). Every adult male member of the subterritorial group participates in this ritual by grasping the *rumbim* as it is planted, thus symbolizing both his connection to the land and his membership in the group that claims the land.

The rituals surrounding the *rumbim* provide an additional criterion for distinguishing the Tsembaga from adjacent groups, for the planting, and later the uprooting of *rumbim* by the three Tsembaga subterritorial groups, and these three groups only, are synchronized, usually taking place on the same day. Moreover, all Tsembaga join together for subsequent rituals. It is on the basis of their coordination of some of these rituals and their joint and exclusive participation in others that we may distinguish the Tsembaga as a single congregation distinct from all others.

Subterritories are subdivided into smaller areas claimed by smaller putatively patrilineal units, either clans or subclans. Each of these groups holds a number of noncontiguous tracts scattered throughout the full altitudinal range of the subterritory. In the arable zone these tracts are further subdivided into garden sites, generally less than an acre, claimed by individual men.

Males have rights in the entire estate in garden land of the subterritorial group by virtue of clan and subclan membership. Although individual men claim title to particular garden sites either through patrilineal inheritance or by clearing virgin forest, adjustments of inequities are readily made. If a man is short of inherited sites, he simply asks a better-endowed member of his subclan for land, and a transfer in perpetuity seems always to be made. An individual's title to garden sites thus amounts to no more than stewardship for his subclan. Similarly, the title of a subclan in a tract of land may be regarded as stewardship for the entire clan. If a subclan is short of land, not only may its individual members ask for and receive grants in land from members of better-endowed subclans, but entire tracts may be granted it by other subclans.

In the case of the subterritorial cluster of three clans, adjustments of inequities in land holdings are also readily made between members of the three separate clans. That is, as far as access to land is concerned, these three clans relate to each other as do the subclans of a single clan. These three clans, at present antigamous in reference to each other, are, or believe themselves to be, related by connections through females in ascending generations when intermarriage among them is either known or believed by them to have taken place. That is, the members of the three separate clans regard each other as cognates, even though actual connections frequently cannot be traced. It could be argued that although this multiclan structure remains de jure a cluster of three agnatic descent groups, since the principle of filiation is patrilineal connection to one of the three constituent clans, it may be regarded as, de facto, a corporate cognatic descent group since its combined membership has rights in a common estate in land. I shall therefore refer to it as a "cognatic cluster." Although there is no term in the Maring language to designate the class of structures I would label "cognatic clusters," it may be noted that the existence of particular cognatic clusters as distinct units are recognized nominally. Thus, the cluster that includes the Kwibigai, Tomegai, and Tsembaga clans is known as "Tsembaga-Tomegai."

Regardless, however, of whether rights to land are based upon agnation or cognation, within the three subterritorial groups serious differences in land holding are ameliorated as quickly as they become apparent. It may be suggested that the ease of transfer displayed by Tsembaga land tenure practices is particularly advantageous among societies organized into small groups, for small groups are highly vulnerable to sudden and drastic demographic fluctuations independent of those experienced by their neighbors. Not only do the transfers avoid social and economic inequities, but they protect the environment from overexploitation in some areas while other areas remain underexploited.

But the subterritorial groups are themselves small and thus highly subject to independent demographic fluctuations. Grants in land are, however, frequently made by members of one subterritorial group to members of another. In a sample of 381 gardens made in 1961, 1962, and 1963, the gardener worked the land of a subterritorial group of which he was not a member in 94, or 24.7 percent, of the cases. Thus, the use of land for gardening is not exclusive to the agnatic or cognatic group that claims the land. To put it in the converse, a man frequently makes gardens on lands to which his agnatic or cognatic land-holding group has no claim. While titles to three distinct areas are recognized by the Tsembaga to be vested in three discrete groups, Tsembaga gardens are very much intermingled.

It should perhaps be made clear that the pattern of residence is largely independent of land use. Distances are not great, and a man may, and usually does, maintain patrilocal residence while making gardens on land received from other subterritorial groups within Tsembaga. The actual residence pattern may be called "pulsating." At a certain point in the ritual cycle there is a high degree of nucleation, when all or almost all houses are located in the general vicinity of a dance ground. However, Tsembaga subsistence procedures, particularly those concerned with pig husbandry, militate against nucleation, and small clusters of houses and scattered homesteads are the rule at most times.

Because of the easy access of all males to garden land all over the territory, it is reasonable to assume that population density figures, which will be presented in the next chapter, reflect a condition existing throughout Tsembaga territory and not averages of what might be a number of very different densities in different areas. In other words, for purposes of estimating intensity of exploitation an even distribution of the Tsembaga over the available land may be assumed.

That all of the Tsembaga, and the Tsembaga alone, enjoy common and almost exclusive access to the resources of a jointly defended territory has a further theoretical and methodological implication. They, separate from neighboring groups, constitute a unit in a set of material exchanges with the populations of other species that also inhabit their territory. They form a population in the ecological sense of the term, and I shall refer to them and similar units as "local populations."[3]

There are, however, differences in the nature and pattern of land transfers between members of constituent units of the same subterritorial group on the one hand and between members of separate

3. My terminology is somewhat different from that employed by Vayda and Cook (1964). *Local population* in my usage corresponds to *clan cluster* in theirs.

subterritorial groups on the other. In contrast to transfers between
members of separate constituent units of the same subterritorial
group, which were in 28, or 85%, of the cases in the sample grants
in perpetuity, only 35% of the transfers between members of separate subterritorial groups were grants in perpetuity. The remainder
were usufructory grants made by men to cognates or to wives' agnates, in most cases. Of the 33 grants in perpetuity made by members of one subterritorial group to members of another, 26, or 79%,
were made by men to *husbands of female agnates.* Such affinal grants
first take place when it becomes apparent that a marriage will be an
enduring one, but in most cases additional grants are made throughout the lives of the principals. These grants, which confer rights
only in specified sites and *not* in the entire estate of the grantor, do
not require the grantee to take up uxorilocal residence, and he seldom does. In most cases sites received from a wife's agnates only
supplement the lands to which a man has rights by virtue of patri-
filiation, lands which he usually continues to rely upon most heavily.
Whether or not he needs lands received through affinal grants, however, he is likely to use them, for he is under pressure from his wife
and his affines to do so. His wife will likely wish to make some of
her gardens on the land of her agnates so that she may visit them
frequently. On the other hand, a woman's agnates encourage her
husband to take up these lands for less sentimental reasons. From
their point of view, indeed, the affinal grant provides a means for
retaining access to a portion of the labor of female agnates after
their marriages. The sites transferred to a woman's husband are
usually adjacent to those being cultivated by her agnates; thus, a
woman can without great inconvenience assist an unmarried brother
or a widowed father with his garden, and she often does.

In light of the considerations involved in cultivating land received
from wives' agnates, it is not surprising that these sites, although said
to be transferred in perpetuity, often revert to the grantors after one
generation. The pressures that induce a man to cultivate land received from his wife's natal group are absent from his relationship
with his mother's natal group. If, however, the lands his father has
received through affinal transfers are convenient to a man's residence
he is likely to continue to use them. Therefore, affinal transfers between adjacent subterritorial groups are likely to endure through

several generations. The result is that the garden sites claimed by members of adjacent subterritorial groups become intermingled. Such intermingling has proceeded far among the Tsembaga, particularly between the cognatic cluster, which occupies the central subterritory, and the Kamuŋgagai clan, which occupies the subterritory to its west. Indeed, the two subterritories seem to be fusing. People say that the land of the two groups is or is becoming one, and many younger men claim to be ignorant of the location of the boundary between them. Older men are in agreement concerning its location but invariably state that this boundary no longer means as much as it did in former times.

It may be noted that the closeness of the relationship between the Kamuŋgagai clan and the Tsembaga-Tomegai cognatic cluster is nominally recognized: the two subterritorial groups are frequently referred to in aggregate as "Kamuŋgagai-Tsembaga." Although there is no corresponding term in the Maring language, I would designate as "affinal clusters" structures such as Kamuŋgagai-Tsembaga, which consist of two adjacent subterritorial groups whose lands are becoming intermingled through affinal transfers.

In connection with the gradual obliteration of the boundary between Tsembaga-Tomegai and Kamuŋgagai it is interesting to note that four of the new transfers in perpetuity of land between them included in the sample were not made on the basis of current affinal connections, but on the basis of affinal connections in ascending generations, that is, cognatic connections. The number is small, but I believe that it both marks a trend and illuminates the processes of group formation. Evidence is insufficient, but it may be suggested that cognatic clusters and affinal clusters represent two points in a continuous process of land amalgamation. Through intermarriage, and then by grants in perpetuity through affinal connections, the land of adjacent groups becomes intermingled. Since neither a man nor his subclan "brothers" should take a wife from his mother's natal clan, there is partial antigamy between the groups in alternate generations; but the intermingling is maintained because sons tend to maintain rights ceded to their fathers by their mothers' brothers in sites near their own patrilocal residences. Thus, they remain in constant contact with their mothers' natal groups and occasionally receive new grants of land on the basis of their maternal connections.

More intermarriage elaborates the web of cognatic relationships for descending generations and results in further intermingling of the garden sites of the two groups. People come to talk of the subterritories of the two groups as being one, and the border becomes indistinct. Eventually members of each group can trace cognatic connections to almost everyone in the other group. Cognatic connections replace marriage as the preferred means for acquiring rights in land and intermarriage ceases. The affinal cluster has become a cognatic cluster. Maring kinship terminology would facilitate this process. Kin terms are Iroquois on ego's generational level and bifurcate merging in the first ascending generation, but generational in the first descending and second ascending generations. Terminological distinctions between members of one's own exogamous group and groups with which it has intermarried are thus obliterated in two generations. Whereas the children of affines refer to each other by special cross-cousin terms, the children of cross-cousins refer to each other by the terms for brother and sister, although they may marry. This usage may be a formal concession to group dynamics: separate intermarrying groups can become a single corporate cognatic group, or cognatic cluster, without requiring a change in the kin terms that people of either group use to refer to the other.

It may further be that cognatic clusters become putative agnatic descent groups with the passage of time. Since a subterritorial clan cluster is functionally equivalent to a subterritorial clan such a transformation requires only a change in "charter." Once again their kinship terminology would facilitate such a change, since it masks the distinction between cognates and agnates after two generations. Ideological consistency would call for such a transformation, for in the Tsembaga view territoriality is ideally associated with agnation. It might be expected, a priori, that when knowledge of actual connections fade agnatic connections between the constituent (clan) units of the (cognatic) cluster will be assumed. This expectation is not, however, supported by the cognatic cluster found among the Tsembaga. A marriage connection between the KwiBigai and the Tsembaga clan is recent and therefore well remembered. In the case of the Tsembaga clan and the Tomegai, however, which have shared the subterritory for a much longer time, specific marriage connections are no longer remembered but the two clans retain their separate agnatic identities.

So far I have only spoken of land amalgamation leading to group fusion. This process is sometimes reversed, however, as may be illustrated from the tradition of the easternmost of the three subterritorial groups, the Merkai. At the time of my fieldwork this group consisted of a single exogamous clan but in the past, before they and the other four clans joined together as the Tsembaga local population, members of one of Merkai's three subclans began to intermarry with members of the other two. Informants say that when the clan was far more populous and occupied less land than it does at present one of the subclans moved its houses away and began to concentrate its gardening activities in the vicinity of its new settlement. Eventually its lands became separate, and intermarriage with the other two subclans began, although common ancestry was still acknowledged.

The process of fission seems later to have been reversed and it may be suggested that this reversal was correlated with a reduction in population pressure. After intraclan marriage began, the Merkai both won additional land and experienced a reduction in numbers as a result of disease, warfare, and emigration. At any rate, in 1963 the lands of the Merkai subclans were again intermingled. However, one intraclan marriage had taken place in the early 1950s, long after any population pressure that the Merkai had been experiencing had been relieved. Informants say that this marriage caused considerable consternation and that no further intraclan marriages would take place. This statement reflects, at least, demographic probability, for the Atigai subclan, which has in the past intermarried with the other two, has been reduced to seven persons.

Returning to the process of fission, what may have induced the removal of the Merkai Atigai residences is beyond the memory of any Tsembaga, and I will refrain from speculating about the mechanisms by which land segregation, if it actually occurred, may have been effected. All that is certain is that intermarriage between what are presently subclans of a single clan did take place, and that in former times a larger population occupied a smaller area.

While it is not possible to be certain, there is strong reason to believe that the Merkai were approaching or exceeding the carrying capacity of their land during at least part of the period when intermarriage was taking place among what are presently its subclans (see pp. 114ff.). Although data based upon my own observations or

the observations of living informants are lacking, I believe that informants' statements relating, at least temporally, the transformation
of antigamous subclans into intermarrying clans with population
pressure should be taken to reflect a systemic possibility if not an
historical fact. This belief is reinforced by Meggitt's observation of
a similar process among the Enga people of the Western Highlands
(1965:16).

In this connection it may be noted that although the practice of
conveying land between members of different subclans of the same
clan and between members of different clans or subterritorial groups
may disperse population evenly over available land, it cannot alleviate a general land shortage. As critical density is approached or exceeded it may be that land-claiming units at all levels discourage
the cultivation of their lands by members of coordinate units. An
increasing emphasis on the primary principle of filiation, in this case
agnation, as the basis for claims to land might then be expected, as
Meggitt (1965:26off) has proposed. Intraclan marriage accompanied
by affinal land transfers might well be part of the associated strategy.
Such marriages transform clan agnates into affines (affinal, rather
than agnatic terms of reference and address are used), and affinal
transfers of land may replace the recipients' residual rights as agnates in the subclan estate of the donors with the more limited
rights of affines in specified garden sites, while leaving intact or
ambiguous the donor's agnatic rights in the lands of the recipient.
Since this post hoc interpretation did not occur to me until after I
left the field, sufficient data to support or refute it are lacking.

Vayda and Cook have suggested concerning social organization
in New Guinea that "it is probably more rewarding . . . to focus
upon . . . processes than to attempt to devise elaborate social ty-
pologies applicable to all the structural variations encountered upon
a single time plane" (1964:802). It may be suggested that the formal structure of the Tsembaga local population at any point in time
is a more or less ephemeral product of continuing processes of population dispersal over available land, and that the discussion here
bears upon the more general discussion of the relationship between
population pressure and agnation in Oceania that has been carried
on over the past decade (cf. Brookfield and Brown, 1963:170ff;
Goodenough, 1955:80f; Meggitt, 1965:26off). Tsembaga data would

suggest that when population densities are low and considerable distances separate neighboring groups there is little permanent intermingling of garden land only because land acquired by virtue of membership in an agnatic group is convenient to a man's residence and other lands are not. With moderate to moderately high densities and reduced distances between neighboring groups, conditions that currently prevail among the Tsembaga, intermingling increases, for conveniently located lands may be obtained through affinal and then cognatic connections. As lands become intermingled, previously distinct social groups fuse, and in doing so they become antigamous. As critical density is approached the primary principle of filiation is emphasized as the basis for rights in land, garden intermingling is inhibited, and social groups are likely to fission or split and may begin to intermarry. This interpretation tends to support Meggitt's argument concerning the relationship between agnation and population pressure in the New Guinea Highlands, but it also reconciles some of the differences between him and Brookfield and Brown.

Clan histories indicate that warfare played an important part in the processes through which the five agnatic descent groups composing Tsembaga emerged as a single distinct unit from a regional population composed of many agnatic descent groups dispersed more or less continuously over the entire Maring area. People say that approximately fifty years before my fieldwork the gardens of the Kamuŋgagai, the westernmost Tsembaga clan, and the Kundagai to their west were intermingled, and litigation that has been initiated since the imposition of government-enforced peace supports their memory. But in a fight over a woman one Kundagai was killed and warfare immediately followed. Each of the embattled clans received, generally, the support of the clans behind it in this encounter. The Kamuŋgagai thus received assistance from the Tsembaga, Tomegai, and Kwibigai, with whom their garden lands were intermingled and with whom they had intermarried frequently, and from many Merkai, with whom they had married less frequently. They also received some support from the Dimbagai-Yimyagai immediately to the east of the Merkai, and the Tuguma local population, which occupied the territory beyond the Dimbagai-Yimyagai. Within days of the successful termination of this round of warfare trouble developed between the Merkai and the Dimbagai-Yimyagai.

In subsequent fighting the Merkai prevailed, with the support of most of the Kwibigai, Tsembaga, Tomegai, and many Kamuŋgagai, and with the further cooperation of the Tuguma who had a grievance of their own against the Dimbagai-Yimyagai. The Dimbagai-Yimyagai were driven from their territory, part of which the Merkai eventually annexed. There is reason to believe that the fight between the Merkai and Dimbagai-Yimyagai, at least, was a response to population pressure (see pp. 114ff.), but whatever its causes warfare seems to have defined the borders of Tsembaga territory, and the Tsembaga as a unit were distinguished from other units by their joint participation in the fighting that defined these borders. This de facto association of previously autonomous units then became a de jure structure through the synchronization of the *rumbim* rituals that follow the successful termination of hostilities. These rituals will be discussed in detail in later chapters.

POLITICAL STRUCTURE

Some of the events to be discussed later depend upon the coordination of the activities of many persons; the means by which such coordination is achieved requires brief description.

There are no hereditary or formally elected chiefs among the Tsembaga, nor are there any named, explicitly political offices. Neither is there to be found a pattern, such as that described by Oliver (1955), in which certain individuals, having achieved the status of "big men," command or coerce the activities of subordinates and vie with each other in feast giving. Among the Maring, to be sure, some men are recognized as *yu maiwai* ("big," or "important" men) and are especially influential in public affairs. They do not, however, compete in feast giving and do not command the obedience of others. The ability of such a man to effect compliance with his wishes depends upon his persuasiveness, and not upon his exclusive occupancy of a particular position in the social or political structure. Indeed, there is no limitation upon the number of big men that may be present in any subclan or clan: the Tsembaga are truly egalitarian in that there are as many big men as there are men whose capabilities permit them to be big men. Moreover, there is not on the part of men in general any abdication, either expressed or tacit, of decision making in favor of big men. Everyone has a voice in decision making, if he cares to raise it, and anyone may attempt to initiate action by himself proceeding to act and thereby instigating others to follow.

If the term *authority* is taken to refer to a locus in communications network from which flow messages instigating actions, then it may be said that among the Tsembaga authority is shifting. Big men may perhaps be defined statistically: they are those who more frequently than other men initiate the courses of action to which a group commits itself. A man is not involved frequently in decision making because he is a big man; he is a big man because he is frequently involved in decision making. It should be made clear, however, that a big man is seldom under an obligation to participate in the making of any decision. He may, and frequently does, leave decisions to others. His motive for refraining from participation in a decision may be lack of interest, inability to arrive at an opinion, or the desire to avoid a thorny issue. But his right to silence is unquestioned, and its invocation, if not too frequent, does not diminish his status.

Whether or not a man is a big man depends upon his personal attributes. Big men, it is said, have "talk" (*čep*). They have talk concerning fighting, women, rituals, and gardens. They have opinions about things concerning the group, which they can express articulately and which their auditors respect. They are, in short, intelligent men of forceful personality. They are usually men of considerable physical strength and vigor as well.

Big men tend to be wealthy, tend to be shamans, and tend to be in possession of knowledge of the rituals concerned with fighting. Wealth and esoteric knowledge and ability are primarily the fruits of the same abilities—intelligence, vigor, forcefulness—that make a man a frequent decision-maker. While the possession of wealth and esoteric knowledge tends to support the status of a big man, it does not per se confer decision-making prerogatives. It does not, moreover, provide a particularly powerful set of tools that a man may use to bend others to his will, as may be the case in societies in which the difference in amounts held by the wealthy and the nonwealthy is great, or where esoteric knowledge surrounds its possessor with great sanctity. The "spheres of influence" of even the most respected big men are very limited. The ability of any such man to effect compliance with his wishes diminishes with structural distance: it is greatest within his own subclan and among the residents of his own men's house, less among other subclans within his clan and among residents of other men's houses, and even less (although perhaps still considerable) among members of other clans within the local population. The renown of such men usually transcends the local population, but their direct influence outside their own local group is restricted to affines, cognates, and nonkin trading partners.

The processes of decision making are as amorphous as the structure within which they take place. Meetings are sometimes called to discuss an issue, but these are rare. At meetings that I attended, furthermore, there was little attempt to reach decisions in any formal way. There was no one to frame propositions in the form of anything like motions that could be put to a vote, for one thing, and besides, the idea of voting itself is unknown. It may be suggested that formal decision making is actually avoided at meetings, for the framing of issues in terms that would allow a decision to be made could lead to confrontations between those holding opposing views. Such confrontations would be difficult to resolve. Meetings are simply events at which there is much discussion about a particular subject going on at the same place and time among an assemblage that is larger than usual. These meetings are strange in appearance. Small knots of men—three or four or five in a group—stand or sit on the ground and talk among themselves. There may be many such groups within a restricted area. A few men move from group to group. Occasionally someone will address the entire assemblage in a loud voice. Some men drift away, others come by. Eventually everyone drifts away. No decision has been reached and no action initiated, but there has been much talk. Concerning most action there is no meeting, but there is discussion in the men's houses and on the paths and in the gardens. A meeting crystallizes sentiment more quickly, but its purpose is limited to forming a consensus and not making decisions or instigating action per se. Its purpose is "to make the talk one" (reach agreement) more quickly than is usually the case. When some man thinks the consensus has been achieved, or when he thinks that there has been enough discussion, without further discussion he initiates the course of action that the consensus suggests: for instance, he puts his eel traps at a traditionally designated place in one of the streams, thus initiating preparations for the final stage of the *kaiko* or pig festival; he begins to collect materials required for the construction of visitors' houses on the dance ground; or he personally visits another local group and, through a kinsman, extends an invitation to the *kaiko*.

It frequently happens that he who attempts to instigate group action has misjudged the consensus and he is not followed. A young man named Borgai, for instance, placed his ritual eel traps in the water in late August 1963. No one else followed suit immediately; indeed, some men didn't place their traps until October, and by the time eels were finally used in November, most of those caught early by Borgai had died. But to find oneself without an immediate following is not the lot of young men of little account only, and to instigate action successfully even a recognized big man must sometimes persevere. In late 1962 there was much talk of the need to build a house on the periphery of the dance ground to shelter visitors to the pig festival, and one morning Yemp, who is both the government-appointed *luluai* and recognized by the people to be a *yu maiwai*, called out that construction would start immediately. Absolutely no one joined him. Undeterred, he proceeded to the forest and began to cut poles and gather *pandanus* leaves for the structure. He continued to work alone for three days, complaining bitterly to those who passed by about the worthlessness of Tsembaga men, their sole interests being gardening and copulating. On the fourth day others, perhaps out of shame or perhaps because Yemp had stimulated their sense of public duty, finally joined him in the work.

CHAPTER 3

Relations with the Immediate Environment

In the last chapter it was suggested that the Tsembaga are a population in the ecological sense since they, separate from neighboring groups, constitute a unit in a set of material exchanges with the populations of other species with which they share their territory. In this chapter Tsembaga territory, its climate, and biota will be described, and the material relations of the people with their non-human coinhabitants will be discussed.

THE ENVIRONMENT

Some measurements of the climate and descriptions of the biota of Tsembaga territory presented here will not enter the later analysis as variables. Nevertheless, they warrant attention. For instance, temperature and rainfall are discussed here not because the quantities themselves will be treated as variables, but because they represent conditions that may possibly affect the presence or absence of the various biotic components of the Tsembaga ecosystem. The cultivation of particular plants, for instance, is limited by temperature, rainfall, insolation, and soil conditions (Brookfield, 1964:20ff.; Kroeber, 1939). Information concerning climate, soils, and vegetation may thus constitute an important empirical basis for comparison between areas.

Climate

Between December 1, 1962 and November 30, 1963, 153.89 inches of rainfall were recorded at an altitude of 4,750 feet on Tsembaga territory. No figures from any earlier period are available. While there was a drier and a wetter season, recognized terminologically by the Tsembaga, in no month did less than 6.76 inches of rain fall. Moreover, three of the months that, according to informants, were supposed to be part of the dry season, August, September, and October, were very wet.

Rain generally fell gently, although on several occasions over 100 points fell in less than a half hour. The highest daily recording was 4.01 inches, and there were forty-three days when over 1 inch of rain fell.

Most rainfall occurred at night, and on most days sunshine was prolonged, although cloud was seldom absent from some part of the sky. From August through November, however, much of the rainfall occurred during the daylight hours, and days of prolonged sunshine were few. Evaporation, consequently, was impeded and the ground remained wet. Fog, technically cloud, is common, particularly above 4,000 feet. Although it appeared most usually between 4 and 7 P.M., it would occasionally persist through the day.

During the year there was sunshine on more than 243 days and rainfall on 253 days. Monthly rainfall figures for Tsembaga, and a summary of five years of rainfall statistics for Tabibuga in the Jimi Valley, are included in Appendix 1.

Seasonal variation in temperature is slight. The diurnal variation ranges from 7° to 16°F, with daily maxima almost always falling in the mid- to high 70s and the daily minima in the low 60s.

No winds of a force sufficient to break small twigs off trees were noted during the year, although Clarke (personal communication) reports that he experienced somewhat stronger winds in 1964. Informants say that they have never known wind to reach a force sufficient to damage houses, groves, or gardens.

Land

Tsembaga territory measured orthographically includes 2,033 acres, or 3.2 square miles, of which 1,690 acres, or approximately 2.5 miles, are in the Simbai Valley, while the remaining 343 acres are in the Jimi Valley. Population density reckoned against total orthographic area is thus about sixty-four persons per square mile.

The terrain is rugged, rising from an altitude of 2,200 feet at the Simbai River to 7,200 feet at the Bismarck Ridge. Slope is about

20° up to 5,000 feet, then rises more steeply to the mountain top. The surface is further complicated by spurs projecting at approximate right angles to the line of the ridge, and by frequent watercourses.

Information concerning soils, which seem generally to be poor, is summarized in Appendix 2.

Vegetation

Hundreds or even thousands of species of plants are to be found within the limited area circumscribed by the borders of Tsembaga territory. Native nomenclature is elaborate. In the case of most non-domesticated plants, the native taxon usually corresponds to a species designation, while among the cultivated plants elaborate distinctions are made at a subspecies level.

This rich flora is distributed over Tsembaga territory in several different plant associations, among which the Tsembaga make clear terminological distinctions, which may form the basis for our discussion here. These associations include:

1. *geni:* forest that is said never to have been cut
2. *korndo:* grassy areas devoid, or almost devoid, of trees, and dominated by *Imperata cylindrica*
3. *riŋgop:* associations of domesticated plants, i.e. gardens in production
4. *riŋgopwai:* secondary growth, of which there are two subtypes
   (a) *kikia:* secondary associations dominated by herbaceous species
   (b) *dukmi:* secondary associations dominated by woody species

Only *geni* and *korndo* will be discussed here; *riŋgop* and *riŋgopwai* will be discussed later in the context of subsistence activities.

GENI

Of the 1,690 acres held by the Tsembaga within the Simbai Valley, 602 by orthographic measurement are in virgin forest, which lies unbroken above a line varying in altitude from 5,000 to 5,400 feet. An additional 28 acres of virgin forest have survived as remnants at lower altitudes, and in the Jimi Valley the entire Tser holding of 343 acres is either in primary forest or very advanced secondary growth. Of the total area of 2,033 acres included by orthographic measurement in Tsembaga territory, 973, or 48 percent, are in virgin forest or in secondary growth resembling virgin forest.

Two different virgin forest associations may be distinguished on structural grounds, although no such distinction is recognized in the Maring language, so far as I know. These are the high forest and the moss forest.

High forest survives only in remnants between 2,000' and 5,000', but it is unbroken from approximately 5,000' to 6,000'. Throughout the high forest, three fairly distinct arboreal strata support an abundance of epiphytes, lianes, stranglers, and small climbers. While there are two lower strata, one of shrubs and young trees, the other composed of low herbaceous forms, the forest floor generally appears open, and it is only in scattered locations that visibility at the ground is less than 100'.

There are some floristic differences between the upper and lower portions of the high-forest range, with the transition occurring between 3,500' and 4,500'. The lower zone is referred to by the Tsembaga as the "*wora*," and the entire area above it is called the "*kamuŋga.*" Information concerning floristic composition will be found in Appendix 3; it is enough to say here that all structural components of both the *kamuŋga* and *wora* high forest are extremely mixed. In a strip 200'x17' at an altitude of 5,000', the "A," or highest, tree stratum was found to include nine named tree types, the "B" stratum four, and the "C" stratum ten. Details concerning the forest census taken on this strip will be found in Appendix 3.

The most striking aspect of the high forest is the size of the trees. The crowns of "A" stratum trees achieve an estimated average height of close to 125', with occasional individuals, particularly *nonomba*, a species of *Eugenia*, reaching 150' or more. Girths are frequently massive; 8' circumferences 3' above the ground, or above the buttresses, which are a common feature, are not unusual. Trees of even greater girth are present.

Three-storied forests composed of trees of such size do not seem to be common at altitudes of 5,000 to 6,000 feet in most parts of the world (Richards, 1964). The forest observed at such altitudes on Tsembaga territory resembles lowland formations more closely than it does montane or submontane associations. The presence of this formation at such an altitude may be regarded as an example of "Massenerhebung Effect," the upward displacement of the altitudinal ranges of plant associations in inland regions as compared to coastal areas, and in the interior of mountain ranges as compared to foothills. Richards (1964:347) states that protection from wind is at least partially responsible for the Massenerhebung Effect, but Clarke in a personal communication suggests that patterns of cloud cover may also be important.

In the moss forest above 6,000' trees are smaller, both in girth and height. The forest ceiling in this range is usually well under 100' from the ground, and stratification is indistinct. Although scattered individuals reach heights of 100' or more, their crowns do not form an unbroken canopy. Herbaceous epiphytes and climbers are less abundant than at lower ranges, but epiphytic mosses are much more luxuriant, completely covering the trunks of most trees to a depth of more than an inch. Information concerning the composition of the moss forest will also be found in Appendix 3.

KORNDO

In several parts of Tsembaga territory apparently stable grassy associations occur. Only one of these, located between 2,800 and 3,600 feet, is of considerable size, covering 41 acres. *Korndo* (*Imperata cylindrica;* p. e.: *kunai*), is the overwhelming dominant, although a few ground creepers are present, as are scattered tree ferns, most of which are *Cyathea angiensis,* and a few small thickets of a very large bamboo called *"waia,"* which have been planted. The oldest Tsembaga informants maintain that neither they nor their ancestors ever made gardens in this area, and that it has always been, as it is now, under *kunai.*

I have already mentioned that there is reason to believe that the Maring occupation of the Simbai Valley is relatively recent, perhaps having begun within the last 200 years. It may be that this association, if it is anthropogenic (Robbins, 1963), is the result of the activities of an earlier population for whose presence there is archaeological evidence in the form of the stone mortars and pestles that are occasionally found in the ground.

The sort of exploitation that would turn the cover over limited areas into *kunai* while surrounding areas remained in high forest is hard to visualize. It is certainly the case, however, that the frequent fires to which such associations are subjected encourage this grass, the rhyzomes of which are undamaged by fire and discourage most other plants.

Fauna

The nondomesticated fauna inhabiting Tsembaga territory is abundant. Placental mammals include only feral pigs, bats, and rats, of which there are ten or more named varieties. At least thirty named varieties of marsupials are present, and there are at least fourteen named snake types. Lizards and frogs are also represented by many named types, and the avifauna is very rich. The Tsembaga say that at least eighty-four named types are present on their territory. These include cassowary, several birds of paradise, many species of parrot, and "bush turkeys." Most of the carnivores are to be found among the avifauna, which include many owls, several species of hawk, and at least one eagle. In the streams both eels and catfish are found, although the latter is rare. Arthropoda are quite varied, and their nomenclature is elaborate.

The fauna includes few forms that imperil human beings. Five of the fourteen snakes are venomous. Only one of them, however, the *rarawa* (unident), is sufficiently poisonous, according to informants, to kill a human being, and the only instance of snakebite death that anyone remembers occurred many years ago, when an old woman succumbed. Wild pigs and cassowaries are capable of injuring seriously or even killing human beings, and gorings by pigs are not infrequent. Informants say, however, that neither wild pigs nor wild cassowaries are ever guilty of unprovoked attacks, and injuries are inflicted by them only when they are hunted.

Of greater danger to the welfare of the Tsembaga than any large animal are anopheles mosquitoes. Most of the Tsembaga suffer what are probably mild malarial attacks from time to time. Data are insufficient concerning intestinal parasites. Stools of only two persons, in addition to the Tsembaga fieldworkers, were subjected to laboratory analysis, and no parasites were found.

Spirits

The Tsembaga regard spirits (*rawa*) to be significant components of their environment, and the reasons they offer for performing many rituals that will be discussed later in this study concern their relations with them. To make the rituals comprehensible a brief introduction to several of the major categories of spirits is necessary.

In the *wora*, the lower part of the territory, a class of spirits called the "*rawa mai*" is said to dwell. The term *mai* appears in a number of other contexts, which illuminate both the usage here and the role the Tsembaga impute to these spirits.

A taro corm out of which rhyzomes have started to grow is a *mai*. A woman who has had a child is an *ambra mai*, and adult females of animals are *mai*. But femaleness is not necessarily implied by the term, for old men are *yu mai*. A meaning that seems common to all of these contexts is something out of which something else has grown.

The spirits of the low ground are concerned with growth and fertility. It is they who look after the increase and growth of people and pigs and the productivity of gardens and groves. They are concerned, too, with that portion of the fauna which inhabits the area below the unbroken high forest, which covers the land above 5,000 feet. Feral pigs are theirs, and when one is shot thanks must be given to them. Of particular importance to them are eels, which are said to be their pigs. As the *rawa mai* are concerned with the lower portion of the territory, so are they concerned with the lower portion of the body—the belly, the genitals, and the legs. Fecundity and strength in the legs derive from them, but so do afflictions of the belly and the groin.

The category of *rawa mai* includes two subcategories of related spirits. There are, first, those called "*koipa maŋgiaŋ*." When informants are questioned they say that the *koipa maŋgiaŋ* of each clan is distinct, and that he dwells in a wide place in one of the streams on the clan's territory. Other contexts, however, suggest a single *koipa maŋgiaŋ* for all Tsembaga or even all Maring. A notion of separate manifestations of a single supernatural entity perhaps reconciles such inconsistencies.

Koipa maŋgiaŋ were never human, but near *koipa maŋgiaŋ* in "A" stratum trees in virgin forest remnants live the spirits of those Tsembaga who have died of illness or accident. They are referred to as

"*rawa tukump.*" *Tukump,* in other contexts, designates the mold that
develops on such articles as orchid fiber belts and the bark rope bind-
ings of stone axes. These spirits, the "spirits of rot," are conceived as
intermediaries between the living and *koipa maŋgiaŋ.*

Spirits of the low ground are said to be *kinim,* which in many contexts means simply "cold." Here, as in some other contexts, it carries
an implication of wetness as well. The juice of sugar cane is *kinim,*
as is water, and women are said to be so because of their vaginal
secretions. Coldness and wetness are said by the Tsembaga to be
conditions that together cause softness and rot, and softness and rot,
in contrast to hardness and desiccation, are thought to be the necessary conditions for growing things. This is recognized in certain important rituals that will be discussed later; for now it is sufficient to
say that the Tsembaga conceive the spirits of the low ground to be
implicated in the cycle of fertility, growth, and decay to which all
animate things are subject.

But in the Tsembaga view while decay is necessary to life it also
implies death, and the spirits of the low ground are dangerous. The
spirits of rot, particularly when newly deceased, may spread a kind
of supernatural corruption, called simply "*tukump,*" which causes
illness and harm to those exposed to it. *Koipa maŋgiaŋ* himself is
particularly fearful. He alone among the spirits of local origin actually kills. Other of the local spirits may bring illness, but it is only
koipa maŋgiaŋ who brings death, even when it is another spirit
whose displeasure is responsible for such punishment. In sum, the
notion of fertility and growth on the one hand and death and dissolution through decay on the other are linked in the persons of the
spirits of rot and *koipa maŋgiaŋ.* The spirits of the low ground seem
to be more than spirits of fertility; they are, rather, the spirits of a
cycle in which life both terminates in and arises out of death.

In the *kamuŋga,* the upper part of the territory, a class of spirits
called the "*rawa mugi*" (red spirits) reside. These are the spirits of
Tsembaga who have been killed in warfare, and Tsembaga say that
they derive their name from the fact that their deaths were bloody.
Much of the moss forest and high forest near the top of the mountain
is considered to be their home, and it is said that they have forbidden
the felling of trees, except for certain ritual purposes, in this sacred
area. The category of mammals termed "*ma*" (marsupials and per-

haps some giant rats), which live in the *kamuŋga geni,* the virgin
forest above 5,000 feet, are, moreover, considered to be their pigs,
and when one is obtained in a trap or through hunting thanks must
be offered to the red spirits. This is also the case when cassowary or
other large birds are taken in the high-altitude virgin forest.

Aside from hunting and trapping in the *kamuŋga geni,* however,
the red spirits are hardly concerned with the subsistence activities
of the living. They are concerned, rather, with the relations of the
Tsembaga to other local groups, particularly in the context of warfare. It is from the red spirits that the rituals associated with warfare are said to have been received by ancestors, and it is to them
that they are mainly addressed. It is the red spirits, furthermore,
who enforce the taboos concerning relations with the enemy during
periods when hostilities are quiescent.

In contrast to the spirits of the low ground, who are said to be
kinim, or "cold," the red spirits are *romba-nda,* or "hot." But as
kinim in reference to the spirits of the low ground denotes wetness
and softness, *romba-nda* in reference to the red spirits denotes dry-
ness and hardness. While the cold, wet, and soft imply fertility, the
hot, dry, and hard imply strength.

While both the hot and the cold, strength and fertility, are recognized to be qualities necessary to their survival and well-being, the
Tsembaga regard them as opposing principles, inimical to each
other. Certain activities therefore must be segregated from each
other in time and space, and certain objects or persons must be prohibited from contact with other objects or persons. Men who have
knowledge of rituals for propitiating the red spirits, for instance,
are forbidden to eat snakes, because the "coldness" of these reptiles
will damage the "hotness" of their rituals.

In further contrast to the spirits of the low ground, the red spirits
are concerned with the upper, nonsexual part of the body: the chest,
the head, and the arms, and afflictions of these parts may result
from the displeasure of these spirits.

The red spirits are not the only supernatural inhabitants of the
kamuŋga. Residing at *komba ku,* a limestone cliff at the highest
point on Tsembaga territory, is a female spirit, or set of spirits,
called the "*kun kaze ambra.*" *Yur kun kaze* is the term for the technique through which shamanistic ecstasy is produced. It involves

smoking locally grown tobacco over which spells have been said, and singing ritual songs. *Yur* is the Maring term for tobacco. The meaning of *kun kaze* is obscure and is probably not Maring. It is the *kun kaze ambra* (*ambra:* woman) whom a shaman consults when he wishes to learn the will of the deceased.

In many contexts it would seem that there is a single *kun kaze ambra*, or "smoke woman," not only for all the Tsembaga but for all Maring speakers. In other contexts, however, it appears that there are many: as in the case of *koipa maŋgiaŋ*, the problem can perhaps be resolved in terms of a concept of local or even personal manifestations of a single supernatural entity.

While the smoke woman, who is said never to have been human, is conceived as female, this conception does not seem to carry any implication of fertility. She is not thought to be antagonistic or dangerous to women, but sexual activities must be segregated temporally from activities having to do with her.

Although she resides in the upper portion of the territory, unlike the *rawa mugi* the smoke woman is not associated with any animals or plants living on the high ground. Neither is she responsible for any portion of the human anatomy, although she is associated with the nose: it is through the nostrils that she enters the shaman's body. She is concerned, rather, with relationships among the spirits themselves and between the spirits and the Tsembaga. She must be contacted when a change from activities implicating the spirits of the low ground to activities implicating the red spirits is contemplated, and again when a change back is projected. Through ʌer comes the consensus of the spirit world, approving, disapproving, advising delay. The smoke woman, in short, is thought to be a link between the living and the dead.

Only one other class of spirits needs to be mentioned here. These are *rawa tukump ragai*. These are the deceased of other clans. Unlike the Tsembaga's own *rawa tukump*, the term *rawa tukump ragai* includes the deceased of other groups who have been killed in warfare as well as those who died of illness or by accident. Particularly dangerous are the spirits of slain enemies, who are thought to lurk about the territory waiting for opportunities to avenge themselves by bringing illness or death to members of their slayer's group.

SUBSISTENCE

Tsembaga subsistence activities will be examined with a view to deriving values for some of the variables suggested in Chapter 1. Descriptions of actual subsistence procedures will form the subject of a separate work, and therefore are, to a large extent, excluded here.

Cultivation

Cultivation is considered to be the complex of behavior by which members of an animal species both propagate and care for the members of other species, either plant or animal, which, in turn, provide them with useful material. Among the Tsembaga cultivation includes horticulture, silviculture, and animal husbandry.

HORTICULTURE

The Tsembaga rely upon the products of their gardens for much the greatest part of their nutritional requirements. Their horticulture is shifting. It is a set of interrelated activities directed toward (1) the establishment and maintenance, in an area previously dominated by other plants, of a temporary association of cultivated plants in which edible species are most prevalent, and (2) the succession of the temporary association of cultivated plants by an association similar to that which it replaced.

The great preponderance of the gardens are made in secondary forest between 3,000 and 5,000 feet. Of the 381 gardens made in 1961, 1962, and 1963 that were surveyed or censused, only 1 had been cut in virgin forest.[1]

Informants say that some Maring people plant garden sites twice before abandoning them, but the Tsembaga plant them only once. Cropping continues for periods varying from fourteen to twenty-four or more months, after which the garden is allowed to revert to secondary growth. The major gardens are cut, for the most part, in the latter part of what is said to be the wetter season (April, May, and early June). Most burning takes place in the drier season

1.   There are indications that other local populations of Maring speakers nearer to large expanses of low-lying virgin forest tend to make a somewhat greater percentage of their gardens in virgin forest.

(between June and September), and planting follows immediately. There is no calendar; the scheduling of gardening activities depends mostly on weather, although some attention is paid to a few indicator plants.

Men and women cooperate in making gardens. Both cut underbrush. Men alone fell and pollard trees, make fences, and lay out logs on the ground as plot markers, planting guides, and soil retainers. Either men or women may burn the refuse on the plot for the first time, but women are usually responsible for the second firing, which disposes of materials not burned by the first. The heaviest burden in planting falls upon women. Men plant bananas, sugar cane, and *maŋap* (*Saccharum edule;* p.e.: *pitpit*); women plant the tubers and greens. Harvesting also falls largely to women, as does weeding, although men sometimes help their wives in these operations.

Gardening pairs overlap; that is, a woman may, and usually does, during the same year, make gardens with more than one man. In addition to her husband, she will frequently make gardens with her own or her husband's unmarried brothers or a widowed father. Conversely, a man is likely to make gardens not only with his wife but also with his unmarried sisters or a widowed mother. It is not unusual, therefore, for a single individual to participate in making several gardens in a single season. An important factor contributing to the pattern of personnel arrangements in gardens is, of course, the disparity between numbers of males and females in particular clans or subclans.

If a gardening pair has many pigs, two kinds of gardens are planted during the dry season. In the lower altitudes, that is, between 3,000′ and 4,000′–4,500′, a *daŋ-wan duk* (taro-yam garden) will be planted, while in the upper altitudes, between 4,200′ and 5,200′, a *bo-ñogai duk* (sugar-sweet potato garden) is made. The native names for the two garden types indicate the crops that are most important in these gardens. Some sweet potatoes and sugar are found in almost all taro-yam gardens and vice versa. The differences in the composition of these gardens are mainly statistical, although some low-altitude crops—certain yams and hibiscus especially—are absent from sweet potato gardens in the higher altitudes. When the number of pigs is small, separate sweet potato gardens are not planted. Instead, mixed gardens (*duk mai yant*), which bear closer resemblance in their composition to taro-yam gardens than to sugar-sweet potato gardens, are planted toward the middle of the altitudinal range.

In the wetter season, between November and April, most people plant additional gardens containing, for the most part, greens that come into maturity during the dry season. These gardens are always small and sometimes are not planted.

Information concerning the crop inventory is summarized in Table 2. Column 1 presents native categories, and column 2 provides

Table 2. Tsembaga *Riŋgop* (Cultivated Species Planted in Swiddens)

Native category	Identification, description, or criterial attributes	Popular name	Number of named varieties	Origin or introduction
1. daŋ-wan	"presentation tubers"			
daŋ	taros			
daŋ	*Colocasia esculenta*	taro	27	Present from time of ancestors, but new varieties appear, old disappear.
koŋ	*Xanthosoma sagittifolium*	taro kong	1	From Karam people in 1957.
wan	Yams			
wan	*Dioscorea alata* and *nummularia*	yam	32	Present from time of ancestors, but varieties change.
man	*D. bulbifera*	yam, mami	4	All varieties said to be present from time of ancestors.
diŋga	*D. pentaphylla*	yam	1	Said to be present from time of ancestors.
ruka	*D. esculenta*	yam	1	Said to be present from time of ancestors.
2. ñogai	"pig tubers"			
ñogai	*Ipomoea batatas*	sweet potato	24	Present from time of ancestors, but varieties change.
baundi	*Manihot dulcis*	manioc	1	Introduced from the Jimi Valley around 1920.
3. bep	Leafy greens not planted in pandanus groves			
čeŋmba	*Rungia klossi*		5	All said to be present from time of ancestors.
rampmañe	*Commelina* sp.		1	All said to be present from time of ancestors.

Table 2 continued:

Native category	Identification, description, or criterial attributes	Popular name	Number of named varieties	Origin or introduction
gonebi	*Brassica juncea*		1	All said to be present from time of ancestors.
rumba	*Cucurbitaceae* sp.		1	All said to be present from time of ancestors.
kiñipo	*Oenanthe javanica*	parsley	1	All said to be present from time of ancestors.
niŋk gonebi	?*Nasturium officinale*	watercress	1	Introduced from Jimi Valley, 1957.
4. komba-čem	crops planted in *pandanus* groves			
komba	*Pandanus conoideus*	*marita*	34	Present from time of ancestors, but varieties said to change slowly
čem	*Hibiscus manihot*	hibiscus	17	Present from time of ancestors, but varieties change.
bep	*Cyathea* spp.	fern	3	All present from time of ancestors.
5. bar	*Psophocarpus tetragonulobus* and *Dolichos lablab*	peas, beans	4	(P. tet) present since time of ancestors, (D. lablab) introduced from the Jimi Valley 1935–40.
6. yobai	*Musa sapientum*	banana	28	Present from time of ancestors, but varieties change.
7. konapa	*Zea mays*	corn, maize	2	Introduced from Jimi Valley, 1945–50.
8. maŋap	*Saccharum edule*	pitpit	16	Present since time of ancestors, but varieties change.
9. kwiai	*Setaria palmaefolia*	New Guinea asparagus	7	Present since time of ancestors, but varieties change.
10. pika	cucumber	cucumber		
pika	*Cucumis sativus*	cucumber	1	Said to be present from time of ancestors.
mop	?*Cucumis sativus*	cucumber	1	Said to be present from time of ancestors.
11. ira	*Cucurbita pepo*	pumpkin	1	From Jimi Valley 1945–1950.

Table 2 continued:

Native category	Identification, description, or crithrial attributes	Popular name	Number of named varieties	Origin or introduction
12. yibona	*Cucurbitaceae ?lagaenaria* sp.	gourd	1	?
13. raŋgo	*Zingiber c.p. zerumbet*	ginger	1	Present from time of ancestors.
14. bo	*Saccharum officinarum*	sugar cane	27	All said to be present from time of ancestors.
15. aramp	succulents eaten raw with salt			
kumerik	*?Pollia* sp.		2	Present from time of ancestors.
kiñkiñmai	*Hemigraphis* sp.		2	Present from time of ancestors.
16. punt	ornamentals			
amame	*Coleus seutellaroides*	green and yellow coleus	1	Present from time of ancestors.
nimp	*Coleus seutellaroides*	purple coleus	1	Present from time of ancestors.
korambe	*Impatiens platypelia*		1	Present from time of ancestors.
17. kañpamp	*?Broussonetia*	paper mulberry	1	Present from time of ancestors.
18. pai pai	*Carica papaya*	paw paw	1	Introduced from Karam people around 1940.
19. rumbim	*Cordyline fruticosa*	tanket	10	All varieties said to be present from time of ancestors.
20. yur	*Nicotiana*	tobacco	1	Introduced from Karam people during (?) 1920s.
Totals	Species: 36+		264+	

translations or meanings for these categories; in some instances English terms or Latin binomials serve adequately. In the case of some of the more inclusive categories (indicated by Roman numerals), this has not been possible, and notes on some of the entries are required.

Daŋ-wan, which translates "taro-yam," are designated "presentation tubers." *Daŋ-wan* figure in ceremonial food presentations, in contrast to *ñogai*, which do not. *Ñogai* are fed to pigs as well as people and are thus designated "pig tubers" here. The plants included in category IV, *komba čem*, are found in swiddens and are thus included here. They are also found separately in *pandanus* groves (see the discussion of silviculture below).

Information concerning the place of origin and time of introduction of the various crops is derived from informants' statements.

The tabulation of harvesting began on January 25, 1963, and daily records were kept for more than thirty gardens from February 16 to December 14, 1963. A schedule of harvesting by crop is provided in Figure 1. Until week twenty-four, this schedule represents a synthesis of observations on several gardens in which planting dates could be fixed within one week. After week twenty-four, however, planting dates could not be fixed with equal accuracy, for the plantings upon which this schedule is based took place before I arrived in the field. They may therefore be inaccurate by as much as two weeks.

It should also be kept in mind that there is variation in speed of growth between gardens that differ in altitude and in other respects. This diagram represents an approximation of the harvesting schedule in gardens at altitudes around 4,000 feet. At higher altitudes maturation is slower.

Quantities harvested per acre are presented in Table 3 for taro-yam gardens and in Table 4 for sugar-sweet potato gardens. These estimations, which are critical preliminaries to an estimation of the amount of garden land required to support the Tsembaga, are based upon the daily harvest records compiled in the field. The weights of major crop categories are presented individually, but caloric values for each, drawn from the literature (see Appendix 8), have been assigned so that there will be a degree of commensurability both between the various crops and between the totals and total figures from other areas in which the crop inventory is different.

These figures, which represent an attempt at estimating the yields of two major types of gardens from first harvesting to abandonment, should be accepted with caution. Because the period of fieldwork was considerably shorter than the period of harvesting, in both cases the figures represent a compilation of harvesting records kept for

Figure 1. Harvesting Schedule of Tsembaga Garden Crops

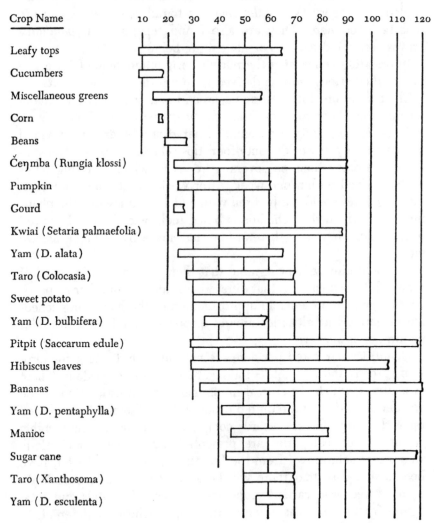

Weeks after Planting

| Crop Name | 10 | 20 | 30 | 40 | 50 | 60 | 70 | 80 | 90 | 100 | 110 | 120 |

Leafy tops

Cucumbers

Miscellaneous greens

Corn

Beans

Čeŋmba (Rungia klossi)

Pumpkin

Gourd

Kwiai (Setaria palmaefolia)

Yam (D. alata)

Taro (Colocasia)

Sweet potato

Yam (D. bulbifera)

Pitpit (Saccarum edule)

Hibiscus leaves

Bananas

Yam (D. pentaphylla)

Manioc

Sugar cane

Taro (Xanthosoma)

Yam (D. esculenta)

three gardens of different ages. For these and other reasons an error of 10 percent is not unlikely. The methods employed in these estimations are outlined in Appendix 4.

The per-acre yields of Tsembaga gardens are not high. Massal

Table 3. Yields per Acre—Tsembaga Taro-Yam Gardens

Crops	Yield in lbs. Torpai, 3.89[b] (0-23 wks.)[a]	Yield in lbs. Kakopai, 3.3 (24-66 wks.)	Total lbs. Torpai & Kakopai (0-66 wks.)	Factor for nonweighed harvest, in %	Adj. total lbs. per acre (0-66 wks.)	Yield in lbs. Tipema, 6.0 (67-120 wks.)	Factor for nonweighed harvest, in %	Adj. total lbs. per acre (67-120 wks.)	Total lbs. per acre (0-120 wks.)	Edible portion, in %	Calories per lb.	Total calories per acre
Colocasia	—	2,349.9	2,349.9	5	2,467.4	306.0	—	306.0	2,773.4	85	658	1,551,169
Xanthosoma	—	971.2	971.2	5	1,019.8	—	—	—	1,019.8	80	658	536,796
Dioscorea alata & nummularia	2.14	806.9	828.3	5	869.7	81.0	—	81.0	950.7	85	486	576,104
D. bulbifera[c]	—	188.9	188.9	5	198.3	18.0	—	18.0	216.3	85	486	
D. pentaphylla	—	159.3	159.3	5	167.3	4.0	—	4.0	171.3	85	486	
D. esculenta	—	53.6	53.6	5	56.3	—	—	—	56.3	85	486	
sweet potato	—	1,356.3	1,356.3	5	1,424.1	390.0	—	390.0	1,814.1	80	681	988,345
manioc	—	546.2	546.2	5	573.6	22.5	—	22.5	596.1	80	595	354,680
Rungia klossi	34.00	165.8	199.8	2	203.8	42.0	—	42.0	245.8	95	136	31,756
misc. greens	178.00	97.5	275.5	2	281.0	16.5	—	16.5	297.5	95	218	61,606
hibiscus leaves	—	636.9	636.9	2	649.6	120.0	—	120.0	769.6	95	136	99,430
beans	33.00	3.3	36.3	—	36.3	—	—	—	36.3	95	440	15,972
banana	—	534.9	534.9	20	641.9	822.0	20	986.4	1,628.3	70	427	486,685
corn	236.30	—	236.3	5	248.1	—	—	—	248.1	29	463	33,336
pitpit	33.00	459.8	459.8	2	468.9	26.6	—	26.6	495.5	40	104	20,612
Setaria palm.	33.00	468.9	501.9	2	511.9	610.5	—	610.5	1,122.4	17	65	12,402
cucumber	566.00	—	566.0	50	854.0	—	—	—	854.0	95	50	40,565
pumpkin	34.00	244.2	278.2	2	283.8	52.5	—	52.5	336.3	68	200	45,740
gourd	20.30	—	20.3	2	20.7	—	—	—	20.7	68	154	2,171
sugar	—	644.3	644.3	200	1,932.9	1,986.0	20	2,383.2	4,316.1	30	263	340,532
Totals									17,968.6			5,197,901

[a] Weeks after planting (entries in column 2, for example, indicate yields between 0 and 24 weeks after planting).

[b] The names (e.g., Torpai) are those of the sample gardens whose yields were weighed. The figures (e.g., 3.89) following the garden names are factors required to adjust the yields of the various sample gardens to yields per acre.

[c] D. = Dioscorea.

Relations with the Immediate Environment

Table 4. Yields per Acre—Tsembaga Sugar-Sweet Potato Gardens

Crops	Yield in lbs. Torpai, 3.89[b] (0–23 wks.)[a]	Yield in lbs. Timbikai, 4.2 (24–66 wks.)	Total in lbs. Torpai & Timbikai (0–66 wks.)	Factor for nonweighed harvest, in %	Adj. total lbs. per acre (0–66 wks.)	Yield in lbs. Unai, 3.3 (67–120 wks.)	Factor for nonweighed harvest, in %	Adj. total lbs. per acre (67–120 wks.)	Total lbs. per acre (0–120 wks.)	Edible portion, in %	Calories per lb.	Total calories per acre
Colocasia	—	445.2	445.2	5	467.5	13.2	—	13.2	480.7	85	658	268,858
Xanthosoma	—	769.6	769.6	5	808.1	16.5	—	16.5	824.6	80	658	434,280
Dioscorea alata & nummularia	—	—	—	—	—	—	—	—	—	—	—	—
D. bulbifera[c]	—	59.5	59.5	5	62.9	1.6	—	1.6	62.9	85	486	⎫
D. pentaphylla	—	38.8	38.8	5	40.7	—	—	—	42.3	85	486	⎬ 86,994
D. esculenta	—	70.3	70.3	5	73.8	—	—	—	73.8	85	486	⎭
sweet potato	—	5,055.0	5,055.0	5	5,307.7	477.7	—	477.7	5,785.4	80	681	3,151,668
manioc	17.0	—	110.2	5	115.7	16.5	—	16.5	132.2	80	595	62,475
Rungia klossi	84.0	53.5	70.5	5	71.9	12.4	—	12.4	94.3	95	136	12,186
misc. greens	—	37.8	126.8	2	129.2	—	—	—	129.2	95	218	26,748
hibiscus leaves	33.0	40.9	40.9	2	41.7	26.4	—	26.4	68.1	95	130	8,799
beans	—	33.0	33.0	2	33.0	—	—	—	33.0	95	440	13,816
banana	236.3	—	45.1	20	54.1	293.7	20	352.3	406.4	70	427	121,482
corn	—	45.1	236.3	5	248.1	—	—	—	248.1	29	463	33,336
pitpit	16.5	405.3	405.3	2	413.4	316.0	—	316.0	729.4	40	104	30,264
Setaria palm.	566.0	266.2	282.7	2	288.4	29.7	—	29.7	318.1	17	65	3,510
cucumber	17.0	—	566.0	50	854.0	—	—	—	854.0	95	50	40,565
pumpkin	10.0	106.0	123.0	2	125.4	—	—	—	125.4	68	200	16,864
gourd	—	—	10.0	2	10.2	—	—	—	10.2	68	154	1,063
sugar	—	386.4	386.4	200	1,759.2	1,372.8	20	1,647.2	3,406.4	30	263	268,686
Totals									13,824.5			4,581,594

[a] Weeks after planting (entries in column 2, for example, indicate yields between 0 and 24 weeks after planting).
[b] The names (e.g., Torpai) are those of the sample gardens whose yields were weighed. The figures (e.g., 3.89) are factors required to adjust the yields of the sample gardens to per acre yields.
[c] D. = Dioscorea.

and Barrau (1956) present a number of estimates of yields of other types of agriculture found in the South Pacific. They state that mounded sweet potatoes produce three million to six million calories per acre within seven months, or a little more, after planting. If Okinawa variety sweet potatoes are planted, the yield might be as high as eight million calories (p. 25). Irrigated taro yields, they state, may reach eight tons per acre within a year of planting (p. 8). At values equivalent to those used for the Tsembaga swiddens, this represents close to nine million calories. Higher yields are also reported from the New Guinea Highlands. Brown and Brookfield (1959:26) report for Chimbu "long fallow cultivation" of sweet potatoes, and "comparatively high yields, certainly higher than the four tons per acre of sweet potatoes which Meggitt estimated in Mae Enga."

Tsembaga yields are not as high as these, but for purposes of comparison it should be emphasized that the great preponderance of the harvest of Tsembaga gardens is taken during the twelve-month period following the initial ripening of root crops. In the period between the twenty-fourth and the seventy-sixth weeks (approximately) after planting, Tsembaga taro-yam gardens yield crops containing 85.0 percent of their total of 5,197,900 calories. During the same period sugar-sweet potato gardens yield 90.7 percent of their total. It may also be noted here that calories are not, of course, all that gardens produce. Tsembaga gardens almost certainly yield larger amounts of plant protein, for instance, than do the gardens of the Chimbu and Enga.

An attempt has been made to estimate the amount of energy expended in producing an acre of both taro-yam and sugar-sweet potato gardens. This estimation is germane to calculations that will be made later in this study, particularly in reference to pig keeping and the timing of the ritual cycle. It also provides an additional dimension for evaluating Tsembaga subsistence procedures and comparing them to those in other areas. The results of these estimations are presented in Table 5, and a discussion of the methods employed in deriving the values will be found in Appendix 5.

Estimations of the lengths of the fallow periods for various gardens were difficult. The Tsembaga are not accustomed to reckoning in years, and in most cases it was necessary to arrive at dates of

Table 5. Energy Expenditure per Acre—Tsembaga Gardens

Operation (in sequence)	Expenditure value (kcals)	Derivation	Taro-yam garden	Sugar-sweet potato garden
Clearing underbrush	.65 cal/sq ft	Timing, H-K[a]	28,314	28,314
Clearing trees	.26 cal/sq ft	Timing, H-K	11,325	11,325
Fencing	46.17 cal/lin ft	Timing, H-K[b]	17,082	17,082
Preburn weeding	.1 cal/sq ft	Timing, H-K, modified	4,356	4,356
First burn	.008 cal/sq ft	Timing, H-K	336	336
Second burn	.11 cal/sq ft	Timing, H-K	4,792	4,792
Laying soil retainers	.168 cal/sq ft	Timing, H-K	7,238	7,238
Planting	.19 cal/sq ft	Timing, H-K	16,553	16,553
First weeding	.69 cal/sq ft	Timing, H-K	30,056	30,056
Second weeding	.69 cal/sq ft	Timing, H-K	30,056	30,056
Third weeding	.69 cal/sq ft	Timing, H-K	30,056	30,056
Tying sugar	1.80–3.60 cal/clump	Timing, H-K[c]	4,500	4,500
Misc. maintenance		(see note [d])	10,000	5,000
Acquiring supplies		Estimate for acquiring supplies, mainly lashing	8,500	5,000
Harvesting sweet potatoes	5.9 cal/lb	Timing, H-K	10,703	34,132
Harvesting taros	1.1 cal/lb	Timing, H-K	4,172	1,436
Harvesting manioc	3.0 cal/lb	Estimate, H-K	1,788	396
Harvesting yams	10.0 cal/lb	Estimate, H-K	13,930	1,770
Harvesting surface crops	1.0 cal/lb	Estimate, H-K	10,373	6,434
Walking to gardens	1.5 cal/min	H-K[e]	12,000	9,000
Carrying from gardens	6.56 cal/min	H-K[f]	59,404	39,360
Total			315,534	287,192

NOTES: Ratio of caloric return to input: taro-yam garden, 16.5:1; sugar-sweet potato garden, 15.9:1; and with carrying and walking reduced 80%, taro-yam garden, 20.1:1; sugar-sweet potato garden, 18.4:1.

[a] Hipsley and Kirk, 1965.

[b] Assumption of 370 ft of fence per acre.

[c] Assumption of 500 clumps per acre. First tie 1.8 cal/clump: second and third 3.6 cal/clump.

[d] Estimate for fence mending, yam house building, propping plants, etc.

[e] Allowance 20-minute walk down hill, 300 trips to sugar-sweet potato garden, 400 trips to taro-yam garden.

[f] 25-kg load carried up slope for 30 minutes, 300 trips from taro-yam, 200 from sugar-sweet potato garden.

previous cultivation by reference to events that themselves could be fixed in time only approximately.

The length of the fallow period varies between sites on the basis of a number of factors. These include local edaphic conditions and convenience to residences, but most important seems to be altitude. The full cultivation cycle measured from one planting to the next on sites between 3,500 and 4,200 feet is in some instances as short as ten years, although the average seems to fall around fifteen. At the higher altitudes fallow periods vary in length from an estimated twenty to forty-five years, with the average falling around twenty-five years. The figures of fifteen and twenty-five years, for lack of more precise estimations, will be used in later computations.

Estimation of the adequacy of fallow periods presents problems of criteria. The soil samples that survived the voyage to the laboratory cannot form the basis of a judgment; they indicate merely that fallow periods are necessary if soil depletion is to be avoided. The factors considered in estimating the adequacy of Tsembaga fallow periods are summarized here.

1. Several of the gardening practices that were observed seem to have conservation value. The Tsembaga practice selective weeding, for instance. From the time that weeding begins, five to eight weeks after planting, second-growth tree seedlings are allowed to remain, while herbaceous forms are uprooted. Not only does this avoid a definite grassy phase in the post-gardening succession, thereby minimizing the danger of a deflection toward a grassy disclimax, but it also provides during the cropping period deep tree roots that penetrate farther into the substrate than the roots of most crops. These roots are able to recover nutrients that otherwise might be lost through leaching. The development of trees over the garden also provides some protection for the exposed soil against tropical downpours and, furthermore, induces the gardeners to abandon the garden before the structure or content of the soil is severely damaged. People abandon gardens not because the crops are completely exhausted, but because the developing trees make the harvesting of the remaining root crops difficult.

The practice of pollarding large trees may also serve to protect the exposed soil during the cropping period. A fringe of leaves is left on the tops of many of the larger pollarded trees, and some of them survive their mutilation. Their roots may also recover some of the soil nutrients that are leached to levels deeper than may be recovered by the roots of the crops.

The practice of placing pigs in abandoned gardens for short periods (two to four weeks) may also contribute to the recovery of the sites. The pigs turn the ground, eliminating both herbaceous growth that has developed since the last weeding and some of the smaller seedlings, which if allowed to develop could provide root and light competition for already established saplings. The contribution of manure by pigs may also be considerable, but is probably offset by the organic materials they remove from the site.

2. Examination of the floristic composition of secondary growth at various stages of development also was relied upon as an indicator of the adequacy of the fallow periods. The absence or rarity of *Imperata cylindrica*, the grass that dominates disclimax areas on Tsembaga territory, on almost all garden sites suggests that deflection toward stable grassy associations is uncommon. On the other hand, the fact that in a census of twenty- to twenty-five-year-old secondary growth 54 percent of the tree species noted are also found in the virgin forest suggests that the secondary forest does not represent a serious deflection from the primary forest. Information concerning the floristic composition of secondary growth is summarized in Appendix 6.

3. The structure of the secondary growth in which gardens were being cut was also taken into consideration. In almost all instances the forest had formed an unbroken canopy over the site, and trees were of substantial size. There were in most plots many trees over 18 inches in circumference, and average heights were usually above 30 feet. The herbaceous species, while present, were for the most part limited to forms less than 2 feet in height.

4. Information from other areas, while not directly applicable, at least suggests the adequacy of Tsembaga fallow periods. Newton (1960:83), in reporting upon experimental work on shifting cultivation in Africa, states that the total quantity of nutrients immobilized within five years of garden abandonment is half that in eighteen years, and leaf development is also rapid. He states that the accumulation of litter on the forest floor reaches a maximum in eight to twelve years, and its soil-restoring decomposition and mineralization is rapid in tropical areas due to high temperature, humidity, and the prevalence of insects. There are, no doubt, differences between conditions in various areas, but if Tsembaga conditions are at all similar to those in which the experiments reported by Newton took place, Tsembaga fallow periods should be sufficient.

In consideration of these various factors, Tsembaga fallow periods were judged to be adequate; it is even possible that they are longer than necessary. In later computations, however, the values of fifteen and twenty-five years will be used.

SILVICULTURE

Tsembaga silviculture is a set of interrelated activities directed toward the establishment and maintenance of a permanent association of trees bearing edible materials in areas previously dominated by associations of other plants. Many kinds of trees are planted on Tsembaga territory; a list of the more important ones will be found in Appendix 71. Attention will be confined here to the two forms that are planted in groves: *ambiam* (*Gnetum gnemon;* p.e.: *tulip*) and *komba* (*Pandanus conoideus;* p.e.: *marita*).

Ambiam, which is planted in groves below 4,000 feet, provides most importantly an edible green leaf. The fruit, which is known to the Tsembaga to be edible, is only infrequently consumed. This tree is less important in the diet of the Tsembaga than it is in those of many other Maring groups, which is at least in part a result of recent military defeat. After the Tsembaga were driven from their territory in 1953 their victorious enemies, the Kundagai, cut down most of their *ambiam* trees. The Tsembaga, however, are fortunate in having many other greens in their diet, many of which they prefer to *ambiam,* and replanting has not been heavy.

The Kundagai also cut down much of the Tsembaga *marita,* but heavy replanting has taken place since the Tsembaga began their return to their territory in 1957, and some men have as many as 700 trees in the ground. Unlike *ambiam,* for which there are many alternative greens, there is no substitute for *marita.* This tree bears a large waxy red or yellow fruit from which a sauce rich in vegetable fats is produced. Most of these trees were not yet bearing during the period of fieldwork, for *marita* planted on Tsembaga territory does not produce fruit until it is about five years of age.

No measurements were made of the amount of land under *marita* groves, of yields per unit area, or of the expenditure of energy involved in their planting or harvesting. The total amount of land under these groves is small, however, probably under fifteen acres, and is located for the most part below 3,000 feet. Some *marita* is also planted at higher altitudes, usually in gullies and ravines unfit for swiddening. Planting density is between 300 and 400 trees per acre.

The amount of work in planting and harvesting *marita* is slight, for the herbaceous cover need not be removed from the site, nor is fencing necessary. Harvesting involves simply knocking down the fruit with a long pole. Both planting and harvesting are men's work. While no estimates were made of per-acre yields, the contribution of *marita* to the diet is significant, as reflected in consumption records (see Appendix 9).

ANIMAL HUSBANDRY

The Tsembaga keep four kinds of animals: pigs, dogs, chickens, and cassowaries (dogs were reintroduced during the period of fieldwork). All dogs previously owned by the Tsembaga had perished in an epidemic of a respiratory disease some years earlier. They were kept mainly for their usefulness in hunting and, in earlier times, for their teeth. Before shells were brought into the area forty to seventy years ago, the incisors of dogs and marsupials served as valuables in bride prices and other transactions. Some Marings, furthermore, eat dog flesh. Others are enjoined from doing so by taboos that not only apply to certain descent groups but also to people who are cognatically connected to those descent groups. Two of the five Tsembaga clans suffered such a prohibition against consuming dog flesh.

Some Maring groups keep large numbers of cassowaries; the Tsembaga do not. During most of the period of fieldwork, the Tsembaga had only one fully grown cassowary. Cassowaries do not breed in captivity. All tame birds are captured as chicks, and the Tsembaga usually trade cassowary chicks shortly after their capture to Jimi Valley people who, in turn, trade them across the Wahgi Divide, where they are important in bride prices. Among Maring groups cassowaries not only provided meat but also feathers, which were used in headdresses worn during fighting. Since pacification, cassowary feathers are not as valuable as they were. Chickens are few in number and hardly cared for. Rats kill many of the chicks, and hawks and other carnivorous birds carry off many of the grown chickens.

Pigs, in terms of their numbers, their contribution to the diet, and the effort required to keep them, are by far the most important of the domestic animals. Tsembaga ritual, moreover, like the ritual of many other people in Melanesia, is closely bound up with pigs. Most ritual occasions are marked by the slaughter of pigs and the consumption of pork. Furthermore, the timing of the ritual cycle and the occurrence of the year-long pig festival, called the *kaiko,* which terminates the five- to twenty-year cycle, depend upon the size, composition, and rate of growth of the pig herd. A more detailed discussion of the place of pigs among the Tsembaga is therefore necessary.

In June 1962, at the beginning of the *kaiko,* the Tsembaga herd numbered 169. At the termination of the festival in November 1963, the herd was reduced to 60 juvenile and 15 adult pigs. All of the surviving adults were scheduled for imminent killing, so that the herd was in effect reduced to 60 juveniles. This latter figure, moreover, is much higher than it would have been had I not been present. Wealth which I provided (by trading salt and beads for food, by paying young men in shillings for carrying supplies, etc.) was used for the purchase of a number of baby pigs that otherwise could not have been obtained. It is likely that in my absence the pig herd at the close of the *kaiko,* the point at which it is smallest, would have consisted of no more than 40 juveniles.

The average size of the animals also differed at the beginning and end of the *kaiko.* The average live weight of animals in June 1962 is estimated at 120 to 150 pounds. The average weight of animals surviving the *kaiko* is estimated at 60 to 70 pounds. The live weight of the herd was, if the surviving adults are discounted, about 5.6 times as great before the festival as after it. If a further adjustment is made to discount 20 of the juveniles present in November 1963, as a result of my presence, the difference becomes even greater. After such an adjustment the ratio of the live weight of the herd before to live weight after the festival is 8.4:1.

In addition to providing their owners with meat, pigs make at least two other contributions to the subsistence and physical well-being of the Tsembaga. It has already been mentioned that pigs confined in abandoned gardens not only utilize root crops that cannot be efficiently harvested by human beings, but also benefit the secondary forest that is developing on the site by uprooting much of its herbaceous component and thinning the arboreal component. Swiddens are sometimes planted twice by Maring groups in the Jimi Valley, and after the first crop is almost exhausted, pigs are penned in the gardens. Their rooting not only eliminates weeds and seedling trees, but it also softens the ground, making the task of planting for a second time easier. The pigs, then, are used by some Maring as cultivating machines.

Pigs make a further contribution to Tsembaga subsistence by eating garbage and human feces. Not only do they thus assist in keeping residential areas clean but they also convert wastes into materials that may be utilized by their masters.

Young pigs are treated as pets. As soon as it is weaned a baby pig begins to accompany its mistress to the gardens each day. At first it is carried. When it gets a little older it is led by a leash attached to its foreleg, but it quickly learns to follow its mistress in dog-like fashion and the leash is removed.

The young animal receives a great deal of loving attention—it is petted, talked to, and fed choice morsels. It shares the living quarters of the woman's house with the humans until it is between eight months and a year of age, when it is given a stall of its own. Even then it is not domiciled separately from its keepers, for stalls are inside the house, separated from the living quarters only by a rail fence through which the animal can thrust its snout for scratching or for morsels of food.

When it reaches four or five months of age the pig is considered old enough to look after itself and it no longer accompanies its mistress to the gardens. Instead, it is turned loose each morning to spend its day rooting in the secondary growth and forest and to return home in the evening, when it is given its daily ration of garbage and substandard tubers, mainly sweet potatoes.

This ration is substantial, but it probably does not comprise the largest portion of a mature animal's intake. The pig provides himself with most of his food in the course of his daily rounds. It is, however, an amount that is at least sufficient to induce most pigs to return home each evening and thus remain attached to the households of their mistresses. That is, it is an amount sufficient to keep most, but not all, animals domesticated in the face of considerable opportunity to become feral.

In this connection it may be suggested that as important to the pig as his ration of garbage and sweet potatoes may be, he may not return home for garbage and sweet potatoes alone. The work of Hendrix, Mitchell, and Van Vlack (1966) with horses indicates that certain kinds of human handling, notably petting and stroking, very early in a foal's life alter its relations with its mother and tie it closely to its human handler. For instance, foals that receive affectionate human handling do not follow closely behind their mothers as do foals that have not been so treated, but move considerable distances away. They also become unusually tractable and responsive saddle horses.

It is important to note that Hendrix et al. suggest that an important factor in the modification of the foal's development is the greater ability of the human handler (because he is equipped with hands) than the mare to provide tactile stimulation to the foal, and it may be that animals thus treated develop attachments to humans as strong or even stronger than attachments to their own species. Similarly, Lawrence K. Frank (1957) has observed that tactile communication is extremely important in the psychic development and socialization of human infants, and there are indications that this is true for the infants of other species as well (see Jay, 1963:119; Frank, 1957:201). It may be suggested that the petting and stroking to which Maring pigs are subjected as infants is an additional factor in keeping them domesticated throughout their lives. Such handling by humans communicates and produces positive affect, through which, along with his ration, the pig is bound to a social group dominated by humans. It is hardly facetious to say that the pig through its early socialization becomes a member of a Maring family.

Small numbers of pigs are easy to keep. To supply one or two animals with substandard sweet potatoes (under four ounces each) requires little extra work, for these tubers are taken from the ground in the course of harvesting the daily ration for humans. When the herd becomes large, however, the substandard tubers incidentally obtained in the course of harvesting for human needs become insufficient. It then becomes necessary to harvest especially for pigs —that is, to work for the pigs and perhaps to give them food fit for human consumption.

Records were kept of rations set aside for pigs at the four households of the Tomegai clan for a period of a little over three months (information concerning the sizes of these pigs is summarized in Table 6). The pig consumption figures were then extended to cover an additional five months for which harvesting and consumption figures were compiled for the Tomegai, and during which the pig and human populations were fairly constant.

Table 6. Roster of Pigs Owned by Members of the Tomegai Clan, 1962–63

Pig name	Size* March 1963	Date of acquisition	Size at acquisition	Month of death (1963)	Surviving size, Nov., 1963	Notes
Aŋgane	5			Nov.		
Gerki	5			Nov.		
Parau	4			Nov.		
Kombom	5			Nov.		
Tereŋ	5			Nov.		Bi-local pig; residing in Bank about 50% of time
Kikia	4			Nov.		
Koč Wai	3			Nov.		
Tambuŋ	2			Nov.		
Jokai	2			Nov.		
Bai	2				3	Scheduled for killing soon
Gi	2				3	Scheduled for killing soon
Grič	1				3	
Yuaneŋa	1				3	
Nameless		Aug.	1		2	
Prim		July	1	Sept.		Accidental death

* Pig sizes: (1) *wamba ñak* ("soft child"), under 40 pounds; (2) *wamba anč* ("hard child"), 40 to 80 pounds; (3) *baka* ("short"), 80 to 120 pounds; (4) *yundoi* ("large"), 120 to 160 pounds; (5) *yundoimai* ("very large"), 160 to 200 pounds.

The thirteen to fifteen pigs received considerably more sweet potato and manioc than did the sixteen humans. Of 9,944 pounds of sweet potatoes brought to the houses between March 11 and November 8, 1963, the pigs were given 5,554 pounds, or 53.7% of the total. Of 1,349 pounds of manioc brought home, the pigs received 1,106 pounds, or 82.0%. The total of all root crops brought home during this period in the four households was 18,574 pounds. The ration set aside for pigs was 6,674 pounds, or 35.9% of the total. An additional calculation suggests that an even larger proportion of root crops carried home eventually finds its way into the stomachs of the pigs. On the basis of observations (which accorded well with published figures on edible portion and wastage in root crops), 15% of the gross human ration of 11,900 pounds, or 1,785 pounds, may be assumed to have been wasted; that is, it was not eaten by humans. If half of this waste was peeling that was consumed by the pigs, the pig ration was 40.7% of the total root crops carried home. The humans received 54.4%, and 4.9% was wasted (burned in cooking, etc.).

It was not possible to weigh the size of the ration given to pigs of different sizes. Using as a basis figures of rations given to European pigs of different sizes under test conditions (FAO Agricultural Study #44:47), size 2 pigs receive about twice as much as size 1, and sizes 3, 4, and 5 receive three times as much. This calculation, which is gross and probably underestimates their rations, yields a figure of 2.6 pounds per day of tubers set aside for the adult and adolescent pigs. If garbage from tuberous portions of the human ration is added, the daily ration of adult pigs approaches three pounds, and it should not be forgotten that they receive other food as well, both other kinds of garbage and morsels from the rations of their masters and mistresses.

To provide such a ration for pigs is expensive. An indication of just how expensive may be derived from an examination of the differences in amount of land put in cultivation by the Tomegai in 1962, when they were supporting fourteen pigs averaging 100 to 130 pounds each, and in 1963, when they were looking forward to the reduction of the herd to three pigs averaging between 85 and 110 pounds. These figures are summarized in Table 7. The reduction

Table 7. Total Area of Tomegai Gardens in Square Feet

Garden type	1962	1963
Taro-yam gardens or mixed gardens	98,859	126,100
Sugar-sweet potato gardens	111,375	8,225
Totals	210,234	134,325

in land under cultivation immediately following the reduction of the pig herd by eleven animals was 75,909 square feet, or 36.1 percent. Since the difference is entirely in sweet potato gardens, and not in taro-yam gardens (out of which visitors to the pig festival are fed), it is reasonable to regard the reduction in garden area as a result of the reduction in the number of pigs being fed. It would seem that 1.65 acres were put into cultivation for the provisioning of eleven adult and adolescent animals. It may be mentioned here that the figure of .15 acres in cultivation per pig falls within the range, computed later in this chapter, for acreage under cultivation per person.

Another computation is of interest here. Figures derived earlier indicate that the energy required to produce 76,000 square feet of sweet potato garden is approximately 495,000 calories. The reduction in the herd was estimated at a live weight of 1,600 pounds at a maximum. This amount was estimated to produce, after dressing, about 800 pounds of uncooked flesh, or 50% of the live weight. At 1,318 calories per pound (FAO Nutritional Study #11:1954), this converts to 1,054,400 calories. The protein content of thin pork carcasses is taken at 10.9%, and fat 27% (FAO #11:1954), yielding for the ten pigs 87 pounds of protein and 216 pounds of fat.

It may not be necessary to point out that the ratio of energy derived from pork to energy expended in raising the pigs was *not* approximately 1,000,000:500,000, or 2:1. This would have been a poor enough figure from the point of view of energy efficiency. The actual ratio was even worse, for most of the pigs were two or more years of age when killed. The ratio could hardly have been better than 1:1 and may, indeed, have been even less favorable. That is, it is quite possible that more energy was expended to raise food for pigs than was returned in the form of pork. Pig raising, furthermore, involves energy costs other than those connected with raising food for them: lost pigs must be searched for, and damage to houses and fences by pigs must be repaired. The destruction of crops caused by invasions of pigs into producing gardens must also be regarded as an energy loss to the human population and, thus, one of the costs of pig keeping.

It is interesting to note that the energy ratio characteristic of the Tsembaga pig husbandry is less favorable than that of Siriono hunting, estimated by Harris (unpublished paper) to be 1.4:1, but probably closer to 2.5:1. Even this latter figure is not very favorable, and probably no human population anywhere could survive with such a ratio characterizing the energy-capturing activities upon which it relies most heavily. In addition to subsistence activities, other activities and basal metabolism must be supported by captured energy, and so must the activities and metabolisms of nonworking dependents: children, old people, and the sick and injured. It is little more than a guess, but I believe that very few techniques employed by human groups *primarily for the purpose of capturing energy* would show energy ratios much below 10:1. Less favorable ratios would barely cover the survival requirements of the population.

But it should not be assumed that energy-capturing activities are the only necessary subsistence activities. The survival and well-being of the human organism depend upon a supply of minerals, vitamins, and proteins as well as upon a supply of calories. In some cases the activity that yields these nutrients is the same as that which captures energy. Activities directed toward the production and harvesting of cereals, for instance, frequently fulfill at one and the same time both energy and protein requirements. But this need not be the case, and there is strong reason to doubt that the production and harvesting of root crops does so. It is not the purpose of this section to discuss the general adequacy of Tsembaga crops for the fulfillment of the protein as well as energy requirements of human beings. It is, however, important to emphasize here that while the details of energy transactions may illuminate some aspects of ecological and, perhaps, economic relationships, explanations that are restricted to the consideration of energy inputs and outputs will in some cases fail. We could only be mystified by a prolonged and laborious procedure, such as Tsembaga pig raising, which resulted in the return of somewhat less energy than was actually invested. We might, indeed, be tempted to construct theories that included among the advantages of the procedure only such empirically undemonstrable qualities as "mystic merit," or the prestige derived from conspicuous waste (Linton, 1955:98). On the other hand, if the frame is broadened so that not only energy input–energy output but also energy input–material output transactions are considered, activities such as Tsembaga pig raising are more clearly understood. The Tsembaga make an investment of energy and get a return of nutrients that are extremely important, but not primarily as a source of energy.

In light of the food and energy requirements of pig keeping and of the energy yield of pork, the applicability to the Tsembaga of a hypothesis recently advanced by Vayda, Leeds, and Smith (1961) concerning Melanesian pig keeping should be examined. These writers suggest that pig keeping may play an important part in the adjustment of Melanesian man to variations from time to time in the availability of foodstuffs, due to unfavorable weather.

A way in which Melanesian populations are able to adjust to such unpredictable variation is through the practice of trying to plant more crops every year than can be or need to be consumed by the planters in a year not appreciably disturbed by adverse weather. Planting what will be more than enough should the weather be good is a means of ensuring that there will be enough . . . should the weather be bad. . . . If, then, the size of the human population is limited by the times of minimal yield, the vegetal surpluses of normal years become available for the feeding of live-stock. . . . The practice of feeding vegetal surpluses to the pigs in the years of normal and maximal crop yields is described as "banking" in Oliver's account (1955:470) of a Solomon Island culture, and the term seems appropri-ate, for the pigs are indeed food reserves on the hoof. . . . In years of minimal yield when the garden produce has to be used entirely for the support of the local human popula-tion, attempts may be made to trade away or ceremonially to give away the pigs to distant and better-supplied com-munities or else to have the pigs agisted at such places. If these attempts are unsuccessful, the pigs must subsist on what they can forage for themselves. . . . Moreover, in the years of minimal yield, not only can the mature pigs in most cases take care of their own subsistence but they can also be a vital source of food for human beings. [1961:70, 71]

The mechanism outlined here does not seem applicable to the Tsembaga case. Weather bad enough to cause crop failures seems never to occur, according to informants. Indeed, they say that crop failures don't seem to occur for any reason. Anything less than a residence of many years' standing does not permit definitive state-ments concerning the occurrence or nonoccurrence of crop failures, but there is little reason in this instance to doubt informants' state-ments. They indicate that the most serious hindrance to cultivation suffered by the Tsembaga and their neighbors is excessive rain during the "drier season' (June–September), when most gardens are burned. Heavy rain during this period makes the task of burning more difficult but does not reduce the acreage placed in cultivation and has no effect upon yields. Field observations tend to support the informants' statements. July, August, and September 1963 were marked by unseasonably heavy rains, but I could detect nothing to suggest that the unfavorable weather resulted in less acreage in cultivation than would otherwise have been the case. No one, for instance, failed to burn gardens that had already been cleared of trees and underbrush. People simply worked harder at burning their gardens than would have been necessary if the weather had been drier. Informants say that comparably heavy rains had fallen during July, August, and September 1962. Very wet "drier seasons" apparently are not uncommon in the Simbai Valley.

Although crop failure caused by weather conditions may not have occurred, it is possible that food shortages could have developed out of the disruption brought by warfare. Informants denied this, however, and generally agreed that even during periods of active hostility garden work could be accomplished during frequent cease-fires.

The mechanism suggested by Vayda, Leeds, and Smith is inapplicable to the Tsembaga case for another reason as well. It posits an adjustment in which the amount of land put into cultivation by a population of constant size will remain more or less constant from year to year. In "normal years" this amount of land will yield food in excess of human requirements, and the excess will be fed to pigs, which may be regarded as "repositories for surplus vegetal produce" (1961:71). It has already been noted, however, that among the Tsembaga the amount of land put into production is not constant from year to year. The amount of land in production in any year depends upon the sizes of both the human and pig populations. As the pig population increases, so does the amount of land under cultivation. Pigs are not only fed from the surplus of gardens planted for humans: acreage may be put into production for the pigs.

The Tsembaga case does not provide a general refutation of the Vayda, Leeds, and Smith hypothesis, however. Their larger point, that Melanesian pig keeping is not wasteful, and that on the contrary "pigs are vitally important to the management of subsistence by

Melanesian populations" (1961:69) is supported. Although their more particular formulation does not fit the Tsembaga case, it deserves to be tested by quantified observations of pig husbandry, cultivation practices, and dietary intakes among Melanesian people living under a variety of weather conditions. It need hardly be said that in different ecological settings practices such as pig keeping should be expected to play different roles in the adjustments of their practitioners to their environments. It would not be surprising to discover that the mechanism suggested by Vayda, Leeds, and Smith corresponds closely to the situations in some areas subject to climatic catastrophe.

But in light of the discussion above concerning the capture of protein and energy, some comment must be made on one further point in the Vayda, Leeds, and Smith formulation: the characterization of pigs as repositories of vegetal surplus. The mere fact that pigs are fed domesticated plant foods not consumed by humans makes them, in a sense, repositories of vegetal surplus. The characterization suggests, however, whether or not it is the authors' intention, that the ration fed to the pigs is material that is in excess of the immediate physiological requirements of their keepers, and that it is merely stored in the animals for future use. The implication is that the material recovered from the animals is of the same sort as, or equivalent to, that which was fed to them at earlier times. In fact, the material recovered from pigs is quantitatively and qualitatively different from that which was fed to them, and it is in these differences that the main significance of the place of pigs in the diet of their keepers lies.

The ration fed to pigs consists mainly of carbohydrates in the form of sweet potatoes and tubers. These are most important sources of energy. However, animals are poor storehouses of energy since most of what they consume is expended in metabolism and activity, and it is unlikely that the amount of calories that can be reclaimed from the flesh of pigs raised by Melanesian practices would exceed one-fifth of the amount that they had received in rations.

It may also be recalled that pig husbandry is expensive in terms of the caloric expenditure demanded of its practitioners, and that the maintenance of pigs may also demand, as it does among the Tsembaga, the cultivation of acreage in excess of that required for the support of the human population. Where swiddening is practiced this could necessitate shortened fallow periods, which might produce changes in either soil structure or composition. These changes might well affect crop yields adversely. To put this in terms of the banking analogy, the "service charges" may be greater than the "savings account."

In view of the shortcomings of pigs as energy storehouses, and in view of the high cost of pig maintenance in both energy expenditure and land, it might well be asked if pig husbandry could be regarded as adaptive if the storage of energy for use in periods of crisis were the main advantage gained by those who practice it. The indications are that in many situations people would serve themselves better by giving up pig husbandry, letting surplus tubers rot in good years, and in years of shortage themselves consuming substandard tubers, which are edible even if undesirable. It may be suggested that only in environments in which even substandard tubers might become unavailable would the emergency energy supply provided by pork justify the high costs of maintaining pigs, and even in such environments pigs alone are of questionable value as a famine food. It is not likely that a Melanesian population would have sufficient pigs on hand to use pork as a substitute for carbohydrates until a new crop of tubers came in. The Tsembaga pig herd, for instance, at the outset of the *kaiko*, probably represented about 13,000 pounds of pork. A minimum of 1,000 to 1,400 calories a day per average person would be required to permit people to carry out even minimal activities. If such a ration had to be provided to a population the size of the Tsembaga by pork alone, the Tsembaga herd would be exhausted in two to three months. It is, of course, unlikely that no other foods would be obtainable, but it is also unlikely that such a quantity of pork would be available during a period of hardship to groups similar in size to the Tsembaga. This quantity reflects maximal herd size; usually the herd is smaller.

Although the advantages of pigs as storehouses of energy are dubious, the animals do render an obvious nutritional service to their keepers. The qualitative differences between the composition of pig fodder, mainly sweet potatoes and manioc in the Tsembaga case, and pork make this apparent. The edible portion of a lean pig yields 10.9% protein and 27% fat by weight (FAO Nutritional Study

#11:1954). The edible portion of sweet potatoes yields 0.9–1.7% protein and 0.3% fat by weight (Massal and Barrau, 1956). Manioc yields 0.7–1.2% protein and 0.3% fat (Massal and Barrau). While the amino acid ratios of sweet potatoes are quite good, those of manioc are extremely poor, and not all of the limited amount of protein that manioc contains can be metabolized by humans except in the presence of other foods rich in the specific proteins that manioc lacks. The disparity, thus, between the protein contents of manioc and sweet potato on the one hand, and pork on the other, is even wider than indicated by the figures. The difference between the fat contents of the root crops and the pork is in the ratio of 89:1. It seems, therefore, that rather than being viewed as a means for storing vegetables, pig husbandry might better be regarded as a means for converting carbohydrates into high-quality protein and fat.

In a later section the role of pork consumption at times of crisis will be discussed. It is sufficient to note here that a ready supply of high-quality protein is of considerable importance to the well-being of the Tsembaga and no doubt other Melanesian populations as well. Melanesian pigs, as Vayda, Leeds, and Smith point out, cannot be regarded as luxuries. They are a very expensive necessity. The lengths to which the Tsembaga go to maintain their animals is striking, but perhaps not extraordinary for horticultural people living on tuberous staples.

It is not only in respect to the amount of work entailed in their care that large numbers of pigs may be, as Vayda, Leeds, and Smith (1961:71) have pointed out, too much of a good thing. This is also true of the sanitary and cultivating services rendered by pigs. A small number of pigs is sufficient to keep residential areas clean and is also sufficient to suppress herbaceous growth and superfluous seedlings in abandoned gardens. A larger herd, on the other hand, may be troublesome—the greater the number of pigs, the greater the possibility of their invading producing gardens, with concomitant damage not only to crops and young secondary growth, but also to the relations between the owners of guilty pigs and the owners of damaged gardens. Furthermore, while exposure to a moderate number of pigs for a limited time directly after the abandonment of gardens may benefit the development of the arboreal component of the fallow by eliminating seedlings that might compete with established saplings, the prolonged exposure of a site to a large number of pigs is detrimental; many seedlings that, being at some distance from already established specimens, could grow to fill gaps in the canopy are constantly eliminated. The establishment of quick-growing, sun-loving herbaceous species, including *kunai*, is thus encouraged. The latter grass, when it becomes dominant, tends to form a fairly stable disclimax, its rhyzomatous subsurface structure making it difficult for other species, arboreal or herbaceous, to gain a foothold.

The effects of concentrating a large number of pigs in a small area could be observed around the Tsembaga settlement. It has already been mentioned that in the past the Tsembaga settlement pattern has been "pulsating," with residential units being of clan or subclan size most of the time. Not only people but also, and perhaps more importantly, their pigs have usually been scattered over the country-side. However, out of fear of their enemies the Tsembaga, upon returning to their territory in 1957 after a three-year exile, built all of their houses in a single nucleated settlement, which they con-tinued to occupy in 1963. For six years 200 persons, rather than the usual 20 to 40, thus resided within an area 200 to 400 feet wide and about 2,000 feet long. Each day about half of their pigs passed through the grounds named "*Pra*" and "*Gerki*" just west of the set-tlement, rooting on their way. These areas were cultivated in 1957, and stumps bear out informants' statements that the sites were in secondary forest previous to that time. But six years later trees were only scattered. No canopy had formed, for the pigs had constantly rooted out the seedlings necessary to its development. *Kunai* seemed to be the most important component of the ground cover.

Usually such concentrations of pigs were not allowed to develop. In earlier times the extent to which settlements were scattered was, it seems, directly correlated with the size of the pig herd. During and directly after the pig festival the degree of nucleation was high. As the pig herd grew, however, people would move away, establish-ing themselves in hamlets. Even these sometimes disintegrated into scattered homesteads as the number of pigs grew even larger.

Factors other than pigs, of course, provided stimulus for this scat-tering. The Tsembaga and other Maring are likely to move their residences because of illness, which is thought frequently to be the result of the contamination of the ground either by supernatural *tukump,* corruption disseminated by a spirit, or by *kum,* a similar sort of areal infection sent by sorcery. But disease among pigs is frequently rationalized in precisely the same way and is probably as frequent a reason for moving as is disease among people.

Arguments concerning pigs also result in removals to isolated locations. These frequently have to do with garden invasion. Residential isolation serves to increase the distance between one's pigs and the gardens of others and the pigs of other people and gardens of one's own, thus diminishing the possibility of damage to both gardens and social relations. This is explicitly stated by some Tsembaga in explaining the location of their residences. Residential removal, usually resulting in the scattering of house sites, is also stimulated by the desire to decrease house-to-garden distances, as has already been mentioned, and the meaning of this in terms of energy expenditure has been presented. The need to reduce house-to-garden distances obviously becomes increasingly compelling with an increased pig herd, for it is necessary to transport food for pigs as well as people from gardens to houses.

While the process of residential "denucleation" mitigates the problems resulting from large concentrations of pigs in limited areas, it also undoubtedly results in less social interaction between members of different small residential groups. Further, the scattered residential pattern opens the group to greater danger from enemy action during periods of open hostility. In short, the Tsembaga pay for their pigs not only in land, food, and energy, but also in loss of opportunities for social contact and in increased vulnerability.

Certain breeding practices inhibit the rapid growth of the pig population. All male pigs are castrated at approximately three months of age. Tsembaga say that this practice produces a larger and more docile animal. It also obviously results in a reliance upon feral males for the impregnation of domestic sows. Matings must be infrequent since most of the sows are domiciled above 4,000 feet, while the feral males are inclined to stay below 3,000 feet. During the period of fieldwork, out of a potential one hundred pregnancies (sows can bear two litters a year) only fourteen litters resulted.[2]

Birth generally takes place in the forest and infants are sometimes

2. I believe that this figure is particularly low and should not be taken to represent the birthrate of Tsembaga pigs over longer periods of time. I suggest that the

lost. Perhaps some of those lost survive in a feral state, if so, they may serve later to impregnate domestic sows or may be recovered through hunting, but most of them probably perish. Mortality among those infant pigs who do find their way home is also high. From the fourteen litters only thirty-two of the offspring were alive at the end of the fieldwork. If the seven littermates born in early December 1963 and still surviving at the end of the fieldwork two weeks later are excluded from the sample, an average of only two animals per litter survived infancy.

Hunting and Gathering

A wide variety of nondomesticated resources, obtained from all of the biotic associations found on the territory, are utilized by the Tsembaga. Information concerning the use and site of occurrence of several hundred of these items is summarized in Appendix 8, but the lists are far from complete.

Reliance upon any single item is not particularly heavy. While no quantitative data on the use of such materials were compiled, it is clear, however, that reliance upon the aggregate of nondomesticated resources is considerable. Of particular importance are firewood, game, and building materials. The land under primary and secondary forest should not be considered to be merely a reserve that could be put into production should the need arise, or land out of production during the fallow period. Such lands constitute important resource areas in their own right. Increase in the amount of land under cultivation not only might damage the environment by shortening fallows or encouraging erosion in the steep higher zone covered by primary forest; it would also reduce the amount of nondomesticated materials available to the Tsembaga.

THE DIET

Estimation of the food intakes of the Tsembaga are necessary to calculations that will be made later. One of the goals of this study

---

birthrate among the pigs is inversely correlated with the degree of residential nucleation. Feral pigs tend to avoid areas that are densely populated by humans, and domestic animals do not seem for the most part to wander very far afield. Moreover, in 1963 the movements of domestic pigs were restricted by the situation of the Tsembaga settlement, which was separated from much of the territory by streams the pigs found difficult to cross. With a more dispersed settlement pattern there would be considerably more opportunity for feral males and domestic sows to meet.

is to show how ritual operates to keep the trophic demands of the Tsembaga and their pigs within the carrying capacity of their territory. To do this, it is necessary to calculate the trophic demands of the population. In most estimations of carrying capacity, this quantification is expressed in terms of acreage per capita per annum put into production. Such a figure does not indicate, however, whether a per capita daily intake of 1,500 or 2,500 or 3,000 calories is allowed for. Estimations of actual intake specify the level at which the individuals who constitute the population are being supported, which quantification in terms of area under cultivation alone does not. Actual intakes, further, may be assessed against estimated requirements and a judgment can be made as to whether the population is being maintained in a state of well-being or at bare subsistence level.

Estimations of intakes, in addition to supplementing carrying capacity calculations, will form one of the bases for another estimation that will be of considerable importance in elucidating the homeostatic function of ritual: the amount of energy available for pig husbandry. The ways in which ritual and taboo tend to optimize the utility of the limited amounts of animal protein available will also be described.

Composition of the Diet

The composition of the Tsembaga diet by percentage of constituent foods by weight is presented in Table 8, along with comparative information from other New Guinea groups.

The data from Busama, Kaiapit, Patep, and Kavataria were collected during the New Guinea Food Survey of 1947. The broad nature of this survey did not permit long observation of consumption in any location, and it is probable that some items included in the diets of these communities were not recorded. It may be, therefore, that the impression of greater variety in the Tsembaga diet is to some extent misleading. It is worth noting, however, that the Tsembaga seem to rely less upon any single starchy staple than do other groups. Furthermore, a much larger proportion of the diet apparently consists of foods other than starchy staples. Slightly more than one-third of the Tsembaga diet by weight, 34.9%, is composed of leaves, stems, and fruits other than banana. Sugar cane (which will be included in later calculations of Tsembaga intake)

The Diet

73

Table 8. Composition of Diets of Tsembaga and Other New Guinea Communities,
by Percentage Weight

	Busama	Kaiapit	Patep	Kavataria	Chimbu	Tsembaga
Taro	65.0	7.3	45.9	8.6	—	25.8
Yam	1.4	9.5	.2	55.2	5.0	9.3
Manioc	—	2.0	.2	1.4	—	1.2
Sweet potato	—	25.7	37.6	14.0	77.0	21.0
Sago	6.8	.28	—	—	—	—
Banana	1.1	31.6	.4	5.5	—	7.8
Fruits and stems	6.1	—	2.6	2.3	13.0	17.3
Leaves	14.0	9.2	8.0	—	2.5	9.9
Coconut	2.2	9.5	—	2.8	—	—
Marita pandanus	—	—	?	—	?	4.2
Grain	.36	—	3.0	—	1.5	—
Misc. veg.	—	3.4	1.8	1.4	—	2.5
Animal	2.9	1.7	.2	9.7	1.0	1.0

SOURCES: Information for Busama, Kaiapit, Patep, and Kavataria from Hipsley & Clements, 1947. Information for Chimbu from Venkatachalam, 1962.

NOTES: Busama is a coastal village on the Huon Gulf. Kaiapit is 6 miles east of the Markham River, about 60 miles northwest of Lae, altitude about 1,000 feet. Patep is about 25 miles from the coast at the mouth of the Buang River, altitude 3,550 feet. Kavataria is a coastal village on Kirawina in the Trobriand Islands. Chimbu is at an altitude of 5,000–7,000 feet in a central mountain range.

has been excluded from this comparison since it is not included in the reports from some of the other communities in which it may be present. If it were included here, the proportion of items other than starchy staples in the Tsembaga diet would approach 50%. In the five other communities with which the Tsembaga are compared, the percentage of nonstarchy items in the diet varies from 15.3% to 25.7%. In further contrast to the others, the Tsembaga diet includes an appreciable amount of *marita* pandanus, the edible portion of which contains 14.0% fat, according to Hipsley and Kirk (1965:38). The nutritional consequences of the greater variety found in the Tsembaga diet will be discussed later.

Tsembaga Intakes

Assessment of the Tsembaga diet is based upon both the quantity of food ingested and its nutritive value. Vegetable and animal foods are treated separately.

PLANT FOODS

Fruits and vegetables comprise approximately 99 percent by weight of the usual daily intake of the Tsembaga. All vegetables brought home to the four hearths of the Tomegai clan were weighed daily by named variety, from February 14 to December 14, 1963. The figures from March 11 to November 8, a period during which both the pig and human populations were relatively stable, formed the basis of the estimations of intake. Details of the methods employed will be found in Appendix 9.

Estimated daily intakes of calories, protein, and calcium for individuals in various age and sex categories are summarized in Table 9, where they are compared to recommendations of both the New Guinea Food Survey (Langley, 1947:134; Venkatachalam, 1962:10) and FAO/WHO (World Food Problems #5, 1964:6).

In comparison to these recommendations, caloric intake for all categories of the population is adequate, but the calcium portions of the younger groups are not. These possible deficiencies are moderate in the case of children three to five years old and five to ten, while the lack possibly suffered by infants up to three years old is made up in whole or part by mother's milk, since children are nursed usually for two years or more.

In a discussion of protein intake, the quality of the protein must be considered. Foods vary in "biological value," that is, in the extent to which they may be utilized for maintenance and growth (Burton et al., 1959:46). This is a function of the proportions in which the various amino acids of which the protein is composed are present: some may not be utilized except in the presence of others, while excesses of some may inhibit the utilization of others (FAO #16, 1957:23).

It is generally the case that proteins of animal origin are "complete," that is, they contain appreciable amounts of all of the amino acids that are essential for growth and tissue repair. This is not the case with many vegetable proteins. Manioc, which contains almost as much protein as the other root crops, is very poor in certain of the essential amino acids and is thus by itself of only slight value as a protein source.

It is not necessary, however, that all the essential amino acids be present in a particular food. The total requirement may be derived from the proteins found in the variety of foods that are ingested together (Albanese and Orto, 1964:143f). Thus, the variety enjoyed by the Tsembaga not only spares them the gustatory boredom to

Table 9. Nutritive Value of Vegetable Portion of Tsembaga Diet Compared with FAO/WHO and New Guinea Food Standards

	Consumers			Calories		Protein				Calcium	
Category	Number persons	Average weight (kgm).	Trophic units per capita	Rec. daily intake (Langley, corrected)[a]	Est. actual daily intake	Rec. daily intake (Langley, corrected)	Rec. daily intake (FAO/WHO, corrected)[b]	Est. daily intake (grams) min.[c]	max.	Rec. daily intake (Langley, corrected) (mgms)	Est. daily intake (mgms)
Adult males	6	43.0	25.0	2,130	2,575	32	37	43.2	58.2	640	1,525
Adult females	4	38.0	21.0	1,735	2,163	32	33	36.3	48.9	640	1,281
Adolescent females	1	27.3	20.5	1,540	2,112	56	27	35.4	47.3	750	1,250
Children 5–10	2	18.6	13.0	1,157	1,334	44–53	21	22.5	30.3	890	793
Children 3–5	2	13.0	12.0	1,000	1,236	42	15	20.7	28.0	840	732
Children 0–3	1	7.7	8.5	800	875	33	10	14.7	19.8	940	519
Per capita average					2,015						

[a] Langley, 1947:134. Recommendations were made for people larger in stature than the Tsembaga. Venkatachalam (1962:10) has applied them directly to the Chimbu, among whom the average weight of adult males is 118 pounds. A correction was made for the difference between Tsembaga and Chimbu average weights.

[b] FAO, World Food Problems, #5, 1964, corrected for the biological value of vegetable protein, taken for the vegetable diet as a whole to be 70 (out of a possible 100).

[c] Minimum and maximum intakes are presented because of ranges in protein content attributed to various vegetables by various authorities. Authorities and values assigned by them appear in Appendix 9.

which some other New Guinea populations must be subject, but it also may improve utilization of the total intake. For instance, the amino acid contents of sweet potatoes are significant, but their utilization is limited by rather low proportions of methionine and cystine (Peters, 1958:40). Taros are good sources of methionine although poor in iso-leucine, in which sweet potatoes are well supplied (Peters, 1958:35). The presence of both items in the diet enhances the value of each, since they are frequently ingested at the same meal. Analyses of amino acid contents of many other Tsembaga vegetables are not available. It may be suggested, however, that the biological value (Albanese and Orto, 1964:140f) of the aggregate protein in the Tsembaga diet, although perhaps remaining low, is higher than would be the case if the diet consisted of fewer items, since it is reasonable to assume that the proteins in the many different foods ingested daily would complement each other to some extent.

There is a further problem, however. It may be noted in Table 9 that the intakes of adults meet the recommendations of the New Guinea Food Survey for protein, but the intakes of those in the younger categories do not. This may well be characteristic of people whose diets include root crop staples. To derive sufficient protein from root crops alone requires the ingestion of a greater quantity of tubers than children may be able to manage easily. While the caloric requirements of a five- to ten-year-old child may be fulfilled by two pounds of tubers, to meet the suggested protein allowances he would have to consume two to four times that quantity. The seriousness of this disparity is directly proportional to the extent to which root crops comprise the diet. Among the Chimbu, for instance, where roots comprise 82 percent of the total intake, five- to ten-year-olds are reported to ingest only 12.8 grams of protein a day (Venkatachalam, 1962:10). This is about half of the estimated Tsembaga intake, while the caloric intakes of the two peoples show nowhere near such a disparity.

The comparative advantage of the Tsembaga diet lies in the fact that starchy staples comprise only 65 percent of it. Furthermore, because the Tsembaga have available to them such protein-rich greens as hibiscus leaves, they need derive only 40 percent of their protein from tubers (see Appendix 8). The Tsembaga child's problem is thus not as serious as that of the Chimbu child, but it still may be difficult for him to obtain protein in a form sufficiently compact to be easily ingested. Animal protein is especially valuable to him not only because it is a more adequate protein but because it comes in a more concentrated form.

It must be kept in mind that the sample includes only five children and one adolescent, and the method used for apportioning the total weighed food sample among the various age and sex categories must have produced some error. A clinical assessment of the nutritive status of the children would have indicated more clearly than the comparison of estimated intakes to standard recommendations whether or not there was sufficient protein in their diets. It was not possible to arrange for such a clinical assessment but it may be noted that a number of the children had soft and discolored hair, frequently a sign of low or inadequate protein intake, and that the parotids of a few were slightly enlarged. No cases of either kwashiorkor or severe emaciation were seen, however, nor did any of the children seem especially dull. It is likely that their growth is retarded, but data are insufficient to assess this matter. Compared to American children Tsembaga children seemed small for their estimated ages. While this is to be expected among the children of a population in which adults average less than five feet in height, it is reasonable to believe that the small stature of the Tsembaga is at least partially attributable to low protein intake among children and, as will be discussed later, adolescents. It may be significant that the adults of the Fungai-Korama, a Maring group occupying a territory on the edge of a large expanse of virgin forest, are taller and heavier than the Tsembaga (Bick, personal communication). It is possible that their greater size is a result of larger amounts of game in their diet, but quantitative data are lacking.

That Tsembaga children do not seem to be suffering from more severe symptoms of protein deficiency, such as obvious kwashiorkor, suggests that Langley's recommendations are unrealistically high. Langley herself suggests care in their application, pointing out that they were derived from experimental work on Caucasian peoples and in addition include a "wide margin of safety" (1947:106). She made corrections for differences in stature and also on the basis of observations of "the mode of life and degree of activity of the New

Guinea native," but they were made without "physiological studies which would give a picture of the metabolism of Melanesian people" (1947:106).

More recent studies indicate that a considerably smaller protein ration may be sufficient even for children, and in column 8 of Table 9 the requirements set forth by the Joint FAO/WHO Expert Group on Protein Requirements (World Food Problems #5, 1964:6) are presented. The low incidence of severe pathology among Tsembaga children suggests that the FAO/WHO requirements may be more in accord with physiological facts than are Langley's recommendations. The FAO/WHO allowances do not, however, explicitly include a wide "margin of safety," and the fact that there is some pathology suggests that the Tsembaga achieve nitrogen balance at a low level. In view of this, the contexts in which the Tsembaga consume the limited amounts of animal protein available to them may be of considerable significance.

ANIMAL FOODS

A variety of domesticated and nondomesticated animal foods is available to the Tsembaga. Domesticated animals, it has already been mentioned, include pigs, cassowaries, and chickens. Nondomesticated animals include, in addition to wild pigs and cassowaries, marsupials, rats, snakes, lizards, eels, catfish, frogs, birds, bird eggs, bats, grubs, insects, and spiders. It might be mentioned that the Tsembaga are not and vehemently maintain their ancestors never were, cannibals.

No records were kept of the intake of nondomesticated animal foods, for a great part of the consumption, particularly of the smaller forms, takes place away from the houses. It is clear, nevertheless, that for certain categories of the population—married women and prepubescent children—small items such as rats, frogs, nestling birds, and insects form a part of the daily diet. The amounts are small, however, and probably do not contribute more than a gram or two to the daily protein intake. The larger items, eels, snakes, and marsupials, although less frequently taken, probably contribute more to the annual diet. Wild pigs, of which six were killed in 1963, contributed most of all the nondomesticated animal food to the diet in that year. Wild cassowaries are only infrequently obtained by the Tsembaga; none were either shot or trapped in 1963. These birds may be more important in the diet of other Maring groups. The apportionment of animal foods throughout the population is not even. Taboos against eating certain animals burden various categories of persons. The most extensive of these are suffered by *bamp kunda yu* (fight magic men), those who perform the rituals associated with warfare. The taboos applicable to other men who have participated in fighting are slightly less extensive. For both of these groups the consumption of many kinds of marsupial and all snakes, eels, catfish, lizards, and frogs is proscribed. The ideological basis for the restriction on marsupials is not clear. It may be mentioned, however, that all of the proscribed varieties live in the high-altitude virgin forest and are associated with the red spirits, with whom the men suffering the proscription have a special relationship. The reptiles, amphibia, and fish are not eaten because their "coldness" is regarded to be inimical to the "hotness" of ritual knowledge and ritual experience. In addition to these supernaturally sanctioned taboos, men also simply avoid certain animal foods. Any man, other than fight magic men, may eat rats, but no man would. They are said to be small things fit only for women and children. The same is said of small birds, bats, and most insects.

Adolescent boys suffer a somewhat different set of taboos and avoidances. The ideological basis for many of them rests upon the effect that eating certain foods might have on the massive coiffure, called a *mamp ku,* which a boy allows to grow shortly after secondary sexual characteristics appear. If a marsupial with loose fur is eaten, for instance, it is said that the hair will become loose. If wild pig is eaten, the hair will be filled with lice, like that of the wild pig.

The restrictions to which adolescent girls and women of childbearing age who have not yet borne children are subject are more limited than those that apply to adolescent boys. They do, however, pertain to the two most important wild animal foods: wild pig, the consumption of which, they believe, will give them lice, and rats, which will impart a bad odor to the vagina, making them unacceptable to men.

Children and women who have borne children are, as categories, subject to no taboos whatsoever. Thus, when a man or adolescent boy kills a snake, lizard, small bird, rat, or marsupial, he gives it to a woman or child.

The taboos operate, in short, to direct most of the subsidiary sources of animal protein to two categories very much in need of them: women and children. The deprivation of adult males, who as an ontogenetic category need the least protein, in favor of women and children may be of some advantage to the population. On the other hand, the deprivation of adolescents in favor of women and children is not as clearly advantageous. Protein requirements during adolescence are high, for this is a period of rapid growth and development. It may be observed that while some of the other possible effects of low protein intake during adolescence (particularly mental dullness, which was not observed among Tsembaga adolescents) are clearly injurious, the inhibition of growth and the retardation of sexual development (Hipsley and Kirk, 1965:14) may not be disadvantageous. The advantages conferred by an additional inch or two and an additional few pounds could not be great, and the delay of menarche for a year or two might even be of advantage to the population as a whole. At any rate, while deprivation of protein at this time may result in suppression of the individual's growth, this may not be a high price to pay for more adequate protein for mothers and small children.

Since the Tsembaga, unlike some other Marings, keep almost no cassowaries and since chickens are few, pigs are the major source of food from domesticated animals. During the fieldwork period a pig festival was in progress, and the usual patterns of pork consumption were obscured by the special demands of various ritual and ceremonial events. Therefore, although it was possible to collect information from informants concerning pork consumption in nonfestival years, quantitative data are lacking.

It should be mentioned first that religious prohibitions suffered by men are not restricted to wild animal foods. During the greater part of the ritual cycle they may not eat the flesh of pigs killed in connection with the festivals of other local populations. Women, children, and adolescents, however, may eat such pork and are thus the full nutritional beneficiaries of these presentations.

Personal preferences also may play a nutritionally significant role in the apportionment of pork. Men receive larger portions of the cuts they deem most desirable. These are the fatter parts of the animal, with the belly being most appreciated. Women, children, and adolescents on the other hand receive larger portions of the lean. In short, the protein intakes of women and children are benefited by preference as well as taboo in the matter of domestic pork.

Pigs are seldom eaten on occasions that are not ceremonial. They sometimes become sick and die, of course, and an animal that has succumbed to disease will be eaten unless its carcass has putrefied before it is recovered. Some also die of arrow wounds, for pigs are not infrequently guilty of invading gardens and are shot by garden owners. No Tsembaga pigs were killed for this reason in 1963 because, informants said, almost all of the gardens were separated from the residences by a fast-rushing and steeply banked stream. But news reached me of six animals being shot among the neighboring Tuguma during the same year. Feelings run high after such killings; the owner of a slain pig is likely to make an attempt on the life of the garden owner, his wife, or one of his pigs. If a peaceful settlement can be achieved the flesh of the slain animal is apportioned among the agnates of the two principals to the dispute, who may redistribute it to others. The owner of the slain pig is then supposed to repair the fence that the animal damaged in breaking into the garden, and the garden owner is supposed to present him with a piglet to replace the one killed. When this animal matures, it is killed and both parties to the dispute share its flesh evenly, according to informants.

Pigs are deliberately killed by their masters during nonfestival years only for the ceremonial fulfillment of obligations or in the context of rituals associated with misfortune and emergency.

The nonfestival obligations requiring the slaughter of pigs are mainly those associated with marriage.[3] Prestations of valuables are made to affines from time to time in connection with the marriage itself, with the birth of children, and with the deaths of either of the marriage partners or their children. These prestations are almost always accompanied by pork, but do not always follow immediately upon the assumption of the obligation. Those made in connection

3. Young men occasionally kill pigs and present the flesh (some of which is salted) to older men from whom they wish to obtain knowledge of important magical procedures. Such transactions are rare. Some men are never involved, while most others enter into them only once or twice in their lives.

with the birth of children are often deferred until the next pig festival, and such delays seem often to occur even in the case of marriage prestations.

The demands arising from misfortune and emergency probably result among the Tsembaga in the greatest amount of pig slaughter and consumption during years unmarked by pig festivals. (This may not be the case with all Maring. Cherry Vayda in a personal communication reports that among the Kauwasi, a Maring group living in the Jimi Valley, more pigs are killed in nonfestival years for affinal prestations.[4]) Most frequently the misfortunes calling for pig slaughter are illness and injury, but during the period of fieldwork the Tsembaga, because they were conducting a pig festival, did not kill pigs immediately upon injury or during the course of illness. Instead, they promised the ancestors that they would give them animals at the termination of the kaiko, when they were planning to kill them anyhow. But all informants agree, and some information from other local populations indicates, that in nonfestival years pigs are sacrificed soon after a person is injured or during the course of an illness that hasn't responded to less radical treatment (magical procedures), and if illness is protracted a number of pigs may be killed.

Death as well as illness and injury demands the slaughter of pigs. If the deceased was a married woman the slaughter is likely to be

4. Data are insufficient, but I believe that this difference may be a function of differences in horticultural practices. Clarke's (1966:350) observations indicate that sweet potatoes are relatively more important among the Kauwasi than the Tsembaga. This may be in part attributable to the somewhat higher altitudes at which the Kauwasi are gardening (up to and a little beyond 6,000 feet), and perhaps to changes in soil structure on Kauwasi territory, which seems to have been occupied for a longer period than Tsembaga territory. At any rate, fallows are shorter on Kauwasi garden sites and there are clear signs of some degradation of Kauwasi land in general: about 20 percent of the territory is under stabilized short grass (Clarke, 1966: 350ff).

The Kauwasi seem to keep more pigs than do the Tsembaga (no censuses have been taken), and the greater importance of pigs is probably not unrelated to the greater importance of sweet potatoes. When one informant was asked why the Tsembaga kept fewer pigs than the Kauwasi, he responded in effect that it is because Tsembaga soil is softer and more fit for taros and yams. Kauwasi soil is harder and more suitable for sweet potato. Since the Kauwasi must grow more sweet potatoes they keep more pigs, which they eat more frequently. It may be that we can see here a long-term succession in horticultural practice. In recently entered areas there is greater emphasis on taro and yam cultivation. With continued occupation there are structural changes in the soil that lead to a greater emphasis on sweet potatoes and pig husbandry. For an excellent discussion of possible successions see Clarke (1966).

of greater magnitude than for other categories of persons. Instances are reported in which men have killed all of their deceased wife's pigs, for there were no other women to look after them. As in the case of illness, the Tsembaga in 1963 killed no pigs at times of death. They merely promised animals at the termination of the pig festival.

The slaughter of pigs is also demanded by the rituals associated with warfare. The number of pigs killed is directly related to the duration and severity of the fighting. This matter will be treated in more detail in the next chapter.

The occasion that defines when a pig is to be killed also designates who is to eat it. Pigs sacrificed during the rituals associated with the actual prosecution of warfare are consumed only by the men participating in the fighting. When pigs are killed in connection with illness, injury, or death, the pork liver is served to the victim, if he is alive. If the sacrificial pig belongs to the victim or his agnates, informants told me, the remainder of the flesh could be consumed only by the agnates or, in the case of a married woman, by her husband's agnates as well. It was said that the sacrifice is made to spirits of deceased ancestors (to the red spirits if the upper part of the body is affected, to the spirits of rot if suffering is in the lower portion of the body) to mollify them if they (or one of them) have visited the affliction, or to strengthen them so that they might assist in recovery if the victim has been the target of a hostile spirit, sorcerer (*kum yu*), or witch (*koimp*). The recipient spirits, informants said, would be angered if the flesh of animals sacrificed to them under these circumstances were to be distributed to nonagnates and they would either withhold their assistance from the victim or continue their attack upon him, with the result that he would die, and they would also afflict illness upon the nonagnatic consumers. Despite these statements, personal communications from Cherry Vayda and Georgeda Bick, who returned to the Maring area in 1966, indicate that resident nonagnates may also receive portions of the sacrificial flesh. It is sometimes the case, moreover, that a cognate or affine contributes a pig to be sacrificed for the benefit of a victim of illness or injury and in such instances a larger but still restricted number of people may partake of the pork.[5] (Such contributions by

5. I did not perceive the full significance of pork consumption in the context of misfortune while I was in the field, and therefore did not collect information on this

nonagnates are expected to be reciprocated at later pig festivals or rewarded in some other way. I know of one instance in which the victim of illness, having recovered, transferred to his nonagnatic benefactor perpetual rights in a number of garden sites.)

In sum, pigs killed in the context of misfortune or emergency apparently tend to be consumed by those who are either victims of or participants in the event, or by those close to them. It is interesting to note, in contrast, that there is a tendency to distribute widely the meat that results from the killing of pigs for reasons other than misfortune or emergency. Pork that is received in bride or child payments, for instance, is consumed not only by members of the recipient exogamous group; some of it is invariably redistributed by them to coresidents and affines. Pork resulting from the death of pigs from accident or natural causes is also widely distributed. It may be mentioned that the consumption of the flesh of wild pigs is also not restricted to the agnatic group of the slayer. There seems to be, indeed, a tendency to distribute the flesh of these animals as widely as possible. At least all of those who participate in the hunt share in the flesh, which is apportioned by the slayer. If the animal is large, others do, too. In the case of the two largest wild pigs killed in 1963 every Tsembaga received a portion.

It is a matter of physiological interest that most pork consumption in years in which pig festivals do not occur probably takes place in contexts of misfortune or emergency, and that the distribution of meat in these instances is restricted. It is reasonable to assume that misfortune and emergency induce in those experiencing them a "stress reaction," a complex of physiological changes that result directly from or in response to the emergency with which the organisms are confronted. In the case of the sick and injured, this is obvious. It is also the case, however, that stress reactions occur among people who are experiencing rage or fear (Houssay, 1955:1096) or even prolonged anxiety (NRC #1100, 1963:53).

One aspect of stress reactions is "negative nitrogen balance" (Houssay, 1955:440), that is, a net loss of nitrogen from the body. This may not, if the stress period is not unduly prolonged, be a

---

subject in the detail that is warranted. Georgeda Bick and Cherry Vayda will publish elsewhere the details of apportionment and context definition for pig sacrifice, based upon their research into this subject in 1966 and 1967.

serious matter for organisms that have previously achieved nitrogen
balance at a high level. Negative nitrogen balance, according to
Moore (1959:439), will not, for instance, impair wound healing in a
normally well-nourished patient.

However, organisms that are in nitrogen balance at a low level
previous to their exposure to stress may experience difficulties. As
long ago as 1919 it was reported that the healing of experimental
wounds in animals on low protein intakes was slower than healing
in animals on high-protein diets (Large and Johnston, 1948:352).
In a more recent discussion Moore also notes differences in healing
between poorly and well-nourished animals and surgical patients,
and states that "it is appealing to explain this . . . in the labilization or translocation theory; the well nourished animal has more
body protein available for labilization or translocation [from undamaged tissues to damaged structures]" (1959:102). Zintel (1964:
1043) has also pointed out that "hypoproteinemia predisposes to
poor wound healing or disruption of wounds, delayed healing of
fractures, including anemia, failure of gastro-intestinal stomas to
function, embarrassment of pulmonary and cardiac function and
reduced resistance to infection." Lund and Levinson, in a discussion
of surgical patients, noted yet other ill effects of protein depletion
upon the injured some years ago. These included decreased resistance to shock, hypotension, lower basal metabolism rates, polyuria,
lack of appetite, weakness, and mental changes including confusion,
lethargy, and depression (1948:349). Lund and Levinson suggest a
"great increase" in the protein intake of individuals traumatized by
surgery (1948:350), and their view is shared by Elman (1951:85,
100). The more recent writers do not necessarily suggest such a
course for individuals who were well nourished previous to trauma-
tization, but Zintel (1964:1043ff) underlines the necessity to alleviate protein deficiency, if it should be present or should develop in
surgical patients.

It is not only victims of trauma who may be put at a disadvantage
by poor protein nutrition. In febrile diseases "the underfed febrile
patient is thrown into a negative nitrogen balance, which is far from
desirable since it predisposes to hypoproteinemia and anemia, interferes with the body's anabolic defense mechanisms, and delays con-
valescence" (Burton, 1959:230). A protein allowance somewhat in

excess of usual requirements may therefore be indicated for fever patients (Burton, 1959:231).

It may be the case that protein intake not only affects the prognosis for ill or injured organisms, but may also have a bearing upon susceptibility to some diseases. While the subject is not well known, Berg (1948:309ff) has remarked that "numerous incidental observations have indicated the possibility that proteins play an important part in immunity," and relates this to their role in the production of antibodies and the part they probably play in phagocytosis as well. It may be of importance here to note that the status of a protein-depleted organism may be significantly improved by the intake of high-quality proteins for relatively short periods of time. Berg (1948:311) states that experiments indicate that repletion of depleted animals "by feeding a high quality protein for as little as two days before antigenic stimulation leads to a detectable increase in antibody production; in only seven days the capacity [of the previously depleted animals] approximates that of the control animals [which had previously been fed an "adequate diet"]." In a more recent discussion Axelrod (1964:654) states that "the detrimental effects of specific dietary deficiencies upon the development of acquired immunity in experimental animals have been amply documented. In particular, the requirements for amino acids . . . are recognized." He warns, however, that "the significance of animal experimentation must . . . be evaluated critically," and remarks that "the relationship of nutritional state to acquired immunity in man remains indeterminate" (1964:655). Zucker and Zucker, in a discussion of the relationship between nutrition and the resistance of uninfected animals to infection, make a similar observation concerning the role of proteins: "The available data are largely inconclusive or uncertain as to interpretation" (1964:643).

It appears, then, that illness and injury are marked by negative nitrogen balance, which can have dangerous implications for protein-depleted organisms. The effects of negative nitrogen balance, however, may be offset rather quickly by the ingestion of large amounts of protein. It also may be, although this is far less certain, that the consumption of high-quality protein for relatively short periods of time may significantly improve the ability of uninfected organisms to withstand infection. I suggest that, given the adequacy of the protein derived from vegetables and nondomesticated animals for maintaining the Tsembaga in nitrogen balance at low levels in the absence of stress, the practice of sacrifice in situations of misfortune and emergency is a highly effective way to utilize the scarce and costly pigs. Individuals who are already traumatized or diseased are provided with high-quality protein, which may go far to offset the nitrogen losses they are already experiencing as a direct result of the injuries to their bodies, and which also assists them in producing sufficient antibodies to resist infection. Those close to the victims also receive protein, which not only may offset the nitrogen loss resulting from the anxiety they may be experiencing but also might possibly prepare their bodies better to withstand the injuries or infections likely to be forthcoming if the victim is suffering from a contagious disease, for example, or was wounded in warfare that must be continued.

In sum, while the protein content of the everyday diet of the Tsembaga is probably adequate for everyday activities, it may be less than adequate in stress situations. The practice of killing and consuming pigs in connection with emergency and misfortune tends to provide physiological reinforcement when it is needed to those who need it. The contribution of pork to the Tsembaga diet thus seems to be of much greater importance than is indicated by the amounts actually consumed. Clearly this suggestion has implications for future anthropological analyses of animal sacrifice, and appropriate physiological tests should be undertaken wherever possible; until they are this formulation must remain hypothetical only. It may be said nevertheless that there are strong reasons to believe that the ritual regulation of pork consumption by the Tsembaga makes an important contribution to a diet that maintains the population in adequate health at a high level of activity.

THE LIMITS OF THE SYSTEM

An attempt has been made here to specify the trophic requirements of the Tsembaga, the procedures by which they fill them, and the effects that these procedures have upon the environment in which they take place. Now a computation will be attempted of the carrying capacity of Tsembaga territory, that is, the maximum number of people and pigs that could be supported on it for a period of indefinite length, through the procedures described above, without any change in the intakes of individual Tsembaga and without depletion of the environment. These estimates must be made before we can examine the role of the ritual cycle in regulating the relations of the Tsembaga with the nonhuman components of their immediate, or territorial, environment.

It should be emphasized that carrying capacity figures presented here do not necessarily constitute approximations of the number of people who could survive on Tsembaga territory. Estimates of carrying capacity, as the term is used in anthropology,[6] do not necessarily provide such information. They are, rather, approximations of the numbers of organisms that may be supported within a given area *without inducing degradation of the environment*. In fact, populations may, and often are, limited by environmental factors that become significant below carrying capacity in this sense. Density-dependent epidemics and predators may be cited as examples. It should also be kept in mind that Liebig's law of the minimum and Shelford's law of tolerance can come into operation at levels below those sufficient to degrade the environment. A carrying capacity figure indicates the numbers of a species that can survive within a designated area only if ranges set by other factors have not been exceeded at lower population levels and the population is limited by its gross food supply, that is, by the production of usable biomass in the area it exploits.

It is impossible to say whether or not the probable limits of Tsembaga population are set by the productivity of their territory or by other factors. Nevertheless, a carrying capacity estimation allows us to approximate the levels at which variables in the Tsembaga ecosystem become destructive of that system.

Difficulties Concerning Carrying Capacity

The advantages that may be gained from a calculation of carrying capacity should not blind us to the difficulties, both conceptual and methodological, hidden beneath the simplicity of the concept. Some

6. In animal ecology the term *carrying capacity* is sometimes used in a slightly different sense: to refer to the maximum number of animals of a particular kind that can survive in an area (Andrewartha, 1961:154). This number is a function of the processes that actually limit the size of the population. These factors do not necessarily include environmental degradation.

of the problems encountered in Tsembaga data are discussed in Appendix 10, but it is useful to call attention to some of the more general ones here.

1. Both conceptual and methodological problems are presented by the concept of environmental degradation. If it is taken to mean reduction in the productivity (measured by the amount of biomass produced within a specified area during a specified time period) or decrease in the organization (complexity and orderliness) of the ecological system, then the mere replacement of a climax community by a community based upon cultivated plants is likely to represent environmental degradation. Cultivated communities are in most cases simpler in structure than the climax communities they replace, and there is strong reason to believe that their productivity is usually lower (Allee et al., 1949:478 passim, 507; Odum, 1959:76). Climatic or edaphic climax communities represent optimal adaptations to their abiotic habitats, and it is only through the alteration of the abiotic habitat (for example, through irrigation or the application of fertilizer) that communities dominated by man are likely to exceed them in productivity.

It is furthermore the case that the cultivated community will, almost without exception, be less stable than the climax community. The climax community together with its habitat constitutes a self-regulating system. As such, it will endure through long periods of time unless it is subjected to such agencies as climatic change, cataclysm, or the intervention of certain organisms such as agricultural man or blight parasites. The cultivated community, on the other hand, is not per se a self-regulating system. Many of the plant species that it includes may not have the ability to propagate themselves and they require protection from competitors, such as weeds and second-growth trees, which are often as well or even better adapted than they are to the local conditions of the garden and field or the general conditions of the region. The maintenance of the cultivated community, like any community, depends upon the constant functioning of its dominant species. Man, however, is less reliable in such a role than the "A" stratum trees that dominate the rain forest. But whether or not cultivation degrades the environment in an absolute sense, it must be remembered that, since the Neolithic, man has not been primarily a member of climax associations. He is, rather, a form that thrives mainly in the highly modified ecosystems that he himself dominates. It is not of direct concern to him that the productivity of such ecosystems is lower than those of the climatic communities they replace. The amount of usable biomass with which they provide him is much higher.

The instability of the cultivated ecosystem is more directly relevant to man. On the one hand there is the possibility of the reassertion of the succession leading to the climatic or edaphic climax characteristic of the region. While this may not be regarded as degradation in the absolute sense, such a process results, at least temporarily, in less land available for cultivation. It also is likely that considerable labor must be expended to reclaim such areas for cultivation. On the other hand, and more likely, there is the possibility of further absolute degradation leading to the establishment of a "disclimax," such as the anthropogenic grasslands found in some parts of New Guinea where forests and gardens once flourished. While gardens made in such grasslands yield well, they do so only if special techniques, which are costly in terms of labor, are employed.

In light of these considerations, in a discussion of the environment of human groups we should distinguish between "absolute degradation" and "anthropocentric degradation," the latter term referring to any process that lowers the productivity of biomass useful to man per unit of area or labor input or both. To put it in slightly different terms, it refers to deviation from conditions that are optimal for the survival of a human population dependent upon a particular set of resources and equipped with a particular set of means for acquiring them.

The question of whether or not degradation, absolute or anthropocentric, is widespread over Tsembaga territory was touched upon earlier in the discussion of the adequacy of fallow periods. Evidence indicated that except in highly localized areas there is no degradation of either sort. The assumption will be made for the purpose of estimating carrying capacity that degradation is not occurring, but it should be reiterated that the evidence falls short of demonstration. As Street has underlined in a recent article (1965), in many instances it is virtually impossible to assess environmental degradation, particularly in the structure and content of the soil: "Deterioration of the land is a cumulative process, and short term processes may be so slight as to be exceeded by errors in measurement."

2. A related problem concerns the lengths of fallow periods when carrying capacity is estimated for people depending upon swidden gardens. Shifting horticulture is frequently practiced by people who are unaccustomed to keeping careful track of the years, and the length of fallow periods may vary from site to site. It often becomes necessary to estimate fallow periods through involved means that may produce inaccurate results. Moreover, even if the estimation is accurate the actual fallow periods may be longer or shorter than they need to be, and their use in carrying capacity computation may produce inaccuracies.

3. Carrying capacity estimates, including those to follow, assume not only that the inventory of crops remains unchanged, but that the proportions in which these crops are planted will also remain constant. People practicing mixed crop, shifting horticulture (and the Tsembaga are no exception) readily accept new crops and new varieties of old crops, as Street (1965) has pointed out. To the extent that new introductions or changes in planting proportions will produce changes in yields per unit area, the assumption of a constant inventory of crops and constant planting proportions will deflect an estimate of carrying capacity from true values.

4. Carrying capacity estimations include as one variable the area of cultivated land required to provide a population with food. The value for this variable is usually derived from the practice of the people under study. It has already been pointed out that an areal figure alone does not indicate the nutritional level at which the population is being supported, or whether this level is adequate. An estimation was made above of the intake of the population and the adequacy of this intake. There remains, however, an associated problem. Except in rare cases local populations of human beings are made up of individuals in a number of age and sex categories, each of which has different trophic requirements. Estimations of carrying capacity are based upon the assumption that the proportion of individuals in each age-sex category will remain constant. This assumption underlies the computations that will follow, but no doubt it differs from reality to some extent. Among all human populations, and especially among small groups living under primitive conditions,

the proportions of individuals in the various categories is constantly shifting.

The Carrying Capacity of Tsembaga Territory

A number of formulae have been proposed for applying the concept of carrying capacity to human populations. Those of Allen (1949:74), Brookfield and Brown (1963:108f), Carneiro (1960:230–31), Freeman (1955:133), and Loeffler (1960:41) are addressed particularly to the problems inherent in arriving at carrying capacity for groups practicing shifting cultivation. Among the variables considered are amounts of land put into cultivation, duration of harvesting, length of fallow, and total area of arable land. Brookfield has further categorized garden land into various types and takes into consideration grazing land.

The formulae proposed are generally simple ones. Carneiro's, which follows, has been used here:

$$P = \frac{\dfrac{T}{(R+Y)} \times Y}{A}$$

Where:

P = The population that can be supported.

T = Total arable land.

R = Length of fallow in years.

Y = Length of cropping period in years.

A = The area of cultivated land required to provide an "average individual" with the amount of food that he ordinarily derives from cultivated plants per year.

Through the application of this formula and subsidiary procedures outlined in Appendix 10, a number of carrying capacity estimates have been derived.

Two values have been used for variable T, total arable land: (1) land that at the time of field study was either in cultivation or under secondary forest, and (2) land deemed arable but under high forest. Because these latter areas have not been cultivated in the recent past, because they are important sources of nondomesticated resources, and because, being at high altitudes and frequently covered by cloud they would doubtless be only marginally productive under cultivation, it was considered advisable to segregate them.

Because pigs have trophic requirements of a magnitude comparable to those of humans, the pig population had to be taken into consideration in estimates of carrying capacity for humans. Estimates were therefore made of carrying capacity for humans with the pig population at its minimum and maximum sizes. Minimum pig population size was assumed to be represented by the number of pigs surviving the pig festival in 1963. At that time the ratio of pigs, averaging 60 to 75 pounds, to people was .29:1. Maximum pig population size was assumed to be represented by the number of animals the Tsembaga had at the beginning of the pig festival in 1962. The ratio of pigs, averaging 120 to 150 pounds each, to people at that time was .83:1.

Because all Tsembaga gardens made in 1962 were measured by chain and compass, only one calculation was made for human carrying capacity with maximum pig population. Only some of the Tsembaga gardens made in 1963 could be measured, however, and it was necessary to calculate the value of variable A, the amount of land put under cultivation per capita. Three methods were used in this calculation. The results produced by using the extreme values for variable A are reflected in the range shown for human carrying capacity with the pig population at minimum size. It should be noted here, however, that two of the three calculations for variable A were separated by a difference of only 4 percent while the third calculation was separated from one of these by 27 percent. The use of the aberrant value for variable A produces the lower figure, 290 persons, for carrying capacity with the pig population at minimum. For reasons discussed in Appendix 10 this figure is deemed to be less reliable than the higher figures.

Carrying capacity for pigs, holding the size and composition of the human population constant, was also estimated. Two methods were used, and in applying one of these methods the two extreme values were again used for variable A. The lower figure, 142 pigs, was produced by the use of the aberrant value for variable A and is deemed to be less reliable than the higher figure, 240 pigs (of 120- to 150-pound size). The results of the various estimates are summarized in Table 10.

Table 10. Estimates of Tsembaga Territory's Carrying Capacity,
Human and Pig Populations

	Secondary forest	High forest	Total
Human population (pig population held to minimum)	290–397	44–60	334–457
Human population (pig population maintained at maximum)	251	38	284
Human population, mean carrying capacity	271–324	42–49	313–373
Pig population (human population held constant)	142–240	62	204–302

Several comments need to be made concerning the figures in this table. It should be repeated that the figure of 290 persons, if the pig population is never allowed to exceed minimum size, is probably too low. On the other hand, the figure of 397 persons may be too high for the number of people that can be supported by land under secondary forest. A calculation employing the intermediate value derived for variable A produces a carrying capacity figure of 383 persons. Averaging the three calculations yields a figure of 356 persons.

It should be emphasized here that the carrying capacities for humans with the pig population at minimum represents an estimate of the number of people that could be supported on Tsembaga territory if the ratio of pigs (of 60- to 75-pound size) to people was *never* allowed to exceed .24:1. Similarly, the figures for carrying capacity for humans, pig population at maximum, is an attempt to estimate the number of people who could be maintained if the ratio of pigs (of 120- to 150-pound size) to people was *constantly* maintained at .83:1. In fact, the pig population fluctuates, and the actual carrying capacity for humans lies between the figures estimated in connection with the extreme sizes of pig herds. Where in this range the actual carrying capacity will fall depends upon demographic processes within the pig population, which itself is dependent upon so many factors, including the changes in the human population, that precise estimation would be impossible. No more could be done here than to strike means between the estimates of carrying capacity with minimum and maximum herd sizes. These have been represented as mean carrying capacity.

Figures for carrying capacities for pigs must be interpreted in a similar way. These figures represent attempts at estimating the number of pigs of 120- to 150-pound size that could be supported *continuously* on Tsembaga territory, if the size and composition of the human population remained constant. Since the size of the pig population fluctuates it could doubtless exceed considerably, for years at a time, the figures presented here without degrading the territory. Thus, although the Tsembaga pig population stood in 1962 above one of the figures derived for carrying capacity this does not mean, granting the correctness of the figure, that the number of pigs had actually exceeded the capacity of the territory to support pigs.

If the estimates presented here are even approximately accurate, the Tsembaga were well below the carrying capacity of their territory in 1962 and 1963. There have been times in the past, however, during which this might not have been the case. In the last chapter it was suggested that a population of 250 to 300 persons is indicated for the period thirty to forty years prior to fieldwork, and at that time the Tsembaga had less land. It was during that period that they annexed about 135 acres (surface area) of arable land by driving out the Dimbagai-Yimyagai, who had previously lived immediately to their east.

It may be that differences in horticultural and pig-herding practices compensated for the larger populations in earlier times. Information concerning this is fragmentary and difficult to quantify. People do say that the number of pigs regarded as sufficient for a pig festival was smaller in earlier times. Considering the amount of labor necessary to make gardens with stone tools, this would not be surprising. People also say that they previously ate more bananas, and it may be that before the arrival of steel tools smaller gardens were kept in production longer, with third- or even fourth-generation bananas making a much more important contribution to the diet than they did in 1962–63; however, information is conflicting and unclear.

It may well be asked why additional virgin forest was not put into cultivation during periods of high population. Use of these lands could have substantially increased the number of people who could be supported on Tsembaga territory. That they were not utilized, at least in fairly recent times, is not sufficiently explained by the fact that cutting gardens is ritually proscribed in much of the area. Other factors may be suggested, however.

First, the Jimi Valley lands are both distant and exposed to enemies. The latter reason was agreed upon by all informants, who said
that their ancestors did make some gardens there, but the area has
been avoided since the development of the enmity with the Kundagai. Even in the absence of such an enmity, however, the regular
utilization of lands three or four hours' hard walk (including climbs
of 2,000 to 4,000 feet in both directions) from other arable lands
could not be very attractive.

Secondly, these are marginal lands. Considering both the low
yields of high-altitude gardens and the long fallow periods they
seem to require, these lands are judged to be less than 40 percent
as productive as the best land that the Tsembaga have under production. Clearing virgin forest without steel tools must have been
extremely arduous, and it may have been that people would have
eaten less, kept fewer pigs, lived or gardened uxorilocally or sororilocally, or seized their neighbors' land rather than expend effort in
cultivating such poor ground.

Third, it should be kept in mind that these areas in their condition
as virgin forest are important sources of animal food, fiber, building
materials, and other items. Data are insufficient to estimate the extent to which the deprivation of these items, resulting from removal
of the present vegetation cover, would adversely affect the Tsembaga. It is surely the case, however, that although the estimations
of carrying capacity here have been based upon domesticated foodstuffs, other items are necessary to the well-being and even survival
of the population.

SYSTEM AND ECOSYSTEM

In this discussion of the Tsembaga and their environment, the
Tsembaga have been taken to be an ecological population in an
ecosystem bounded by the limits of what is recognized as their territory. My purpose has been to describe and, where possible, assign
values to components of this system, rather than to analyze its
functioning.

The designation of dimensions of the phenomena described above
as variables in a system has an advantage beyond that of facilitating
the expression of their interrelations. It also makes it possible to
specify approximately the limits within which the system—that is,

a particular set of dynamic interrelationships among specified variables—can continue to exist.

First, the parameters of the system may be designated. These are abstracted from conditions that affect variables within the system but which vary independently of them. Included among the parameters of the system that is emerging here are aspects of such factors as terrain, altitude, temperature, rainfall, and insolation.

The presence or absence of variables within a system cannot be explained in terms of the other variables in the system. Presence or absence can, however, sometimes be explained in terms of the parameters of the system. Brookfield's (1964) discussion of insolation, sweet potato cultivation, and population density in the New Guinea Highlands is a recent example of the explanation of presence or absence by reference to the parameters of systems. Kroeber's (1939) discussion of maize is another example. The specification of parameters is, of course, especially important in comparative studies. A description of the ways in which the Tsembaga relate to their immediate environment may be adequate without reference to rainfall, temperature, or altitude. The same is the case for the Chimbu people. In comparing Tsembaga and Chimbu subsistence procedures, diet, and nutritive status, however, we would note important differences. These are in large measure due to parameters of the system: for instance, the limits of toleration of certain plants, notably many protein-rich greens, probably exclude them from the Chimbu crop inventory, and therefore from the Chimbu diet, from which they are apparently absent.

In addition to designating limiting conditions or parameters, it may also become possible, when dimensions of phenomena are regarded as variables in a system, to discover the "system-destroying" levels of these variables.

The formulae for computing carrying capacity may be regarded as summary statements of the interrelations of the variables that they include. They do not, however, elucidate the mechanisms by which the values of the variables are regulated. A carrying capacity figure indicates ranges of values within which variables must remain if the system is to endure, but it does not indicate how values are kept within those ranges. In the course of the descriptions in this chapter, some processes and mechanisms that contribute to maintaining variables with "ranges of viability" have been mentioned; for example, the effect of selective weeding upon the length of time required for the fallow on garden sites was suggested. In a later chapter the ritual means by which other variables are kept from reaching system-destroying levels will be discussed.

CHAPTER 4

Relations with Other Local Populations

Just as the Tsembaga form part of a network of relationships with nonhuman components of their immediate environment, so do they participate in relationships with other local populations similar to themselves living outside their territory.

THE LOCATION OF OTHER GROUPS

The population size and territorial area of the Tsembaga fall around the middle of the ranges of Simbai Valley Maring groups. The small size of territories and the relatively large numbers of people who occupy them result in the proximity of both the residences and subsistence activities of adjacent groups. The houses of one of the clans belonging to the Tuguma local population immediately to the east are not more than a half mile from the houses of the Tsembaga. The residences of the Kundagai, the local group to the west of the Tsembaga, are about one and one half miles away. Both the eastern and western borders follow certain watercourses from near the top of the Bismarck Mountain to the Simbai River.

The Tsembaga refer to the Tuguma, along with themselves, as "*amaŋ yindok*" ("inside" or "between" people), meaning that they and the Tuguma form an enclave of friendly people occupying a continuous area bordered by hostile groups. The territory to the east of the Tuguma is occupied by their enemies of long standing, the Kanump-Kaur, and the Tsembaga fought four wars against their western neighbors, the Kundagai, during the forty or fifty years before 1962.

This spatial distribution of friends and enemies seems to be typical of the Maring. According to Vayda, almost every Maring local population shares at least one border with an enemy, and in almost every case the antagonists are located on the same side of the valley. Enmities between groups separated by the major rivers in the valley bottoms, the Simbai and the Jimi, do occur, but they are rare and short-lived. Enmities between groups separated by the mountain ridge do not, according to Vayda, occur at all.[1] It is no doubt relevant that the trade routes generally run across the grain of the land. Commodities that are not provided in a group's own territory, or are provided only in insufficient quantities, are obtained from people living across the river or over the ridge in the next valley.

It may also be relevant that a man would find it difficult to exploit land separated from his residence by a major ridge or river. Because residences are in the middle altitudes, the walk to land across the river or in the next valley is long, and a climb of several thousand feet is inevitable. During some parts of the year, moreover, the major rivers become impassable for days or weeks at a time. Only by moving his residence can a man conveniently utilize such distant ground for regular root crop gardens, and this alternative is not likely to be attractive to most people, even when they are short of land.

It is not surprising, then, that friendly relations generally prevail between groups separated by mountain ridge or river. Their relationship is mutually advantageous in that they supply each other with needed or desired commodities, and they are noncompetitive because their lands are not of great use to each other.

Conversely, it is not surprising that relationships between groups living side by side on the same valley wall are frequently antagonistic. Such adjacent groups do not depend upon each other for commodities. They are not bound together by the material exchanges that characterize the relationships of people whose territories are separated by mountain ridge or river. Their proximity, furthermore, increases the probability of friction between them. While it is extremely unlikely, for instance, that the pigs of groups separated by mountain or river will damage each other's gardens, it is a common occurrence among groups living adjacent to each other on the same valley wall.

1. The term *enmity* refers here to the relationship between groups who have opposed each other as principal combatants (see p. 117) in rounds of warfare.

It is also the case that some of the garden land of the neighboring group is likely to be as close to a man's residence as some of his own. If a group were short of land its members would look to the conveniently located land of the adjacent group rather than to land across the river or the mountain.

In contrast then to relations between groups located across the grain of the land from each other, the relations of groups occupying adjacent territories on the same valley wall may become competitive in respect to land and are not mutually beneficial in exchanging those goods in which the territories of each might be lacking.

FRIENDLY RELATIONS

Relations with friendly groups are concerned with and bound by exchanges of women and goods and may therefore be discussed in terms of marriage and trade.

Marriage

Detailed information concerning Maring marriage will be presented elsewhere; a brief summary is sufficient for the purposes of this study. It has already been mentioned that the Tsembaga state a preference for wives who are also Tsembaga by birth, and that this preference is reflected in practice. Of the fifty married women, including widows, among the Tsembaga in 1962 and 1963, twenty-two were Tsembaga by birth.

Some of the reasons for this preference have already been suggested. A man receives landrights from his wife's agnates. Only if this land is close by, however, may it be effectively used. Conversely, Tsembaga say that they prefer, other things being equal, to give sisters and daughters to local men so that even after her marriage a girl may continue to participate, to some extent, with her unmarried brothers or widowed father in gardening activities. Women and widowers, moreover, want at least one of their daughters to be married close by so that they may be assured of the funerary services that women perform.

Forty-one married women of Tsembaga birth were known to be alive during the fieldwork period. In addition to the twenty-two who were married to Tsembaga men, seven were married to the Tuguma. The remaining twelve had gone either to Jimi Valley men or to men north of the Simbai River.

Full satisfaction of a preference for local women is unlikely among groups the size of the Tsembaga. Even if the Tuguma, who number 225 people, are added, the population remains too small for easy local endogamy. Groups of such size are subject to imbalance in the numbers of persons in each sex available for marriage, especially when the sexes are subject to different mortality and, perhaps, different birth rates.[2]

While unions between men and women of a single local origin confer certain advantages upon both parties and their natal agnatic groups, unions between people of different local origins confer others. Unions across the grain of the land serve to strengthen trading relationships, for one thing. Perhaps more important to the welfare of the group is that allies are recruited through affinal ties. Thus, while it may be that the Tsembaga depend upon other groups for women for simple demographic reasons, the resulting interlocal ties enhance their ability to obtain commodities in trade and support in warfare.

Most marriages are arranged between the natal groups of the principals. In some instances an immediate direct exchange takes place: the two women are exchanged the same day. More common are delayed direct exchanges, in which a man, when he receives a woman, promises to reciprocate by sending to his wife's natal group at some future time a specified sister who is as yet too young to marry. A few women are given in what may be regarded as a transgenerationally delayed direct exchange. There is a rule stipulating that one of a woman's granddaughters is to be returned to her natal group. This is, in effect, a prescribed second patrilateral cross-cousin marriage (between a man and woman who call each other "brother" and "sister"). Such marriages are actually contracted in very few

2. The majority of nonlocal marriages are with members of other Maring-speaking groups, but four of the living wives and widows resident among the Tsembaga in 1963 came from nearby Karam-speaking groups. Conversely, two living women of Tsembaga birth were married to Karam men and another to a Gainj man. While no Tsembaga were married to Narak speakers prior to November 1963, marriage between Jimi Valley Maring and Narak speakers is frequent. It may be that propinquity, rather than linguistic affiliation, is the decisive factor in intergroup marriage. This question is likely to be resolved with the analysis of marriage data collected by A. P. Vayda during a pan-Maring census conducted in 1963 and 1966.

cases. Indirect exchanges are most common. The bride's natal group uses the wealth received from her husband to make payments on a woman procured elsewhere. Women are also sometimes given as compensation for certain services, such as revenging homicides, and figure in wergild settlements. This will be discussed later in the contexts of ritual and warfare.

Prestations must always be made by the groom and his kin to the bride's group even when the bride is given as wergild or in compensation for services. In most instances, however, no prestation, or only a small one, is made at the time the bride goes to the groom. It is said that the first substantial payment should be made soon after the bride and groom have harvested the first garden they have planted together; but it is frequently delayed much longer, sometimes until the next pig festival staged by the groom's group. Further payments are also made for both a woman and the children she bears throughout their lives and upon their deaths. The first marriage prestation is the largest, however, and may consist of over thirty wealth objects, as well as a whole cooked pig. Live pigs are never included in affinal prestations.

Wealth objects, or "valuables," form a named class, *muŋgoi*, which has traditionally included *meŋr* (shells: gold-lip, green sea snail, and bands of small cowries), *kabaŋ an* (feathers: most importantly bird of paradise plumes and parrot and eagle feathers), *ma wak* and *ma an* (animal pelts, used mainly as head bands, and loose animal fur used to embellish loin cloths), *čenaŋ* (cutting implements: steel axes and bushknives; previous to the arrival of steel, some stone axes[3] served only as *muŋgoi*) and *miña* (earth pigments). Austral-

---

3. Working axes are characterized by heavy, usually short blades, and are used for clearing, gardening, and fighting. Bridal ax blades, on the other hand, are long and sometimes extremely thin. One in my possession is 10″ long but nowhere more than .3″ thick. Such thin blades were not suitable for gardening, woodworking, or fighting, but were sometimes wielded during dancing, and they often figured in bride prices and other payments to affines. The distinction between the two types is recognized terminologically: bridal axes are referred to as *ambra poka čenaŋ* (woman payment ax), while a variety of working types are designated by their primary function (e.g. *ap čenaŋ*, tree felling ax). In fact, bridal axes are not separated from working axes by any sharp discontinuity. They form one end of a continuum with heavy working blades on the other. Intermediate forms both figured in bride wealth and were used for work.

While a variety of stones were used, *daŋunt*, black basaltic blades, were most common. *Gema*, blades of light green, grey, or white stone were also common (Chappell 1966).

ian money (*ku:* stone, including *ku meŋ,* stone pieces, and *ku wunt,* stone leaves), cloth (*ãlap*) and trade beads (*budz*) have recently been incorporated into the *muŋgoi* class.

In the Simbai Valley in 1963 the items most prominent in affinal prestations were gold-lip and green sea snail shells and steel axes. Cowrie shell bands were going out of style but still were included, as were beads, bushknives, a few animal pelts, and occasionally pigments. Small amounts of money were included in two of the nineteen affinal payments that took place at the termination of the pig festival in 1963. Bird plumes figure in affinal prestations in the Jimi Valley, particularly among the neighboring Narak people (E. A. Cook, personal communication), but not in the Simbai Valley.

Although most marriages are the products of agreements reached by male members of the natal groups of the bride and groom, a girl's wishes in the matter are given serious consideration. Furthermore, it must not be imagined that the bride-to-be necessarily remains passive while her future is being arranged. It is often reported that girls refuse to go to the men whom their brothers or fathers select for them or, having gone, run away. Moreover, it not infrequently happens that girls run off to men without the prior consent of their male agnates. Fourteen, or 28 percent, of the fifty living married women and widows included in the sample were obtained by their husbands without the prior consent of their male relatives. This figure, which represents only those elopements that became enduring marriages, does not, of course, reflect the frequency of such occurrences, which must be much higher, for marriages are brittle previous to the birth of children. One Tuguma man who had two wives in 1963 reported that he had previously taken seven other women, only one of whom had died. Some of the remaining six were sent back to their natal groups by him and others left of their own accord. This number of unions for one man may approach the extreme, but other men also report several short-lived marriages.

Girls not only have considerable prerogatives in the final decisions concerning their marriages, but they also exercise considerable choice in the earlier stages of the process of mate selection. It is the female who initiates courtship, and young men attempt to make themselves appealing so that their advances will be invited. In this the *kaiko* plays an important part, as will be discussed in the next chapter.

Trade

A variety of goods comes to the Tsembaga through exchanges with other local groups and, in recent years, through exchanges with Europeans as well. While a number of other items figure in intergroup exchanges, most important during the period of fieldwork were bird of paradise plumes, axes, bushknives, European salt, shells, furs, and pigs. Previous to the arrival of Europeans and European goods, native salt manufactured from the waters of salt springs by Simbai Valley people, including the Tsembaga, and stone axes manufactured in two locations in the Jimi Valley were of great importance.

The importance of pigs in intergroup trade during 1962–63 was exaggerated by my presence. During that period the Tsembaga obtained in trade from other local groups 31 baby pigs (pigs above the age of three or four months are almost never traded). Most of these were obtained, however, with salt, face paint, or beads obtained from me in trade for food, or with shillings men earned by carrying supplies or equipment for me. It is doubtful if half that number would have been obtained in my absence. Of the 169 pigs constituting the herd at the beginning of the pig festival in June 1962, 56 were born elsewhere. Only 22 of these, or 13 percent of the herd, were obtained in trade from other places, however. The remaining 34 were brought to Tsembaga by their masters upon return from their exile following the military defeat of late 1953 or early 1954. To put it in a slightly different way, 87 percent of the pigs constituting the Tsembaga herd at the beginning of the pig festival were born on the territory of their masters.

Plumes and some furs come to the Tsembaga from northerly directions just as they did before their contact with Europeans. The Tsembaga themselves still add a few furs and plumes to the flow of goods, but in pre-contact times the most important contribution they and their Simbai Valley neighbors made to the trade was salt of their own manufacture. All of these items were sent to the south for commodities that came from that direction: pigs, shells, and both working and "bridal" stone axes.

Two of the items, native salt and stone working axes, are no longer produced by the Maring, but when they did figure in the exchange apparatus they were necessary or important to survival. Most of the

other items were not. Bird of paradise plumes, fur headbands, shell
ornaments, and bridal axes play no direct part in human subsistence.
Neither do the minor items figuring in the exchanges: green bettles,
pigments, and loose animal fur, all used to ornament the person,
shields, or clothing.

Aesthetic considerations perhaps should not be overlooked in a
discussion of this trade. To the Tsembaga and their neighbors, all
of whom are without sculpture, ornamentation of the self or of
shields is a form of artistic expression. They consider fine plumes
and shells, gold-lip or green sea snail, to be among the most beauti-
ful of objects, and men enjoy possessing them for their own sakes.
They also, however, want the plumes so that they will be enticing
to women when they dance, and they want the shells so that they
can pay for the women they obtain.

It is also important that these valuables could be freely exchanged
for stone axes and native salt. It may be suggested that the inclusion
of both the nonutilitarian valuables and utilitarian goods within a
single "sphere of conveyance" (Bohannan, 1955) stimulated the production and facilitated the distribution of the utilitarian goods.

Trade among the Maring is effected through direct exchanges between individuals. It may be questioned whether a direct exchange
apparatus that moves only two or three items critical to subsistence
would be viable. If native salt and working axes were the only items
moving along a trade route, or were the only items freely exchangeable for each other, sufficient supplies of both might be jeopardized
merely by inequities in production. Insufficiencies would develop
because the production of each of the two commodities would not
be determined by the demand for that commodity, but by the demand for the commodity for which it was exchanged. That is, the
production of native salt would not be limited by the demand for
salt, but by the demand for axes. If all that the Simbai people could
obtain for their salt were working axes they would be likely to
suspend the manufacture of salt if they had a large supply of axes
on hand, regardless of the state of the salt supply in the Jimi Valley.
The converse might be the case if the ax manufacturers had large
stockpiles of salt.

It may be asked if the relationships of the people who regularly
traded with each other would not in themselves be sufficiently im-

portant to the participants to compel them to supply each other's needs as a matter entirely separate from the fulfillment of their own needs (see Sahlins, 1965). In the case of the Maring salt–stone ax trade the answer is probably "no." The salt producers and stone ax producers were in almost all cases separated by at least two intervening peoples. A man may be able to bring moral pressure successfully to bear upon a kin or nonkin trading partner to supply his needs, or conversely, a man might feel morally bound to fulfill the needs of a trading partner. If, however, a man must put pressure on a trading partner to put pressure on a second, who will in turn put it on a third, who will attempt to get an ax from the manufacturers, success is less likely. It may be suggested that formal trading partner arrangements are sufficient to effect necessary exchanges in situations in which the trading partners exchange goods that they themselves have produced. But when a number of trade links separate the producers, other mechanisms may have to be employed. In other words, trading partnerships may adequately distribute needed exotic materials when each trader or each local group is the center of a *web-like* trading network. When, however, each trader or local group is a link in a *chain-like* exchange structure, the trading partnership by itself may not be sufficient to maintain an adequate supply of exotic materials. In such a situation the producers and consumers of a particular commodity may be separated from each other by a number of links and are usually unknown to each other. Moral pressure, which might induce production on the part of a trading partner, becomes too diluted between producers and consumers remote from each other to be dependable.

Although salt and working axes are both necessary to survival, the demands for them are limited. A man can eat just so much salt or use just so many axes, even if he is supplying some to kinsmen. If only salt and stone axes could be exchanged for each other the maintenance of a supply of both throughout the population would require a balance between the quantities of each produced and between their respective exchange values, both of which constantly fluctuate in response to such processes as local demographic changes. Without some kind of coordinating or directing managerial agency it seems hardly likely that such balance could be maintained. Where "redistributive systems" operate, that is, in populations in which supralocal authorities may demand production and enforce deliveries, exchange sets of such narrow scope may work. They might even work in "reciprocal systems" in which the parties to the transactions are *groups* in which production may be commanded by a local authority who might, conceivably, take into consideration the requirements of other groups. Among the Maring, however, the exchange apparatus was, and continues to be, based upon reciprocity between *individuals,* and no authority, local or supralocal, exists which may demand production or enforce deliveries.

The exchangeability of plumes, shells, and bridal axes with native-produced salt and working axes alters the relationship between these commodities. While the demands for salt and working axes were limited by the amounts required for specific processes of production, extraction, or metabolism, this is not the case with valuables. Plumes are perishable and there was, therefore, a constant demand for new ones. The size of bride prices is unspecified in advance, but a man is usually under pressure from his affines to pay well for his wife and is shamed if he is not able to do so. The unlimited demand for the valuables required to entice or pay for women, most importantly shells and "bridal axes," provided a mechanism for articulating the production of each of the two items critical to metabolism or subsistence to its own demand. As long as it was possible to exchange salt for shells or bridal axes, commodities for which the need was large but indefinite, salt would be produced. The production of salt would be suspended only with the suspension of the demand for it, and this demand presumably would reflect its status as a physiological necessity or near necessity. Conversely, as long as it was possible to obtain feathers for working axes, the latter would be produced. The demand for working axes, it may be assumed, would depend on the numbers of individuals gardening, the total area under production, and the kind of vegetation in which gardens were being cut.

Furthermore, the indefinite nature of the demand for valuables could serve to cushion fluctuating inequalities in the demand for salt and working axes. If, for instance, local population increases in the Simbai Valley increased demands for working axes at a greater rate than increases in the demand for salt developed in the Jimi Valley, the differences could be absorbed by an increased flow of valuables from the Simbai to Jimi Valleys. Any accumulation of valuables that the ax manufacturers might begin to amass would represent no threat to the continuation of ax production. Such accumulations might be drawn off by enlarged bride payments. They also might permit the ax manufacturers to obtain more wives. This could mean that women would move from the Simbai Valley to the Jimi Valley, which would suppress the birthrate in the Simbai Valley and augment it in the Jimi. Not only might the valuables have facilitated the distribution of axes and salt; they also might have thus provided a mechanism for distributing people more or less evenly over a broad area by adjusting differences in local population dynamics. Pig festivals also form an important part of this equalizing mechanism, as will be discussed in the next chapter.

No direct quantitative data in support of this interpretation of Maring trade are available, unfortunately, since the production of both native salt and stone axes ended some years before this fieldwork began. These suggestions may, however, serve as hypotheses that could be tested in areas where there has been less contact with Europeans.

HOSTILE RELATIONS

Hostile relations between Maring groups are characterized by long periods of ritually sanctioned mutual avoidance interrupted by armed confrontation or conflict. The last engagements in which Tsembaga participated as a principal combatant occurred in late 1953 or early 1954. Their enemy was Kundagai-Aikupa, the local population occupying the territory immediately to their west. Tsembaga men have taken part in warfare more recently, but only as allies or members or other local populations; on the most recent occasion, in 1958, they assisted the Tuguma against the Kanump-Kaur. This was among the last armed encounters to take place in the Maring area. Fieldwork did not begin until four years later, and information concerning fighting and the rituals associated with it therefore rests mainly upon informants' statements.

The Causes of Warfare

The proximate causes of Maring warfare may be inferred directly from accounts of fights and the events preceding them. The ecological-demographic conditions that may have underlain much of Maring fighting must remain hypothetical, since reliable quantified data concerning such conditions at the time of, and preceding, outbreaks of warfare are unavailable.

Accounts of hostilities suggest that a distinction exists between events that originate hostilities between two groups and acts that merely maintain previously established enmities.

In every instance for which I have collected information, hostilities between previously friendly groups followed violence between members of the two groups. The violence, in turn, was induced in the particular instances reported by informants by (1) taking a woman without the prior permission of her agnates, (2) rape, (3) shooting a pig that had invaded a garden, (4) stealing crops, (5) poaching game and stealing scarce wild resources, and (6) sorcery accusations. Surely, however, there must be other acts that also have induced violence leading to intergroup fighting.

A violent episode between single or a few members of a pair of groups did not in all cases lead to intergroup armed conflict. Whether or not it did seems to have been mainly dependent upon (1) the results of the violence, and (2) the previous relationship of the two groups.

If the violence resulted in homicide, armed conflict between the groups of which the participants were members was more likely than if it resulted in mere wounding. Sometimes, however, homicides were settled peacefully and, conversely, less-than-fatal injuries occasionally led to intergroup fighting. The previous relationship of the groups to which the antagonists belonged is significant here. If the antagonists were members of different clans within a single local population it was likely that the trouble would be resolved without battle. When, for instance, the Tomegai and Merkai clans of the Tsembaga had a confrontation many years ago, members of the other Tsembaga clans stood between the shields of the antagonists, admonished them that it was wrong for brothers to fight, and implored them to break off the struggle, which they did.

That such fights, which are referred to as "inside fights" (*ura amaŋ*) or "brother fights" (*gui bamp*), were usually contained may well have been due to the great number of affinal and cognatic ties binding the several agnatic groups that form a local population. These ties not only provided a set of relationships through which composition might be attempted but also provided strong incentives for local neutrals as well as antagonists to seek settlement. It is likely that every, or almost every, local neutral, because of the high degree of local endogamy, would have close relatives among both sets of antagonists. If "brother fights" were allowed to proceed, these relationships would be seriously damaged. If armed hostilities were not speedily resolved, a pair of full brothers from a netural clan who had wives from the opposing antagonists would be likely to find themselves staring at each other across raised shields on a fighting ground, for military assistance is recruited through affinal connections. Even if the situation did not quite come to this, normal intercourse of those related to the antagonists might well be inhibited. There are taboos against eating food cooked over the same fire or grown in the same garden as that of one's enemy, and neutrals must make a choice. If the natal groups of the wives of brothers become enemies, either the brothers must choose between eating with each other or with their respective wives, or one or both of the wives must refuse to adopt the interdining taboos of her natal group. If a woman refuses to adopt the taboos of her natal group she may no longer dine with them. In any case, dyadic relations, which are heavily loaded both economically and with sentiment, are subjected to rather serious symbolic and behavioral impediments by unresolved disputes.

There are other incentives for the peaceful settlement of interclan disputes within the local population. It was shown in an earlier chapter that the local population as a unit exploits the territory. All individuals have access to nondomesticated resources existing anywhere on the territory, and garden land is intermingled. A dispute between the subclans of a clan, or between two clans within a single local population could, if it were not settled or at least contained, make it necessary for the population to redisperse itself radically over these resources. Members of the groups involved know that parcels of land upon which they are presently gardening or upon which they plan to garden would have to be abandoned in case of a continuing dispute; usually they do not desire such a redispersal and are anxious to see any hostility resolved.

Furthermore, the local population forms a single military formation, which faces the enemy as a unit. Intrapopulational disputes debilitate such a unit and may even diminish it in size, for it sometimes happens that one of the parties to a dispute departs from the local population. Such a loss may jeopardize the position of those remaining in later confrontations with the enemy. As the maximum size of local populations is limited by the carrying capacities of their territories, so are minima set by the size of the groups whom they confront as enemies. This principle seems not to be lost upon the Maring: depleted groups have several times invited people from elsewhere to join them on their land. Informants reported that three such events occurred within the Tsembaga and Tuguma local populations during the fifty years previous to fieldwork, and Vayda and Cook (1964:801) suggest that such invitations were common throughout the Maring and Narak areas.

Local populations may also be regarded as congregations, in that the performances of certain important rituals by constituent subterritorial groups are coordinated, and it may be that the Maring regard the necessity to continue performing these rituals together as another imperative for resolving disputes within the local population.

Peaceful settlement of disputes is less likely between friendly adjacent groups that do not form a single local population, that is, do not share rights in the nondomesticated resources of a combined territory, do not form a single military unit in confrontations with the same enemy, and within which all constituent units do not plant and uproot their *rumbim* at the same time. While there is considerable intermarriage between such adjacent groups, it is usually less than that which takes place within each of the local groups; there are thus fewer channels through which peace may be effected and less incentive to do so than is the case within the single local population. Moreover, disputes between adjacent but separate local populations endanger neither patterns of dispersion over resources nor military capability to the same extent as intrapopulational strife. While there may be some intermingling of garden land between adjacent local populations, unless they are in the process of fusion it seldom reaches the proportions that it does within single local populations. And while the adjacent groups act as allies to each other in the military encounters that each have with their separate enemies, there is a difference between the ways in which principal combatants and allies participate in fights.

It may be said, thus, that fighting between separate territorial groups is more likely to occur than fighting between descent groups that are constituents of a single local population. Settlement of disputes within the local population is more likely because of the mutual interests not only of the antagonists but also of other agnatic groups forming part of the same local population. Furthermore, all of the members of the local population are closely bound to each other in a web of kinship connections that serve as channels through which problems may be solved. "Inside" or "brother" fights do occur and sometimes lead to fission and the adoption of formal enmity relations, but we shall be concerned here with fighting between separate local populations, not internal fights.

Once an enmity is established, the requirements of vengeance play an important role in maintaining it. A principle of absolute reciprocity is supposedly in force; every death at the hands of an enemy group requires the killing of one of that group's members, and peace should not be made until both antagonists have revenged all of their losses. A series of military engagements may be terminated, even though the homicide score remains unbalanced, but only by a truce, with arms to be taken up again in the future. The periods of truce may last for ten years or more, however, depending upon a number of factors, which will be discussed in the next chapter.

An even score in killing is not easy to achieve, even though for purposes of vengeance all men, women, children, and babes in arms are considered to be equivalent, and most military episodes terminate with blood debts remaining. Since this is the case, each round of fighting contains within it the seeds of the next. The Tsembaga–Kundagai-Aikupa hostilities in 1953, for instance, were set off by an attempt on the part of some Tsembaga to erase a blood debt by killing a Kundagai. This blood debt was the product of the previous series of engagements, perhaps ten or twelve years earlier, which in turn had been set off by blood debts arising out of a yet earlier conflict.

Some practices may act to preserve the principle of homicidal reciprocity while mitigating the rigorousness of its application. A distinction between the responsibilities of allies and those of the principal combatants has such an effect, as may certain magical and religious procedures, which will be discussed later. Here we are concerned with the ways in which the Maring assign responsibility for revenge and credit for homicide and how they may serve to temper the requirement of absolute reciprocity. A clan is responsible for the vengeance of deaths sustained by its own members and their wives. If in the course of a battle an enemy is brought down, it is usually the case that a number of men participate in administering the coup de grace. Each, claiming credit for the homicide, may regard vengeance accomplished for a member of his own clan. One corpse, thus, may fulfill the reciprocal requirements of several homicides.

On the other hand, the way in which responsibility for the initial homicide is assigned serves to extend and exacerbate enmities and, perhaps, to increase killing. The agnates of the victim of homicide hold as responsible not only the agnatic group of the slayer but the entire local population of which the slayer is a member. Vengeance can be wreaked against any member of this larger group. A previously uninvolved agnatic group may thus become embroiled in a vendetta by suffering revenge for a killing that was not committed by any of its members. Obliged to repay such a homicide, its members will seek vengeance against the local population of the slayer, perhaps victimizing a group that was not party to the aggression they themselves had suffered.

UNDERLYING CAUSES: POPULATION PRESSURE

Although data are deficient, and informants deny fighting over land, there are indications that at least one of the fights in which Tsembaga have been involved was a response to population pressure.

No census material is available for the period during and immediately preceding a fight between the Tsembaga, primarily the Merkai clan, and the Dimbagai-Yimyagai thirty to forty years ago. It was estimated in Chapter 2, however, that the Tsembaga population probably stood between 250 and 300 persons at the time. Estimates also suggest that such a number would have been pressing upon the carrying capacity of a territory, which was at the time smaller than in 1962–63. People say, furthermore, that at the time of the fight there were many people and not much land. The circumstances surrounding the fight itself also suggest that land shortage was the cause. The dispute that may be regarded as the proximate cause of the fight should have been easily resolved since it did not result in homicide. The garden of a man named Paŋwai, who lived with the Dimbagai-Yimyagai, lay close to the path that Merkai men followed to their trapping and collecting grounds in the high forest. Located at about five thousand feet, it was the last garden one would pass before entering the forest and the first one would come upon on the way home, and men often rested by it and slaked their thirst with its sugar cane. Paŋwai was annoyed by what he regarded to be their thievery, and when he caught Kati "drinking" his sugar cane, he shot him. Kati was not seriously injured: the wound was in the buttock and the arrow was unbarbed. Nevertheless, the Merkai took up arms against the Dimbagai-Yimyagai. It was their position that Paŋwai would have been correct to shoot a man whom he caught taking taro from his garden, for to take taro is indeed stealing. But Kati, who had taken only a little sugar to quench his thirst, did not deserve to be shot.

A striking aspect of the affair was the agnatic affiliations of the principals. While Paŋwai was living with the Dimbagai-Yimyagai, he was actually a Merkai by birth. Although Kati was living with the Merkai, he was actually a Karam-speaking man living with the husband of a sister married into Merkai. No Dimbagai-Yimyagai was party to the dispute. The Merkai could have regarded the incident as an intraclan dispute rather than an interlocal population matter. Moreover, they were not required to avenge Kati, for Kati was not an agnate.

Another point of interest is that at the time the fight broke out there were nine Merkai men living and gardening uxorilocally, sororilocally, or matrilocally upon the territory of the Dimbagai-Yimyagai, while only one Dimbagai-Yimyagai man was gardening on Merkai territory. Informants, while they do not make clear why these Merkai did not maintain patrilocal residence while gardening on Dimbagai-Yimyagai ground, state that their reason for gardening on ground other than that of their own clan was land shortage. These men, it should be noted, fought on the side of the Dim-

bagai-Yimyagai against their own agnates. This indicates either that
they had accreted to the Dimbagai-Yimyagai or, more likely, that
the Dimbagai-Yimyagai and the Merkai were fusing when fighting
broke out between them. The possibility of fusion being aborted is
consistent with the density-dependent sequence of land amalgamation and structural arrangements suggested earlier (page 27). At
moderately high densities the lands of adjacent groups become intermingled through affinal and then cognatic grants, which serve
to even out the dispersal of persons over wider areas than is possible through reliance upon unilineal descent principles alone, and
the process of fusion proceeds through the stages of the affinal and
then the cognatic cluster. However, if densities become very high
during this process and an absolute shortage of land develops in the
total area occupied by the fusing groups, it is reasonable to expect
that the fusion process will cease, and fighting, leading to the expulsion of one of the previously fusing groups, is perhaps likely.

Even less information is available from which we would or could
infer environmental or demographic conditions at the time of other
fights. It may be suggested here, however, that the frequencies of
some kinds of disputes are dependent on population densities.

If twenty men, for example, each own one pig and have one garden, there are 400 possibilities for pigs to cause disputes between
men by damaging gardens. If the number of men is raised to forty,
each of which still has one pig and one garden, the number of possibilities for disputes has increased to 1,600, other things being equal.
Likewise, doubling the numbers of unmarried males and unmarried
females also, perhaps, more than doubles the possibilities of woman
stealing and other dispute-producing incidents. Sources of irritation
thus increase at a greater rate than population size. If population
increase were taken to be linear, the increase in some causes of dispute, if not actual dispute, might be taken to be roughly geometric.
It might even be possible to find some way to express mathematically
an "irritation coefficient" of population size.

This increasing irritability should begin to express itself in disputes well below the actual carrying capacity of an area. However,
there is little information relevant to this hypothesis concerning the
Tsembaga, even of an anecdotal sort. The earliest fight about which
Tsembaga informants have any clear recollection took place fifty or

sixty years before this fieldwork, when the Kamuŋgagai and Tsembaga clans together fought the Kekai, a group living across the Simbai River. Informants say that all of the parties to the fight had sufficient land.

Previous to this, in the time of their grandfathers, middle-aged and old informants say, fights were infrequent and enmities were brief, and there are also indications that the population was smaller. There is some evidence, although equivocal, in genealogies, in the flora, in clan histories, and in accounts of the removal of virgin forest from extensive tracts below 4,500 feet within the past sixty years, to indicate that the Tsembaga and their neighbors have arrived in the Simbai Valley within the past two hundred years, that they were relatively peaceful for a long while after their arrival, and that when intergroup fighting began, the population had already expanded considerably but had not yet approached carrying capacity.

It is possible that increasing irritability accompanying a growth in population size might serve, if some of the disputes result in the movement of individuals or groups, to protect the environment from degradation by continually redispersing populations over available land before the carrying capacity is reached.

Composition of Fighting Forces

Fighting forces almost always include two categories of men. The first may be referred to as principal combatants. These are members of the local populations that are parties to the dispute from which the armed conflict has arisen. The second are allies—members of other local populations who are recruited by the principal combatants through cognatic or affinal ties. In some instances men also give armed assistance to nonrelated trading partners.

Because of frequent intermarriage between the Tuguma and Tsembaga through a number of generations, almost every member of each has affines or cognates in the other. The result is, in effect, that the Tuguma as a unit assist the Tsembaga in their fights against the Kundagai, and the Tsembaga as a unit come to the aid of the Tuguma in their encounters with the Kanump-Kaur. While it may be the case that Tuguma-Tsembaga form a single military unit for the defense of a continuous area, the rationale of recruitment of one by the other remains that of kinship ties between individuals.

Kinship ties are less numerous between groups separated by mountain ridge or river. The result is that military assistance rendered by these geographically more distant groups to each other is on a smaller scale, consisting of men who are closely related to the principal combatants and, if these men are influential, some of their relatives as well.

Principal combatants are responsible for casualties sustained by their allies,[4] and they must compensate the agnates of a slain ally with, among other things, a woman, whose first son will bear his name. The practice of assigning the responsibility for casualties sustained by allies to the principal combatants whom they assist, rather than to enemies, may serve to diminish the frequency of fighting throughout the Maring area. It frequently occurs that enemies of long standing find themselves confronting each other as allies of other principal combatants. The Kanump-Kaur, for instance, who are the enemies of the Tuguma, have many affinal connections with the Kundagai and therefore turn out in large numbers to assist the Kundagai in their fights against the Tsembaga, who are assisted by the Tuguma. The Tuguma and Kanamp-Kaur face each other in such situations not as principal combatants but as allies of opposing principal combatants. If in the course of such an encounter the Tuguma slay a Kanump-Kaur, they may regard this as revenge for a previously slain Tuguma. The Kanump-Kaur, on the other hand, would not charge this slaying to the Tuguma, but look to the Kundagai for redress. If such a killing fulfills the revenge requirements of a group it will not be necessary for it to seek vengeance on its own and set off another round of warfare.

Fighting and Its Rituals

Accounts of fighting and the rituals associated with it sometimes conflict. This is true particularly with respect to the sequence and details of prefight ritual procedures. Differences in accounts may in part be explained by variations in the practice of different groups and even different men. A simplified account of ritual performances is sufficient here; variations will be discussed elsewhere. What follows reflects the practice of two of the three Tsembaga subterritorial

4. Glasse (1959) reports very similar assignments of responsibility among the Huli people of the Southern Highlands of New Guinea.

groups; the practices of the third differ in some details, according to informants.

THE "SMALL" OR "NOTHING" FIGHT

Most fights have two stages, which are distinguished by the weapons employed and the rituals performed. The first of the two stages is referred to as the "nothing fight" (*ura auere*), or "small fight" (*bamp ačimp*). A local population that has suffered injury calls out to the enemy to prepare for an encounter on a designated fight ground. One or two days' notice is usually given, providing ample time for both sides to mobilize their allies and to clear the fight ground of underbrush. This task falls equally upon both antagonists but encounters between the bush-clearing details of the hostile groups are avoided. Informants say that if members of one of the groups arrive at the fight ground to find their opponents already at work they will withdraw for some distance until their opponents retire, after which they will enter the fight ground and finish the clearing.

Prefight rituals are performed separately by the three separate Tsembaga subterritorial groups. On the night previous to a "small" or "nothing" fight, informants say, the warriors convene by clans or subclans in men's houses to inform the spirits of both the high and low ground of the next morning's encounter. As they sit chanting in a darkness illuminated only by the embers of small fires, shamans (*kun kaze yu*), of whom there are several in each clan, induce in themselves an ecstasy by inhaling deeply and rapidly the smoke of bespelled cigars made from strong native tobacco.[5] When his *no-mane* (his animated, immortal, thought stuff) departs through his nose to seek out the smoke woman (*kun kaze ambra*) in high places, the shaman begins to tremble and gibber. Soon the smoke woman "strikes" him. Led by his *nomane* she enters the shaman's head by way of his nose, and his ecstasy reaches its height. Rising to his feet he dances about the embers in a low crouch, sobbing, chanting, and screaming in tongues. It is through the smoke woman that the ancestors are now being informed by the living of the fight and it is

---

5. While I have not witnessed the performance of shamans in connection with fighting, I have seen shamans perform in a number of other situations. Informants assure me that their performances in the context of fighting are similar to those I have witnessed.

through her that they are now signifying their endorsement of the
enterprise and sending assurances of their protection. It is, informants say, the smoke woman who speaks in tongues through the
shaman's mouth.

The protection of the ancestors is bestowed upon the warriors
through the shaman's body. As he dances within the circle of men,
the shaman takes each of their extended hands in turn, and with
it wipes sweat from his own armpits. This sweat, driven from his
body by the heat of the entering spirit, is said to be hot and therefore imparts strength. No pigs are killed at this time, informants
agree, but slaughter is promised in the event of a satisfactory outcome of the fight.

It is not clear whether the smoke woman is asked at this time to
name those members of the enemy group who may be easily killed
and to warn those members of the local group who are in special
danger. Some say that this forms part of the ritual preceding the
more deadly second stage of fighting only.

In the morning spells are said by "fight magic men" (*bamp kunda
yu*),[6] of whom there are one to three in each clan, and who are
usually, but not necessarily, shamans as well. The spells are said
over the bows and arrows so that they will be strong, accurate, and
sharp, and over the shields so that they will stop the arrows of the
enemy. Small bundles, called "fight packages" (*bamp yuk*) or "fight
bags" (*bamp kun*), are pressed to the hearts and heads of each
warrior by the fight magic man. These packages contain the thorny
leaves of the males of a rare, unidentified tree growing in the
kamuŋga, called the "fight tree" (*ap bamp*), and personal material
belonging to the enemy, such as hair, fragments of leaves worn over
the buttocks, and dirt scraped from the skin. It is said that pressing
the "fight leaves" (*bamp wunt*) contained in the packages to the
heart and head of a man diminishes his fear, and that control over
the personal items of enemies, and their confinement within the same
package as the leaves, enhances the opportunities for killing those
who are represented. These materials are obtained from neutrals who
have kinship connections among the enemy and therefore may visit

6. I have used *magic* as a translation for the Maring term *kunda*. *Kunda* refers
to procedures involving the repetition of conventional formulae, or spells, that are
said to derive their power from the words themselves, rather than from any other
agency. Spirits are not invoked in any of the *kunda* spells I have collected.

them. A neutral himself may, if he suspects a man of being a witch (*koimp*) or sorcerer (*kum yu*), acquire such objects by stealth, but it is said that sometimes a man's own clan brothers, suspecting him of witchcraft or sorcery, will give some of his exuviae to a neutral to deliver to the enemy.

While one fight magic man is pressing the fight package to the hearts of all men, another is ritually applying a gray clay (*gir*), obtained from the *wora*, or low ground, to their legs so that they will remain strong throughout the day.

When treatment of both the heart and legs is completed, lengths of green bamboo are laid on a fire. With the warriors gathered in a circle around them, one or more fight magic men kneel by the fire and talk to the ancestors, sobbing as they implore protection. When the bamboo explodes, the men stamp their feet and, crying "ooooooo," leave in single file for the fight ground, carrying shields, bows, and arrows. They sing a song called "*wobar*" as they proceed in a peculiar prancing gait toward battle.

In the small fight only bows and arrows, and perhaps throwing spears, are used. Some informants say that hand-to-hand weapons such as axes and jabbing spears are not even brought to the fight ground.

The antagonistic groups line up on the fight ground within easy bow shot of each other, according to informants, who also say that allies and principal combatants are intermingled in the formations. The shields, which are very large, averaging 2.5 by 5 feet, are propped up, permitting bowmen to dart out from behind them to take shots and leap back again. To demonstrate their bravery, men also emerge from behind the shields to draw enemy fire. Casualties are not numerous and deaths infrequent, for the unfletched arrows of the Maring seldom kill.

It may be that the "small" or "nothing" fight is less a serious battle than a device for ending a quarrel before more lethal fighting, with its attendant ritual constraints, develops. The relative harmlessness of a bow and arrow engagement from stationary positions with cover well provided by shields itself suggests such a possibility, but there are even more cogent reasons for seeing the small fight in such a light.

First, small fights are protracted. Accounts of engagements in the past indicate that in some instances there were four or five days of such fighting before escalation took place. Such a period might allow tempers to cool while satisfying the bellicose imperatives of manhood.

Second, while there are no third parties with either the power or authority to adjudicate disputes, the formations of the antagonists include allies, men less committed to the quarrel than the principal combatants. These men often have a considerable interest in seeing the quarrel settled before it goes any further, for they themselves have no direct grievance and may have close relatives in the enemy formation. When the Tuguma fought the Tsevent, for example, some Tsembaga went to the assistance of both of the antagonists. In one instance, this split two full brothers who had sisters married into each of the opposing groups. Although they take their places in the military formations of the antagonists, such men may serve to dampen the martial ardor of the principal combatants by obliquely counseling moderation. Allies seem to have behaved in this way during at least one confrontation between antagonists who had previously been friendly. During the Tuguma-Tsevent fight, informants say, some of the Tsembaga allies of both antagonists, instead of hurling insults at their opponents, lamented loudly and continually about the evil of brothers fighting. Their laments in this instance were unheeded, perhaps because two or three Tuguma are reported to have been killed by arrows during the little fight. If there had been no fatalities, or if only one Tuguma had been killed in reciprocation for the homicide that had led to the fight, the preachings of the Tsembaga may have had more effect.

Third, the small fight affords an opportunity for nonallied neutrals to attempt to intervene between antagonists who have previously been friendly. Reference has already been made to the fight between the Dimbagai-Yimyagai and the Merkai clan of the Tsembaga. At the initial engagement neutrals stood on a knoll, informants say, overlooking the fight ground, admonishing both sides that it is wrong for brothers to fight, demanding that the combatants quit the field and throwing rocks at both formations. Their efforts were unavailing, it must be reported, and the fight escalated.

Finally, the "small fight" brings the antagonists within the range of each others' voices while keeping them out of the range of each others' deadlier weapons. Informants say that this opportunity for communication was used mainly to hurl insults at each other, but there is some evidence to indicate that in some fights, at least, the opportunity was used to resolve the quarrel. Information on this aspect of the small fight is ambiguous. There are several reported instances of small fights being terminated by shouted negotiations after one side had sustained a fatality that the other side could regard as full reciprocation for a homicide it had sustained and which had set off the fight. In such instances the termination of the conflict should be attributed to the fulfillment of revenge requirements, rather than to the negotiations, but the small fight at least provided an opportunity to fulfill the revenge requirements without recourse to deadlier fighting, which would have been more likely to compound grievances than to cancel them.

When information is derived mainly from the war stories of old campaigners it is difficult or impossible to know what actually occurred. There are, nevertheless, indications that the small fight operated, albeit in an inefficient way, to suppress rather than to encourage hostilities. Such an interpretation acquires additional plausibility when the small fight is compared to the deadlier encounter that usually follows it, and when the process of escalation is examined.

ESCALATION

Informants' accounts indicate that from the first day of the small fight, or certainly after one or two days, some members of one or both of the antagonistic groups would begin to shout to both their opponents and their comrades that they had had enough of the "nothing fight" and that the time had come for a serious engagement. It may be that such sentiments formed a kind of counterpoint to the laments of allies, in the case of fights between erstwhile friends, for the lost peace. The small fight may perhaps be viewed as a debate, held in a setting that minimized the danger of casualties while satisfying martial imperatives, between those eager to fight and those hoping to preserve the peace. All the interested parties, both the antagonists and their less-committed allies, were present and in a position to contribute opinions and sentiments.

Furthermore the small fight is a show of force. The antagonists are given an opportunity to assess the strength of their enemies and to shape their policy accordingly. There is little information on this point, but an apparent equivalence of forces may encourage settlement of the quarrel. Conversely, an apparent disparity may induce the weaker group to flee without putting the matter to a further test of arms. Some informants say that this is what happened in the second round of engagements between the Dimbagai-Yimyagai and the Merkai, but agreement among informants is not complete.

As a show of force, the small fight may resemble in certain respects the war games and military displays of more complex societies. It bears an even closer apparent resemblance, however, to the agonistic territorial displays of other animal species and may well have had an effect similar to that which some scholars (e.g., Wynne-Edwards, 1962) attribute to this kind of animal behavior: maintenance of optimum population dispersal at minimum expense in blood.

The success of such exercises in diplomacy in avoiding escalation depended largely on two factors. These were, first, the previous history of the relationship between the antagonists. If their hostility were long standing or if the homicide score between the two were seriously out of balance, those eager to fight would no doubt prevail. Also important was the extent to which the events of the bow and arrow fighting exacerbated or assuaged hostilities. It may be that if casualties were few tempers would cool and voices would be added to those speaking in the cause of peace.

Eventually the talk would, as the Tsembaga say, "become one." If those in favor of peace prevailed, the fight would be dropped, and if the antagonists had been friendly until this engagement, they could resume their friendship without going through elaborate ritual procedures.

However, it was frequently, perhaps even usually, the case that a consensus in favor of fighting crystallized. If it did, the antagonists withdrew from the fight ground for at least two days to prepare ritually for the forthcoming encounter.

THE AX FIGHT

The second, more serious stage of the fight has no native designation; it is simply called by Tsembaga the "*ura kuñuai*," "fight itself,"

or "true fight." It will be referred to here as the "ax fight," although
jabbing spears, throwing spears, and bows and arrows are also
employed.

The rituals preparatory to the ax fight are much more elaborate
than those preceding the small fight. In the last chapter it was
mentioned that each land-holding group periodically plants a ritual
Cordyline fruticosa bush called the *"yu miñ rumbim"* or "men's
souls *rumbim*." [7] A group may not participate as principal combatants in ax fights with its *yu miñ rumbim* in the ground. There are
periods when land-holding groups do not have *yu miñ rumbim*
growing, and fighting is generally confined to such periods (this
will be discussed in the next chapter). It occasionally has happened,
however, that a group who has uprooted its *rumbim* has initiated hostilities while the *yu miñ rumbim* of its opponents has remained in
the ground. If a group has suffered an attack while its *yu miñ
rumbim* continues to grow, it must, before proceeding to the other
rituals preparatory to the ax fight, uproot this plant. The elaborate
rituals that surround the uprooting of the *rumbim* under peaceful
conditions are abbreviated when a group is forced into the procedure by enemy action. Description of the procedure will be
reserved for the discussion of the *kaiko*, the context in which it
more frequently occurs.

After the *rumbim* is uprooted, the ritual hanging of the "fighting
stones" (*bamp ku*) is begun. Each of the land-holding groups owns
at least one pair of "fighting stones." These are also sometimes referred to as *"aram ku"* (the meaning of *aram* is obscure). These
stones are in the care of one or two of the fight magic men, who
are referred to as *"aram* stone men" (*aram ku yu*) or, because of
the large number of ritual restrictions under which they labor,
"taboo men" (*aček yu*). Fighting stones, which are in fact stone
mortars and pestles made by a vanished and unremembered people,
are occasionally found in the ground in both the Jimi and Simbai
Valleys. Informants believe, however, that all of them originated
at the first home of the smoke woman, Mount Oipor, in the upper

7. In contrast to the *nomane*, which is immortal, the *miñ* is lost at death. Conversely, its abandonment of the body, an occurrence that may be induced by sorcery,
bewitchment, or fright, results in death. The *miñ* is thought to walk abroad in
dreams, and the moment of waking is particularly dangerous, for a sudden awaken-
ing may not allow it to return to the body. The *miñ* may, in short, be regarded as
mortal life stuff.

Jimi Valley, and say that their ancestors obtained them from people in that vicinity.

The fighting stones are ordinarily kept in a small, round house called *riŋgi yiŋ* (*riŋgi*/fighting ash; *yiŋ*/house). During the portion of the ritual cycle preceding hostilities, the stones are kept in a small net bag on the floor of the house, where they also remain during the small fight. When the ax fight is agreed upon, the net bag is taken from its resting place and hung near the top of the center pole. Informants say that this is done by the taboo men unceremoniously, but it is a momentous act. By hanging up the fighting stones, a group places itself in a position of debt to both allies and ancestors for their assistance in the forthcoming ax fight. These debts can be fulfilled only through the prolonged ritual procedures that will be discussed in the next chapter.

The act of hanging the fighting stones signifies the assumption of a large number of taboos by the entire local population or various of its members. These include, for all members, females and children as well as adult males, prohibitions against trapping marsupials, eating eels, or eating marsupials and *marita pandanus* fruit together. Adult males may not eat the flesh of pigs killed for the *kaiko* of other groups, many kinds of marsupials, some yams, and a number of green vegetables. A number of other foods may be eaten by both men and women, but not shared by them. Drums may not be beaten, and the movements of some men are severely restricted. Some informants say that the taboo men may not depart from the territory of the local population, although others say they may visit the adjacent Tuguma, but not groups whose territories lie across the Bismarck Mountain ridge or the Simbai River. Furthermore, the fires over which their food is prepared, or which serve to heat stones for the ovens from which they partake, may not be used to cook food for members of other local populations.

Most important, the opposing group, which may have been until this moment referred to as "brothers" (*gui*), if they had previously been friends, now become, formally, "ax men" (*čenaŋ yu*), or enemies. Their territory may no longer be entered except in battle, and outside of the context of battle members of the enemy group may not be touched or even addressed. One is not even supposed to look at their faces. No cultivated food grown on enemy ground may be eaten, nor may food grown elsewhere by a member of the enemy group. Should fatalities be suffered, food grown by allies of the enemy must also be avoided, and, while they may be addressed and even visited, their houses may not be entered. If no fatalities are suffered, food that allies of the enemy have grown may be eaten, but dining from the same fire with them is forbidden. The act of hanging the fighting stones, in short, not only terminates any kind of mutually supportive relations between the principal combatants, but also places restrictions upon the future relations of principal combatants with the allies of their opponents. Moreover, some prohibitions, particularly in the area of food sharing, affect relations between allies of the opposing principal combatants if they suffer fatalities.

Hanging the fighting stones, furthermore, also pushes far into the future any possibility of reconciliation between the principal combatants. Truces are possible while the fighting stones hang, but reconciliations are not. The time for quick settlement of the dispute has passed.

After the stones have been hung on the center pole one of the fight magic men climbs to the roof of the *riŋgi* house, where he ignites a stick of wood taken from a tree called "*kawit*" (*Cryptocarya* sp.). This is obtained from the dwelling places of the red spirits near the top of the Bismarck Mountain ridge. *Kauit* is one of the varieties of trees said to be the houses of the red spirits. It is particularly difficult to ignite, and the fight magic man sobs as he recounts to the red spirits the circumstances that have led to this performance and implores them to come into the fire. When he succeeds in igniting the *kawit* he returns to the ground and uses it to ignite a fire that has been laid inside the *riŋgi* house to heat oven stones and in which the ritual ash, *riŋgi*, will be prepared from logs of *kanam* (*Albizzia* sp.), *kamukai* (*Colona scabra*), and *pokai* (*Alphitonia iacana*). These second-growth trees have themselves no ritual significance; they are used, informants say, only because their combustion produces good black charcoal. Their ash, or charcoal, is supernaturally powerful only because the red spirits themselves have been brought into the fire upon which it is prepared. The oven stones also partake of the supernatural power of this fire, and the fighting stones, always strong, are fortified by the smoke surrounding them, as they hang from the center pole.

A second fire is laid outside the house for the purpose of heating cooking stones for a second oven. This is ignited at the same time as the indoor fire, but not with the *kawit*. The red spirits do not enter or ignite this fire, and no *riŋgi* is prepared in it.

Two pigs are now slain. One of them is to be offered to the red spirits and must be a male. The second, to be given to the spirits of the low ground (*the rawa mai*, a category, it will be recalled, which includes both *rawa tukump*, spirits of rot, and *koipa maŋgiaŋ*), may be either male or female.

When pigs are sacrificed to them, spirits are usually addressed in a peculiar screaming style. The message is delivered in staccato phrases, interrupted with increasing frequency by meaningless, loud, sharp yells until, just before the pig is struck on the head with the club, the staccato "Ah! ah! ah! ah! ah!" has replaced words completely. Informants say that the addresses to the spirits in connection with the killing of the pigs in preparation for the ax fight follows this pattern, which I have observed in other contexts on several occasions.

The red spirits are first approached. They are not addressed as *rawa mugi*. Instead a series of allusive terms referring to their characteristics and activities, and pseudonyms that may also be allusive but remain obscure, are used. Allusive designations include "sun-fire" (*ruŋga-yiñe*), referring to their hotness and, therefore, strength; "orchid, cassowary" (*norum-kombri*), referring to their habitation of high places and fighting qualities, and *niñ niñ koramon*, which designates the act of lighting the fire on the roof of the *riŋgi* house. After being addressed as a class, individual red spirits—the slain brothers, fathers, and perhaps grandfathers of the living—are addressed and told to bring their associates to watch and listen.

Having alerted the red spirits, the slaughterer, who is one of the fight magic men, proceeds with his address. The burden of his message is to tell the spirits that an ax fight is about to start. He promises that the living will attempt to avenge their deaths and asks their help. He invites them to eat the pig that is about to be killed for them and to come into the heads of the living. He promises that only members of the local population will join them in eating the flesh of this pig. Men from other places, he tells the red spirits, will be given other pigs.

His short address finished, the screaming slaughterer runs back and forth in front of the pig, which is tethered by one leg only, and strikes the animal with his club while on the run. The first blow usually kills the pig.

The spirits of the low ground are approached in a similar way, although they are addressed neither as *rawa mai* nor *rawa tukump*, but as ancestors (*ana-koka*, literally, father-grandfather) and as *koipa mangiang*. These spirits are also told of the forthcoming encounter, and they are invited to eat the flesh of the pig offered them and to take hold of, or strengthen, the legs of the living.

The pigs are then placed in the ovens for cooking. The pig that has been dedicated to the red spirits, sometimes referred to as the "head pig," is cooked in an oven built entirely above the ground out of wood and leaves. Stones heated on the fire made inside the *ringi* house, which had been ignited by and entered into by the red spirits, are used in this oven.

After the pigs have been put into the ovens, the men retire into their houses. They spend a substantial portion of the night chanting while the shamans contact the smoke woman, whom they ask to name those enemies who may be easily killed and to warn those of the local men who are in especially great danger. It is usually the case, informants say, that only one or two enemy men are designated easy marks in each of the three to six Tsembaga men's houses in which shamans perform. Similarly, only a few of the locals are warned. Informants say that a warned man is urged by his fellows to stay away from the fight ground, but his usual response is to refuse, saying that he will kill one of the enemy first, after which it is all right if he himself is killed. He may add that it makes little difference if he is killed, for many clan brothers will survive him. If a warned man survives the fighting, his reputation is enhanced, for his *miñ*, his life essence, is said to be strong.

A second procedure is also used to mark those of the enemy who may be easily killed. A separate, small above-ground oven is built in the *ringi* house to cook the head of the pig killed for the red spirits. During the night, informants say, the *miñ* of some of the sleeping enemy, which wander abroad while they dream, may be lured by the pleasant odor of cooking pork into the *ringi* house, where they will partake of the pig's head. Such men may be killed. The taboo man sits by the oven and recites the names of enemy men. The head of the pig, it is said, whistles when the name of an enemy whose *miñ* has partaken of it is enunciated. The whistling of the pig's head is said to be audible not only to the taboo man but also to others, most of whom cannot be in the *riŋgi* house, but are rather in nearby men's houses or, less likely, out of doors.

Several aspects of these two types of divination ritual should be discussed. It is of interest that only a few of the enemy are marked for easy killing by the two procedures. It may be that this is simply the expression of a realistic appraisal of the situation, i.e. that it would not be easy to kill a larger number. There is some suggestion, however, that the number designated, although not large, represents "sufficient" homicides—enough, that is, as far as the local group is concerned, to halt the fighting. This is not necessarily a reflection of the "homicide score" existing between the antagonists, for the group that has suffered fewer fatalities in the past also goes through such divining procedures. The data are far from sufficient, but it may be that such divination sets up a rough "killing quota." The possibility that such quotas are established through ritual or other means could be explored by anthropologists working in areas where warfare still occurs.

The designation of certain enemies as easy marks also may serve to direct the homicidal attentions of the entire force to them. That is, such prophesies in effect may be self-fulfilling. If this is the case, both shamanistic practices and pig's head divination may be constantly reinforced by their apparent successes.

Clear information relevant to this matter can no longer be obtained. Conversations with shamans would indicate that many of the enemy who are marked actually are slain in battle. Shamans, however, boast about their own successes and, in confidence, disparage the abilities of other practitioners. The actual facts of particular cases cannot be known for certain.

It may be that the use of enemy exuviae, combined with the practice of predicting who among the enemy are easy prey, may act as part of a social control mechanism. As in the matter of the accuracy of predictions made by shamans, data are deficient concerning fight packages because their owners, while sometimes boastful about their efficacy, are always secretive about their specific contents. Only they and the intermediaries from whom they have obtained material know whose exuviae is held by a fight magic man; the following must remain, thus, no more than a suggestion. Among the Tsembaga, all men who are in possession of fight packages happen to be shamans as well (although this need not be the case). I was informed by one of these men that those enemies whom the smoke woman marked for killing through him were among those whose exuviae, or whose father's exuviae, were contained in his fight package. If it is the case that designations of the smoke woman are to some extent self-fulfilling prophesies, then those whose exuviae are contained within the fight package are more likely to be killed than other members of the enemy force.

The declared motive of a man's betrayal of another to his enemy by giving them his exuviae—suspicion of witchcraft or sorcery— is suggestive. While it is entirely possible that the victim of such a betrayal may be the innocent object of unprovoked antagonism, it is also possible that he has departed sufficiently from certain approved modes of behavior to arouse covert, but not general, animosity. Widespread antagonism toward a member of the group is likely to lead to general agreement that he is a witch, and when such agreement exists, betrayal to the enemy is unnecessary; a man's own clan brothers may kill him. No such killings took place among the Tsembaga during the period of fieldwork, but grumblings frequently were heard concerning who would have been killed for a witch had the government not arrived, and descriptions of the personalities of individuals killed for witchcraft in the past indicate that the victims are likely to be bad-tempered, argumentative, and assertive.

Information is both insufficient and general, but it does suggest that those likely to incur covert but less than general suspicion of witchcraft include those who have plenty of women, valuables, pigs, and crops, but who are not generous. For reasons they do not make clear, the Maring regard especially marked success in pig husbandry or gardening to be associated with witchcraft or sorcery. If a man's pigs and gardens prosper out of proportion to those of his neighbors, he invites suspicion. It is the exuviae of such a man, it is suggested here, that is likely to be sent to the enemy, and he is thus expected to be killed in battle. There are strong reasons then for a successful man to be sufficiently generous to allay the envy of those around him. At the least, fear that through treachery one's exuviae might come to rest in the fight package of an enemy, like fear of sorcery and witchcraft and fear of being suspected of sorcery and witchcraft, is a factor in maintaining the social and economic egalitarianism that characterizes Maring society.[8] The fight packages of the enemy may indeed be worthy of the fear in which they are held, because those whose exuviae are contained in them may be in greater physical danger than their clan brothers.

This suggestion must apply mainly to the practice of shamanism by men possessing a fight package, for it is not clear how the whistling of the pig's head is produced. Taboo men say, of course, that it is the head of the pig that whistles, and other people don't know. Few people, or none at all, watch the taboo man's face during the procedure, and it is possible that he simply puckers his lips and blows. It is also possible that the steam of the oven is in some way made to produce the sound.

It may be the case that warnings, like designations of who among the enemy may be killed, are correct in a greater than chance number of cases. If a shaman could judge who in his clan would be marked for killing by his counterpart in the enemy group, or whom the enemy might try especially hard to kill, he could warn this man.

While any member of a local population may be slain in retaliation for a homicide committed by one of its members, it is sometimes the case that the victim's group marks one of the killer's group as the preferred object for revenge. This may be the killer himself, or one of his sons, although according to Vayda it is the custom among some Maring groups to designate a member of the enemy group who physically resembles the victim. Such a practice carries the ideal of absolute reciprocity to the extreme.

Sometime during the night two *rumbim* are planted in the enclosure shared by the *riŋgi* house and the men's house in which the warriors are assembled. These *rumbim*, which are also, according to some informants, called "*yu miñ rumbim*," are planted to keep the *miñ* of the men inside the enclosure when, on the follow-

8. Both Wolf (1954:46) and Kluckhohn (1944:67–68) have made similar suggestions concerning the functions of fear and suspicion of witchcraft in other kinds of communities in other parts of the world.

ing day, they themselves leave it for battle. That is to say, the men leave their *miñ*, their life stuff, behind when they go to battle. Tsembaga say that if their *miñ* were exposed to the powerful spells made by enemy fight magic men, they would surely succumb, causing their possessors to fall victim to enemy weapons. The *miñ*, therefore, must be left in a safe place and kept from following their possessors into battle or running off if frightened. The *rumbim* prevent them from leaving the enclosure. Informants say that no Tsembaga knows the spells that must be enunciated over these *rumbim*, and that one old Tuguma man comes to perform this ritual for all the Tsembaga.

During the night the fight magic men paint and bespell a number of small stakes. Before dawn they go quietly to the fight ground and push them into the earth far enough so that they cannot be seen. These stakes are said by informants to cause the enemy to lose their *miñ* if they are brought to the battlefield. Informants do not report any encounter of opposing fight magic men on the fight ground. Whether there were conventions preventing such meetings was not investigated.

At dawn the pigs are taken from the ovens. The fat belly of the "leg pig," the pig dedicated to the spirits of the low ground, is covered with salt. When the allies arrive, as soon as possible after dawn, they are given portions of this salted pig fat, which they eat immediately along with the green vegetables, mostly ferns, with which the pig was cooked. The remainder of the pig will be recooked and given to them in the evening, after the day's fighting.

The procedure involving the pig offered to the red spirits, the "head pig," is more elaborate. Before its salted belly is eaten by the principal combatants, they blacken their bodies with the *riŋgi*. The heart and lungs of the pig are placed on a small table in the *riŋgi* house, and the fighting stones are removed from their net bag and laid on top of them. One informant says that the red spirits have themselves come into the stones through the fire. Placing the stones on top of the heart and lungs permits the red spirits to partake of these parts. The men then enter the house two or three at a time to take the *riŋgi*, the black ash made in the fire ignited by the red spirits. They are asked if they prefer to take *riŋgi* from the male fighting stone, the *wai*, which is the pestle, or from the *mai*, meaning in this instance the female, which is the mortar. Their choice has a bearing upon the permanence of some of the taboos, to be discussed below, which are assumed at this time. If the *mai* is selected, the taboo man uses it to apply a little of the *riŋgi* to the shoulders and forehead of the warrior. If the *wai* is chosen, the taboo man applies some of the ash to it and the warrior licks it off. It is unclear whether it is the contact with the stones, the reception of the *riŋgi*, or both which brings the red spirits into the head, but informants agree that this is the effect of the procedure. When men go to battle, their *miñ* are left behind, but the hot, dry, hard red spirits are thought to have come literally into their heads where they burn, informants say, like fires, imbuing them with strength, anger, and the desire for revenge.

After having received the *riŋgi* ritually from the taboo man, the warrior retires from the house with a handful of ash so that he may blacken his entire body. Now that the red spirits are inside him and he himself is "hot," he may apply the "hot" protective and strengthening ash to his skin. Had he done this before being marked by the female stone or licking the male stone, informants say, his skin would have come up in blisters from the supernatural heat of the *riŋgi*.

Riŋgi is also applied, Tsembaga say, so that the face of the warriors may not be seen by the enemy, in accordance with one of the taboos assumed when the fighting stones were hung a few hours earlier. It is said that if the enemy can see a man's face, they will be able to kill him.

The taboos assumed with application of the *riŋgi* are extensive and include both limitations on social intercourse and prohibitions against certain foods. The taboos on social intercourse refer mainly to relations with women. A man cannot, while he is wearing *riŋgi*, eat food from the same fire as a woman or cooked by a woman. While he may speak to women, he may not touch them; sexual intercourse is, of course, forbidden. Women, and anything touched by women, are said to be "cold." Contact with them would extinguish the fires burning in the men's heads. Conversely, contact with the hot men would, it is said, literally blister the skins of the women.

Food taboos are extensive. All wild animal foods are forbidden. Snakes, eels, catfish, lizards, and frogs are proscribed because they are "cold." Marsupials are not eaten because they are the pigs of the red spirits and cannot now be taken until the living are in a position to give their masters pork in return for them. Some green vegetables are also forbidden. These include *Setaria palmaefolia* and hibiscus leaves. The latter are forbidden because they are wet and slippery; their ingestion will not only extinguish the fires in the head but also make it difficult to grip an enemy in hand-to-hand combat. No explanation for the taboo against *Setaria* could be obtained, and it may be that it was merely imported with the plant itself or else developed in a former home area long ago. Taboos against the ingestion of this plant by males are in effect elsewhere in the highlands (see Newman, 1964:263–66). Some bananas and yams are also tabooed. These are, in the main, soft varieties, which it is said would injure the hardness or strength of their consumers. All food grown in the *wora* must be avoided, and unless the fight ground is located there men must not enter the *wora*.

All of these taboos remain in effect until, at the earliest, the *riŋgi* is ritually removed at the end of the fight. If a man has taken *riŋgi* from the male stone some taboos remain for the rest of his life or at least until he is a very old man. These permanent taboos include prohibitions against the ingestion of snakes, eels, catfish, lizards, frogs, and many of the marsupials that live in the high forest. Since most men take *riŋgi* from the male stone the great bulk of these subsidiary protein sources are, as it has already been mentioned in an earlier chapter, reserved for women and children.

Permanent prohibitions also apply to certain vegetables. These include all varieties of *Setaria palmaefolia*, some yams, and some bananas. There are, in addition, a number of other plants which may be eaten, but never from the same plant that has fed a woman. Several varieties of *Pandanus conoideus* fruit fall into this category, as do sugar cane, banana, and *Saccharum edule* varieties that have red skins or leaves.

After the *riŋgi* has been applied, a hasty meal is made of the greens with which the pig has been cooked. The pork, however, except for the bellies, is returned to the ovens for recooking with fresh greens, in preparation for the meal at the end of the day. According to information I received, the men then form a circle and consume fighting leaves and heavily salted belly fat. Georgeda

Bick (personal communication) received slightly different information from some of the same informants in 1966. She was told that the salt was not taken on pig belly, but wrapped in the leaf of the succulent *komerik* (?*Pollia* sp.). Informants say that eating the fighting leaf makes them wild and bloodthirsty, but the effect is probably psychological rather than physiological, for the ingestion of the prescribed amount produced no effect upon me. No explanation involving specific supernatural or natural processes could be elicited about the consumption of pig belly. Bick, however, was told that the ingestion of salt and *komerik* would ward off enemy spears.

Whether the salt was ingested with pig or with *komerik*, the practice may have some important consequences. First, the consumption of salt is accompanied by an absolute taboo upon drinking any liquid whatsoever while on the fight ground. Certainly no man who wears *riŋgi*, and perhaps no allied warrior, although this is not clear, may drink water or the juice of sugar cane, or eat cucumbers or papaya while the engagement continues. The rationale for this taboo, in light of previous discussion, is apparent. These cold, wet foods will extinguish the fire that burn in a man's head, leaving him weak and defenseless. A man, therefore, does not drink from the time that he consumes the salted pig belly until he leaves the fight ground later in the day. To note that the resulting thirst might well limit the length of the fighting day is not to be facetious, particularly in light of the fact that fighting takes place usually on sunny days. (Fighting is postponed if there is rain, for rain would extinguish the fires in the men's heads.) Indeed, some Tsembaga men have admitted that fighting would cease for the day when the warriors became too thirsty to fight any longer. The ingestion of salted pig belly and the associated taboo on taking fluids may thus mitigate the consequences of combat by shortening the fighting day. Other consequences of salt and fat consumption, however, may operate to increase the intensity of the fighting while it does last.

The Maring diet is deficient in sodium. This is obvious because most Maring will eat pure table salt by the handful, and sodium appetite appears to be directly correlated with sodium need (J. Sabine, personal communication, 1965). The manufacture of native salt was discontinued some years before fieldwork began and no samples could be obtained. Because the native salt was made from the waters of mineral springs and not reduced from plant ash, however, it is quite certain that it was a sodium salt, despite the lack of samples. Eating large amounts of sodium just before fighting would have permitted the warriors to sweat normally while maintaining normal blood volume. If they lacked this additional sodium they might well have experienced a lowering in blood volume and a consequent weakness as they lost sodium through sweating (W. V. Macfarlane, Frederick L. Dunn, personal communications, 1965).

Sabine (personal communication, 1965) points out that the salt may also play a part in the catabolization of the fat, which, according to Macfarlane (personal communication, 1965), would then become available as energy about two hours after consumption, thus providing a "second wind" to the tiring warrior.

The consumption of the lean pork at the end of the day, it may be mentioned, would offset to some extent the nitrogen loss caused by the stress of fighting.

After eating the fighting leaves and salted belly, the men form a circle and fight magic men press the fight packages to their hearts and their heads, to the cassowary plumes adorning their heads, and to the weapons as well. Another fight magic man applies bespelled *gir*, a gray clay, to their ankles and feet. The taboo men rub *riŋgi* on all of the jabbing spears and axes.

Having finished applying the fighting package to men and weapons, the fight magic men build a fire outside of the circle formed by the men and lay lengths of green bamboo on it. Both sets of ancestors are asked again for their aid and protection.

In the meantime, the men have enclosed the inside of the circle by making a fence of their shields. The taboo men are inside this circle, and when the bamboo explodes they begin to scream out to the red spirits, asking again who may be killed among the enemy and who among the locals are in great danger. Informants say that this is the only occasion upon which the red spirits themselves communicate with the living without going through the intermediary smoke woman. The taboo man screams, leaps in the air, hurls himself against the wall of shields. His eyes roll up into his head showing only the whites and his tongue protrudes. He screams out the names and, after writhing on the ground, lies still for a moment or two. He is assisted to his feet by one of the fight magic men while the men yell war cries. More bamboo is exploded and the men, led by a fight magic man waving his fighting package in the direction of the fight ground, leave for battle brandishing their weapons, singing a song called "*de*," and shouting war cries. The taboo men, who recover quickly, join the procession.

In contrast to the weapons of "small" or "nothing" fight, both axes and two types of jabbing spear are employed in the "ax" fight. The point of one type is armed with a sharpened beak of a hornbill, which remains in the wound when the weapon is withdrawn. The other is barbed for half of its seven-to-nine-foot length. Below the barbs three or four prongs project forward and outward at an angle to the shaft. Such a weapon seems designed for defense against headlong charges, which informants say were not a regular feature of Maring warfare.

On the fight ground formations were mixed; both principal combatants and allies stood side by side, it is reported. The taboo man remained in the rear, heavily protected by the men closest to him. The slightest wound sustained by a taboo man supposedly portended the inevitable death of one of the men of his group, and if he were killed it meant that his side would be routed. Such a belief could operate, of course, to mitigate the severity of fighting if both sides spent their energy in trying to shoot the taboo men of their opponents and if his men fled when he was killed. There is no suggestion from any informant, however, that ax fights degenerated into attempts to shoot the enemy taboo man while others of the enemy were being ignored.

There is little information concerning leadership on the fight ground. It is quite clear, however, that discipline was not tight nor control close. Formations were several ranks deep, and the men in the front row were relieved by those behind them from time to time. While the opposing men in the front ranks were fighting a series of duels from behind their enormous shields, bowmen in the ranks farther to the rear gave support to the men in the first rank and shot at those who exposed themselves. Fatalities generally occurred when a man in the front rank was brought down by an arrow. His opponent, supported by nearby comrades, would then rush in to finish him off with axes. The fallen man's comrades would also rush to his defense, protecting him with their shields if possible.

Informants' accounts give the impression that this static positional fight was most common. In most engagements the opposing forces stood toe-to-toe behind their huge shields with no tactical or strategic movement taking place. A series of such engagements frequently continued sporadically for weeks, with neither side suffering more than light casualties. The antagonists, it seems, were waiting for the day when their enemies would arrive on the fight ground without the support of their allies. On the day that a group found itself with a clear numerical advantage, instead of taking up the usual static positions it would charge.

Maintaining the support of allies seems to have become increasingly difficult as the fighting went on. Informants say that they simply tired of participating in a fight that was not their own. Victory, thus, must have often gone to the group who could continue to mobilize its allies the longest. There are two clear-cut instances of this involving the Tuguma and the Tsembaga. In their last conflict with the Kundagai, it was on the day that their allies, the Tuguma, did not appear that the Tsembaga were routed. The Kundagai, heavily supported by the Kanump-Kaur and other groups, took advantage of the absence of the Tuguma to mount a charge. The Tsembaga suffered eighteen fatalities on this one day, six of them being women and children, and many other people were wounded. Thus casualties sometimes were heavy.

The Kanump-Kaur avoided the more dire consequences of the failure of their allies to appear for an engagement against the Tuguma. When they heard that the Kandembent-Namikai, their most important supporters, were not going to arrive, they themselves didn't go to the fight ground. They simply gathered up their women, children, and pigs and fled their territory. Vayda has gathered accounts of similar behavior among a number of Jimi Valley Maring groups.

Waiting for a numerical advantage and then charging, according to informants' accounts, was the most frequently employed strategic and tactical procedure. There were others as well, however. An example of ambush is to be found in Tuguma history. Night-time raids were rare but did occur. Accounts of battles indicate, furthermore, that flanking and surrounding movements were sometimes attempted; by stealth a force would gain its enemy's rear or flank, opening him to either cross fire or charges from two directions. These latter maneuvers were probably only attempted by forces with some numerical superiority.

Informants' accounts indicate that an ax fight often went on for weeks, or perhaps even months; however, engagements did not take place every day. Rain confined the men to their houses, and the requirements of ritual also produced interruptions. The frequency of ritual performance was, to a large extent, directly correlated with the frequency of casualties, for most of the rituals were performed in connection with casualties.

After a fatality, fighting was discontinued while the group that suffered the loss mourned the deceased and performed the necessary funerary rites, which included killing one or more pigs. Those who inflicted the fatality also had to undertake ritual performances to protect themselves from the spirit of their victim. It is said that the *miñ* of the slain man follows the killer home, menacing not only the killer himself but all of his coresidents. If the killer sleeps in the men's house the spirit of the slain man might follow him inside, wreaking vengeance upon all who are present. When a man kills an enemy, therefore, he sleeps away from his fellow warriors to keep from exposing them to danger. To protect himself, he sleeps in the *riŋgi* house.

In the morning the killer slaughters one of his own pigs for the red spirits. In his address he tells them that with their help he has killed an enemy and he now gives them a pig in thanks for their assistance. He asks that the *miñ* of the slain be prevented from killing him or any of his brothers. He invites the red spirits first to eat the pig being offered them and later to assist the living in killing more of the enemy. Since the allies may not partake of pig offered to the red spirits, a second pig may be killed and dedicated to the spirits of the low ground, but it is not clear that this is the case.

While the pig is in the oven the fight magic men prepare to drive the spirit of the slain man from the territory through a procedure called "extraction and disposal magic" (*kunda guio warumbon*). They fashion brooms from *rumbim* and obtain from the forest several 4- to 6-foot lngths of the vine *deraka* (*Pipturus* sp.), leaves of *močam* (*Aglaomena* or *Alocasia* sp.), and a few 3- to 5-foot poles that are 1 to 2 inches in diameter of *ganč*, a tree of the *Rubiaceae*

View north across the Simbai Valley to the gardens of the Kekai (light areas) from above the Tsembaga dance ground. The woman's house in the foreground was later demolished to enlarge the dance ground.

The author, who is 5'10", with a group of Maring men and boys.

Large pigs being led to slaughter.

Joints of a wild pig are distributed by a successful hunter. Every Tsembaga shared in the flesh of this animal.

Members of the Tomegai and Kwibigai clans join to feast on the wild pig in a men's house enclosure.

Bespelling sections of bamboo before their use in a stake planting ritual. The stakes (left foreground) and the močam leaves (behind the bamboo) are also treated.

Tsembaga men ready to leave for Tuguma to participate in the Tuguma stake planting ritual. When the bamboo being placed on the fire at the right explodes, they will depart.

(*Opposite*)
The trail crosses a boundary between local populations. It is rare for shields to be set at boundaries, but stakes (left foreground) are always planted.

Erecting the *timbi* house. Bark is scraped from the center post so that it will fall on the wealth objects, causing them to increase.

(*Opposite*)
A man leaps onto heated cooking stones to pierce the *marita* fruit (in his left hand) with a cassowary bone.

A medium-sized pig is sacrificed to the Red Spirits. (Photo taken by Mrs. Cherry Vayda among the Fuŋgai-Korama, a Maring group living east of the Tsembaga in the Simbai Valley.)

(*Opposite*)
A woman renounces a taboo.

The Auŋdagai charge onto the Tsembaga dance ground.

Men bedecked for dancing. The young man in the center wears a *mamp gunč*.

Trade follows dancing. Two men discuss the merits of a gold-lip shell.

family. The posts are sharpened on the bottom and painted at the top with earth pigments. Spells are said over these four kinds of objects and they are passed out among the men. Bamboo is laid in a fire and the ancestors are asked to assist the living in driving away the spirit of the slain man. When the bamboo explodes the men stamp their feet and cry out. Those who are carrying the bespelled objects run all over the enclosure. The men with *rumbim* make sweeping motions as they run. Those carrying the vine *deraka* whip the ground, while the men with the sharpened *ganč* posts thrust their points into the earth at frequent intervals. The *močam* are carried by their 2- to 3-foot stems with the leaf held a foot or so above the ground. As the men run they occasionally shout, "*Pio!*" ("Go!").

After having covered the enclosure thoroughly, they go out through the gate and head for the houses of the women. Other men follow, brandishing weapons and shouting battle cries. Every house and every enclosure is visited so that the spirit of the slain man, wherever it is, and the supernatural corruption (*tukump*) it has spread, may be beaten by the *deraka*, pierced by the *ganč* posts, "bitten" by the *močam* leaves (which contain oxalic acid), and swept by the *rumbim* toward the boundary. There, amidst battle cries, the four plants are deposited, after spells are again recited over them to bring harm to the enemy by sending to their territory not only the spirit of the dead man, but also his *tukump*.

While neither rituals performed by the victim's nor the killer's group require more than a day or two to complete, fighting may be discontinued for considerably longer; a period of five to seven days, informants say, was not unusual. It is the victim's group that calls out the challenge for a new engagement but sometimes they delayed, since fatalities, it is admitted, do damage to the faith of the victim's group in the efficacy of its ritual performances. After a death, therefore, requests might be sent to renowned fight magic men in friendly groups, asking them for their assistance. By the time that the invitations reached such men and they had traveled to the territory of those who had sent for them, several days might have passed. These "cease-fire" periods were used by combatants on both sides to take care of garden work if necessary. Another day might then be spent in preparation for the visitor's rituals and in their performance. After their completion the challenge for a new round of fighting could be issued. Both sides again killed pigs for the red spirits and the spirits of the low ground and sent word to their allies that the time for a new engagement had been set.

Wounding, when it was serious, also required interruptions of the fighting, according to informants. The victim's group would on these occasions kill a pig for the red spirits, which would be eaten by the victim and his agnates. New engagements might be delayed until it was clear whether the injured man would live or die.

Several obvious advantages of "ritual cease-fires" may be summarized here. First, interruptions in the fighting provided the combatants with an opportunity to perform necessary subsistence tasks. Second, they relieved the psychological and physiological stress that must have accompanied an ax fight. The requirement of the rituals for the slaughter and consumption of pigs, furthermore, may also have served to mitigate the ill effects of the increased catabolization of protein brought about by this stress. Third, it is possible that such interruptions may have enhanced the opportunities for reestablishing peace on a more prolonged basis. For one thing, each cease-fire resulted in a partial or full demobilization of the allies, who returned to their own territories. Informants' accounts suggest that remobilizing allies became increasingly difficult as fights dragged on. A group having difficulty rallying its supporters for a new encounter might choose not to issue the challenge, or, if the homicide score was not too uneven, to send word to the enemy, either through intermediaries or by shouting, that a truce was desired. This was likely to be acceptable if the fighting had been protracted and some casualties had been suffered. Informants report that men would say that enough had been killed or wounded for the present, that if the fighting continued everyone would be killed, and that it was better to perform the truce rituals now and to resume the fighting again sometime in the future.

TERMINATING THE FIGHT

Most ax fights ended in a truce. Sometimes, as suggested above, termination of the hostilities was arranged during periods when fighting had already been interrupted by the necessity to perform rituals. At other times it was arranged while both sides were on the fight ground.

Informants say that such agreements were reached at least three times by the Tsembaga and their enemies the Kundagai. Evening the homicide score, while not necessary, no doubt facilitated the invocation of truce. Old informants say that in the first fight against the Kundagai, when the score was evened by the slaying of a Tsembaga man (each side had then suffered four deaths), the Tsembaga called out to the Kundagai that their requirements for revenge had now been fulfilled and that both sides should return to their respective houses to plant the *yu miñ rumbim*, signifying truce. On the other two occasions when truces were declared, there were disparities in the homicide score but the contestants agreed that killing had been sufficient for the time being and that the pressures of gardening and pig herding required a cessation of the fighting.

Truces continued for the duration of the ritual cycle. The description and timing of this cycle will be discussed in the next chapter; it is sufficient to note here that these ritual cycles were protracted, as were the truces that coincided with them. They sometimes endured for fifteen or even twenty years, although ten or twelve years was probably the average.

Not all fights ended in truces, however; it sometimes happened that one side was routed. The victors, in such instances, after killing every man, woman, and child unfortunate enough to be caught, laid waste the territory of the vanquished. After the defeat of the Tsembaga in 1953, the Kundagai tore up the Tsembaga gardens, cut down most of the *pandanus* and *ambiam* (*Gnetum gnemon*) groves, desecrated the *raku*, the burial places where pig sacrifices are made, burned the houses, and killed all the adolescent and adult pigs. Their depredations were directed toward making it as difficult as possible for the Tsembaga to return to their own territory, rather than toward the acquisition of booty. Since the Tsembaga were *čenaŋ yu*, or formal enemies, to them, foodstuffs grown by the Tsembaga were supernaturally proscribed. Their booty was therefore limited to baby pigs, which could be taken home to be raised, and perhaps to wealth objects, such as plumes and shells, which the fleeing Tsembaga had left behind. The slain pigs were not allowed to rot, however. Neutrals, seeing the smoke of the burning Tsembaga houses, immediately came and carried the carcasses back to their own houses for cooking.

Having done what they could to lay waste Tsembaga territory, the Kundagai retired to their own ground. The immediate occupation of Tsembaga territory was tabooed to the Kundagai. It will be recalled that when the fighting stones are hung up, a taboo against entering enemy territory except in anger comes into effect. Once the armed conflict had come to an end and despoliation had been completed, the Kundagai not only returned to their own ground, therefore, but were restrained from reentering Tsembaga territory by fear of both the ancestral spirits of the Tsembaga, who were thought to remain at least for a time on the ground lost by their living descendants, and also by fear of their own ancestral spirits from whom the injunction emanated.

If the defeated do not return to their territory, it remains vacant while the fighting stones of the victors remain hanging from the center poles of their *riŋgi* houses. I know of only one instance in Maring history in which the territory of the routed group was immediately occupied by the victors. In 1955 the Kauwasi, a Jimi Valley group, routed their neighbors, the Cenda. Some members of the victorious forces announced their intention to make gardens immediately on the ground abandoned by their opponents, but they were actually prevented from doing so by the Australian government, whose presence was first being felt in the area.

This case may illustrate the limits beyond which a particular set of supernatural constraints cannot contain demographic and ecological pressures. The Kauwasi are the most numerous of all Maring local populations. They numbered, in 1963, nearly 900 persons, according to Vayda, and there is no reason to believe that they were fewer in 1955. In 1955, moreover, their numbers had been swollen by refugees from the Tsembaga, Ambrakwi, and Tsengamp. There must have been at the time over 1,000 persons living on Kauwasi territory, and 1,100 is not unlikely. The land of the Kauwasi, moreover, is poor. Large areas are in grass, and much of the gardening takes place in very young secondary growth. There are indications, in short, that the Kauwasi were pressing the carrying capacity of their territory, a state of affairs that could only have been worsened by the influx of refugees.

It is further interesting to note that some but not all Kauwasi informants deny any intention of occupying the territory of the Čenda themselves. They say that it was not the Kauwasi but the

Tsembaga, Tsengamp, and Ambrakwi refugees who were going to take Čenda land, and that they could do so because they were not themselves enemies of the Čenda but were merely assisting the Kauwasi in the fight as allies. This statement is inconsistent with other statements which indicate that the refugees were considered principal combatants, and not allies.

Accounts of routs suggest that in some instances the members of the vanquished group do not return to their territory. The group fragments as the survivors flee to affines or cognates. The Tsembaga who survived the 1953 disaster took refuge with seven different local populations, two of which were across the Simbai River to the north, while three were to the south, across the mountain in the Jimi Valley. To rally these small and scattered remnants for an attempt at reoccupation would have been difficult in light of their dispersion, their abiding fear of the Kundagai, and their ruined *pandanus* and *ambiam* groves. The Tsembaga ceased to exist as a group after their defeat, and, if it were not for agents of the newly arrived Australian government who offered to protect them, it is unlikely that they would as a group have returned to their territory. Not only was their return discouraged by the dangers and difficulties of such an enterprise, but continued residence with their hosts was encouraged by participation in rituals that had the effect of converting their de facto membership in these local populations to de jure membership (this will be discussed in the next chapter).

While accounts indicate that the return of an entire local population to its abandoned territory often did not occur, frequently, and perhaps usually, a fraction of that territory would be reoccupied by remnants of the vanquished group under the cover of one or more of the groups among whom they had taken refuge. Some Tsembaga, for example, after being driven off their territory by the Kundagai, took refuge with the Tuguma immediately to the east. As members of the Tuguma group, or under their protection, they reentered the eastern portion of their territory and made a few gardens. They were accompanied in this enterprise by a few Tuguma who had been told by Tsembaga relatives living elsewhere to avail themselves of their lost ground. So far as I know, the reoccupied Tsembaga territory was used for gardening only; houses remained at a greater distance from the enemy border. Such limited reoccupation of abandoned territory is reported in two other instances in Tuguma-Tsembaga history.

Even when truces have been arranged on the battlefield, the antagonists remain uncertain of each other's sincerity. If after a protracted period active hostilities are not resumed, truce-making rituals are performed. Informants, who it must be admitted are inaccurate in such matters, indicate the period is a month or so. In addition to a sufficient time lapse since the last engagement, it may be that word certifying the resolve of their opponents to terminate the fighting comes to each of the principal combatant groups through neutrals. In light of the reticulate nature of intergroup relationships throughout the Maring area this is likely, but no statements from informants give support to the possibility.

Truce rituals are performed only by groups that remain on their own territory after the fight. The scattered survivors of a rout simply remove the *ringi* from their bodies with little ceremony. The antagonists do not participate together in truce rituals; each conducts them separately. When a group is assured that its opponents have given up any intention of prolonging the hostilities, word is sent to the allies to assemble for the killing of the pigs and the planting of *rumbim*.

The number of pigs slaughtered depends upon the size of the herd, the length of the conflict, and the number of casualties. The sacrifices take place at the *raku*, where ancestors' houses had been located. These are scattered throughout the territory, and every man has a number at which he sometimes sacrifices pigs. The specific *raku* at which slaughter is to take place are designated on this, as on all other occasions by shamans, who tell each man where the ancestors wish to eat their pork. On pig-slaughtering occasions during the period of fieldwork shamans' advice directed most of the members of a subclan to the same *raku*, but there were always some men killing all or some of their pigs by themselves in isolated *raku*. Informants say that this was also the case when *rumbim* was planted. The locals are accompanied to the *raku* by their affines, cognates, and, perhaps, nonkin trading partners from other places who assisted them in the fight.

Some of the pigs killed are for the red spirits, but most are offered to the spirits of the low ground. The burden of the addresses to both categories of ancestors is to thank them for their assistance in the fight. Most of the pork from animals dedicated to the spirits of the low ground is immediately presented to the allies, who take it home with them when the rituals are concluded. The fat bellies are first removed, however, for formal presentation. This belly fat, along with that taken from the pigs dedicated to the red spirits, is brought to the men's enclosure, where the *riŋgi* house stands. This is the scene, on the following day, of the planting of the *rumbim*.

Everyone, including allies, women, and children, assembles for this ritual. In preparation all varieties of wild animals are captured: marsupials, snakes, lizards, frogs, rats, insects, grubs, and birds. A special oven (*pubit*) is prepared out of bark. It is about three feet square and rests directly on the ground. This oven is loaded with greens, the wild animals, and the belly fat of the pigs dedicated to the red spirits, which is cut into little pieces. While this is cooking the presentation of the belly fat of the pigs dedicated to the spirits of the low ground is made to the allies. These men sit in a circle and, as each man's name is called his local affines, cognates, or trading partners push handfuls of the now cold salted belly fat into his mouth. A second local relative assists by pushing additional salt into his mouth and by sprinkling more on his shoulders. There is a vague order of precedence in these proceedings: the sons of men slain in the fighting, if there are any, will be called first, and men who have killed enemies next.

After the presentation to their allies has been made, the principal combatants may remove their *riŋgi*. The fight magic men bespell the cloth-like tents of certain tree caterpillars, which are used as wash cloths, and the sap taken from the tree *yiŋgam* (unident), which serves as a soap.

These spells are among those included in the category of *kunda*, known as "turning word" (*andik meŋ*). Throughout the remainder of the entire ritual cycle, *andik meŋ* is performed from time to time to "turn off," or reverse, magic performed or the ritual states assumed in connection with fighting.

As the oven is opened the taboo man addresses both categories of ancestors, recounting the circumstances of the fight and announcing

to them that the taboos associated with the *riŋgi* will now be removed. The men then cleanse themselves of *riŋgi*. The removal of
the *riŋgi* signals the end of the taboos against sexual intercourse,
food cooked by women, and some of the foods forbidden during
the time of fighting. The men, along with the women and children,
may now eat the food in the oven. Informants say, when questioned
about it directly, that those men who took *riŋgi* orally from the *wai*,
or pestle, avoid the snake, lizard, rat, and other forbidden foods that
the oven contains, while those who received *riŋgi* from the mortar,
or *mai*, eat everything, as do the women and children. This may
not be the case, however. It must be hard to distinguish a small
piece of forbidden cooked rat from a small piece of perhaps acceptable marsupial, and it must be impossible to distinguish pieces of
acceptable marsupial from marsupials that are tabooed. This may
be, in short, an occasion when food taboos are in fact abrogated
simply because mistakes may be impossible to avoid.

    After the contents of the oven are consumed, the *yu miñ rumbim*,
always a red-leafed variety of *Cordyline fruticosa*, called "tundoko,"
is planted. After it has been bespelled with *andik meŋ*, it is placed
directly in the middle of the square bark oven in which the food
has just been cooked. The ancestors are addressed by one of the
fight magic men, who thanks them for both preserving the lives of
the men who survived the fight and for not allowing them to be
dispossessed of their territory. He repeats that the fight is over and
tells them that the *rumbim* is now being planted on their own territory. He assures them that while it remains in the ground the living will not fight or turn their thoughts to fighting. He deprecates
the amount of pigs given to them and to the allies, but promises
that while the *rumbim* remains in the ground the thoughts and
efforts of the living will be directed only toward raising taro and
more pigs so that some time in the future, when the pigs are of
sufficient size and number, the *rumbim* may be uprooted and pork
in great quantity can be given to them and to the allies for their
assistance in the fight.

    He also asks the spirits to care well for the *rumbim*, for if it does
not flourish neither will the men. All of the local males are then directed to place a hand on the plant as the earth is tamped around
its roots. The taboo man tells them that intercourse with their wives

will now result in children and that the children will be strong and grow quickly.

Some informants say that the laying of hands on the *rumbim* actually introduces the *miñ*, the life stuff of the men and boys, into the *rumbim*, where they remain for safe-keeping. Others deny that this is the case and explain that while this *rumbim* is planted for the sake of the men, their *miñ* remain either in the *rumbim* planted the night previous to the ax fight or confined by that *rumbim* to the men's house enclosure. It has already been mentioned that both are sometimes referred to as "*yu miñ rumbim*" (men's "souls" *rumbim*), but the exact whereabouts of the men's *miñ* is not a matter of great concern here. It is clear, however, that the *rumbim* is associated with males; in fact, women may not touch this plant.

Another plant, *amame* (*Coelus sentellariodes*), a low, fragrant, herbaceous, in this case green-leafed, ornamental, is planted for women. When the men unclasp the *rumbim*, the taboo man plants the *amame* around the outside of the oven. Some informants say that small pieces of fat from the belly of the pig are planted with the *amame*, and all agree that it is referred to as the "pig belly *amame*" (*konj kump amame*). While planting it the taboo man asks that the spirits of the low ground care well for the *amame*, that the pigs grow fat, that the women be fertile, and that gardens flourish.

The sexual and fertility content of this ritual seems apparent. The spatial placement of the ritual objects associated with male and female may represent the procreative act, which in turn symbolizes fertility in general. It is in the receptacle that later received the *rumbim* that the varied fruits of the land were cooked, and pigs and gardens are associated with the same plant as are women. It must be mentioned here, however, that *rumbim* and *amame* are also planted over graves, and death as well as fertility might also be symbolized here. It has already been noted, however, that death and fertility are not antithetical in the Maring view.

It seems apparent too that this ritual, following as it does the removal of the *riŋgi*, which terminates the supernatural restrictions associated with fighting, reorients the participants toward peaceful activities. Their attention and efforts are directed away from their borders and those who live across their borders. They may now turn inward and devote themselves to prospering within their successfully defended territory. The cleansing of the *riŋgi from their bodies*, followed by the planting of the *rumbim* and *amame*, ends war and begins peace.

Another important aspect of the ritual planting of *rumbim* is its affirmation of the connection of the individual to the group, and the group to its territory. The ability to plant *rumbim* indicates the successful defense of the territory against outside threat. *Rumbim* may be planted only on the territory. Groups who have been driven off their land cannot as groups perform this ritual elsewhere. Survivors of routs, after having taken *riŋgi* from the fighting stones of their hosts during their hosts' fights, participate in planting *rumbim* with their hosts. This act attaches refugees to the land of the groups who have harbored them, and, moreover, clears the way for the annexation of their abandoned territory by those who drove them off it. When a refugee sacrifices a pig in connection with the *rumbim* planting of his hosts, he invites his ancestors to leave their old residence and partake of pork in the new place. Thus, even the ancestors of a routed group eventually vacate the territory from which their living descendants have been driven.

The peace that follows the planting of *rumbim* is a truce only. Men say that it is still the "time of the fighting stones." These objects remain hanging from the centerpole of the *riŋgi* house, and intercourse with the enemy remains forbidden. Moreover, the time of the fighting stones, that is to say, while the stones remain suspended from the centerpost and the *rumbim* remains in the ground, is a period of indebtedness, for the allies and ancestors have not yet been fully repaid for their assistance in the fight that has just been concluded.

Several taboos remain in effect during this time. Eels, which are said to be the pigs of *koipa maŋgiaŋ*, may not be eaten, and marsupials, which are said to be pigs of the red spirits, may not be trapped. Before the living may again avail themselves of these "pigs" raised by the spirits it is necessary for them to raise pigs themselves to give in return.

It has already been mentioned that pigs killed in connection with the pig festivals of other groups may not be eaten by men. Informants say that men would be ashamed to eat the festival pig of other people when they have not yet raised sufficient pigs to conduct a festival themselves, and such a pig, when it is received, is given to the women and children.

A taboo on beating drums also prevails. While their *rumbim* remains in the ground the members of a group, when invited to dance elsewhere, dance with weapons rather than drums in their hands.

Further taboos remain that seem to segregate some of the components of the community associated with the red spirits (and thus warfare) from some of those associated with the spirits of the low ground (and thus peaceful activities). Marsupials may not be trapped; although they may be eaten, they may not be mixed with *pandanus* fruit, which is associated with the spirits of the low ground. Red-skinned sugars, bananas, and *Saccharum edule,* as well as certain varieties of *pandanus* and certain species of marsupials, may be eaten by both men and women, but men and women may not share the same plant or animal. Men, moreover, may not eat certain soft tubers, particularly some varieties of *Dioscorea alata, D. bulbifera,* and *D. esculenta,* which grow in the *wora.*

Two of these taboos have certain empirical effects. First, as was mentioned in the last chapter, the taboo against the consumption of "festival pig" from other places applies only to adult and adolescent males. Women and children, who are most in need of protein, are the physiological beneficiaries of this taboo. Second, the taboo against trapping marsupials can only redound to the advantage of the marsupial population. During the period of fieldwork, although no count was kept, it was clear that almost all marsupials taken were taken in traps, rather than by shooting. The yields of trapping, moreover, seemed substantial. When trapping is permitted, several hundred animals may be taken in the course of a year. There are no data concerning the population dynamics of marsupials inhabiting Tsembaga territory, but it may be that the prolonged prohibition on trapping permits these animals to recover from exploitation that might otherwise decimate them.

While these taboos may enhance the well-being of the local population, they are unimportant in comparison to another concomitant of the local group's debtor status, acknowledged with the planting of the *rumbim. The spirits and the allies must be rewarded for their assistance in the recent fight before aggression may again be undertaken.* If a group attacks its enemy before these debts are paid, help will be forthcoming from neither spirits nor allies. Informants agree that both allies and ancestors would be sufficiently angered to refuse to assist a group who initiated new hostilities before fulfilling obligations accrued in the last round of fighting. These sanctions are sufficiently frightening to make breaches of the peace rare.[9] A "truce of God" thus prevails until there are sufficient pigs to present to the allies and spirits and to uproot the *rumbim*. The next chapter will discuss what constitutes "sufficient pigs," how long it takes to acquire them, and the festival during which they are sacrificed.

9. Out of a corpus including information on more than twenty fights, three cases of violations are known. It is interesting that in two of these three cases the chief violators were the Kauwasi, who, it was mentioned earlier, are the largest of the Maring local populations and who may well have been pressing the populational limits of their territory at the time. It is further interesting to note that violation of the *rumbim* truce did not necessarily involve a simple abrogation of the *rumbim* convention, at least in the case of the Tukmenga, a large Jimi Valley local population who joined with the Kauwasi in an attack upon the Monambant several days after the Kauwasi routed the Čenda. According to Vayda, who revisited the Maring area in 1966, the Tukmenga, although sympathetic to the Kauwasi proposal for a concerted attack upon the Monambant, were hesitant because their *rumbim* remained in the ground, and thus they feared an adverse reaction from their ancestral spirits, who had not yet been repaid for their assistance in the last fight. Their solution was to slaughter a small number of pigs, at least some of which were laid on the roof of the *riŋgi* houses as offerings, no doubt, to the red spirits. In other words, the sanctified *principle* that obligations to ancestors must be fulfilled before new hostilities are initiated may have remained unchanged, while the *rule* concerning how those obligations are to be fulfilled was modified. Informants later said, according to Vayda, that the procedure adopted by the Tukmenga had always been acceptable, but no precedents were cited. Data, although insufficient, warrant the suggestion that the Tukmenga were reinterpreting the behavioral requirements of sacred tradition in terms of contemporary conditions, a process well known in Western societies.

CHAPTER 5

The Ritual Cycle

THE DURATION OF THE CYCLE

The length of the ritual cycle, and thus the length of the truce that depends upon the ritual cycle, is largely regulated by the demographic fortunes of the pig population. The *kaiko*, the year-long festival which culminates the ritual cycle, is initiated by uprooting the *rumbim* that was planted after the fight. To uproot the *rumbim* requires that the people have "sufficient" pigs. We must first, therefore, define this quantity and discover how "sufficient" pigs are accumulated.

The Origin of the Pigs

The question of the origin of the pigs constituting the herd when it is of "sufficient size" to stage the *kaiko* is of importance here. It has already been pointed out that only 13 percent of the pigs constituting the herd at the outset of the Tsembaga *kaiko* in 1962 were purchased from people outside the local population. Accumulation of sufficient pigs to uproot the *rumbim*, therefore, seems to depend largely upon the natural increase of the local herd, rather than upon the purchase of animals from members of other local populations.

"Sufficient" Pigs

The obligations of members of the local population to make presentations of pork to others do not define the number of pigs sufficient to uproot the *rumbim* initiating the *kaiko*. Such obligations exist, and they must be fulfilled, but they set only a lower limit on the number of pigs that need be killed. This becomes clear when

153

it is understood that except in instances in which a presentation of pork will be made in reciprocation for an equal amount of pork previously received, the size of presentations are at the discretion of the donor. It is certainly the case that he gains prestige if he makes large presentations, but there is in most cases no specific amount required to meet a man's obligations. Moreover, in those instances in which a man has specific requirements, his herd is likely to include more animals than required to meet his obligations; these will be consumed by himself and his family. The fulfillment of obligations to spirits, similarly, does not require the slaughter of a specified number of animals. Pigs must be killed in certain contexts, but the number is not specified.

It seems clear that the definition of a "sufficient" number of pigs must be sought in areas other than that of obligation to the living or dead. In earlier chapters the role of the pig in Tsembaga subsistence was discussed; it will be useful to turn here to a brief review of this information.

Perhaps the most important contribution made by pigs to the welfare of the Tsembaga is the protein they provide during periods of stress. They also provide certain other services to the human population: by eating feces and garbage they keep residential areas clean and also improve the efficiency of the use to which crops are put. The foraging of small numbers of pigs for limited periods of time not only utilizes tubers that might otherwise be wasted, but it might also benefit the arboreal component of the developing second growth.

Small numbers of pigs are easy to keep, since they are fed substandard tubers harvested along with the ration for humans. It may, in fact, be said that by eating the ration presented them the animals provide a further service to their masters: they convert tubers of only marginal usefulness as human food to high-quality protein.

There are, on the other hand, trying consequences of population expansion among the pigs. First, as the pig population expands, residential groupings become more and more fragmented. Just prior to a *kaiko* the pattern is likely to be one of subclan hamlets and scattered homesteads. The number of people with whom any individual has frequent social contacts is thus diminished. This must represent a deprivation to the Tsembaga, who, like most other people, enjoy meeting and talking, and it may also result in a lowered effectiveness of the social structure. It will be recalled, for instance, that consensus formation is achieved through informal conversations, the "talk" eventually "becoming one." Residential proximity may accelerate this process, residential dispersion inhibit it.

Perhaps more important, in a scattered settlement pattern people are vulnerable to attack. A truce prevails with the antagonists of the last fight as long as the *rumbim* remains in the ground, but there may be other groups across other borders who do not have *rumbim* in the ground and who would be free to initiate armed hostilities if a dispute should develop.

Second, the increased pig population requires additional work. The magnitude of the labor requirements of pig husbandry has already been pointed out, but some aspects of the matter must receive additional discussion.

A third disadvantage, also mentioned earlier, is that the possibilities of garden invasion by pigs are increased as the herd increases. Such events frequently result not only in damaged crops but also in slain pigs and serious fights. Slain pigs and serious fights, in turn, accelerate further the scattering of residences.

As Vayda, Leeds, and Smith have said of Melanesian pigs in general, they "apparently are in the category of those good things of which there can be too much" (1961:71). The question is not how many pigs are required to uproot the *rumbim* and stage a *kaiko;* it is, rather, how many pigs can be tolerated, and how long it takes to acquire them.

Tsembaga say that if a place is "good" it doesn't take very many years to accumulate sufficient pigs to uproot the *rumbim.* If a place is "bad," however, it takes much longer. A good place, they say, is a place where people remain well. It thus may be inferred that a good place is one in which the pig population expands because its natural increase exceeds the demands made upon it for ritual slaughter, most of which are associated with misfortune. A "bad" place, on the other hand, is one in which people often sicken or die. It is, thus, a place requiring frequent pig sacrifices. In a bad place the herd increases slowly, or not at all, or even may sometimes diminish over considerable periods of time.

While misfortune sometimes directly befalls pigs themselves, and while some pigs are killed during nonfestival periods for presentations to affines or in connection with cyclical rituals that have nothing to do with misfortune,[1] the dynamics of a Maring pig herd may be regarded as a rough index of the well-being of the human population with which it is associated.

It is difficult to translate statements concerning good and bad places into years. Informants who, it has already been pointed out, are not usually accurate in estimating lengths of time, indicate that sufficient pigs to uproot the *rumbim* may be accumulated in five or six years if a place is good.

Between two and three years is required for Tsembaga pigs to reach maximum size. Five or six years would allow both the juveniles surviving the slaughter that accompanied the planting of the *rumbim* and some of their offspring to reach maturity. A third generation might also be well grown. It may be remembered, however, that pregnancies among Tsembaga pigs are infrequent. Only fourteen litters were conceived out of approximately 100 possibilities in one year during the period of fieldwork. Infant mortality among pigs is also high. It may also be recalled that little more than 2 pigs per litter survived to the age of six months between October 1962 and December 1963. Thus, the indications are that the increase of the pig population is likely to be slow even if the ritual demands for slaughter are few. In short, a place would have to be very good indeed for a pig population of 60 juveniles, the number surviving the *kaiko* in November 1963, to expand in six years to a size approximating the 169 animals constituting the herd at the outset of the *kaiko* in June 1962.

The Tsembaga staged four previous *kaiko* during the fifty- to sixty-year period ending in 1963, which means that there were on the average approximately twelve to fifteen years between festivals. It is not clear in most cases, however, how much time elapsed between one *kaiko* and the next fight, although indications are that fighting usually did break out fairly quickly. An average of eight to

1. There are two rituals that regularly take place during the *rumbim* truce. The first of these, occurring a year or two after the planting of the *rumbim*, is concerned with transplanting· *konj kump amame* (pig belly *amame*), a ritual plant, from the men's houses to the women's houses. Each land-holding group kills one pig at this time. Some time later some young men are "struck" by the shamanistic spirit, the smoke woman, and several pigs are also killed. Neither of these events, however, constitutes an important demand upon the pig herd.

twelve years between the planting of *rumbim* and the accumulation of sufficient pigs to uproot it is, perhaps, not too inaccurate an estimate for the Tsembaga.

It must be emphasized that ritual cycles of durations well outside the mean of twelve to fifteen years suggested for the Tsembaga are known. In 1963 Vayda reported that some groups had not staged a *kaiko* in over twenty years. If the number of misfortunes during a given period is either abnormally high or abnormally low, or even if there are chance variations of a sufficient magnitude in pig natality or mortality from injury or illness, the length of the ritual cycle may depart considerably from those suggested here.

PIGS, LABOR, AND WOMEN

It may be recalled that the Tomegai clan, which numbered sixteen persons, had 36.1 percent more acreage in production when the herd was at its maximum than it did when the herd was at its minimum. The difference, in square feet, was approximately 75,000, and it was estimated that this acreage required for production, harvesting, and transport a labor input of about 495,000 calories. Since the reduction in the herd amounted to eleven adult or adolescent animals, it may be assumed that the energy expense for keeping each of these pigs was approximately 45,000 calories per year, or, on an average, approximately 125 calories per day.

Since sweet potato and manioc are fed to the pigs, the burden of the labor for supplying their food falls mainly upon the women. Aside from felling the trees, making the fences, helping in the clearing of underbrush, harvesting some of the surface crops and caring for the sugar cane, men do little in the sweet potato gardens, which constitute the additional acreage. It is the women who plant and harvest the root crops and do much the greater part of the weeding and almost all of the carrying. Exact computation is difficult, but it seems fair to assume that 100 of the 125 calories that are expended as a daily average for each pig are expended by women. The question becomes, "How many pigs can a woman care for?"

In our calculation of the amount of food Tsembaga consume, it was estimated that the daily ration of a woman provides her with about 2,150 calories. Since women of Tsembaga body size need about 950 calories for basal metabolism, approximately 1,200 calo-

ries is left for expenditure in all activities. Beside caring for the pigs
these include gardening for herself and her family, cooking, tending her children, and manufacturing such items as net bags, string
aprons, and loin cloths, to say nothing of socializing and procreating.
It is little wonder that the 66 Tsembaga females estimated to be
over ten years of age were, at the outset of the *kaiko* in 1962, caring
for only 169 pigs. That is, there were only 2.4 pigs of 120- to 150-
pound size to each female. The range in the number of animals
cared for by individual women was from 0 to 8. When the latter
figure is adjusted to an equivalent in 120- to 150-pound animals,
however, the range becomes 0 to 6. On the basis of the rough calculation of 100 calories per day per pig, the care of 6 pigs would
demand 50 percent of the energy a woman would have available
for all activity. It is not surprising that only one woman was keeping
such a number unassisted, and only four women were keeping five.
These numbers, it is not unreasonable to assume, approximate the
maximum number that a strong adult female can care for. Since
ten- to fifteen-year-old girls and old women are also included among
the pig-herding females, and since these categories are not capable
of as much exertion as females between fifteen and fifty, the maximum number of animals that can be cared for by the "average female" should be lowered to 4. Since there were 66 females over the
age of ten among the Tsembaga during the period of fieldwork, a
herd of 264 animals could have been supported. It has already been
pointed out, however, that the *kaiko* started with far fewer animals,
and it is probable that pig populations never approach the maximum number that can be supported by all the women in a local
population. Since pigs are individually owned, some women find
themselves burdened with several pigs before others have any at all.
It is with the husbands of women already burdened with pigs that
public agitation to uproot the *rumbim* and stage the *kaiko* apparently starts.

According to informants, as early as 1960 or 1961 certain men
were already urging that a *kaiko* be staged. These men included the
owners of the largest numbers of pigs. Among the reasons these men
gave me for wanting to have the *kaiko* was that they were tired of
planting sweet potato gardens. One, however, was frank enough to
state that it was his wife who was tired, and that she had been tell-

ing him so incessantly. Close observation of the domestic scene at the house of the wife of another of these men suggests that he too must have been subjected to complaints from his wife concerning the arduousness of maintaining five pigs as well as her family. Also prominent in the agitation was a widower who had been left with the equivalent of between five and six animals of 120- to 150-pound size and only a thirteen-year-old daughter to attend them. He had been forced into planting and harvesting sweet potatoes himself and on several occasions complained pathetically to me about this aspect of a widower's lot.

Men with few or no pigs responded to the talk of an approaching *kaiko* by attempting to acquire animals. Only shoats, usually under the age of three or four months, are traded, and they are always in short supply. Some were available from local litters, however, and some were obtained from other groups, particularly those residing in the Jimi Valley. As more people obtained more pigs, voices were added to those favoring the uprooting of the *rumbim*.

While it is not possible to specify a precise number of pigs that is sufficient to uproot the *rumbim*, a general statement in ecological terms can now be made. Agitation for a *kaiko* starts when the relationship of some pigs to their owners changes from one of support (emergency protein supply, conversion of substandard tubers, etc.) to one of parasitism (burdensome or even intolerable energy demands).[2] There are sufficient pigs to uproot the *rumbim* when this unfavorable change in relationship occurs in enough cases to produce a consensus within the local population.

The *kaiko* thus provides, among a group in which the slaughter of pigs is in large measure advantageously restricted by ritual to stress situations, a ritual means for disposing of a parasitic surplus of animals. In somewhat different terms it may also be said that the *kaiko* provides a means for limiting the amount of calories expended in acquiring animal protein. That the pig festivals of the Chimbu people of the New Guinea Highlands also serve to rid people of pig populations that have become parasitic has been implied by Brown and Brookfield (1959):

2. The term *parasitism* is used here, *senso latu*, to refer to a relationship between two or more individuals through which one or more are benefited or supported at the expense of others, to whom their return is significantly less than equivalent, or to whom injury is done in the process, or both.

its [the pig ceremony's] timing depends upon the rate of growth and increase of pigs, as the main feature is a massive pig killing and distribution of cooked pork. [p. 46]

The peak of the pig cycle . . . occurs immediately before a *bugla gende* [pig ceremony] when an adult pig population several times the size[3] of the human population makes heavy demands on land and labour, . . . much more and much stronger fencing is required to keep pigs out of cultivated land. . . . Large additional areas must be planted, not only for ceremonial foods demanded by the *bugla gende*, but also to provide more sweet potatoes for the pigs. [p. 22]

THE DESTRUCTIVENESS OF PIGS

In addition to preserving the people from further parasitism by the pigs, the *kaiko* in some instances may be a response to and a protective reaction against their destruction of gardens. This function of pig festivals has already been suggested by Vayda, Leeds, and Smith (1961):

the pig population may . . . increase to such an extent as to become more and more a menace to the people's gardens. Among New Guinea highlanders and some other Melanesians, the fact of having a large pig population on hand is the "trigger" for holding great festivals in which so many hundreds or sometimes even thousands of pigs are slaughtered . . . whether intended as such or not by the people themselves, these massive slaughters are a way of keeping the land from being overrun by pigs. [p. 71]

Brown and Brookfield (1959:22) have emphasized the social consequences of such depredations by pigs and have suggested that among the Chimbu the disputes they cause "must be innumerable."

Because the people and their pigs were kept on one side of a steeply banked stream while all of their gardens were on the other

---

3. In a later publication (Brookfield and Brown, 1963:59) the same authors revise downward their estimate of the pig population at the time of the pig ceremony to approximately one pig per person. This approximates the Tsembaga figure of .83 pigs per capita.

side, there were few cases of damage to Tsembaga gardens by domestic pigs during the period of fieldwork. This geographical segregation of pigs from gardens was, however, both unusual and transitory. Informants say that there had never before been such separation, and it is unlikely that it will occur again.

Events among the neighboring Tuguma during 1963 are doubtless more representative of the extent to which the herd menaces
the gardens just previous to *kaiko*. Tuguma human and pig populations were roughly comparable in size to those living on Tsembaga
territory. During the period of fieldwork at least six Tuguma pigs
were shot and killed after having damaged gardens. There may
have been other shootings that I did not hear about, and there must
have been other garden invasions in which the guilty animals were
not caught.

Some of these incidents formed the basis of serious disputes. In
one of these, further pig killing resulted when the owner of a slain
pig took revenge by shooting an animal of the man who had killed
his. One of the principals in this affair talked bitterly of moving
away from Tuguma to take up permanent residence with his wife's
brother, a Tsembaga. He didn't move his residence, but he did make
his most extensive taro-yam garden for the year 1963 on Tsembaga
land received by usufructory grant from his wife's brother, and he
very clearly stated that he had chosen to plant in this location to get
away from Tuguma pigs. Another man, a Tsembaga who had been
living uxorilocally with the Tuguma, moved back to Tsembaga territory during 1963 after one of his pigs had been killed in someone
else's taro-yam garden. It is likely that he would have eventually
returned to Tsembaga anyway, but he said that it was this incident
which was decisive.

Another Simbai Valley Maring group, the Kanump, were evidently
experiencing tribulations similar to those of the Tuguma during 1963
just before they too expected to stage a *kaiko*. Informants there told
Vayda that they wanted to have their *kaiko* soon because the pigs
were ruining the gardens.

While it is the damage to the gardens that the pigs are directly
guilty of, the effects of their depredations are frequently more serious than loss of foodstuffs. Garden damage sometimes leads to violence between the pig owner and the garden owner. More often it

results in interpersonal taboos between the principals: they refuse to eat food cooked over the same fire, and each refuses to eat anything grown by the other. Parties to such disputes sometimes threaten to leave the territory and no doubt occasionally do. The process of residential dispersal that accompanies the expansion of the herd from the time shortly after the planting of the *rumbim* threatens to reach its logical conclusion: people may move to residences out of the territory and perhaps be permanently lost to the local group. Pigs may, in short, become competitors (for the planted crops) as well as parasites of the human population, and their competition can drive people off the land. It may be suggested that the *kaiko*, in addition to being a regulatory response on the part of the people to the parasitism of their pigs, may also be a regulatory response to the growing competitive ability of the increased pig population.

Population Densities and the Triggering of the Kaiko

Data from the Tuguma and Kanump-Kaur local populations are insufficient, but it may be that the relative importance of the two aspects of large pig herds, their parasitic requirements and their competitive abilities, vary with population densities. In less densely populated areas, or in situations like that of the Tsembaga, in which the gardens were protected from pigs, their parasitism may trigger the *kaiko*. In more densely settled areas, and in areas such as those occupied by the Tuguma and Kanump-Kaur, in which the gardens are more easily accessible to pigs, it may be their competition that determines the consensus. In other words, where population density is high and the gardens are accessible to the pigs, the number of animals required to reach an intolerable level of destructiveness might be fewer than the number required to reach an intolerable level of energy expenditure on the part of the women.

In either case the *kaiko* is likely to be triggered by population levels of pigs and people below the carrying capacity of the territory. In the case of the Tsembaga *kaiko* of 1962-63, which was clearly triggered by the parasitism of the pigs, this is obvious. It was estimated in an earlier chapter that with a human population of the size and composition displayed by the Tsembaga in 1963, the pig population could reach cyclical maxima considerably in excess of the number present without exceeding the carrying capacity of the territory. While a precise estimate cannot be made, 250 to 300 animals at the cyclical maximum would perhaps not exceed the territorial limits. A pig population within such a range would require each woman and girl to care for 4 to 4.5 animals of 120- to 150-pound size. The estimates presented here indicate that such a number is not likely to be achieved; the physiological capacity of women to care for pigs is below the capacity of the territory to provide the animals with sustenance.

Unlike situations in which the *kaiko* is triggered by the excessive labor demands of pigs, the triggering of *kaiko* by the destructiveness of the animals may be regarded as a process directly related to the density of the human population. It seems clear that with any expansion in human population there will be an increase in the number of gardens if tools, techniques, crop inventories, and planting proportions are held constant. If the area is limited, as the territories of Maring local populations are, the greater will be the number of gardens and the shorter will be the distance between them and the domiciles of pigs. That the opportunities for pig damage increase geometrically while the populations of people and pigs increase only arithmetically has already been suggested. It may be suggested here that as the human population expands, its members, increasingly troubled by the destruction of gardens, will progressively define fewer pigs, in proportion to numbers of people, as sufficient for the *kaiko*. As the human population approaches carrying capacity the number will be small. Data from local Maring populations other than the Tsembaga are insufficient, and this construction must remain hypothetical at present. It may be recalled, however, that the Tsembaga say that when, in previous times, their numbers were greater they staged the *kaiko* with fewer pigs. It may be suggested cautiously that if the carrying capacity of a territory is to be exceeded it will be exceeded by people and not pigs. The mode of population limitation posited here may not be unusual. Density-dependent processes may, and probably often do, operate at levels below carrying capacity. This has been pointed out with respect to human populations by Birdsell (1957), and Wynne-Edwards (1962, 1965) has suggested that in populations of other animals it is rare for their numbers to be affected only after increase to the level of carrying capacity. Regulation is more commonly effected at much lower population levels through density-dependent processes, such as suppression of ovulation, dispersion, and inhibition of copulation.

Whether the *kaiko* is triggered by the parasitism of the pigs or by their competition, it does seem clear that the regulation of the relationship between the pig and human populations that is accomplished by the ritual cycle helps, by periodically reducing the pig population, to keep the combined demands of people and pigs below the carrying capacity of the territory. It helps, in other words, to maintain adequate fallow periods in the secondary forests and to preserve the virgin forest cover over areas, however marginal, that might otherwise be turned to cultivation.

A further regulatory aspect of the ritual cycle may be suggested here. While the *kaiko* cannot prevent an expanding human population from exceeding the carrying capacity of its territory, it may serve to relieve local population pressure by affording increased opportunities for expansive aggression. If it is the case that, as a population grows, fewer pigs are sufficient to uproot the *rumbim*, truces should be shorter for denser populations, for the fewer the required number of pigs the less time it should take to accumulate them. To put this in the converse, the occasions when it is permissible to attack one's neighbors become more frequent with increasing population density. Data collected by Vayda should throw considerable light on this question, although unequivocal answers may never be gained due to the difficulties inherent in estimating such things as population sizes prior to fights that took place long ago and the precise intervals between fights among a people unaccustomed to reckoning in years.

While some of the suggestions that have been made here must remain hypothetical, it may be said that the ritual cycle may be regarded as a mechanism that, by responding to changes in the relationships between variables in a system, returns these variables to former and more viable levels. These variables include the number and size of the pigs and the rate of their increase, and the size, composition, and caloric intake of the human population, as well as the amount of land available to them, the distances between gardens and the domiciles of pigs, and, perhaps, other items as well. Information from the Tsembaga and other Maring groups support the suggestion made by Vayda, Leeds, and Smith (1961:72) that pig festivals "help to maintain a long-term balance between Melanesian man and the crops and fauna from which he draws his sustenance."

The Ritual Cycle of the Enemy

While the size and rate of growth of the local pig population are clearly the most important determinants of the timing of a *kaiko*, the ritual cycle of the enemy may be a perturbing factor. Both the accounts of informants concerning the time prior to contact with Europeans and the observation of events in the Simbai and Jimi Valleys in 1962 and 1963 indicate that the *kaiko* of antagonists were held at the same, or close to the same time. Rarely, it seems, were the initiation of festivals by the two principal parties to the same fight separated by more than one or two years.

Informants deny that the imminence of the enemy's *kaiko* affects their own plans, and it is likely that the near coincidence of the *kaiko* of antagonists is sometimes the result of similar processes operating in similar populations. Nevertheless, the fact that a group that has completed its *kaiko* is free to initiate hostilities, while one that has not completed its *kaiko* is not, suggests that informants' denials are expressions of ideals, rather than reports of actual motivations.

Being one year behind the enemy in initiating the *kaiko* does not expose a group to danger. Since the *kaiko* usually lasts for a little more than a year, the tardy group begins its *kaiko* shortly before or after the enemy completes its festivals. Attacks may not be mounted by a group until its *kaiko* is completed, and attacks on groups engaged in the *kaiko* seem not to have occurred. Reasons for this are not clear, but it is perhaps because *kaiko* are a matter of supralocal interest. The services rendered by any and all *kaiko* to the entire Maring and adjacent populations in terms of the movement of goods and the exchange of personnel, as well as the pork distributions, will be discussed later. It is sufficient to say here that these services are considerable and that their disruption would be regarded even by members of neutral groups as inconvenient, if not intolerable. It is doubtful that a group could rally the support of allies for an attack upon another that is engaged in a *kaiko*.

An interval of two years between the *kaiko* of enemies places the tardy group in danger, however. Their *rumbim* remains in the ground during a protracted period in which their enemies are free to attack them. The renewal of old hostilities is thus at the sole discretion of an enemy who may choose the time, place, and manner of attack. In at least one instance in Maring history an old antagonism was renewed by a group that, having finished its *kaiko*, mounted a surprise raid upon their old adversaries, whose *rumbim* had not yet been uprooted.

The implications of tardiness are apparent to the Maring. There can be little doubt, furthermore, that all groups frequently receive through neutrals information concerning events occurring on enemy territory. It may thus have been the case that in some instances groups chose to stage the *kaiko* with somewhat fewer animals than they could have tolerated.

THE KAIKO

Under the pressure of the increasing pig herd, and, possibly, in consideration also of events occurring within the enemy group, a consensus to stage the *kaiko* is finally achieved. The various events that together comprise the *kaiko* affect population dispersion, the movement of food, goods, and personnel, and both intra- and interlocal social and political relations.

Planting the Stakes at the Boundary

Preparations for the *kaiko* are initiated by planting stakes at the boundary of the territory. This ritual is performed during the earlier part of the drier season, after the trees have been cut for the new taro-yam gardens, but before planting has begun. Among the Tsembaga in 1962 this ritual took place in June or July, some three or four months before fieldwork began. Performances that were reported to be, and doubtless were, similar were observed among the Tuguma, who planted stakes for their *kaiko* in June 1963.

As in the case of all important rituals, shamans first sought the ancestors' approval for the matter at hand and asked them to designate those pigs they wanted to receive, to specify the *raku*, or pig-killing places, at which they wanted to receive them, and to appoint the day on which the killing should take place. Allies of the previous fights, in both the Tuguma and Tsembaga cases, were informed of the appointed day so that they could prepare for their parts in the proceedings.

The number of animals killed for stake planting is small. Informants agree that the Tsembaga killed only seven in 1962 and say that in earlier times only three were killed, one by each land-holding group. That a larger number were killed in 1962 was due to taboos that had come into effect during the exile of 1953–56 making it impossible for all members of any single land-holding group to share either food or cooking fires.[4]

In the addresses accompanying the slaughter of the pigs the ancestors are thanked for caring for both the people and the pigs, and they are told that there are now sufficient animals for the *kaiko* and that the people wanted to plant stakes at the boundary.

The bodies of the slain animals are cooked in earth ovens at the *raku* and apportioned to all members of the local population, regardless of age or sex. The head, heart, and lungs, however, are brought back to the *riŋgi* houses, inside of which they are cooked in *konj bint*, above-ground ovens.[5]

While the head, hearts, and lungs are cooking, the stakes are planted. The preliminary portions of the procedure need not be described here, for they are similar to those employed after an enemy has been killed during active hostilities. Spells are made upon the *rumbim, močam, deraka,* and painted stakes, and the territory is rid of both the spirits of slain enemies, who may have returned to work evil, and the corruption that such spirits spread.

4. During their exile many Tsembaga fled to the Jimi Valley, where they took refuge with the Monambant and Kauwasi local populations. These groups were enemies of long standing, and while the Tsembaga were in residence fighting between them broke out. The Tsembaga not only fought in the ranks of their hosts but, as residents, fought as principal combatants and two were killed. At the time of the Tsembaga *kaiko* in 1962–63 those who had fled to Kauwasi and those who had taken refuge in Monambant were still prohibited from eating any food grown by each other. Those who had gone elsewhere were also affected by taboos growing out of the battle between the Monambant and Kauwasi. They could eat foodstuffs grown both by those who had refuged among the Monambant and the Kauwasi but could not share cooking fires with both. If, for instance, they shared cooking fires with those who had gone to the Kauwasi they could at no time eat food cooked over the same fire as food eaten by those who had stayed with the Monambant. These taboos split all three land-holding groups, three of the five clans, and even four subclans.

5. This procedure was modified in Tsembaga in 1962. When they were returned from their exile by the Australian government the Tsembaga built no *riŋgi* houses because, informants say, the government had imposed peace and *riŋgi* could no longer be worn. The fighting stones were hung in men's houses, and it was there that the heads, hearts, and lungs were cooked.

The processions that have started from the various *riŋgi* houses and separately rid their residential areas of supernatural danger meet in the newly cut but not yet planted taro-yam gardens, which are made in one or several large clusters. During the *kaiko* year among the Tsembaga this resulted in a continuous swidden covering an area of over twenty acres. Especially careful attention is given to these gardens since it is from them that visitors to the *kaiko* will be fed. Because illness suffered by visitors would be blamed upon the locals, these gardens are deemed to be likely targets for the mischief of antagonistic spirits who sometimes make crops poisonous, and it is not considered safe to plant them until they have been thus ritually cleansed.

After they have finished with the new garden, the assemblage, led by men waving *bamp yuk* (fight packages) before them, proceeds to the enemy border. They follow the path they took to the fight ground during the hostilities, and on the way they are joined by contingents from allied groups, who also bring stakes and who, if they killed any of the enemy, have gone through similar preliminary procedures at home. On the way to the boundary all sing *welowe*, the song that was sung during hostilities on the way home from the fight ground only on the days when an enemy was killed.

At the border the new stakes are planted. These, together with the old stakes and growing *rumbim* to which the cleansing objects are tied, form a gate to the territory. Spells are made to send both the enemy spirits and their corruption back to the enemy territory from which they came. Large trees are then designated for felling, one for each enemy killed. The groups responsible for the killings, both local patrilineal groups and allies, chop them so that they fall across, or at least in the direction of, the border. While they chop, the men sing *welowe*, and the fight magic men rub the trees with their fight packages.

Some informants say that the act of cutting down the trees is simply a celebration of the power of the fight packages, with the aid of which men "as big as trees" were killed. Others say that the trees are being offered to the spirits of the slain men to use as residences. Cutting them so that they fall across the border, moreover, sends the spirits (*rawa*) of the trees[6] across the border, where, it is

---

6. This is the only context, to my knowledge, in which *rawa* are attributed to trees.

hoped, their presence will induce the spirits of the slain men to remain. The procession then returns home, the allies dispersing to their various territories, the locals to their several *ringi* houses.

With the opening of the ovens at the local *ringi* houses the taboo against trapping marsupials is abrogated.[7] *Andik meng*, "turning word," spells are made on cuttings of the shrubs *gañingai* (*Elatostema* sp.). These are held in the steam of the newly opened oven by a fight magic man who, in a conversational tone, addresses both the living and the deceased and recounts the story of the fight, the subsequent planting of the *rumbim*, and enumerates the taboos that have remained in effect ever since. He says that now that the stakes have been planted the men would like to trap marsupials so that drum heads can be made, but when they fought, he continues, they said, in obedience to tradition (*nomane*), that they could not trap marsupials and these words remain inside of them. Before they set their traps, therefore, they must rid themselves of these words. The *gañingai* is then passed among the men and boys, each throwing back his head and brushing himself upward from the navel to the mouth. While brushing, each announces that he is ridding himself of the words of the taboo and he makes a spitting sound. The pig is then eaten and the ritual concluded, therby terminating the "closed season" on marsupials.

There are two other aspects of stake planting that should be commented upon. First, the assemblage that joins to plant stakes is supralocal. The territory being redefined by the planting of the stakes belongs to only one of the assembled groups, but the participation of several of them seems to signify joint defense of the territory. Stake-planting rituals may perhaps be regarded as cyclic ratifications of mutual assistance agreements between members of several local populations.

They also may be regarded as display behavior. Every participant in the stake-planting procession has an opportunity to gauge the size or strength of the entire assemblage and of its constituent units, and the enemy is also exposed to this display. Enemies are said to be afraid to come to the border, or anywhere near it, to witness the spectacle. They therefore view the procession only from a distance at best, and if the terrain is very broken, as at the Tsembaga-Kun-

7. I did not witness this part of the ritual in Tuguma in 1963. I have, however, seen similar performances in other contexts on several occasions.

dagai border, or thickly wooded, as is the border between the Kanump-Kaur and the Tuguma, the enemy does not see the procession at all. He hears it, however. Some enemy men, while remaining out of eyeshot, come close to the border to make counter-magic against the evil that is being sent to them by the stake planters. Even those who remain at a greater distance hear the procession, for the sound of two hundred men or more singing and shouting battle cries carries far in the quiet valley.

The enemy also hears about the procession either from eye witnesses or, more likely, from those to whom eye witnesses have spoken. These reports are inevitably impressive simply because the Maring have no terms for quantities larger than twenty. Most second- or third-hand accounts of events among the Maring are exaggerated, and it is likely, despite the lack of numerical terminology, that these are too. At the least, the enemy gets the impression that a very large number of men participated in the ritual, and this might serve to temper any bellicose plans he might entertain for the future.

The most important aspect of the ritual is not that of agonistic display, however; it concerns where the stakes are planted. If the enemy was not driven off its territory in the last fight, but remained to plant *rumbim*, or if, having been driven out, the enemy has returned and planted *rumbim*, the stakes are planted at the boundary that existed before the fight.

If, however, the enemy was driven out of its territory and never returned to plant *rumbim*, the procession does not stop at the old border. It proceeds into the territory of the former enemies and the stakes are planted at a new location. A new boundary is thus established, incorporating into the territory land previously held by the enemy.

The Tsembaga and most other Marings say that fights do not take place over land and that land occupied by other groups cannot be annexed. To signify its occupation, however, a group must plant *rumbim* upon its land. Areas annexed in stake-planting rituals are areas upon which no *rumbim* is planted; they are, therefore, not lands belonging to the enemy, but lands the enemy has presumably abandoned—they are vacant.

A simple rule may be presented here: *if one of a pair of antagonistic groups can plant its stakes before its opponent can plant its* rumbim, *it may annex land previously held by its opponent.*

It is not only the vanquished who have abandoned their territory; it is assumed that it has now been abandoned by the ancestors of the vanquished as well. The surviving members of the erstwhile enemy group have by this time resided with other groups for a number of years, and all or most of them will already have had occasion to sacrifice pigs to their ancestors at their new residences. When they do so they invite these spirits to come to the new place of the living, where they will continue to receive sacrifices in the future. Ancestors of vanquished groups thus relinquish their guardianship over the territory, making it available to the victorious groups. Meanwhile, the de facto membership in the groups with which they have taken refuge is converted to de jure membership. Sooner or later the host groups will have occasion to plant *yu miñ rumbim,* and the refugee men as coresidents will participate, thus ritually validating their connection to the new territory and the new group. A second rule of population redistribution may thus be stated: *a man becomes a member of a territorial group by participating with it in the planting of* rumbim.

There are two processes that modify or complicate the lasting effects of these rules. The first is the partial reoccupation of its territory by a routed group before the victorious group plants its stakes. It is often the case that some members of a routed group will take refuge with an adjacent group, under whose cover they will reoccupy some of their lost territory. This has happened at least twice in Tuguma-Tsembaga history. When the Dimbagai-Yimyagai, many years ago, were first driven from their land by the Tsembaga on their west, some took refuge with the Dinagai, then a local population immediately to their east. As members of the Dinagai they reoccupied the eastern portion of their territory. The Merkai clan of the Tsembaga recognized this as an annexation of part of the territory by the Dinagai, with whom they were friendly, rather than as reoccupation by their former foes. They therefore planted their stakes to incorporate only part of the territory from which they had driven their enemies. Similar processes took place following the rout of the Tsevent by the Tuguma.

Second, while the planting of stakes to annex abandoned territory provides what might be characterized as de jure rights to that territory, anxieties seem to remain with the conquerors concerning the use of this land for gardens and residences. These anxieties apparently become explicit during times of misfortune. During 1962–63 almost all of the Tsembaga residences were on land that had, at one time, belonged to the Dimbagai-Yimyagai. In 1962 five Tsembaga men and one Tsembaga woman of middle age or younger died of illness, and in early 1963 two more young men, a young woman and a child, became sick and quickly died. After each death there was much talk of giving the land back to the Dimbagai-Yimyagai. Some people said that the Dimbagai-Yimyagai ancestors, wanting to return to their own land, were sending illness. Others blamed the deaths on living Dimbagai-Yimyagai who, they said, were sending the illness magically. Consensus in favor of abandonment seemed to form rapidly, but it could not be acted upon immediately because the *kaiko* dance ground, in addition to the residences, happened to be on the old Dimbagai-Yimyagai territory. Their departure, therefore, had to be delayed until after the *kaiko*.

This delay permitted the consensus to dissolve. After most of the deaths, talk in favor of removal seemed to remain firm for one or two weeks. After a month or a little longer, however, those who had advocated removal were frequently surprised when they were reminded of their position. They would point out that the Dimbagai-Yimyagai had all planted *rumbim* elsewhere, that the Dimbagai-Yimyagai ancestors had long ago vacated the territory, and that the matter was ancient history. Statements to the effect of, "It was our fathers who drove them out, and now we ourselves have children," were common.

If they hadn't been detained by the presence of the dance ground, however, the Tsembaga may well have given the territory back to the Dimbagai-Yimyagai. Because of Australian pacification they no longer needed to fear the presence on their border of a reconstituted Dimbagai-Yimyagai, who at any rate would not be numerically strong. Furthermore, all indications are that the Tsembaga had experienced considerable depopulation since they annexed Dimbagai-Yimyagai land. They now had, or at least said they had, sufficient land without the old Dimbagai-Yimyagai territory, and estimations of carrying capacity support their view.

History thus indicates that annexation of land through conquest and the subsequent stake planting is reversible through peaceful processes. It further suggests that the mechanism through which the annexation is reversed, involving both native theories of disease etiology and native behavior when suffering an especially high incidence of death, depends on the population density. Groups which, because of depopulation, no longer need land they have conquered may abandon it under the impact of further depopulation.

Preparing the Dance Ground

In the weeks before and just after the planting of stakes, the settlement pattern changes from one of scattered homesteads and subclan and clan hamlets to one of relative nucleation around a traditional dance ground. This, of course, results in the concentration of a large number of pigs in a relatively small area. This concentration is temporary, usually lasting little more than a year, and its ill effects upon second growth are therefore limited. It may also be that the threat of pigs to the gardens during this period is offset by the practice, during *kaiko* years, of planting the taro-yam gardens in large clusters. Clustered gardens require fewer linear feet of fence per unit of cultivated area because of a reduction in total periphery. Fencing around the taro-yam gardens in *kaiko* years seems to be exceptionally stout, and it may be that the reduction in linear requirements for fencing permits this sturdier construction.

It may also be usual for gardens during festival years to be planted at a greater distance from the residences than in other years, thus placing them beyond the usual daily range of pigs. Almost all of the gardens planted by the Tsembaga in 1962 were at least a thirty minutes' walk away from the residences. It is not possible, however, to generalize from Tsembaga procedures in 1962, because, as has already been mentioned, their settlement had been, contrary to usual arrangements, nucleated for some years before the *kaiko*, and most of the arable land close to the settlement was under secondary forest too young to cut. The Tuguma gardens planted in 1963, the year of the Tuguma *kaiko*, were generally not as far from the settlement as those of the Tsembaga.

While the Tsembaga settlement was nucleated long before the *kaiko*, it was far from any of the old dance grounds. Instead of moving their residences to the proximity of one of the traditional dance grounds they prepared a new one within the area encompassed by their settlement. The work was considerable, for the site sloped at an angle of more than twenty degrees. Instead of the easy task of removing weeds and saplings from a place previously used for dancing, they were faced with the necessity of leveling a considerable area. Since no one could do more than exhort others to work, and since enthusiasm for the task waxed and waned, it took months to level (roughly) an area of about 150′x200′. Improvements were being made and additional areas were being cleared on the slope deep into the *kaiko*.

The work was not confined to preparing the ground. Two large houses, each about 25′x35′, and 8′ or 9′ high at the center, also had to be built at the edge of the dance ground to accommodate visitors if it rained. Two houses, rather than one, are necessary at almost all *kaiko* because a man may never enter a house into which an enemy has ever set foot, and some of the groups to be entertained are almost always enemies of others.

Immediately after the stake planting and before leveling had actually begun, a fence was built around those portions of the area where the ground did not fall off so steeply as to make approach difficult. At the gate, the root of a variety of *rumbim* called *dawa*, the leaves of which are used to cover the buttocks when dancing, was buried after a spell was said over it. This ritual, which included an address to the ancestors, had two purposes, according to informants: to induce the ancestors to look kindly upon the dance ground, that both local and visitors alike might dance strongly and that their drums might sound rich; and to keep within the fence the *miñ*, the life stuff, of the local girls while the *kaiko* continued. The men often express the fear that some of their unmarried girls might elope with visitors whose strong dancing and finery had captured their fancies.

Uprooting the Rumbim

With the ripening of the first *marita pandanus*, a yellow-fruited variety called *yambai*, preparations for uprooting the *rumbim* begin. In Tsembaga territory this fruit is ready to eat in late August or early September, by which time two months or a little more has elapsed since the stake planting, and the bulk of men's work in the new gardens should be finished or close to finished.

When the *yambai*, which is a scarce variety, becomes ripe it is eaten once, after which a taboo on further consumption of it is assumed by everyone. Even the word for *marita*, *komba*, must be avoided, and a circumlocution is used until the taboo is renounced during the rituals immediately preceding the uprooting of the *rumbim*. *Marita*, informants say, is associated with the spirits of the low ground, and it is now time to trap *ma* (most marsupials and perhaps some giant rats are included in this category), which, it may be remembered, are said to be the "pigs of the red spirits." Undivided attention must now be turned to these spirits, and the ingestion of *marita*, or even the enunciation of its name, would make this difficult or impossible, either because the act would annoy the red spirits or because it would have some direct effect upon the body or mind. This temporary renunciation of *marita*, it must be said, costs the people little, for after the few *komba yambai* fruits are consumed virtually no *marita* becomes ripe until middle or late October.

Ma trapping is carried on separately by the least inclusive agnatic units, clans in some cases, subclans in others, in their own *komoŋ*, tracts in the high-altitude virgin forest which are said to be the homes of their red spirits. While at ordinary times a man may set his traps anywhere on Tsembaga territory, he may now set them only in the *komoŋ* of his own minimal agnatic unit because it is only with one's own ancestors that "pigs" may be exchanged.

Before the traps are placed, shamans contact the red spirits, saying to them that the pigs of the living are now sufficient in number to be exchanged for the red spirits' pigs. They ask the smoke woman to designate those trees in which the red spirits will place the marsupials they wish to give to the living, and it is in these trees that the traps are placed. During the course of the period the smoke woman is asked from time to time to designate further trees.

Adolescent boys and men through middle age participate in the trapping. Because this is an activity associated with the red spirits, the trappers are subject to many of the same taboos as they are during warfare. They may not have sexual intercourse, or even touch women, nor may they eat food prepared by women. They should not set foot in the *wora*, the lower portion of the territory, and food grown in the *wora* should be avoided. They may not leave the territory, and they may not share food cooked over the fires of other local populations.

The trapped *ma* are skinned, and then smoked by the old men and the boys too young to join in the trapping. Some of the animals taken early are preserved for two months or more. Informants say that it is only in the context of this ritual trapping period that meat is thus preserved; smoking was never observed during the fieldwork period.

Special smokehouses are built for this purpose. While the actual trapping is conducted independently by minimal agnatic units, smokehouses are usually built, informants say, by sub-territorial groups. There was some modification of this among the Tsembaga in 1962, however, because of the food and fire taboos, mentioned earlier, which split these groups.

When the variety of *marita* called "*peŋgup*" ripens in mid-October the men stop their trapping and prepare to uproot the *rumbim*. The preparations are elaborate, for pigs must be slaughtered at the *raku*, which means that shelters and above-ground ovens must be built, and vegetables and firewood must be obtained. Allies also must be informed so that they may attend.

The rituals performed at the *raku* on the day before the *rumbim* is uprooted are both elaborate and exotic. Pigs are sacrified for both the spirits of the high ground—the red spirits and the smoke woman —and the spirits of the low ground. In the address preceding the sacrifice for the spirits of the high ground, in addition to being thanked for their help in warfare, the spirits are thanked for the *ma* they have provided and are told that they will now be given pigs in exchange for them. Among some Maring local populations cassowaries are also commonly sacrificed to the red spirits, but the Tsembaga keep very few of these birds.

After the pigs are killed, oven stones are laid on a large fire to heat while the butchering of the pigs and the preparation of the smoked *ma* for cooking proceeds. When these preparations have been completed two large red *pandanus* fruits, harvested with great care on the previous day from groves in the low ground, are brought forth. The groves from which the fruits are obtained may either be those planted by persons now deceased, or those in which the remains of dead are buried. A procession forms, composed of all those present.

Led by two men who continually raise and lower the *pandanus* fruits they are carrying, the group circles the fire chanting:

komba ku komba   *yaŋga yaŋga muŋga muŋga*
kam ku komba   *yaŋga yaŋga muŋga muŋga*
bri komba   *yaŋga yaŋga muŋga muŋga* . . .

(*Marita*, ascend to and come down from *komba ku*
Marita, ascend to and come down from *kam ku*
Marita, ascend to and come down from *bri* . . .)

Komba ku and *kam ku* are high places on Tsembaga territory where the smoke woman is said to dwell. *Bri*, another of her dwelling places, is a mountain in the Jimi Valley. The chant continues, naming many other high places in the Jimi Valley that are said to be homes of the smoke woman, and becomes more frenzied as it proceeds. The voices of some of the men break into sobs. When the catalog of the homes of the smoke woman is almost completed the procession halts. All males take hold of one of the *marita* fruits, while the females grasp the other. When the chant is completed, one of the adult men seizes the *marita* of the males and with it leaps onto the oven stones that have now been heating for well over one hour. Bounding up and down on the hot stones, he stabs the fruit with a cassowary bone, then leaps off. He repeats the performance with the *marita* of the females.

The various foods are now put into the ovens. The pig dedicated to the red spirits and the smoke woman is cooked in an oven constructed above ground, while that for the spirits of the low ground is placed in an earth oven. Marita and marsupials are cooked together, but two special ovens are made for this mixture because fight magic men suffer an enduring taboo on consuming some marsupials with women.

When the ovens are opened, the men who have participated in warfare gather around the above-ground oven. The head of pig cooked in it is raised high while one of the men recounts the story of the last fight, thanks the spirits of the high ground for their assistance, tells them they are being given this pig and that more will be given to them at the end of the *kaiko*. The address concludes with the request to the spirits to take this pig, which is now being offered them, and return to their high places. The oven of the spirits of the low ground, that made in the earth, is opened without ritual.

All of the greens and some of the flesh from both ovens is consumed at the *raku,* but most of the flesh is brought to the residences for later consumption or, in the case of the pig cooked in the earth ovens, for distribution to members of other groups.

Several taboos must be abrogated before the *marita* and *ma* may be eaten. One of these applies to novice shamans, who have been prohibited from eating any *marita* since being "struck" by the smoke woman, in some cases years before. The others apply to all persons. These are, first, the prohibition, in effect for several months, against the consumption of *marita* during the trapping period. The other, in effect since the last fight, has forbidden the cooking and consumption of *marita* and *ma* together. All three of these taboos are ended by spitting out a mouthful of *pandanus* seeds and throwing away the tails of the *ma* in the nearby forest. This latter act is also said to ensure the future proliferation of the *ma.*

After the taboos have been nullified some *pandanus* oil is rubbed on the legs and buttocks of all persons so that their legs will be strong, and on the bellies of the females so that they may be fertile. The cassowary bone previously used to pierce the fruit is used as a spoon to feed each person his first mouthful of the *marita.* The consumption of the *marita* and *ma* is the last ritual act of the day.

The day-long proceedings at the *raku* have two stated purposes. On the one hand they enhance fertility, and on the other hand they nullify a number of taboos. In addition to those restricting the consumption of *marita* and *ma* by all or some categories of persons, the taboos renounced include those, in effect since the last fight, that have prohibited all men who have worn *riŋgi* from sharing with women certain foods including certain species of *ma* and certain varieties of *marita* as well as sugar cane, bananas, and *pitpit* having red skins. The men who wore *riŋgi* also renounce their taboos against the consumption of certain other foods, notably soft varieties of *Dioscorea* grown in the *wora,* the lower part of the territory. The taboos on beating drums and eating pigs slaughtered in connection with the *kaiko* of other local populations are also terminated.

It should be mentioned that these taboos (except that against drum beating) are not renounced by all men. Fight magic men are burdened with them for life. Furthermore, the taboos against the consumption of snakes, lizards, frogs, and other "cold" animals also remain in effect for all men for life.

It was suggested earlier, in reference to their assumption, that some of these taboos serve to segregate ideologically those components, both living and dead, of the total community that are associated with warfare from those associated with peaceful activities. This segregation, it was suggested, is an aspect of the local population's debtor relationship with both the ancestors and allies from whom they received assistance in warfare. The termination of these taboos and, thus, the partial reintegration of the previously segregated elements is concomitant with the partial repayment of the outstanding debts.

Explanations of the significance of much of the ritual could not be elicited from the Tsembaga, but the forms of some of the procedures, particularly those concerned with *marita,* support the notion of reintegration. *Marita* is clearly associated with the spirits of the low ground. Indeed, the fruits used in the ritual must be taken either from trees planted by the deceased on low ground or from groves where the remains of the deceased lie. But before it is placed in the ovens the *marita* is offered to the smoke woman, a spirit of the high ground in whose name novice shamans had suffered an absolute prohibition against its consumption. The fruit, moreover, is pierced with a cassowary bone before cooking. Cassowaries are associated with the red spirits, for whom *norum-kombri* (orchid sp.—cassowary), is often used as a term of address. *Ma,* now cooked with *marita* for the first time since the last fight, are also associated with the spirits of the high ground, being regarded as their pigs.

The relationship of the living to the two categories of spirits seems to undergo transformation in the new reintegration. This is signaled by the ritual consumption of the *marita,* an act, the Tsembaga say, which is like taking the spirits of the low ground inside of one. This is not said of the consumption of the *ma.* These animals are regarded to be the receipts of an exchange with the red spirits, and this is made explicit in the address preceding the slaughter of the pig dedicated to them. What may be regarded as an analogous communion with the red spirits took place when, before the ax fight, the fighting men put on *riŋgi* and took these spirits into their heads. Performances undertaken now, renouncing taboos that were assumed with the *riŋgi*, may be regarded as expunging some of the vestiges of that communion. This interpretation is supported by the address to these spirits when the head of the cooked pig is offered to them: they are asked to take the pig being offered them and to leave. This behavior in reference to the spirits of the high places, in short, seems to suggest not a communion, but its opposite: the expulsion of spirits with whom a burdensome communion was previously effected. It further supports the interpretation that the abrogation of the taboos associated with the wearing of the *riŋgi* requires the transformation of the simple debtor-creditor relationship that has prevailed since the last fight into a relationship that, although obligations remain, is becoming more equal. That the ability to transform the relationship from one of debt to one of equivalence depends upon the demographic and ecological success of the local population is apparent in light of earlier discussion.

The number of pigs killed at this time was substantial—the Tsembaga killed thirty on November 1, 1962. Those killed for the spirits of the high ground, in most cases smaller animals, were consumed by the local population. With the exception of the heads and entrails, pork derived from those killed for the spirits of the low ground was carried back to the residences, where it was presented to the waiting allies. For the most part this flesh was given unceremoniously by each man to those men among the allies, usually his own affines or non-agnatic cognates, who assisted in the fight because of their ties to him. The belly fat was first removed, however, to be salted for formal presentation.

On the following day, after the salted belly fat was presented to the allies, the *rumbim* was uprooted.[8] Both allies and local men were in attendance. *Andik meŋ* spells were first made upon the stacked drums, so that they might be beaten and so that they might sound well, after which they were returned to their owners. Painted stakes, about six inches long, upon which spells had also been made, were then buried near the gate of the enclosure. Now that the *rumbim* was to be uprooted these would protect the *miñ*, the life stuff of the

8.   This ritual was performed only seven days after our arrival among the Tsembaga and I was permitted to watch only from a distance. It was also not possible for me to attend its performance at Tuguma; therefore this account depends in part upon informants' statements.

men, preventing both the spirits of enemies and the corruption that flows from them from entering the house enclosure.

After the stakes were buried, the *amame* was unceremoniously pulled out. The *rumbim* was then uprooted by the man who planted it. This task always, it is said, falls to the man who planted it if he is alive, and to his son if he is not. A digging stick upon which *andik men* spells had been made was used. The address, broken by sobs, recounted the history of the planting and the fight preceding it. Both categories of ancestors were told that they had been given some pigs, but only a few; later, at the end of the *kaiko,* they would be given more. In previous times, informants say, the red spirits were also told that after the *kaiko* their deaths would be avenged. Since pacification, apologies are made to the red spirits because revenge is no longer possible.

While the *rumbim* was being uprooted, bamboo was heated over a fire. When it exploded the *rumbim* was torn from the ground and all the men pounded their drums, yelled, and stamped their feet. Led by men carrying the *rumbim,* they all charged over the stile and headed for the territorial boundary. On the way they were joined by groups who had uprooted *rumbim* at other *riŋgi* houses, as well as by a contingent from Tuguma bringing bespelled stakes.

While most of the array proceeded to the boundary where the stakes were planted, some fight magic men dropped out to dispose of the *rumbim* and *amame* elsewhere. These are traditionally taken to shallow places in certain streams where they are placed on flat rocks with their roots covered by water but with their foliage on dry land. They are oriented so that the foliage points in the direction of the enemy, while the roots point in the direction of the local settlement. Spells are made upon them so that the desiccation which, it is said, will overtake the foliage, will go to the enemy, bringing him illness and death. The roots, on the other hand, rot, and from rot comes new life. Since the roots are pointed in their direction it is the local population that benefits in fertility and growth from their decay.

After the stakes had been planted at the boundary and the *rumbim* and *amame* disposed of in streams, the procession returned to the dance ground. Dancing, accompanied by drumming and singing, continued throughout the night. The *kaiko* had begun.

Kaiko wobar and kaiko de

The year-long *kaiko* is divided into two periods, the first called *wobar*, the second *de*. It may be recalled that these are the names of the songs that were sung on the way to the fight ground, *wobar* during the earlier "nothing fight" and *de* for the ax fight. During the *wobar* period of the *kaiko* only *wobar* may be sung; during the *de* period both *de* and *wobar* may be sung.[9] The two stages of the *kaiko*, informants say, recapitulate the two stages of warfare. The earlier, less important, *wobar* phase continues while work remains to be done on the dance ground, and, more importantly, until there are enough large taros and yams in the new gardens to entertain visitors properly. When there are enough tubers fit for presentation, the rituals inaugurating *kaiko de* may be performed. The first taro and yams may be harvested about six months after planting, but at least another month is required for them to become sufficient in size and number. The Tsembaga had enough of these tubers in late March or early April 1963 to perform the *de* rituals, but were delayed by a number of extraneous events until early May.

As the two stages of the *kaiko* recapitulate the two stages of warfare, so do the rituals preceding the two stages of the *kaiko* reverse the effects of the rituals undertaken in connection with the two stages of fighting. In the case of the bow and arrow fight the prelimimary rituals, which are minimal, are reversed, according to most informants, as one of the effects of the uprooting of the *rumbim*. Two informants also stated that as part of the reversal procedure the arrows and spears used in the small fight are brought to the *raku* on the day before the *rumbim* is uprooted, where they are treated with the ritual *marita*. I did not witness such a performance, however, among either the Tsembaga or the Tuguma.

The details of the rituals inaugurating *kaiko de* need be sketched in only briefly. As always, the shamans contact the smoke woman to ask the spirits' approval and to ask her to designate the *raku* at which the pigs should be killed.

9. *De* and *wobar* refer to melodies, for each of which there are standard refrains but innumerable verses, with new ones constantly being composed or imported. Not all of these are in the Maring language; many of those sung to the *wobar* melody are in Karam, while some of the *de* verses are in Narak. The *de* refrain, moreover, is reported word for word by Luzbetak (1954) in his description of a pig festival among the Nondugl people of the Eastern New Guinea Highlands.

Five animals were slaughtered by the Tsembaga, all of which were consumed by themselves. During the night the *rumbim* that was planted outside the men's house on the night before the ax fight is uprooted. Extraction and disposal spells are then made not only on the usual stakes, *rumbim* brooms, wild taro leaves, and vine whips, but also on bamboo torches, which are then lit on fires made inside the *riŋgi* houses. The dance ground and the entire residential area are then rid of the spirits of slain enemies and the corruption emanating from them as well. When the men return from depositing the uprooted *rumbim* and other objects at the border, the fighting stones are removed from the center post of the *riŋgi* house or, in the case of the Tsembaga, from the rafters of men's houses, and placed on the low tables from which they were taken years before during the night before the ax fight.[10]

The lowering of the fighting stones is not accompanied by the immediate termination of remaining taboos. It does not now become possible, for instance, to enter the territory of the enemy or to speak to the enemy, much less make a permanent peace. However, lowering of the stones is a prerequisite to making peace at a future time and also to the more immediate trapping of eels, which precedes the final pig slaughter. Eels are said to be the pigs of the spirits of the low ground, for which pigs of the living will be exchanged. As it was necessary when *ma* were being trapped to avoid contact with the spirits of the *rawa mai*, so is it necessary before taking eels to continue the process of turning away from the red spirits by lowering the stones. It was mentioned previously that hanging the stones signified the assumption of a debt to both allies and ancestors. Their lowering, conversely, signifies that the debt is soon to be paid.

On the following day another ritual is usually performed. The allies assemble on the dance ground, and small trees that were, when the area was cleared, allowed to remain growing for his purpose are assigned to each group responsible for slaying an enemy in the last fight. After these trees are rubbed with the fight packages they are uprooted while the men sing *welowe*, the killing song.

The killers, or, if they are no longer alive, their sons, are then carried around the dance ground on the uprooted trees, and *de* is

10. I was at the Simbai patrol post recuperating from illness when *kaiko de* was inaugurated by the Tsembaga. This brief sketch is based upon informants' accounts and the account of my wife.

sung. All informants agree that this is a celebration of the power of the fight package, and some say that the spirits of the enemy slain actually inhabit the trees, which apparently symbolize them. The rite also, of course, honors those men who have killed enemies in the service of the local population.

The Tsembaga chose in 1963 to forego this ritual. Men said that they would be ashamed to uproot trees after a fight in which they had killed only two of the enemy while losing twenty themselves.

Differences between the style of entertainment of visitors during the *wobar* and *de* periods are actually minor. During the latter period there is a second melody at the disposal of the dancers and the food presentations become more elaborate as taro and yams become increasingly available. This distinction becomes blurred, however, if the inauguration of *de* is delayed. The Tsembaga were including taro and yams in their presentations for more than two months before they undertook the *de* rituals.

A Kaiko Entertainment

The occasions on which friendly groups are entertained, in addition to the year-long festival, are called "*kaiko*," a term also used to refer to the dancing, which is one of the features of these events. During the course of the year the Tsembaga entertained thirteen other local groups on fifteen separate occasions, exclusive of the final *konj kaiko*, "pig *kaiko*," which terminated the entire festival. On several of these occasions two or more local groups were entertained at the same time, and three local groups attended more than once.

INVITATIONS AND PREPARATIONS

The atomistic nature of the organization of local populations is clearly expressed in the extension of invitations to a *kaiko*. Invitations are not extended by a local population as a whole to another local population as a whole, but rather by one or several individuals in one local population to one or several individuals, either kinsmen or trading partners, in another. Usually the men who have such connections in a particular group will together decide when to issue invitations to these kinsmen or trading partners. They may, in their planning, take into consideration commitments made previously by other members of their local population, but decisions are likely to be made without the counsel of others. Indeed, in instances in which kin or other ties with another group are few, the issue of an invitation may be the decision of a single man who has taken no counsel but his own.

Although invitations are formally extended by individuals to individuals, they are in fact invitations to entire local populations, for the invited are expected to bring at least some of their coresidents. Indeed, the formally invited men would be ashamed to attend if they could not bring with them dancers in a number commensurate with the size of their local population and with the strength of the relations between their local population and that of their hosts. The invited men gain prestige by making a strong showing, and it is to this end that they themselves often extend invitations to members of yet other local populations, to "help them dance" at the *kaiko* to which they have been invited.

As the extension of invitations to a *kaiko* reflects the atomistic character of local organization, so do preparations for these events. It is the responsibility of those men who have kinsmen and trading partners among the visitors to accumulate the firewood and sugar cane required for their entertainment, and of their wives to harvest and prepare the tubers and green vegetables with which the visitors will be fed. Others may contribute effort or garden produce to the preparations, but such contributions are phrased as assistance to those upon whom the responsibility for entertainment falls and through whom the food presentations are made. While some of those who have no direct ties to the visiting group may assist those who do, it is usually the case that some people take no part whatever in the preparations.

THE ENTERTAINMENT

Although days are appointed, temporal arrangements remain vague. Young men are sent in advance to keep the hosts informed of delays and revised times of arrival of the rest of the group. On the day on which the hosts are reasonably certain that the visitors will arrive, extraction and disposal magic is performed on the dance ground. This is usually a perfunctory proceeding, and after the spells are made upon the usual objects the task is turned over to whatever young men happen to be in the vicinity. The object of the extraction and disposal magic is to rid the dance ground of both *tukump*, the corruption that flows from spirits, and *kum,* which is similar but is introduced into the ground by living sorcerers.

After the dance ground has been treated, those men who wish to participate in the dance bathe in streams and then return to the men's houses to adorn themselves. Those who ready themselves for the dance include all or most of the young men and adolescents, and at least those older men who have direct kinship or trading connections with the visiting group. Other older men without direct connections to the visitors may also participate, either to assist those who do have direct connections or simply because they wish to dance.

As invited groups receive support or assistance from other groups when they go to a *kaiko,* so does the host group. On most occasions at Tsembaga young men of Tuguma would swell the ranks of the Tsembaga dancing contingent.

Adornment is painstaking, and men often take hours to complete their dressing. Pigments, formerly earth colors of native manufacture, more recently powders of European origin, are applied to the face in designs that are subject to frequent changes in fashion. Beads and shells are worn as necklaces, and garters of small cowries encircle the calves. The best orchid fiber waistbands and dress loin cloths enriched with marsupial fur and embellished with dyed purple stripes are put on. The buttocks are covered with masses of accordion-folded leaves of a *rumbim* called "*kamp*" and other ornamentals. A bustle, made of dried leaves obtained in trade, which rustles during dancing, is attached on top of the mass of *kamp* leaves.

Most attention is given to the headdress. A crown of feathers, eagle and parrot being most common, encircles the head. The feathers are attached to a basketry base, which is often hidden by marsupial fur bands, bands made of yellow orchid stems and green beetles, or festoons of small cowrie shells. From the center of the head rises a flexible reed, two or even three feet long, to which is attached a plume made either from feathers or an entire stuffed bird. The lesser bird of paradise, the Princess Stephanie bird of paradise, the greater sickle bill, and (?) Pescot's parrot are most common. Plumes, particularly those of the King of Saxony bird of paradise and the racket-tailed kingfisher, are worn through the pierced septum from which also may be suspended a shell disk and gold-lip crescent. Unmarried girls, some as young as nine or ten years of age, also may be adorned.

When their preparations are completed the dancers, both men and girls, congregate at the dance ground, where they dance for practice or pleasure before the visitors arrive and where they may be admired by spectators who are already assembling. These include the local married women and men from many other places who, having heard of the *kaiko*, have come to watch and to trade.

The visiting dancers signal their approach by beginning to sing. When they reach a point about one hundred yards from the gate, the local dancers retire to a vantage point just above the dance ground, where their view of the visitors is unimpeded and where they continue singing. The visitors approach the gate silently, led by men carrying fight packages, swinging their axes as they run back and forth in front of their procession in the peculiar crouched fighting prance. Just before they reach the gate they are met by one or two of those locals who have invited them and who now escort them over the gate. Visiting women and children follow behind the dancers and join the other spectators on the sidelines. There is much embracing as the local women and children greet visiting kinfolk. The dancing procession charges to the center of the dance ground shouting the long, low battle cry and stamping their feet, magically treated before their arrival both to counteract any *kum* or *tukump* which may linger in the ground and to enable them to dance strongly. After they charge back and forth across the dance ground several times, repeating the stamping in several locations while the crowd cheers in admiration of their numbers, their style, and the richness of their finery, they begin to sing. Their first song, to the appropriate melody, either *de* or *wobar*, should be one composed in honor of the occasion.

While the visitors are thus displaying themselves, fight magic men among the hosts apply magic to the feet of the local dancing contingent so that they may dance strongly, and fight packages are applied to their headdresses, so that the beauty of the feathers may attract the fancies of the visiting girls. Bamboo is heated while the presiding fight magic man, his voice broken by sobs, asks that both categories of spirits help the locals, that their dancing not be outdone by the visitors'. They also ask that visiting girls be attracted by the dancing and the feathers of the locals, but that the local girls remain unmoved by the charms of the visitors. When the bamboo explodes the locals charge onto the dance ground pounding their drums and singing. Their numbers include at first the girls who have decorated themselves for the occasion. They dance inside the male ranks for a few minutes before retiring to the sidelines. The formations of the locals and the visitors remain separated at first.

It is usually late afternoon when the visitors arrive. Just before dusk the locals stop dancing and assemble the food that has been prepared for the visitors in the middle of the dance ground. It includes bundles of sugar cane, net bags full of cooked tubers, bamboo tubes of greens mixed with *marita* sauce, and bananas. The visitors are asked to stop dancing and gather around while a presentation speech is made by one of the men responsible for the invitation. As he slowly walks around and around the food that has been laid out in a number of piles, the speechmaker recounts the relations of the two groups: their mutual assistance in fighting, their exchange of women and wealth, their hospitality to each other in times of defeat. He then points out the piles of food being presented to each of the invited men. While the form of the presentation ceremony is corporate, with one or sometimes two men speaking for the entire local population about the relationship of the two local populations, the piles of food are presented by individuals to individuals. The recipients do not make speeches in return. When the speech of presentation is finished they gather their portions and distribute them to those men who came to help them dance, and to their women.

Dancing continues throughout the night around low fires on the dance ground or, in case of rain, in the two large houses at the edge of the dance ground. As the night progresses the formations of visitors and locals becomes more and more mixed as men frequently switch back and forth. By dawn almost everyone has danced with everyone else.

Many of the women and girls retire to women's houses long before dawn. Others, however, remain huddled around the fires, where they may watch the dancers and where they themselves remain under the surveillance of their own menfolk. Opportunities for direct contact with eligible members of the opposite sex of the other group are thus limited. Indirect contacts, however, are made. A vis-

iting girl may talk freely with her cross-cousins, either male or female, among the locals, for instance, and may ask one of them to
tell a local young man whom she finds appealing to come to court
her on an appointed day. Local girls may not receive suitors from
other local populations until the entire year-long *kaiko* is finished,
but they may express their admiration for particular young men to
their visiting kin, who may be depended upon to report their sentiments to the admired men.

On the other hand, it is said that men do not make direct overtures to women. Young men say that a rejection would be bruited
about, making them objects of ridicule. A *yu wundi* (good man)
—one who dances strongly, whose plume waves bravely, and whose
adornment is rich—will attract women. It is for men to entice
women, not to approach them.

At dawn the dancing slackens. The dancing ground now becomes
a trading ground as men from the Jimi Valley, from across the Simbai
River, and from up and down the valley offer their wares. Bird
feathers, gold-lip shells, green sea snail shells, marsupial furs, axes,
and bushknives are, in terms of value and the frequency of exchange,
the most important items entering transactions. Baby pigs, cassowaries, and salt are occasionally traded, and a number of minor
items, including pigments, tobacco, loose marsupial fur, green beetles, and orchid fiber waistbands are also offered. In recent years
money, usually in the form of one shilling coins, but occasionally in
one pound notes, has entered into transactions. During 1962 and
1963, however, it had not yet become a universal medium of exchange. While it could be exchanged for every kind of commodity,
it was not always acceptable. If a man was firm in his desire to
obtain a gold-lip shell for his Princess Stephanie plume he would
not accept money for it. Money, in short, was traded like other items.

The transactions that take place on the dance ground are completed on the spot; a man both gives and receives at the same time.
Moreover, the exchanges are impersonal. The relationship between
the parties to a transaction, who may have never seen each other
before, may last no longer than the time it takes to complete the
trade. At the men's houses, however, a different kind of exchange
takes place. Here men from other places give to their kinsmen or
trading partners in the local group valuables for which they do not

receive immediate return. Men from north of the Simbai River leave plumes with the Tsembaga, who will, after wearing them, exchange them with Jimi Valley men for shells or axes. Jimi Valley men, conversely, leave shells and axes with the Tsembaga, who will exchange them, at future *kaiko* or on future visits to the Simbai's northern banks, for plumes, or in earlier times, native salt. It is often months before such transactions are completed, that is, before a man receives a return for a valuable he has left with a trading partner.

Trading generally lasts for an hour or two. Toward the end some of the young men, although footsore and hoarse, begin to dance again, thus demonstrating their endurance to whatever spectators remain. The dancing is sporadic, however, and ceases altogether by mid-morning. By this time the guests, except those lingering on to visit a little longer with kinsmen, have departed for home.

THE KAIKO, WOMEN, AND GOODS

It is obvious that the supralocal *kaiko* assemblages facilitate mate selection and marriage by providing settings in which marriageable, or soon to be marriageable, girls and young men are brought together. At least seven of the twenty-eight wives and widows of other-than-Tsembaga origin living on Tsembaga territory during 1962–63 made their first overtures to the men they married after being attracted to them at a *kaiko*. It is also obvious that the *kaiko*, by providing market-like settings, facilitates the exchange of goods, some of which, particularly axes and salt, are necessary for survival.

The *kaiko* also facilitates the exchange of goods, and, perhaps, the movement of women, in a less direct and more subtle way. In the last chapter the supralocal exchange system was described. It was suggested that an exchange apparatus in which only two items, in this case salt and axes, critical to either metabolism or subsistence are exchangeable for each other might well be unworkable, since the production of each of the two items would be determined not by its own demand, but by the limited demand for the item for which it is exchanged. It was further suggested that the introduction into the exchange system of valuables, the demand for which is unlimited, provides a mechanism for regulating the production of each of the two critical items in accordance with their own demand.

Valuables, thus, although themselves nonutilitarian, are crucial to provisioning the population with utilitarian commodities.

That valuables should flow from a locality of greater population increase to a locality of lower population increase was also hypothesized. The accumulation of valuables in the locality of lower population increase might be used to obtain women from one of higher population increase, adjusting differences in population between the two localities and thus contributing to the long-term adjustment of population dispersal over the entire area.

The nonutilitarian valuables upon which the Maring exchange system depended most heavily in earlier times were bird feathers, shells, and "bridal" axes. In 1962 and 1963 the importance of shells and bird feathers remained undiminished. The demand for shells is created by their use as payments to affines. It is also the case that shells, being durable, may and do form part of the ordinary daily costume. Bridal axes were also in demand because they could be included in payments to affines, and although they did not form part of a man's daily accoutrements they were carried during visits to friendly groups. Informants say that to appear at the houses of another group bearing only a bridal ax indicated both friendship and reliance upon the host's hospitality, for such implements were hardly fit for either fighting or chopping wood. Valuable bird feathers, however, did not, except occasionally in the Jimi Valley, figure in affinal payments, nor, since they are perishable, did they form part of the daily or even the visiting costume.[11] Their use is confined almost exclusively to their display at the *kaiko*. It may thus be said that the *kaiko* contributes to the movement of critical commodities, and perhaps to the movement of women as well, by creating a demand for one class of valuables upon which the operation of the exchange system depends.

RITUAL AS DISPLAY BEHAVIOR

The term *ritual* has been taken in this study to refer to the performance of conventional acts explicitly directed toward the involvement of nonempirical or supernatural agencies in the affairs of the participants. Although they may have social, demographic, nutri-

11. Less valuable bird feathers may form part of daily or visiting dress. Men will frequently wear a single parrot or eagle feather, for instance.

tional, and ecological consequences, the events already described in this study—from the hanging of the fighting stones to the inauguration of *kaiko de*—are comfortably accommodated by this description, for each is undertaken explicitly to effect changes in the relationships of the participants with various categories of supernaturals. Together with other events that remain as yet undescribed these rituals form an articulated series through which the changes occur in a certain sequence. Because the relationships among the relevant natural and supernatural entities at the termination of the sequence are such as to permit, encourage, or even demand its repetition, the sequence may aptly be termed a ritual cycle.

Kaiko entertainments, like the other events, have a prescribed place in this cycle. They occur only after the uprooting of the *rumbim* and before certain other events that will be described later. But these entertainments, although they include addresses to the spirits, are not primarily directed toward the involvement of non-empirical or supernatural agencies in the affairs of the participants. The dominant and explicit concern of the participants lies in their relations with other participants. Although the entertainments are intrinsic elements in a series that may in its totality be oriented toward the supernatural, their explicit aims are secular. But the term *ritual* is not restricted in its application to events involving the invocation of supernatural or nonempirical agencies. Indeed, the stereotypic or conventional aspects of acts are likely to be more fundamental than their sacred or supernatural aspects in identifying them as rituals, and both anthropologists (e.g., Goffman, 1956:478 passim, and Leach, 1954:10ff) as well as ethologists (e.g., Blest, 1961; Elkin, 1963; Hinde and Tinbergen, 1958; Tinbergen, 1952, 1963) have used the term to designate certain events, occurring among both men and other animals, in which one or more participants transmit, through conventional sign or symbol, information concerning their own physiological, psychological, or sociological states to other participants. They have used the term *ritual*, in other words, to refer to a class of communication events.

There are, of course, many kinds of communication events, and no purpose is served by regarding them all as ritual. But ritual may be distinguished from other modes of communication by its special language, which is conventional display. Put in terms of communications models, if ritual is regarded as a channel, conventional display is the code appropriate to that channel.

Kaiko entertainments, although explicitly secular in intention, may be regarded as rituals not only because their most obvious characteristic is conventional display, but because the displays communicate among participants certain information that, given other aspects of Maring culture, can hardly be communicated in any other way.

The notion of display behavior has already been introduced several times in this study. It has been suggested the "small" or "nothing" fight may be regarded as agonistic territorial display, similar to that which has been observed among species other than man, rather than as sanguinary fighting. It was also suggested that agonistic display is one aspect of the stake-planting ritual, which demarcates or ratifies the territorial boundary. The messages transmitted through such displays are, obviously, ones of threat. Other messages are transmitted by the displays in which friendly groups participate at *kaiko* entertainments.

Thése displays have two main aspects. The first of these, following V. C. Wynne-Edwards, may be termed *epigamic*. Speaking of non-human species Wynne-Edwards uses this term to refer to "displays that characterize the marital relations of the sexes and typically culminate in fertilisation" (1962:17). They are in other words amatory displays, which form all or part of a courtship procedure. The dancing of males at a *kaiko* constitutes the first phase of a conventionalized courtship procedure that, if the female spectators respond favorably, may continue for some of the participants in other contexts.

Certain information is imparted by the massed dancing of the males. First, it presents to the female spectators larger samples of the males of unfamiliar local groups than they are likely to see assembled at any other time or place. The males, fruthermore, signal by their participation in the dance their general interest in the females as a class. It would be difficult to conceive a more economical means for communicating information concerning the availability of males than the sample presentation of the dance. Through it females are able, on a single occasion, to gain some familiarity with all or most of the eligible males of local populations in which they themselves are not resident and which they may visit only rarely.

The amatory display of the males does more than present a sample to the females, however. It also provides them with a basis for differentiating among the males. The appearance of the individual men—their dancing and the richness of their adornment—indicates to females their strength or endurance and their wealth or the wealth of their connections.

Wynne-Edwards suggests that such displays in the animal kingdom are selective mechanisms, since "individuals that were undernourished or depressed would presumably have greater difficulty in achieving mating than the dominant and well-fed" (1962:251). Whether or not the choices that Maring females make are usually responses to the comparative quality of the performances of the individual males cannot be answered here, for the data are insufficient. A number of men maintain, however, that their wives were first attracted to them because of the admirable figures they cut in the dance. It may be pointed out, moreover, that characteristics displayed in dancing are not irrelevant to more prosaic activities. Endurance or strength is as vital to gardening and fighting as to dancing, and the richness of a man's adornment gives some indication of his ability to pay for the woman whom he may attract. This information, it may be added, is not only communicated to the eligible females, but also to their male agnates, whose attitudes toward suitors, although sometimes ignored, are germane to all matings.

It is only the behavior of the men that may be characterized as amatory display, but of course it is also the case that the marriageable women of the hosts and guests are made available for inspection by men at *kaiko* entertainments. While the display behavior of the dancing men may elicit overtures from the women, the presence of the women may also prompt the men to make overtures to the male kinsmen of the women. A man seeking a wife for himself, his son, or his younger brother may approach the father or brothers of a girl who attracts him and for whom he is either able to exchange a sister or daughter or make substantial payments.

The *kaiko*, in short, forms part of two procedures that facilitate sexual pairing. First, by providing a setting in which massed amatory display takes place, it offers an opportunity for females to invite courtship from specific individuals among a large and perhaps previously unfamiliar sample of available males. Second, it is an occasion upon which large numbers of females are presented for inspection, thus providing a basis for negotiations between males concerning the disposal of females. The two procedures, one involving selection by females, the other by males, sometimes conflict, for girls' choices do not always coincide with those of their fathers or brothers, but this need not be considered here.

Following Wynne-Edwards (1962:16), the term *epideictic* may be applied to the second major aspect of displays at *kaiko* entertainments. Epideictic displays are those that impart to the participants information concerning the population's size or density prior to behavior that may affect that size or density. Included by Wynne-Edwards are the "dancing of gnats and midges, the milling of whirligig-beetles, the manoeuvres of birds and bats at roosting time, the choruses of birds, bats, frogs, insects and shrimps" (1962: 16). Epideictic displays usually occur at conventional times and frequently at "traditional places" (1962:17).

The specification by Wynne-Edwards that such displays precede events that "restore or shift the balance of population" justifies the use of the term *epideictic* in reference to *kaiko* entertainments. One of the ways of restoring or shifting the balance of population is by adjusting the dispersion of organisms over the land. It must not be forgotten that the occurrence of the *kaiko* immediately precedes the termination of the truce. After the *kaiko* the existing pattern of population dispersion may again be tested through renewed hostilities. In anticipation of renewed hostilities it is important for the members of a local population to assess the extent to which it will be supported by its allies. Among the Maring it is not possible to base such assessments upon promises of support from authoritative political leaders, men who can command the performance of others, for such do not exist. The decision to participate in fighting as an ally is at the discretion of each individual male.

The Tsembaga say that "those who come to our *kaiko* will also come to our fights." This native interpretation of *kaiko* attendance is also given expression by an invited group. Preparations for departure to a *kaiko* at another place include ritual performances similar to those that precede a fight. Fight packages are applied to the heads and hearts of the dancers and *gir* to their feet so that they will dance strongly, just as, during warfare, they are applied so that they will fight strongly. It has already been indicated that these acts have amatory aspects, but it is also said that dancing is like fighting. The visitors' procession is led by men carrying fight packages, and their entrance upon the dance ground of their hosts is martial. To join a group in dancing is the symbolic expression of willingness to join them in fighting.

The size of a visiting dancing contingent is a product of many factors. Most important of these are the size of the local population to which the invitation has been extended, the number of kin or formal trading connections between hosts and guests, and the extent to which the formally invited men can induce others to support them. The last is itself a product of the relations of the formally invited men to members of their own and other groups.

These are also the factors that most importantly affect the recruitment of allies in time of warfare. Mobilization to attend a *kaiko* thus exercises the connections through which mobilization for warfare is accomplished, and the size of the dancing contingent signals the total strength and effectiveness of these connections. The hosts, thus, can base assessments of the extent to which friendly groups will support their belligerent enterprises upon the samples that are presented to them in the form of dancing contingents. Given the absence of authoritative political leaders, it is difficult to imagine how this information could be economically communicated without display or some other means for presenting a sample.

It is true, of course, that participation in a dance is different from participation in a fight, and men who may be pleased to attend the former may be reluctant to engage in the latter. Display accommodates deception and dissembling, but so does language and the more specialized codes that depend upon language. Indeed, the ability to transmit lies is common to all means of communication that employ symbols. In this connection, however, it should be recalled that although *kaiko* entertainments are essentially secular, visitors do address their ancestors before arriving, and that these addresses and the acts accompanying them are similar to those that are undertaken prior to assisting another group in warfare. It may be suggested that the involvement of the spirits in the *kaiko* participation of the visitors sanctifies the information they transmit to their hosts through display. The sanctification of messages may be of importance in a communication system that can easily accommodate falsehood: on the one hand men may be loath to sanctify information they do not take seriously, and on the other hand statements that have been sanctified may be more credible to recipients than mere promises.

In addition to the epigamic and epideictic messages, display at *kaiko* entertainments transmits other information. Before the food presentation, for instance, a formally invited man watches his host assemble his portion, thus learning how many men his host has been able to induce to assist him in this effort. The invited man's followers, from the size of their portions, may estimate the strength of the connections between the host and the man whom they are "helping to dance." The hosts, at the same time, may assess the influence of the formally invited men by observing the number of people to whom each redistributes the food presented him. The displays thus transmit information concerning not only the strength or size but also the structure of the participating groups.

The Culmination of the Kaiko

With the coming of the "dry" season, in May or June on Tsembaga territory, new gardens are cut. Ordinarily, the greater part of the men's work would be finished by late August, but in 1963 unseasonable rains, falling mainly in the daytime, and heavy overcast seriously impeded burning. Preparations for the *konj kaiko*, the "pig *kaiko*," the event culminating not only the year-long festival but also the entire ritual cycle, were nevertheless initiated by some men in mid-August, and by early September most other men had followed them.

TRAPPING EELS

As preparations for uprooting the *rumbim* begin with the trapping of *ma*, the "pigs of the *rawa mugi*," so preparations for the *konj kaiko* begin with the trapping of eels, the "pigs of the *raua mai*."

The minimal agnatic groups, either clans or subclans, form the trapping units, as they did for the trapping of *ma*, and similar to the trapping of *ma*, the locations in which each agnatic group may place its traps are restricted. Although at other times men may place traps anywhere, they now must set them in traditional places associated with their own spirits of the low ground, for it is only with them that pigs may be exchanged.

The personnel participating in the trapping of eels differs to some extent from those involved in taking *ma*. Fight magic men, who remain for life dedicated to the *rawa mugi*, are precluded from even touching with their hands the cold, wet eels, and they therefore take no part in trapping them.

The prohibitions burdening the men engaged in eel trapping are similar to those under which they labored when trapping *ma*. Now, however, it is the high ground, the *kamuŋga*, which is to be avoided, and the people suffer no prohibition against *marita*.

As the flesh of the trapped *ma* is preserved, so, in a sense, is that of the eels. After being taken from the traps they are kept alive in individual cylindrical bark cages left submerged in the streams. Although they are not fed, some of the captured fish maintain life for as long as two months, apparently subsisting on whatever bits of plant and animal material is carried to them by the current.

As in the case of *ma* and pigs, there is no particular number of eels required for the performance of the rituals in which they figure. A sufficiency of eels seems to be defined, rather, by the toleration of these fish for captivity. As the trapping period continues, the trappers suffer mounting losses among the imprisoned eels, due perhaps to possible lowered food intake and lack of exercise. Sometimes, too, in the heavy run-off of water following downpours, both traps and cages are carried away. With each loss there is increased talk of getting on with the remaining preparations for the *konj kaiko* before all of the eels are lost.

PREPARATIONS AT THE RAKU AND DANCE GROUND

By early October 1963 some men, not waiting for the "talk to become one," after being advised by shamans of the wishes of the ancestors, began to make preparations both at designated *raku* and on the dance ground for the *konj kaiko*, the event that brings the festival and the cycle to a close.

On the dance ground repairs were made to the two houses, and late in the middle of the month a ceremonial fence, called the *pave*, was built on the slope above one end of the dance ground. Constructed of saplings and covered with foliage, this light three-sided structure, about 15' high, enclosed an area of about 30'x50'. This area was increased by the incorporation into it of the large men's house enclosure that stood directly above it. The longest dimension of the *pave*, that facing the dance ground, was broken near its center by a single window about 1' square and approximately 4' above the ground.

By mid-October work had started at the *raku* of all of the minimal agnatic units. These included sites where the residences of men slain in the last fight had stood, for it was these men specifically to whom pigs were to be dedicated. These *raku* were in some, but not all, instances separate from those at which pigs were to be killed for the spirits of the low ground. Most of the latter were to be killed at *raku* that had always been used for this purpose. If the slain men had lived near these traditional sites a single *raku* might be used for both categories of ancestors.

Anomalies in the general pattern of a separate *raku* for each of the minimal agnatic units gave, perhaps, some evidence of past or on-going changes in agnatic structure and residence patterns. Three of the adult males of the Wendekai subclan of the Merkai clan prepared a *raku* separate from that of the other eight adult males. The three had been separated by food and fire taboos from their subclan brothers, but such taboos, it has already been mentioned, split other groups that did maintain the use of single *raku*. Some members of the Atigai subclan of the Tsembaga clan, on the other hand, joined with the Atigai subclan of the Kamuŋgagai clan, as had their fathers, who, they said, had lived sororilocally with the Kamuŋgagai Atigai. The remaining Tsembaga Atigai shared a *raku* with the Tsembaga Wendekai subclan and the unsegmented Tomegai clan.

Early preparations at both kinds of *raku* included the clearing of underbrush and the erection of roofed but unwalled structures for the storage of firewood and vegetables, and for shelter from rain. Additional structures were erected at those *raku* where pigs were to be killed for the spirits of the low ground. These were *timbi* houses, named after the trees that formed the center posts (*Myrtaceae*, ? *Cleistanthus* sp.), which, frequently found by wide still places in streams, are said to be *koipa maŋgiaŋ*'s own trees. *Timbi* houses are round, six to nine feet in diameter, and the *timbi* center posts, with some leaves remaining, project several feet above the conical roof.

It was in these houses that the eels were to be cooked with pig bellies in one or two earth ovens, depending upon whether food taboos split the group.

The erection of the center post is accompanied by a brief ritual, the object of which is fertility and abundance. A sleeping mat is laid upon the earth floor of the still roofless *timbi* house, and valuables to be offered to *koipa mangiang*, "he who gives us eels," are spread upon it. The butt end of the center post is placed upon the mat, and one of the older men, singing in a soft falsetto voice, first cleans moss off its bark with a bamboo scrapper then, with an ax, marks its length with a zig-zag line, representing, informants say, an eel. The debris falls upon the wealth objects, and the song is concerned with the increase of wealth and the thoughts of trading partners. "Let him think of me and send one gold-lip shell. Let him think of me and send one ax," etc. When the work is finished, the moss and bark are gathered up to be cooked with vegetables and eaten by all but fight magic men to enhance both fertility and growth.

The spirits of rot, the fathers and grandfathers of those present who died from causes other than violence, are then addressed by name. They are thanked for the eels and told that they are now being offered valuables at this place where they, when living, killed pigs, and where those presently living would soon kill more. They are told to accept the valuables and give some to *koipa mangiang*, and are asked to look after the women and children, each of whose names are mentioned. The red spirits are then addressed. They are reminded that wealth was previously given to them but that now it is being given to "those who gave us eels." They are asked, however, to continue to look out for the men, all of whom are named. All the men and boys then place their hands on the *timbi* center post as it is thrust in the ground. The shells and beads are then hung from a low branch left on the center post for this purpose, and the axes are planted in a circle around the base of the post. After the roof is completed, the valuables are returned to their owners.

As in the case of the planting of *rumbim* and *amame*, the symbolism of the ritual paraphernalia, particularly the *timbi* house itself, seems sexual. Of greater interest is the further adjustment in the relations of the participants with both categories of ancestors. With the hanging of the fighting stones and the taking of the *ringi*, the dominant relationship was with the red spirits. This was modified when *rumbim* and *amame* were planted, but a heavy debt to both categories of ancestors was acknowledged. When these plants were uprooted a further adjustment between the living and the two categories of spirits was expressed in the abrogation of most of the taboos remaining from the time of the fight, in the reestablishment of reciprocity with the red spirits, and, perhaps, in a commuion with the spirits of the low ground. A further adjustment takes place when the *timbi* center post is set. Reciprocity, to be bound by a forthcoming "pig exchange," is being reestablished with the spirits of the low ground. However, it is important to note that the red spirits are also addressed during the planting of the *timbi*. The Tsembaga say that if they weren't they might grow jealous and desert the living, leaving them open to slaughter in the next round of fights. The goal of the rituals through which the Tsembaga and other Marings proceed does not seem to be the replacement of the red spirits by the spirits of the low ground, but rather a redefinition of the balance in the relationships of the living with the two categories of supernaturals.

THE EFFECT OF THE PLANS OF OTHER GROUPS ON THE TIMING OF THE KONJ KAIKO

The plans of other groups sometimes affect the timing of the *konj kaiko*. The Tuguma uprooted their *rumbim* when their *pengup* variety *marita* ripened in October 1963, one year later than the Tsembaga's. It has already been mentioned that men of local populations who have *rumbim* in the ground may not eat the flesh of pigs killed in connection with the *kaiko* of other groups. The Tsembaga, who might otherwise have been able to stage their *konj kaiko* several weeks earlier, were forced to wait until their most important allies and closest neighbors had uprooted their *rumbim*, thus becoming free to eat the pork to be presented to them.

Delays in terminating *kaiko* for this reason must have been common if not the rule, considering the frequency of fighting throughout the Maring area and the number of groups from which allies were usually drawn. Their consequences in recent years have been trivial. The Tsembaga complained only about increasing deaths among their captured eels. Before pacification, however, they may have had more important consequences. In situations in which the *kaiko*

of a pair of enemies were separated by one year, such delays may
have served to eliminate entirely any period during which one was
free to attack while the other was not.

When all but the final preparations at the *raku* are completed
some of the young men undergo ritual dedication to the red spirits.
The initiates are secluded in the men's house enclosure behind the
pave and their hair is worked into constructions called *mamp gunč*.
Round frames, about six inches high, made of the bark of the *kirim*
tree (*Lauraceae* sp.) are placed on their heads like crowns. The
hair, which has remained uncut since puberty, is pulled up through
the center and down over the sides of the frame, hiding it completely. The melted sap of an unidentified tree called *gunč*, which
gives the construction its name ("head *gunč*"), and which, upon
cooling, leaves the surfaces hard, is then applied. Finally, the headdress is dyed red, with trade pigments now.

Only a few of the fight magic men possess the skill of making
mamp gunč, and the procedure is protracted. The arrangement of
the hair over the frame takes almost a day for each novice, and the
application of the melted *gunč*, bit by bit with an arrow point, takes
another day. It is also highly ritualized, but the details of the rituals
need not be discussed here. It is sufficient to say that the red spirits
are told that the boys are putting on these "red things" for them and
their help is asked in making them shapely, hard, and bright. All
of the remaining ritual procedures have the same goal.

As might be expected of anything associated with the red spirits,
the young men assume a number of stringent taboos along with their
mamp gunč. These proscribe, among other things, sexual intercourse
and visiting the *wora* while the *mamp gunč* remain attached to their
heads. More notable, however, are absolute prohibitions against
drinking water, chewing sugar cane, and eating cucumber, paw
paw, and hibiscus leaves. These prohibitions lasted, in the case of the
Tsembaga boys, for eight days. They did not exert themselves during
this period, and the roots and greens they were allowed to eat evidently contained sufficient moisture to prevent serious dehydration.
Some violations of the taboos did occur, however. I know personally
of two instances in which *gunč yu*, as young men wearing *mamp
gunč* are called, took liquids. One drank a few sips of coffee, and the

other, after complaining of a cough, took cough syrup with a water chaser. Both of these exotic liquids were available only from us and were so uncommon and unfamiliar that the fight magic men had not thought to proscribe them.

When work on their headdresses is finished, the new *mamp gunč* men are "brought out"; that is, they end their seclusion by dancing publicly for the local women and whatever visitors from other places care to watch.

It has already been mentioned that only some of the Tsembaga men took *mamp gunč* at the 1963 *kaiko*. In fact, only five did so. This was an unusually small number, but it seems to be the case that seldom, if ever, did all young men put on *mamp gunč* at the same time.

Mamp gunč, first, are associated with the killing of enemies. Some informants say that *mamp gunč* may be worn only by young men whose agnates have killed enemies in the last fight. Others say that if a member of the subterritorial group has killed, they may be worn, while yet others maintain that the *mamp gunč* may be put on if any member of the local population has slain an enemy. It is not possible to derive any rule from what went on among the Tsembaga in 1963, for the proceedings were unusual. The five young men who put on *mamp gunč* either had taken refuge among the Kauwasi or were agnates of those who had. They justified their *mamp gunč* on the basis of the slaying, during the Kauwasi-Monambant fight, of a Kundagai allied to the Monambant. The Tsembaga who took refuge in Monambant, however, said that they had killed no Kundagai and would await the Monambant *kaiko* to wear *mamp gunč*, for they had helped Monambant kill Kauwasi.

Even in situations in which all young men are related to killers in such a manner as to be eligible to put on a *mamp gunč*, it is unlikely that all would do so. It is said that two brothers, for instance, cannot take *mamp gunč* at the same time, for a man who is wearing a *mamp gunč* cannot assist with the slaughter of the pigs, the gathering of firewood and vegetables, and the other tasks associated with the *konj kaiko*. Those who do not take the *mamp gunč* at the *kaiko* of their own local population, however, may put them on at the *kaiko* of other local populations to which one's own has been allied. To qualify to put on a *mamp gunč* at the *kaiko* of an allied group it seems sufficient to belong to the same local population as any man who has participated in the killing of one of that group's enemies. It is not necessary to be an agnate of the killer.

It is interesting to note that the young men who join in putting on the *mamp gunč* may, although they seldom do, refer to each other as "brother." It could be said that the *mamp gunč* procedure is a device producing supralocal age classes. The political and structural potentialities of such age classes, if they may be so termed, remain unutilized, however.

Another kind of group may also be crystallized by, or at least become apparent in, the *mamp gunč* rituals. While there are at the time of most *kaiko* probably many young men who are eligible to put on *mamp gunč,* there are always certain of them who must do so. These are the young men who have been designated by each of the fight magic men to be heirs to their ritual knowledge. Whenever possible they are the biological sons of the fight magic men, but if a fight magic man has no son he will designate a brother's son, the sons of true brothers being selected before the sons of classificatory brothers.

If a priest is one who performs prescribed rituals at specified times for the benefit of a congregation, it may be said that fight magic men are priests. The putting on of the *mamp gunč,* it may further be said, specifies a group of young men who will inherit priesthood. Hereditary priesthoods, even more than age classes, have served as foci of political activity in many societies. Among the Maring, however, the extent to which ritual knowledge has been converted into secular authority is minimal. Continuity of ritual knowledge is maintained, but the political possibilities of hereditary priesthood remains, like that of age classing, potential. It is beyond the scope of this study to discuss the reasons underlying the lack of development of either age classes or heredity as bases of political organization. It may be suggested, however, that the ritual cycle itself defines sufficiently the tasks that require aggregated effort, and that in groups as small as those of Maring local populations the efforts of entire groups may be mobilized without recourse to the formal structures or positions that could be yielded by age classes or hereditary priesthoods.

FINAL PREPARATIONS

In the last days before the *konj kaiko,* activity reaches a high pitch. Above-ground ovens must be built for pigs to be dedicated to the red spirits and firewood must be gathered at the *raku*. Women must gather large quantities of the ferns and other greens with which pigs are cooked. Many of the visitors who were to receive pork arrived in advance, for they are expected to help in the preparations. It is also necessary to assemble captured eels at locations convenient to the *raku*, so they were deposited in their cages in nearby streams. New paths were cut from their places of deposition to the *raku*, and at their termini light archways were constructed.

Before the pigs are killed, the ground must again be rid of any corruption deriving from spirits or sorcerers. To this end, two days before the *konj kaiko* a number of fight magic men gathered on the government walking track, where they bespelled large bamboos full of water. These were distributed to representatives of each of the minimal agnatic units to use at the *raku* and on the paths. While sprinkling the contents of the bamboos over the ground the men recounted, to both the living and the dead, the story of their defeat and departure and the subsequent pollution of the ground by Kundagai spirits and sorcerers, and announced that they were now counteracting this pollution with magical water.

THE ABROGATION OF TABOOS

On the day before the major pig slaughter fourteen *aček konj*, "taboo pigs," were sacrificed. Although both categories of ancestors were told in the addresses before the killing that the living wished to terminate taboos, the slaughtered animals were cooked in above-ground ovens, for the taboos that applied most generally, those arising from warfare, were associated with the red spirits.

With the opening of the oven each individual brushed himself with the *gañiŋgai* shrub, made the spitting sound, and announced separately the taboos he was terminating. The pig was then eaten by those who had participated in the ritual. The variety of taboos abrogated was great, and it is convenient to separate them into three classes: those associated with mourning, intralocal disputes, and warfare.

During mourning a woman is separated by fire taboos (*aček*) from nonmourning women and from men, because the bones of the deceased remain in her house, by taboos against touching or even conversation. If the deceased was a man, moreover, the woman is burdened with all of the food taboos he suffered when alive.

Just before the *konj kaiko* women who have been keeping the
bones of deceased persons at their houses bury the remains at the
raku, so that the spirits of these deceased may partake of the flesh of
the pigs soon to be killed. Burying the bones at the *raku* effectively
terminates the mourning period, and the taboos associated with it
are abrogated with the killing of the taboo pigs.

Mourning taboos apply to people other than the women who look
after the bones. It is customary for the deceased's close kin (members of his families of orientation and procreation) to give up, as an
expression of sorrow and loss, one of the deceased's favorite varieties
of each of the major categories of foodstuffs (i.e., one variety of taro,
one of banana, etc.). These voluntary renunciations are termed *moi*.
If the deceased was a woman, moreover, the men whose pigs she
looked after customarily give up the consumption of pork for the
duration of the mourning period, and widowers also often announce
that they will neither marry nor engage in sexual intercourse for an
indefinite period. These restrictions are also abrogated with the killing of the taboo pig.

Antagonisms between members of the group arising out of serious
arguments, disputes, and hurts are given symbolic expression in the
form of interdining and food-sharing taboos also known as "*aček*."
The principals refuse to eat food cooked over the same fire, and
each refuses to eat food grown by the other. Taboos arising out of a
variety of incidents ranging from obscene name calling to homicide
were terminated with the killing of the taboo pigs.

Some of the taboos arising out of warfare (also referred to as
"*aček*") are also terminated with the killing of the taboo pigs. To
abrogate the full range of taboos applying to intercourse between the
agnatic groups of the slayers and the slain takes four generations.
Children of the opposing principals may neither eat foodstuffs raised
by their opposites nor share a cooking fire. Grandchildren may eat
food grown by each other, but may not eat food cooked over the
same fire. Great-grandchildren may, after renouncing the taboo,
share the same cooking fire. Individuals who are related through
wives or mothers to erstwhile enemies constitute an exception to the
general applicability of this rule, but this will be discussed later in
another context.

In 1963, young people of the Kamuŋgagai clan terminated the

taboo on food grown by the Kekai clan, who had killed a member
of their grandparental generation during warfare perhaps fifty years
earlier. On the same day, men of the Merkai clan renounced a taboo
upon the fires of the Raweŋ clan of Tuguma, who had killed two
members of their great-grandparental generation so long ago that
no one could provide information concerning the circumstances surrounding the deaths.

The Tsembaga also terminated some of the restrictions on intercourse with their enemies of the last fight, the Kundagai, with the
sacrifice of the taboo pigs. These were the taboos on walking through
Kundagai territory, talking to and touching Kundagai, and visiting
(but not entering) Kundagai residences.

The abrogation of taboos on intercourse with the Kundagai at this
time was irregular. In earlier times the restrictions would have remained in effect until peace-making ceremonies could be conducted
some time in the future, but the establishment of a Simbai patrol post
and the administration policy of drawing people into control by requiring of them corporate effort made the abrogation of these taboos
ex post facto as it was. While carrying cargo for government patrols,
for instance, most Tsembaga had crossed Kundagai territory, as most
Kundagai had crossed theirs, and in building a bridge ordered by the
government across the stream separating their territories members
of the two groups had already been forced into cooperation.

It has already been mentioned that taboos arising out of the warfare of other groups may split local populations. Those Tsembaga
who had fought on opposite sides of the Monambant-Kauwasi fight
terminated their taboo on each other's foodstuffs with the killing of
the taboo pigs. The taboo on each other's fires, however, was to remain in effect until the Monambant terminated their *kaiko* in 1964.

TABOOS, SOCIAL CONTROL, AND INTERGROUP RELATIONS

Taboos on interdining, food sharing, and on other social relations
are a pervasive aspect of Maring social and political life. Interpretations of the nature and function of ritual advanced by Bateson
(1936), Freud (1907), Gluckman (1962), and Reik (1947), although
they cannot be tested, suggest certain ideas concerning the role of
taboo in these relations. The extension of interpretations of ritual to
an examination of taboos is warranted because taboos, which may

be defined as supernaturally sanctioned proscriptions of physically feasible behavior, form a logical pair with ritual; indeed, they may be regarded as "negative rituals." Among the Maring, moreover, the relationship is not only logical but actual, for taboos are also both ritually assumed and ritually abrogated.

Gluckman has suggested that "social rules and values, established by diverse relations, themselves move individuals and sub-groups to dispute with their fellows in their main group of allegiance," and that "ritual operates to cloak the fundamental conflicts which are set up" (1962:40). He does not suggest that rituals settle conflicts. "The whole point of the analysis is that they cannot do so" (1962:46). He suggests instead that conflicts between parties may be concealed by rituals, which "in fact may lead to temporary truces." The ability of ritual to perform such a function, Freud's writings suggest, may lie in the nature of ritual itself. In remarking upon the similarity between the obsessional ceremonials of neurotics and the religious rituals of the pious, Freud notes that both represent compromises between opposing forces. At one and the same time they both suppress and give expression to feelings that may be dangerous to an individual or to a group.

These formulations suggest that the taboos that prevail within Maring local groups are an important means of social control. Among the Maring these taboos arise out of antagonisms. I have already mentioned the basis of some of the antagonisms giving rise to the taboos prevailing among the Tsembaga in 1963. Some were generated by events that are the frequent concomitants of coresidence: insult, assault, woman-stealing, and so on. Others arose out of what Gluckman would call the fundamental constitution of Maring society, that is, out of diverse affiliations and conflicting responsibilities. Thus, taboos to which all Tsembaga were subject resulted from the Monambant-Kauwasi war of 1955. Maring rules of participation in warfare are such that some Tsembaga men could not avoid fighting on each side and thus fighting each other. The Tsembaga were in exile at the time of the war, and those who were living with the Monambant and Kauwasi had to join, as principal combatants, their hosts, who had provided them with land and shelter, and two Tsembaga men were killed and several were wounded in the fighting. When, however, the Tsembaga exile ended and they reassembled on their own territory it was necessary for those who had fought against each other in the Monambant-Kauwasi war to become again members of a single cooperating and coresidential group.

It may be suggested, following Freud and Gluckman, that taboos played an important part in this reamalgamation. The taboos served to define areas of behavior in which the anger and bitterness generated by death and injury could be expressed, while permitting cooperation in most of the important tasks of living. In Freud's terms the taboos represented a compromise between the needs to express and to suppress socially dangerous feelings. They required or allowed antagonism to be stated frequently and formally in controlled circumstances: by men cooking their food side by side, but over separate fires; by the refusal of one man to enter another's house; by the refusal to eat food grown by another. It may be suggested that the frequent but relatively harmless statement of antagonism in areas of behavior narrowly defined by taboos inhibited their more generalized, less predictable, and therefore more dangerous, expression. The supernatural nature of the taboos, moreover, may have relieved tension between antagonists by transferring animus from a mundane to a supernatural plane. These effects of observing taboos, I think, prevented ill-feeling from contaminating all aspects of the relationships of parties between whom grievance lay and thus permitted their cooperation in important tasks. It was in fact the case that men who refused to eat each others' food or at each others' fires helped each other in forest clearing and hunting, granted land to each other, assisted each other with affinal payments, and would have, had the need arisen, fought side by side in defense of the common territory.

It is interesting to note that it is to taboo rather than to ritual that the task of expressing and suppressing antagonism is assigned. I suggest that taboo is better fitted to the purpose than ritual, for the very act of expressing antagonism by observing a taboo turns the principals *away* from each other. Antagonism is thus stated through a means that avoids potentially dangerous confrontations.

This formulation is in some respects applicable to the relations between hostile local populations as well as to interpersonal relations within local populations. The ritual truce inaugurated by the planting of *rumbim* is reinforced by prohibitions on all intercourse between the hostile groups. These taboos, while expressing the hostility symbolically, minimize the possibility of actual truce violations. Although no active or conscious cooperation between the groups is facilitated or even allowed by these taboos, they at least make it possible for the members of each group to live in some security.

However, although taboos may play an important part in maintaining order within the local population, obviously there must be some means of abrogating them, otherwise their accumulation would eventually damage the coresidential and cooperative structure they help to maintain.

The renunciation of taboos involves the killing of pigs. Such slaughter, however, awaits the accumulation of a parasitic or competitive quantity of animals. To sacrifice animals sooner for the purpose of terminating taboos among members of the local group would diminish the quantity of pigs available for emergency and misfortune and it would delay the *kaiko*. Therefore it awaits the *kaiko*, when people can afford to put pigs to this purpose. The expressed attitudes and behavior of the Tsembaga suggest that by this time the taboos have fulfilled their function. The antagonisms that gave rise to them have cooled considerably and have been replaced by annoyance with the taboos themselves. Informants said that by the time of the *kaiko* they no longer bore any animus toward those with whom their relations were restricted by taboos, but continued to observe the taboos merely because their ancestors would punish them if they did not. With the renunciation of taboos people who had long been separated by them frequently embraced.

The *kaiko*, then, which is part of a mechanism for regulating relations between groups, may also be part of a mechanism, which includes taboos, for regulating relations between members of the same local group.

PIGS, EELS, AND FERTILITY

On the day following the abrogation of taboos, eighty-two more pigs were killed. Of these, fourteen were dedicated to the red spirits, one for each man killed in the last fight, and sixty-eight to the spirits of the low ground.

At former *kaiko*, informants say, the red spirits were told, when pigs were offered to them, that their deaths would soon be avenged. In 1963, however, they were told that because of the new presence of the government it was now impossible to avenge their deaths by natural means, and they were asked to eat the pig offered them so that they themselves might become strong enough to avenge their own deaths by visiting illness upon their slayers.

Addresses to the spirits of the low ground recounted the story of the defeat, the subsequent depredation of the land and desecration of the *raku* by the Kundagai, and finally, the return of the people to their own territory. Specifically named ancestors who had been invited to other places to receive sacrifices of pork while the living were in exile were now asked to return to their traditional places on their own territory to receive pig. The spirits as well as the living were thus resettled upon the territory they had previously abandoned.

All pigs were butchered and cooked at the *raku* shortly after their slaughter. Men, usually affines, from other places who were to receive entire pigs were at the *raku* to cook them themselves. The presentations were unceremonious. No speeches of either presentation or acceptance were made. The recipients, after giving their benefactors the return gift of an ax, bushknife, or shell,[12] simply proceeded to butcher and cook the animals presented them. Those recipients who had been allies in the last fight, however, returned the bellies of their animals to the donors to be salted and publicly presented to them on the following day. Men who were to receive less than an entire animal did not come to the *raku*. They received their portions on the following day already cooked.

At each *raku* at least one, and sometimes two, female pigs dedicated to the spirits of the low ground were further designated "*koipa* pigs." These animals played a part in a ritual the Tsembaga regard to be of great importance. As the *koipa* pigs were killed, the names of specific spirits of rot were called out, and they were asked to take this pig and pass it on to *koipa maŋgiaŋ*, "the man who gives us eels." After the *koipa* pigs were killed, the eels were brought from nearby streams by processions of young men and boys who carried the cages, decorated with *timbi* leaves, along the newly cleared paths. Women and girls awaited them at the light archways, made of *timbi* and other plants, at the end of these "roads of *koipa maŋgiaŋ*" on the edges of the *raku*. The men, women, boys, and girls then pro-

12. These presentations cannot be regarded as payment in any strict sense. A single wealth object may be traded for an infant animal. A full-grown pig is worth many times as much. It is not possible to be precise, since full-grown pigs are not traded.

ceeded together to the bodies of the slain *koipa* pigs, where the eels were removed from their cages. Holding them by their tails, women, children, and unmarried young men flailed the dead pigs with the eels until the eels too were dead. The bodies of the dead pigs were then rubbed with the eels. Informants say that the shoulders of the participants should also be rubbed with the eels, but I did not see this done.

The eels were then hung, along with shell valuables and beads, on the center post of the *timbi* houses, so that wealth might increase. Later in the day the valuables were returned to their owners, and as night fell the bellies of the *koipa* pigs were placed in the earth ovens inside the *timbi* houses along with the eels. When the ovens were opened in the morning, if the food was well cooked (as it invariably was), it was said that *koipa maŋgiaŋ* had come in the night and eaten, and that the people might now partake of the oven's contents so that they, their pigs, and their gardens would be fruitful. The spirits of rot were addressed first, being told that the living have given them many pigs, and now that they had eaten their fill they might return to their houses, the large trees in the low-altitude primary forest. They were asked to care for crops, pigs, and people so that these might be fertile and fast growing and were promised that when the crops came up they would be fed. They were finally told to take the contents of the ovens and give them to *koipa maŋgiaŋ*. Everyone, with the exception of fight magic men, ended their taboo on the consumption of eels by eating from this oven.

The purpose of this ritual is made explicit both in the addresses to spirits and in the statements of informants, all of whom agree that the performance is undertaken to ensure the fertility and growth of people, pigs, and gardens and the increase of wealth in the coming years. It is significant that this ritual occurs more or less concurrently with the final fulfillment of obligations incurred during the ritual cycle just ending, and with the termination of the taboos associated with these obligations. The slate has been, or is being, wiped clean. The local population now stands, or will shortly stand, in a relationship of equivalence or reciprocity rather than obligation to the spirits and allies, and a new cycle is beginning.[13]

13. It has not been the purpose of this study to discuss the psychic symbolism that may underlie Maring ritual objects or performances. A brief excursion into this

A Maring ritual cycle may be regarded as a series of adjustments in the relations of the people to two generally antithetic sets of spirits. The dominance of the red spirits is continually tempered as the debtor relationship is transformed into one of reciprocity. With the lowering of the fighting stones the way is paved for the reestablishment of reciprocity with the spirits of the low ground and the implication of *koipa maŋgiaŋ* in future fertility and prosperity.

Each adjustment in these relationships, from the hanging of the fighting stones to the rituals initiating the new cycle, requires the slaughter of pigs. It has already been pointed out that the size and rate of growth of the pig herd serves as an index to the well-being of the human population. For a local population to retain its territory after warfare obviously indicates its viability in opposition to similar local aggregates. For it to accumulate sufficient pigs to fulfill its obligations indicates its viability as an ecological and demographic unit as well.

THE DISTRIBUTION OF PORK AND THE SURVIVING PIGS

Ninety-six pigs were killed in connection with the rituals of November 7 and 8, 1963. Their total live weight is estimated to have been between 13,500 and 17,000 pounds, yielding between 6,750 and 8,500 pounds of edible meat.

area is, however, warranted because it may throw additional light on the structure of the ritual cycle.

What follows, it should be made clear, is my interpretation. I did not explore the possible symbolic significance of what I had observed until I had returned from the field, and it has not been possible, therefore, to learn to what extent these notions are in error, or even, perhaps, made explicit by the Tsembaga.

It may be that the entire eel ritual symbolizes the procreative act, to which it bears some detailed correspondences. The young men and boys first gathered the captured eels, which are said to be the pigs of *koipa maŋgiaŋ*, a spirit who lives in streams and who, like the water in which he lives, is explicitly associated with fertility. They carry the eels up a newly cut path through an archway where they are met by women. It is not far-fetched to regard this as sexual penetration. It is further not implausible to regard the flailing of the carcasses of the female pigs with the eels as orgasm and fertilization, with the pigs representing the female contribution to the foetus and the eels the male. Gestation is perhaps symbolized by hanging the wealth (so that it may increase) with the eels in the *timbi* house, and by cooking the eels with the pig bellies overnight. It is also significant that the path up which the young men carry the eels *must* be a new one; this suggests defloration.

The ritual, in total, seems to me to symbolize a process of cosmic procreation, a new fertilization of both the human population and those populations of plants and animals upon which the human population most heavily depends. As such, the place of this ritual in inaugurating a *new* ritual cycle becomes apparent.

The flesh of animals dedicated to the red spirits, contributing between 1,900 and 2,400 pounds of pork to the total, was retained by the Tsembaga, as were the entrails, heads, and sometimes other parts of some of the animals dedicated to the spirits of the low ground. Exact calculation is impossible, but it may be estimated that the Tsembaga kept for themselves approximately one third, or between 2,275 and 2,635 pounds, of the pork resulting from the slaughter of their animals. This estimate of 11 to 13 pounds of pork available for every Tsembaga man, woman, and child may be lowered by about a pound per capita in consideration of the presentations made to my household. Consumption continued for five days; the meat was preserved by being suspended over fires.

The remaining 4,475 to 5,965 pounds of pork were given to members of other local populations in at least 163 separate presentations in amounts ranging from several pounds of fat or flesh to entire animals. While members of 17 other local populations were among the recipients, the Tuguma, Auŋdagai, Kauwasi, and Monambant received much the greatest part of this pork. The recipients, of course, redistributed their portions to members of their own and other groups. Almost all Tuguma, Auŋdagai, Kauwasi, and Monambant, totaling in population about 2,000, must have received some Tsembaga pig, and it is not unlikely that over 3,000 people eventually received portions from the Tsembaga slaughter.

Seventy-five animals survived the slaughter of November 7 and 8. Of these, forty were infants and juveniles, twenty-five were adolescents (weighing 96 to 120 pounds) and ten were adults (120 to 200 pounds). Of the adults, four survived sacrifice only because they had escaped to the forest and remained marked for imminent killing, two were being saved for the Tuguma *kaiko*, one belonged to a young man who was away at work and would be killed upon his return, and two were spared because, having just littered, they were thin and therefore considered to be unfit for sacrifice. Of the adolescent animals, at least four were being held for presentations to affines, with whom food taboos still prevailed at the termination of the *kaiko*. While those who had taken refuge in Kauwasi and Monambant formally abrogated the taboos on each other's foodstuffs, those who had Kauwasi or Monambant parents or grandparents were to maintain these taboos until the Monambant uprooted their *rumbim*.

The Kauwasi finished their *kaiko* between one and two years before the Tsembaga began theirs. Several of the other adolescent animals, informants said, were to be killed for the uprooting of the *rumbim* in Monambant two or three months after the Tsembaga slaughter.[14] In short, at least fifteen of the surviving pigs were scheduled for slaughter in the near future, and the surviving herd might better be regarded as comprising sixty animals averaging 60 to 75 pounds each rather than seventy-five animals.

PRESENTATION OF VALUABLES

The *konj kaiko* is the occasion for wiping the slate clean of obligations to the living as well as to the spirits, and in addition to the pork distribution, twenty-four prestations or exchanges of valuables took place at the Tsembaga *konj kaiko*.

Fourteen prestations, ranging in quantity from six to forty-two items, were made to affines for living wives or for living children that their wives had born. Two death payments were also made to affines. In one instance the brother of a woman dead over twenty years was given thirteen objects. In the other a young man made a payment for the death of his brother to his mother's clan. In addition, three exactly equivalent exchanges of valuables took place in reference to old Tsembaga women. Such exchanges between a woman's sons and her brothers or brothers' sons, end the series of payments and nonequivalent exchanges that begin shortly after marriage.

Other kinds of payments also took place. Two men who had not done so previously made prestations to men who had given them land during the exile of 1953–56, and two prestations were made in appreciation of certain services rendered. In one of these the recipient was being rewarded for carrying home from the battle ground the corpse of the donor's father. In the other a man made a small prestation to the local government-appointed head man for bringing food to his wife when a government medical patrol ordered her into the Simbai patrol post infirmary.

14. The Monambant are a Jimi Valley group. The annual cycle of plant development is somewhat different in the Jimi and Simbai Valleys, and *kaiko* in the Jimi Valley are likely to begin and end in January or February, rather than in October or November.

In one instance members of one clan "bought out" the rights of another to a young girl. Upon the death of her father, a member of the Tsembaga clan, her mother had taken up residence with her own brothers, members of another local clan, the Kamaŋgagai. Members of her deceased father's clan, wanting eventually to exchange her for a woman for one of their own boys, but recognizing that her mother's clan had rights to her because they had raised her, made a substantial payment (nine valuables) for her to her mother's brothers and their sons.

Seventeen of the twenty-four transactions were between Tsembaga and members of other local populations. I know of no instance in which a man obligated to a member of another local population did not succeed in making the payments expected of him, although in one case the amount was thought by the donor to be almost shamefully small.

It has already been suggested that the ability to stage a *kaiko* indicates the viability of the local population as an ecological and demographic unit. By fulfilling their affinal and other obligations at the *konj kaiko* through gifts of items of wealth, the members of a local population demonstrate that they comprise a viable unit in the supralocal exchange network as well.

THE KONJ KAIKO

The pig festival comes to its climax in the *konj kaiko*, when salted pig belly is publicly presented to allies and the *pave*, the ceremonial fence, is breached.

Many members of other local populations had been among the Tsembaga while the pigs were slaughtered, and during the following day many more people poured in, both in dancing formations and as individuals, from all friendly groups. By mid-afternoon the dance ground was packed with spectators and dancers; attendance may well have exceeded one thousand people by the time that the heroes' portions of salted pig belly were presented.

In the late afternoon all of the Tsembaga, with the exception of married or widowed women and infants in arms, assembled inside the *pave* enclosure and the presentation packages of salted fat were heaped behind the *pave* window. Several men climbed to the top of the structure and from there proclaimed one by one to the multitude the names and clans of the men being honored. As his name was called, each honored man charged toward the *pave* window swinging his ax and shouting. His supporters, yelling battle cries, beating drums, brandishing weapons, followed close behind him. At the window the mouth of the honored man was stuffed with cold salted belly fat by the Tsembaga whom he had come to help in the last fight and who now also passed out to him through the window a package containing additional salted belly for his followers. With the belly fat hanging from his mouth the hero now retired, his supporters close behind him, shouting, singing, beating their drums, dancing. Honored name quickly followed honored name, and groups charging toward the window sometimes became entangled with those retiring.

Between twenty-five and thirty men were publicly honored by presentations from the *pave*. Their number did not include all of those who had assisted the Tsembaga militarily in the last fight, but rather those members of other groups to whom Tsembaga were directly connected through kinship or trade and through whom support had been mobilized, as well as others who had sustained wounds and the sons of those slain. A rough order of precedence prevails, with the wounded and sons of the slain being called first. To be called last is sometimes considered an insult by the recipient, and the Tuguma who found himself in this position refused his portion. Although the Tsembaga *kaiko* was unmarred by such a conflict, it is sometimes the case that members of one local population may become angered if members of another are called before them. Vayda was witness to such a development in 1962 at the *kaiko* of the Kandambent-Namikai, at which the members of the Fungai-Korama group not only refused their pig belly but departed early.

After the presentations were completed, the visitors resumed dancing. The Tsembaga, however, still remained inside the *pave* enclosure, a section of which they now began to push down. As it fell, the men, led by those wearing *mamp gunč*, charged through the breach pounding their drums. They were followed by the unmarried girls. As they emerged the Tsembaga became a dancing formation, one of the many on the dance ground. Breaching the *pave* and subsequently dancing with contingents of friends and allies expressed, it may be suggested, breaking through the confines of debt and taboo that had long separated them from other groups.[15]

All that now remained to conclude the *kaiko* was to dig up the root of the *dawa* variety of *rumbim*, which was buried by the gate when the dance ground was built. This was quickly done, and one of the fight magic men took it and ran off the dance ground, dangling it from a string. All the Tsembaga followed him to a nearby bluff, where he disposed of it. This site overlooks enemy territory and it was in the direction of the enemy that the *rumbim* root was thrown. Then the Tsembaga removed leaves of the *rumbim* variety, *kamp,* from their buttock coverings and flung them after the exhumed root, calling out the names of enemy men and yelling, "We have finished our *kaiko,* we are here." Dancing continued through the night, and next morning, after a massive trading session, the crowd departed and the five young men, without ceremony, cut off their *mamp gunč.* The *kaiko* was finished.

THE TERMINATION OF THE TRUCE AND
THE ESTABLISHMENT OF PEACE

With the termination of the *kaiko* truces that have prevailed since the last fight are also terminated, and in former times warfare usually broke out again in short order. The fighting in late 1953 or early 1954, for instance, began within three months of the end of a Tsembaga *kaiko.*

There are, however, means for reestablishing permanent peace. Peace has been made among Maring groups only very few times within the memories of even the oldest informants, and statements concerning the details of the procedure are vague and conflicting. In another publication (Rappaport, 1967) I outlined what I understood to be the practice more definitively than seems to be warranted now in light of more recent inquiries made by A. P. and Cherry Vayda. I shall first repeat my earlier account, then note the details in which it is likely to be erroneous or at least questionable.

The wreckage of the *pave* is not cleared away at the end of the *kaiko* but is allowed to rot. Its complete dissolution is said to take two to three years, about the length of time, it may be noted, that

15. In light of the previous day's eel ritual, it may have symbolized the rebirth of the local population as well.

it takes to raise a pig to full size. If fighting has not broken out by this time all adult and adolescent pigs are killed and *rumbim* and *amame* are planted after a ritual called "*pave gui*" ("black," "dead," or "rotted" *pave*). The pig herd is again allowed to reach the limits of toleration but, before the uprooting of the *rumbim*, peace-making ceremonies are jointly held by the erstwhile enemies. I shall return to these shortly.

I derived this outline, in reasonably coherent form, from the account of a single informant, a knowledgeable man, but by his own statement too young to be speaking from first-hand experience. However, it seemed to jibe with the statements of other informants, gratuitously volunteered earlier in my fieldwork, that *rumbim* would again be planted in several years (although some Tsembaga said that because of the government presence *rumbim* would never be planted again), and with the report that the Kauwasi, who had completed their *kaiko* in 1961 had *rumbim* in the ground in 1963. Because I received this information on almost the last day of my fieldwork I did not have the opportunity to investigate the matter further.

Inquiries made later by the Vaydas indicate that *pave gui* is performed to benefit the fertility and growth of pigs and requires the sacrifice of some animals, but fewer than I understood to be the case. Furthermore, they were informed that *rumbim* is not planted during or after this ceremony. Even my informant, when questioned by them, denied that *rumbim* was planted at *pave gui*. He had either been corrected between the time he spoke to me and to the Vaydas, or I misunderstood him. At any rate, it is probably the case that my earlier statement concerning this matter is incorrect.

Informants do agree, however, that peace-making rituals are put off until the pig herds of the antagonists are of large, perhaps maximal, size. This is in accordance with informants' statements to me that soon after peace is made the erstwhile antagonists attend each other's *kaiko*, and the rule I stated in the earlier publication seems generally to hold: if a pair of antagonists are able to proceed through two ritual cycles without the resumption of hostilities, they may make peace. It should be made clear, in qualification of this rule, that the rituals constituting the second cycle would be somewhat different from those constituting the first, and that the *kaiko* ending the second are, according to some informants, less elaborate. Furthermore, it is not clear that truce is assured by ritual means during the second cycle. The duration of both cycles, however, is a function of the demography of the pig herds of both parties.

Data concerning the details of the actual peace-making ritual are also deficient. Informants do agree, however, that the two sides, after each consults its own ancestors and offers them sacrifices of pig, convene at their common border where they exchange pig livers. Only those whose mothers or, in the case of long-standing enmities, those whose grandparents were members of the enemy group may eat these pig livers. The interdining taboos under which other members of the two populations labor are abrogated over four generations in accordance with the procedures described earlier.

Women are also exchanged or promised at this time. These women are explicitly regarded as "*wump*" (planting material), through which the slain can be replaced, and the children they bear are named after those whom their brothers, fathers, or grandfathers have killed. Ideally one woman should be given for each of the slain, but the Tsembaga say that this will not be possible when peace is made with the Kundagai, for the deaths have been too many. They add that many women bear more than one child, however, and it will not take many years for all the slain to be replaced by children bearing their names.

The peace-making procedure thus not only terminates the old enmity; it also, through the requirement that women be exchanged, establishes ties between former enemies. The number of new ties established by marriage is likely to be directly correlated with the severity of the former enmity, as measured by the number of deaths each of the participants has suffered at the other's hands, even when the ideal of one woman for each dead man cannot be realized.

THE RITUAL CYCLE AND AREAL INTEGRATION

The role of the ritual cycles of the Maring in interlocal relations bears upon recent discussions of areal integration in Melanesia. These discussions have focused mainly upon the ways in which the movement of goods either in trade (Schwartz, 1962) or in ceremonial exchanges (Bulmer, 1960; Salisbury, 1962) bind together groups who recognize no common superordinate authority. That the exchange system of the Maring, in which the *kaiko* is implicated, operates, like those described by other authors, to integrate all or many of the groups in an area has been implicit here. The ritual cycles of the Maring, however, provide more than a means for elaborating the relationships that arise out of economic interdependence or for formalizing in ceremonial exchanges noneconomic interdependence. When attacks may be launched, land annexed, affiliation of personnel changed, and truce or peace established are all specified in terms of the completion of events that form components of the ritual cycle. It has been shown, in turn, that the completion of these ritual events reflects the state of the relationships of the local population to both human and nonhuman components of their environment. Events in the cycle, furthermore, particularly during the *kaiko* itself, serve to assemble, bind together, and transmit information among the autonomous local populations forming the supralocal aggregates that will participate in the exercise of force. In short, the ritual cycles of the Maring provide both a means for aggregating groups of supralocal magnitude for forceful enterprises and a set of conventions governing these enterprises.

The numbers of persons whose activities are articulated through the ritual cycle of any local population are substantial. It was estimated that over 1,000 persons were present at Tsembaga for the culmination of the *kaiko*, and the groups from which dancing contingents were entertained during the course of the festival totaled over 3,000. Tsembaga pork, it was estimated, also reached 3,000 people. Simply in terms of the numbers of people involved, the aggregations formed by ritual cycles rival some of the hierarchical structures of Polynesia. The Polynesian chiefdoms may also be rivaled in the frequency with which large numbers of people are mobilized for joint activities. Information presented by Marshall Sahlins (1958:132) concerning ceremonial food redistributions in Polynesia, for instance, indicates that these events may not have occurred more often on some islands than once a year. While the *kaiko* of any local population of Maring occur with less than annual frequency, it is not unlikely that in most years a local population would be the beneficiary of a distribution arising from the *kaiko* of another group.

There are, of course, important differences between the organizations of Polynesia and the organization of the Maring. In the hier-archical, centralized organizations of Polynesia, it is reasonable to as-sume, system regulation was accomplished through the activities of discrete authorities, chiefs, to whom flowed information concerning system-endangering changes in the values of variables forming com-ponents of the system, and from whom flowed directives meant to return these values to safe levels. Among the Maring a consensus concerning whether or not the states of variables are in fact en-dangering the system must be reached, but when it is, corrective action, in accord with the conventions of the ritual cycle, follows more or less automatically. To put it in slightly different terms, the locus of the *total* ordering function in the Polynesian chiefdom is in a discrete human authority, the chief, who both *detects* deviations of variables from "safe" levels and initiates *corrective* action. Among the Maring, however, the locus of the *detecting* function is diffuse; the signals (in the form of overwork, garden damage, etc.) are re-ceived or experienced by many people and finally produce con-sensus that there has indeed been some system-endangering change in the state of a variable. The locus of the *correcting* function is in the ritual cycle. But in light of the fact that the activities of large num-bers of people are articulated by both the highly centralized Poly-nesian organization and the acephalous organization of the Maring, we may ask what are the factors that account for the development or evolution of these two types of organization; in what ways might they affect differently the ecosystems in which they exist; what pre-cisely are the differences in their capacities for articulating the activ-ities of large numbers of people; where lie their comparative strengths and weaknesses. Similar questions have been posed re-cently by Sahlins (1963) and Schwartz (1962). These questions require further research. It may be suggested, however, that the Polynesian form of system regulation is considerably more sensitive than the Maring.

First, the strength of the signal required to initiate corrective ac-tion in the chiefdom can be considerably weaker than is likely to be required in the Maring system, for only one man, and not the number of people sufficient to form a consensus, need detect system-endangering trends in the states of variables. Second, a variety of corrective programs, differing from each other both formally and in magnitude, may be initiated by the chief, in contrast to the stereotyped ritual response of the Maring. In short, Polynesian system regulation operates more rapidly and more flexibly than that of the Maring. This might permit the tighter and more continuous coordination of the activities of larger numbers of people than is possible among the Maring. It might also be argued that more sensitive system regulation, such as that found in Polynesia, might avoid the wide fluctuations in the value of variables noted in the Maring area (e.g., in the size of pig herds and the amounts of land in cultivation). It must be emphasized, however, that in the Maring case the fluctuations themselves are of great value, for they are critically important in the regulation of intergroup relations.

Maring system regulation also has its advantages. No special personnel, such as chiefs and their retainers, with elaborate requirements (sumptuary goods, elaborate assembly structures, and the like) need be supported. Furthermore, the corrective responses set by the conventions of the ritual cycle, although they are slow and stereotyped, have a certain merit, given a more or less stable cultural environment: they provide little room for human error. It may also be suggested that it is their very inflexibility that makes it possible for ritual cycles to regulate relationships between autonomous local groups, particularly in respect to warfare.

CHAPTER 6

Ritual and the Regulation of Ecological Systems

The place of ritual in the ecology of the Tsembaga has been the focus of this study. In the earlier chapters the material relations of the Tsembaga with their environment were described, and in the preceding chapter the regulatory functions of ritual were discussed. The Tsembaga ritual cycle has been regarded as a complex homeostatic mechanism, operating to maintain the values of a number of variables within "goal ranges" (ranges of values that permit the perpetuation of a system, as constituted, through indefinite periods of time). It has been argued that the regulatory function of ritual among the Tsembaga and other Maring helps to maintain an undegraded environment, limits fighting to frequencies that do not endanger the existence of the regional population, adjusts man-land ratios, facilitates trade, distributes local surpluses of pig in the form of pork throughout the regional population, and assures people of high-quality protein when they most need it.

Despite the importance attached to religious ritual, which is, so far as we know, a specifically human phenomenon, the frame of reference within which it and other components of culture have been viewed in this study has been borrowed from animal ecology. The Tsembaga, designated a "local population," have been regarded as a population in the animal ecologist's sense: a unit composed of an aggregate of organisms having in common certain distinctive means whereby they maintain a set of shared trophic relations with other living and nonliving components of the biotic community in which they exist together.

Tsembaga territory, moreover, has been regarded as an ecosystem, a demarcated portion of the biosphere that includes living organisms and nonliving substances interacting to produce a systemic exchange of materials among the living components and between the living components and the nonliving substances. This demarcation was guided by particular analytic goals but it is not completely arbitrary. Ecosystems are defined in terms of trophic exchange, and the Tsembaga alone among humans are directly involved in trophic exchanges with the nonhuman entities with which they share their territory. Conversely, the Tsembaga are not directly involved in trophic exchanges with nonhuman entities in the territories of other local populations. This demarcation of ecosystem boundaries is not unduly anthropocentric, for the cycle of materials in which trophic exchanges result is generally highly localized in tropical rain forests.

Although it is possible, through the application of criteria borrowed from animal ecology, to designate the territory of the local group as an ecosystem, it must not be forgotten that the environment of any local human group is likely to include more than those entities in its immediate locality upon which it subsists and which subsist upon it. Other components of the external world affect its survival and well-being in other ways. Neighboring human groups are hardly less significant to Tsembaga survival than the secondary forest in which they plant their gardens and are perhaps more significant than the primary forest in which they trap marsupials. As they participate in a set of trophic exchanges with the members of other species with which they share their territory, so do they exchange genetic materials, personnel, and goods with members of other local populations occupying other territories. Furthermore, it is within this larger field that land is redistributed through warfare. These supralocal relations, it seems to me, can hardly be ignored in ecological analyses, and I have given them as much attention in this study as the more localized trophic relations.

The concept of the ecosystem, however, which provides a convenient frame or model for the analysis of trophic exchanges between ecologically dissimilar populations occupying single localities can accommodate only by the introduction of analogy nontrophic material exchanges between ecologically similar populations occupying separate localities. Instead of extending the concept of the ecosystem (a system of localized trophic exchanges) to include (typically nontrophic) exchanges between distinct local populations of humans exploiting separate areas, I suggest that we recognize that local populations of humans (and many other species as well) are also likely to participate in regional systems. These systems, as I have already indicated, will include among their most important components the several local human populations that occupy distinct areas within general regions. Such aggregates of local populations may be called "regional populations."

It is worth noting that regional populations—aggregates distinguished by the criteria of regional continuity and exchanges of personnel, genetic material, and goods—may in some instances be more or less coterminous with other aggregates distinguished by anthropologists, ethologists, and geneticists by application of other criteria. These are "societies," aggregates of organisms that interact according to common sets of conventions; and "breeding populations," aggregates of interbreeding organisms capable of persisting through an indefinite number of generations in isolation from similar aggregates of the same species. Societies, breeding populations, and regional populations are similar in that they are likely to persist and evolve through long periods of time while their constituent subunits (such as the Tsembaga) are relatively ephemeral. It may be, therefore, that in long-range evolutionary studies these more inclusive aggregates, rather than one or another of their constituent subunits, should be central to the analysis.

It is as difficult to establish boundaries for the regional population as it is for the society or breeding population by any nonarbitrary means. Therefore we can only say that these differently defined aggregates may, in some instances, be roughly coterminous. The notion of clines may be as useful in social and ecological anthropology as in genetic inquiry, but in a study such as this we are concerned only with the ways in which a single local population relates to others of its kind during a particular period in its history, and precise definition of the extent of the regional population is not necessary. It is sufficient to note that the regional population of which the Tsembaga are a constituent unit includes the Maring speakers and their neighbors.

The analytic strategy I have followed in this study involves, then, the discrimination of two systems, the ecosystem and the regional system, with the local population participating in both.[1] I believe that this procedure has certain advantages. First, it protects the power of the ecosystem concept by preserving it from the analogies that would inevitably become necessary if it were extended to include all external relations of human groups. Second, it enhances the utility of the ecosystem concept by enabling us to designate as ecological (local) populations and ecosystems units of sufficiently small size to permit convenient quantitative analysis. These can often be "natural units," units with an existence independent of our discrimination, such as recognized social groups and their land holdings. In this study, named local communities were taken to be populations and the areas they exploit in subsistence activities as ecosystems. Because of poor group or territorial definition, economic complexity, or other reasons it may not always be possible to find such convenient natural units, but where it is possible the advantages may transcend mere convenience. It has already been mentioned, for instance, that the Tsembaga and coordinate groups, being territorial, are in fact the most inclusive human groups directly involved in trophic exchanges within the Maring area. Therefore, their identification as local populations has descriptive validity as well as analytic utility, for it reflects the manner in which the Maring and their neighbors are distributed in space and in relation to their resources.

The discrimination of the regional system and the ecosystem also aids us in illuminating the systemic functions of certain cultural phenomena. I have distinguished the regional system from the ecosystem by differences in the material exchanges that typify them. These differences imply a more abstract criterion by which the two systems may be distinguished: the criterion of internal coherence.

Fully coherent systems are those in which a change in the state of any single component immediately results in proportional

1. I believe that the discrimination of two (sub) systems is sufficient to accommodate the relatively simple Maring ecology, but I recognize that other, more complex, situations might well require more elaborate discriminations.

For example, in the case of a coral atoll, it might be analytically useful to designate that portion of the biosphere within which the human population is directly involved in trophic exchange as the "immediate environment," and to regard it to include three more or less distinct ecosystems, the terrestrial, the reef-lagoon, and the open sea. Such a procedure would recognize both the important differences in the biotic communities in the three areas, and differences in man's participation in them.

Similarly, it may sometimes be necessary or useful to regard the "nonimmediate" environment to be composed of several regional exchange systems.

changes in the states of all other components. At the opposite extreme are completely incoherent systems, for which the term "heap" is sometimes used; the state of any entity in the heap may vary without affecting the states of any of the others. It is obvious that no system in which organisms participate which is not trivial to their survival can be completely incoherent. Conversely, too much coherence may also endanger the survival of participating organisms.

So far as I know no measures of coherence have been devised; nevertheless we may discern in nature collections of entities that affect each other more markedly and more rapidly than they affect or are affected by others. Individual organisms, for instance, show great internal coherence, but less coherence with respect to entities external to themselves. I believe that a high degree of internal coherence also characterizes the ecosystem on the one hand and the regional system on the other, and that it is therefore legitimate to distinguish them from each other.

Nevertheless, the systemic discontinuities that enable us to distinguish sets of highly coherent phenomena from each other (and designate them as systems) are only relative. Nature is continuous, and the several systems one may establish are not likely to be independent of each other. For one thing, they are likely to share some components, and, through these, events in one system eventually are likely to affect events in others. In this study events in the separate ecosystems of the local populations eventually affect the regional system, and vice versa. Since this is the case, the systems we discriminate by application of material criteria, such as types of exchange, or abstract criteria, such as coherence, are properly regarded to be *subsystems* of larger systems that together they comprise.

I would suggest that the strategy of distinguishing subsystems has more general applicability than the ecological use to which it has been put here. It has been useful in this study to distinguish two subsystems, but doubtless several could be distinguished among the phenomena considered in any ethnographic study, and important questions would follow. How are the various subsystems in which any human aggregate participates articulated? That is, through what mechanisms do changes in one subsystem effect changes in others? What items in the culture are involved? Are the effects of changes in one subsystem reflected in others continuously, periodically, or only when some threshold value is transgressed? In the subsystems that are involved, are the changes proportional? "Classical" functionalism, with its assumption of the interrelatedness of phenomena, generally has been concerned with questions similar to these. It can nevertheless be asserted that the search for mechanisms that articulate subsystems and the elucidation of how such mechanisms work can be made more strictly operational by specifying as precisely as possible the subsystems that are in fact being articulated.

It has been argued in this study that Maring ritual is of great importance in articulating the local and regional subsystems. The timing of the ritual cycle is largely dependent upon changes in the states of components of the local ecosystem. But the *kaiko*, which culminates the ritual cycle, does more than reverse changes that have taken place in this subsystem. It also affects relations among the components of the regional subsystem. During its performance obligations to other local populations are fulfilled, support for future military enterprises is rallied, land from which enemies have earlier been driven is occupied, and the movement of goods and women is stimulated. Completion of the *kaiko* permits the local population to initiate warfare again. Conversely, warfare is terminated by the *rumbim*-planting ritual that prohibits the reinitiation of warfare until the state of the local ecosystem allows the *kaiko* to again be staged and completed; participation in the *rumbim* planting also ratifies the connection of men to local populations to which they were not previously affiliated.

Maring ritual, in short, operates not only as a homeostat—maintaining a number of variables that comprise the total system within ranges of viability—but also as a transducer—"translating" changes in the state of one subsystem into information and energy that can produce changes in the second subsystem. It should be recalled here that the transduction operation of the ritual cycle is such that the participation of local populations in respect to warfare, which is important in the redistribution of land and personnel but is also dangerous, is not continuous. It could therefore be argued that the ritual transducer maintains coherence between subsystems at levels above or below which the perpetuation of the total system might be endangered.

In the functional and cybernetic analysis of the ecological relations of the Tsembaga that has been attempted here, variables have been abstracted from events or entities in the physical world and treated as components of an analytic system. If the method of functional analysis is to meet the criticisms of Hemple (1959) and others, quantitative values must be assigned to all variables, and in the case of those variables that define the adequate functioning of the system their tolerable ranges of values must also be specified.

This study, however, has left some variables unquantified. No values were assigned, for instance, to the frequency of warfare, much less to its tolerable limit. While upper limits were assigned to the tolerable range of size of the human and pig populations, lower limits were not. It was suggested that a population's tolerance for the destructiveness of pigs is limited, but this limit was not assigned any quantitative value. Since these and other quantitative data are lacking, this study remains in part what Collins (1965) terms an "explanatory sketch."

Appropriate cautions about the reliability of values assigned to variables were issued or were implicit in the course of discussion as the values were assigned, and the methods by which the values were derived have been spelled out in the appendices. It bears repeating, however, that the measuring techniques were sometimes crude and in some instances statistically insufficient. It should be kept in mind that these data result from the efforts of an anthropologist without special training in such fields as botany, nutrition, physiology, and surveying. To point this out is neither to defend nor to denigrate the worth of the data. It is simply to characterize them and to draw attention to the need, if ecological studies are to show increased refinement, for anthropologists either to broaden their training or to be supported by personnel with training in other fields.

The systemic role of ritual in the ecology of the Tsembaga has been the focus of this study and I have offered no suggestions concerning the origin of these rituals or any of the other phenomena described here. As Durkheim pointed out in 1895:

> To show how a fact is useful is not to explain how it originated or why it is what it is. The uses which it serves presuppose the specific properties characterizing it but do not

create them. The need we have of things cannot give them existence, nor can it confer their specific nature upon them. It is to causes of another sort that they owe their existence. [1938:90]

It may be mentioned, however, that ritual components that are formally similar to those of the Tsembaga are found among other New Guinea highland groups. Massive pig slaughters are, of course, widespread, and such elements as "red spirits," ceremonial fences, and structures resembling *timbi* houses have been reported for a number of groups (Bulmer, 1965; Luzbetak, 1954; Read, 1955; Reay, 1959; Newman, 1964). The ritual use of *Cordyline fruticosa* is also extremely widespread, being found as far away as the Philippines (H. C. Conklin, personal communication). The way these components are arranged in particular events and in particular ritual cycles, however, seems to show considerable variation. The data are not sufficient, but it may be suggested, in light of the functions of ritual among the Tsembaga, that ritual regulation may be widespread in New Guinea, and that variations in ritual may be the result of changes brought about by differences in the ecological circumstances of various populations. Random cultural changes, analogous to gene drift, may of course be involved, but it is not implausible to suggest that as variables and the relations among them change so do the mechanisms that regulate them.

Another point should be made explicit here. This study has been concerned with aspects of Tsembaga and Maring environment, physiology, demography, psychology, the economic, social, and political structure, and religion: phenomena falling into classes that have frequently been assigned to several ontological "levels" (inorganic, organic, superorganic). Some social scientists have argued strongly that events or processes occurring in each level are essentially autonomous in respect to events and processes occurring on other levels, and that explanations that cut across levels are either reductionistic or the opposite.

The notion of levels has been a useful device for organizing science, dividing the study of nature, so to speak, among the various disciplines. The sociologist O. D. Duncan has recently recognized the importance of the concept of levels in the sociology of science, stating, somewhat pejoratively, that "its major contribution to the history of ideas has been to confer legitimacy upon the newer scientific approaches to the empirical world that, when they were emerging, had good use for any kind of ideological support" (1961: 141).

Duncan is perhaps too harsh. In addition to its usefulness in the organization of science, the concept of levels may also be of use in the ordering of data, particularly when explanations of form are sought. But at best it is only one way of ordering data. The concept of the system, which presupposes the interdependent variation of a number of elements, is another. Those who would argue for the functional autonomy of levels apparently assume that organic phenomena, for example, as a general class show greater internal coherence than do any of its members (e.g. organisms, populations) with superorganic, or cultural, phenomena. It seems to me that such a position confuses ontological status with systemic interrelations—confuses what things are "made out of" with causes and effects of their behavior. Systems discovered in or abstracted from relationships observed in nature may, and frequently do, cut across ontologically defined levels.

"Manifest" and "latent" functions have been suggested for many of the rituals discussed in this study. Some of these proposals, particularly those concerned with the role of ritual and taboo in the containment of conflict, have been in the nature of post facto interpretations of observed or reported events and are probably difficult to validate empirically. As such, they are vulnerable to the criticisms leveled against "classical" functional analysis by such writers as Carl Hempel (1959). But these suggestions have been only incidental to the main concern of this study. The emphasis here has been upon the homeostatic function of ritual, and upon the ways in which it links subsystems.

Religion as a homeostatic mechanism has been discussed by Miller (1964), who argues against a growing tendency to discriminate in human phenomena separate ontologically defined "systems" (e.g. cultural system vs. social system, religious system vs. secular system) and states that "cultures are the viable systems for study, and are the *only* wholes we can isolate. Cultures have a 'command pattern,' a structure which is extended throughout the system . . . and keeps it viable as a system" (p. 94, his italics). "Command" is earlier defined as "the locus of the ordering operation," and is identified by Miller with religion.

That ritual and the understandings that elicit ritual behavior comprise the "locus of the ordering operation" in the systemic relationships with which this study has been concerned does not need further reiteration. The examination of the role of ritual among the Tsembaga would suggest disagreement only with Miller's assertion that "cultures are the viable systems for study, and are the *only* wholes we can isolate." Culture has been regarded here not as itself a whole, but as a part of the distinctive means by which a local population maintains itself in an ecosystem and by which a regional population maintains and coordinates its groups and distributes them over the available land. That which is regulated by the command pattern of belief and ritual does not consist merely of the interrelations of other components of the culture, but also includes biological interactions among organisms not all of which are human. Indeed, it would not be improper to refer to the Tsembaga and the other entities with which they share their territory as a "ritually regulated ecosystem," and to the Tsembaga and their human neighbors as a "ritually regulated population."

In light of the analysis presented in this study it may be asked whether rituals have peculiar virtues that make them particularly well suited to function as homeostats and transducers. I can offer only brief and highly speculative suggestions here.

It is worth noting, first, that in mechanical, electronic, and physiological systems, in which the states of other components may vary through a continuous range, the range of states of the regulating mechanism is frequently limited to two. A thermostat, for instance, is basically a switch that, in response to a particular amount of change in the medium in which it is immersed, goes "on" or "off," thus activating or deactivating a source of heat. If we were to represent a heating system in the abstract we would regard the thermostat as a two-valued, or binary, variable, while the other components of the system would be treated as continuous, or many-valued, variables. One of the great advantages of the binary regulating device is simplicity. Indeed, its response to the continuously changing states of other components of the system is the simplest conceivable:

if these changes exceed certain limits, the binary mechanism switches from one to the other of its two possible values.

It may be that the very simplicity of the binary mechanism minimizes the likelihood of its breakdown, but a more important aspect of binary operation has already been suggested in another context. Binary control eliminates the possibility of error from one phase of system operation: an inappropriate response cannot be selected from a set of possible responses because the set of possible responses has only one member. To put it in anthropomorphic terms, the regulating mechanism, once it receives a signal that a variable has transgressed its tolerable range, does not have to decide what to do. It can do only one thing or nothing at all.

Like thermostats, rituals have a binary aspect. As the thermostat switches on and off, affecting the amount of heat produced by the furnace and the temperature of the medium, so the rituals of the Tsembaga are initiated and completed, affecting the size of the pig population, the amount of land under cultivation, the amount of labor expended, the frequency of warfare, and other components of the system. The programs that should be undertaken to correct the deviation of variables from their acceptable ranges are fixed. All that need be decided is whether in fact deviations have occurred. The Tsembaga reach such decisions through discussion and then the formation of a consensus.

It must be recognized that while Maring ritual regulation enjoys the advantages of simplicity, it also suffers from simplicity's limitations. Consensus regarding a deviation from acceptable conditions is likely to be slow to form and the programs initiated to correct such changes are inflexible and unlikely to be proportional to the deviation. In a stable environment slow and inflexible regulation may not produce serious problems, but the novel circumstances that are continuously presented by rapidly changing environments may require more rapid and flexible regulation.

The binary aspect of rituals is also important with respect to their role as transducers. The mere occurrence of a ritual can be regarded as a signal. Since a ritual can, at a particular time, only be occurring or not occurring, its occurrence transmits binary information.[2] Binary

2. It was only when this study was already in proof that I read Anthony F. C. Wallace's *Religion: An Anthropological View*. Wallace states (p. 233) that "ritual

information is qualitative in that it is information of a "yes-no," rather than a "more-less," sort. The performance of a ritual, however, may depend, as many Maring rituals do, upon a complex set of quantitative relationships among many variables. Thus, *the occurrence of the ritual may be a simple qualitative representation of complex quantitative information.*

The importance of this aspect of ritual function may be illustrated by reference to the uprooting of *rumbim*. This ritual can be regarded as a statement concerning the complex of quantitative conditions prevailing in a local subsystem (ecosystem) at a particular time. Now the quantitative information that the qualitative ritual statement (uprooting the *rumbim*) summarizes is not available to populations other than the one performing the ritual, and even if it were it would be subject to perhaps erroneous interpretation. Being summarized are not merely the constantly fluctuating values of a number of separate variables but the continually changing relationships among these variables. It would be difficult indeed to translate quantitative information concerning the constantly fluctuating state of the local subsystem directly into terms that would be meaningful to other populations in the regional subsystem. The information would be ambiguous at best. But this difficulty is overcome if a mechanism is available to summarize the quantitative information and translate it into a qualitative signal.

Uprooting the *rumbim* is such a mechanism. The virtue of this ritual is that it signals *unambiguously* that the local subsystem has achieved a certain state, and that, therefore, the local population may now undertake previously proscribed actions that are likely to affect the regional subsystem. The absence of ambiguity from this message derives from the binary character of the ritual trans-

---

may . . . be classified as communication without information: . . . each ritual is a particular sequence of signals which, once announced, allows no uncertainty, no choice, and hence, in the statistical sense of information theory, conveys no information from sender to receiver." My discussion here does not refer to the sequence of signals *within* a ritual. It takes the *occurrence* of the ritual to be a signal. I am arguing that the occurrence of a ritual, even one that occupies a particular position in a fixed sequence of rituals, does convey information if (1) the time of its occurrence is not calendrically fixed or (2) if the time of its occurrence is not separated by a standard interval from the preceding or subsequent ritual in the sequence. Despite this possible disagreement the remainder of this discussion, as well as preceding ones (particularly that concerning *Kaiko* as display), would have benefited from a consideration of Wallace's enlightening study.

duction device, which reduces a great complex mass of "more-less" information to a simple "yes-no" statement. It is interesting to note here that control transduction in physiological systems may rely heavily upon binary mechanisms and information (Goldman, 1958: 116ff).

Binary mechanisms thus make suitable regulators and transducers. But why is it that such mechanisms should be embedded in religious practice? In other words, what advantages does sanctity confer upon transducers and homeostats? As far as transduction is concerned, I can only elaborate here a suggestion made earlier in the discussion of ritual as display. A ritual, such as uprooting the *rumbim*, has only a conventional relationship to the ecosystemic state that it is taken to represent. As such, it can be regarded as a symbol. Any form of communication that employs symbols can accommodate lies. But a ritual is not only an act of communication; it is also a sacred performance. Although sanctity inheres ultimately in conceptions that are not only assumed by the faithful to be true but whose truth is placed beyond question or criticism, objects and activities associated with these conceptions partake of their sanctity. Since that which is sacred is taken by the faithful to be unquestionably true, sanctified messages are more likely than unsanctified messages to be accepted as true. Conversely, the transmitter's fear of supernatural sanctions may induce him to refrain from deliberately sanctifying and transmitting false information. Sanctification, in short, may enhance the reliability of symbolically communicated information. (For a similar discussion see Waddington, 1960.)

Another aspect of sanctity is important with respect to homeostats. It may be noted that the Maring are without powerful authorities, authorities which have at their disposal men and resources that can be organized to exert force upon the physical and social environment.[3] Indeed, if authorities are defined as discrete loci in communications networks from which directives emanate, it is difficult to identify authorities among the Maring at all. In the near absence of authorities the conventions of the ritual cycle specify the courses of action (such as sacrificing pigs) or inaction (the observance of truces) to be undertaken at specified times or during specified

3. Following Bierstadt's suggestion (1950:737), I regard political power to be the product, in a mathematical sense, of men, resources, and organization.

periods. In the absence of power vested in discrete authorities, compliance with the conventions is ensured, or at least encouraged, by their sanctity. Sanctity, thus, is a functional alternative to political power among the Maring, and no doubt among other people as well. Among the world's peoples we perhaps could discern a continuum from societies, such as the Maring, that are governed by sacred conventions in the absence or near absence of human authorities through societies in which highly sacred authorities have little power to societies in which authorities have little sanctity but great power. It would be plausible to expect this continuum to correlate roughly with technological development, for technological sophistication is likely to place highly effective weaponries in the hands of authorities, weaponries not generally available to their subjects. An authority with great power can dispense with sanctity— as Napoleon said, "God is on the side of the heavy artillery."

Although this study has been primarily concerned with the role ritual plays in the material relations of the Tsembaga, it is nevertheless the case that the Tsembaga say that they perform their rituals to rearrange their relations with spirits. It would be possible in an analysis of the empirical consequences of ritual acts to ignore such rationalizations, but anthropology is concerned with elucidating causes, as well as consequences, of behavior, and proximate causes are often to be found in the understandings of the actors. It seems to me, therefore, that in ecological studies of human groups we must take these understandings into account.

I have suggested elsewhere (Rappaport, 1963:159; 1967:22) that two models of the environment are significant in ecological studies, and I have termed these the "operational" and the "cognized." The operational model is that which the anthropologist constructs through observation and measurement of empirical entities, events, and material relationships. He takes this model to represent, for analytic purposes, the physical world of the group he is studying. The Tsembaga environment has been represented as a complex system of material relationships composed of two subsystems distinguished from each other by differences in the materials exchanged in each, but affecting each other through mechanisms amenable to direct observation.

The cognized model is the model of the environment conceived by the people who act in it. The two models are overlapping, but not identical. While many components of the physical world will be represented in both, the operational model is likely to include material elements, such as disease germs and nitrogen-fixing bacteria, that affect the actors but of which they may not be aware. Conversely, the cognized model may include elements that cannot be shown by empirical means to exist, such as spirits and other supernatural beings.

Some elements peculiar to the cognized model may be isomorphic with elements peculiar to the operational model. The Tsembaga say, for instance, that they are loath to build houses below 3,500 feet because certain spirits that are abroad at night in low areas give one fever. The behavior of these spirits—and the consequences of their behavior—corresponds closely to that of anopheles mosquitoes, which the Tsembaga do not recognize to be carriers of malaria. But elements, and relationships among elements, in the two models need not always be isomorphic or identical. The cognized and operational models may differ in some aspects of their structure as well as in the elements included in each.

This is not to say, of course, that the cognized model is merely a less adequate representation of reality than the operational model. The operational model is an observer's description of selected aspects of the material world. It has a purpose only for the anthropologist. As far as the actors are concerned it has no function. Indeed, it does not exist. The cognized model, while it must be understood by those who entertain it to be a representation of the material and nonmaterial world, has a function for the actors: it guides their action. Since this is the case, we are particularly concerned to discover what the people under study believe to be the functional relationships[4] among the entities that they think are part of their

4. The difficulties of attempting to discover the native, or cognized, model of the environment are even more severe than the difficulties of trying to construct an operational model. The method of ethnoscience pioneered by Conklin (1957), Frake (1962), and others, while valuable, has largely been directed toward the elucidation of native taxonomic distinctions, and taxonomic distinctions do not necessarily indicate folk notions of functional processes (Vayda and Rappaport, in press). The exploration of native ideas about functional relationships still rests, it seems to me, on the rather impressionistic methods that have long prevailed in anthropology, although it may be that a structural approach similar to that advocated by Claude Levi-Strauss

environment, and what they take to be "signs," indicating changes in these entities or relationships, which demand action on their part; but *the important question concerning the cognized model, since it serves as a guide to action, is not the extent to which it conforms to "reality" (i.e. is identical with or isomorphic with the operational model), but the extent to which it elicits behavior that is appropriate to the material situation of the actors, and it is against this functional and adaptive criterion that we may assess it.* Maring notions of disease etiology are certainly inaccurate, but the slaughter and consumption of pigs during illness is just as effective when undertaken to strengthen or mollify spirits as it would be if it were specifically undertaken to alleviate stress symptoms.

It may even be that lack of correspondence between some aspects of the cognized model and the real world which it is taken to represent confers a positive advantage upon a population (Vayda and Rappaport, in press). For instance, it might be to the immediate material advantage of a large local Maring population to attack a weaker neighbor in violation of the ritual truce or without signaling the possibility of such an attack by uprooting the *rumbim* and staging a *kaiko*. Although there have been exceptions, Maring populations are not likely to act in this fashion because their members believe it would be to their disadvantage. They would fear that their ancestors would not support them and that their enterprise would therefore fail. It has been asserted that ritual truces are advantageous to the Maring as a whole because through them the occurrence of warfare is limited to tolerable frequencies. This advantage is achieved by masking from some constituent local populations an appreciation of where their own immediate material interests lie. It can thus be argued that the cognized model is not only not likely to conform in all respects to the real world (the operational model) but that it must not.

The cognized model of the environment, then, is understood by the functional anthropologist to be part of a population's means of adjusting to its environment. It may be suggested that the place of the cognized model in the material relations of a population is analogous to that of the "memory" of a computer control in an

and Edmund Leach or the "cultural grammars" suggested by some other writers could be of use.

automated system of material exchanges and transformations. In the automated system, signals concerning the states of variables are received in the memory, where they are compared to "reference" values or ranges of values. (These values, although they are stored in the memory, may themselves be continuously adjusted in response to signals from other parts of the system.) In response to discrepancies between actual and reference values, programs are initiated that tend to return the deviant variable toward states approximating reference values or within reference ranges. Ideally, a corrective program is discontinued when the discrepancy between the signal emanating from a system component and the reference value is eliminated. Powers, Clark, and McFarland (1960) argue that similar information feedback governs the behavior of individuals, and I have suggested here that it is important in group behavior as well.

It is reasonable to assume that people compare the states of components of their environment, *as these states are indicated by signs*, with their notions (reference values or ranges) of what these states should be. For example, I have stated that a ritual cycle culminates when women's complaints and garden invasions by pigs, both signs that the pig herd is becoming burdensome, transgress the limits of a reference range. No value could be assigned this limit; it was only defined as complaints and invasions of significant number, magnitude, and frequency to affect enough people to shape a consensus. The transgression of this limit is itself a sign that there are sufficient pigs to repay allies and ancestors, and a *kaiko,* which is, among other things, a program directed toward returning the values of pig-related variables to the reference range, is initiated. With the completion of the *kaiko,* garden invasions by pigs are reduced to zero, or nearly so, and the women are left to complain about other things. The discrepancy between signals (complaints of overwork and damage) emanating from system components (affected members of the group) and the reference range has been abolished.

Some important questions follow. First, what is the relationship between signs and the processes they are taken to indicate? Is it the case, for instance, that such processes as environmental degradation are detected (indicated by signs) early, or only when they are well advanced? Second, to what extent do reference values, which are likely to reflect people's wants rather than their needs, correspond to the actual material requirements of the local population, the ecosystem, or the regional population? In other words, *what is the relationship between the reference values or ranges of values of the cognized model and the goal ranges of the operational model?* Concerning the Tsembaga I have noted, for instance, that the upper limit of the reference range for pigs (as defined by complaints) is likely to be below the limit of the goal range, as defined by the carrying capacity of the territory.

This study has been concerned with regulation, or processes by which systems maintain their structure, rather than adaptation, or processes by which the structure of systems change in response to environmental pressures. I shall therefore only suggest here that if cognized models are important components of control mechanisms their consideration in evolutionary as well as functional studies is warranted. We may ask in what ways cognized models change in response to environmental pressures, what differences there may be in the abilities of various cognized models to modify themselves, and how change, or resistance to change, in the cognized model affects the material relations of a people. In other words, native epistemology may be of considerable importance in evolutionary processes. Lawrence, for example, has recently argued (1964), in effect, that the inflexibility of the cognized models of various peoples of the Madang District has seriously hampered their efforts to adapt to material changes in their environment following contact with Europeans.

I have hardly touched upon change in cognized models here (one relevant suggestion was made in passing in footnote 9, Chapter 4), and I have not treated the relationship between Maring cognized and operational models adequately. Nevertheless, it is worth raising such questions, even at the end of this study, for through them we may, in future studies, be able to inquire, in reasonably well-defined ways, into the functional and adaptive characteristics of ideology.

My belief that it is not only possible but preferable to examine man's ecological relations in terms that also apply to noncultural species has been reflected throughout this study. Anthropology has been mainly concerned with phenomena unique in man, but it seems to me that if we are to understand what is uniquely human we must also consider those aspects of existence which man shares with other creatures. This conviction has led me to set religious rituals and the beliefs associated with them in a frame of reference that can also accommodate the behavior of animals other than man. It is this frame of reference that has exposed the crucial role of religion in the Marings' adjustment to their environment. The study of man the culture-bearer cannot be separated from the study of man as a species among species.

APPENDIX 1

Rainfall

Table 11. Rainfall in Tabibuga and Dikai (Tsembaga Territory)

	Tabibuga				Dikai		
Month	Lowest monthly rainfall 1959–1963 in points*	Highest monthly rainfall 1959–1963 in points	Average monthly rainfall 1959–1963 in points	Monthly rainfall Dec. 1, 1962–Nov. 30, 1963 in points	Monthly rainfall Dec. 1, 1962–Nov. 30, 1963 in points	Number of days rain fell	Number of days sun shone
December	664	1,626	1,226	1,626	1,879	29	18
January	550	2,167	1,216	586	770	22	27
February	365	2,001	1,386	365	676	14	28
March	1,420	1,823	1,511	1,432	1,106	incomplete	incomplete
April	568	2,044	1,437	568	1,171	26	20
May	391	1,410	832	391	873	18	20
June	199	799	507	779	900	24	21
July	260	1,211	589	410	703	18	24
August	338	873	637	733	1,495	28	24
September	610	1,401	897	1,401	2,020	26	20
October	676	1,769	1,107	1,769	1,919	27	23
November	974	1,734	1,086	943	1,877	21	18
	Lowest yearly total	Highest yearly total	Average annual total	Annual total	Annual total		
Totals in points	11,003	14,068	12,888	11,003	15,389	253+	243+

* 1 inch = 100 points.

APPENDIX 2

Soils

Data on soils are scanty. One hundred eleven samples were taken from various locations on Tsembaga territory. Unfortunately these were delayed in transit for almost one year, during which time they were damaged; only nine could be salvaged. The results of their analysis by Dr. Hugh Popenoe, director, Department of Soils, University of Florida, are presented in Table 12. Dr. Popenoe's discussion of these results is summarized here.

The fact that the pH values of the soils are low, although the nutrient contents are high in comparison to them, would indicate that the samples are probably very high in organic materials. In most tropical forest soils high organic matter contents are found in the top soil, in the surface litter, and A horizons, below which the organic material diminishes and the mineral content increases. Samples 2, 3, and 4 constitute examples of this point. Although sample 3, from the A horizon (*gi miña:* black earth), which terminates at a depth of only six inches, has a low pH, its nutrient content is much higher than that of samples 2 and 4, which were taken from the B horizon (*miña añeŋgi:* red earth) at the same site (sample 2 was taken from the same boring).

The nutrient contents of all three of these samples is low, although that of sample 3 is adequate for crop production. Since, however, this is the top soil, and fertility is mostly tied up in the organic fraction, these nutrients would, according to Dr. Popenoe, probably be lost in a year or two of heavy cropping. (Street and Clarke question this point.) The surface litter from this location was among the samples lost. In this location it was 1 to 1.5 inches in depth, and if it were of a richness comparable to either sample 42 or 69 it would enhance fertility, at least in the short run, considerably. The site from which these samples were taken was a newly cut but not yet burned garden in secondary forest estimated to be twenty to twenty-five years old.

244

Table 12. Tsembaga Soils

Sample number	Swidden number	Year planted	Altitude	Ground name	Vegetation when sample taken	Depth	Horizon	Native soil type	pH	CaO ppm	MgO ppm	P₂O₅	K₂O	NO₃	O.M.
2	68B	1963	4,400	Tipema	advanced second forest (not yet cut)	Below 6"	B	añengi (red)	5.2	619	218	Trace	24		very low
3	68B	1963	4,400	Tipema	advanced second forest (not yet cut)	1"–4"	A	gi miña (black)	4.5	1,029	880	0.5	501		very high
4	68B	1963	4,400	Tipema	advanced second forest (not yet cut)	4"–7"	B	?	4.4	208	382	1.0	232		very high
13	Oa	1960	4,400	Gomrup	young second-growth trees	1"–4.5"	A	gi	4.8	833	428	1.0	459		very high
42	25A	1961	4,800	Yindokai	sweet potatoes, secondary growth	0–1.2"	litter surface	ñeñuŋ	5.1	8,928	3,676	14.0	666	very high	high
67	—	1958	4,200	Gerki	Imperata; few trees	1.2"–3.4"	A	gi	4.6	645	382	1.0	146		very high
69	19A	1962–63	5,000	Tendopeŋ	crops	0–1.2"	litter surface	ñeñuŋ	5.2	7,526	702	6.0	542	very high	high
74	—	1959	4,400	Gomrup	Imperata; few trees	Below 10"	B	añengi	5.0	99	498	Trace	73	very low	
89	—	1943	3,500	Porakump	advanced secondary forest	Below 8.1"	B	añengi	5.3	4,995	1,562	2.5	792	very high	high

Sample 13 is top soil and also would be impoverished after a year or two of cropping. (This sample was taken about one year after the garden had been abandoned following two years of cropping. Its poverty as compared to sample 3 cannot, however, necessarily be ascribed to gardening, since the sites are separated by more than 1,000 feet.)

Sample 42 is sufficiently rich to support a permanent agriculture if no water table or erosion problems exist. Sample 69 is also very rich. (Both of these samples are of surface litter, however, and are only 1.2 inches in thickness. It is doubtful whether this would be sufficient for permanent cultivation.)

Sample 74, which was taken from the B horizon in a garden abandoned two years earlier after two years of cropping, is very poor.

Sample 89 appears to be "the best general soil" for agriculture. Despite the fact that this sample came from the B horizon, it is quite high in nutrients and might support a "very good agriculture."

Dr. Popenoe concludes that "in general the soil samples appeared to be very low in nutrients and for these soils one might suggest that the crop rotation or swidden cycle helps to maintain the fertility of the soil for crop production."

APPENDIX 3

Floristic Composition of Primary Forest

LOW-ALTITUDE HIGH FOREST (*Wora Geni*), 2,200'–4,000'

Low-altitude high forest survives only in remnants. These are limited in size (the largest covering less than five acres) and are found only in special locations, such as on the crowns of knolls and on the saddles of ridges. Man's removal of the primary forest from adjacent areas has resulted in the increased penetration of sunlight into the lower strata of the remnants of this association, which has undoubtedly affected the floristic composition of these strata. It may be that the composition of the lower strata has also been affected by the absent-minded hacking of those who walk through with ax or bushknife in hand.

No forest census was undertaken in the low-altitude high forest. In one knoll-top location, 3.2 acres in area, the presence of "A" stratum trees was noted, however. These included six native taxa in at least four families: *nuŋ* (*Fagaceae, Quercus* sp.); *banč* (*Magnoliaceae, Elmerrillia papuana*); *kinde* (*Sapindaceae*); *aŋa* (*Sapotaceae, Planchonella* sp.); *tuem* (unident); and *dambi* (unident). Other common "A" stratum trees noted elsewhere in the low-altitude high forest included *Spondias dulcis, Pangium edule, Aleurites moluccana, Araucaria hunsteinii, Eugenia* spp., *Ficus* spp., and representatives of the *Lauraceae* family.

HIGH-ALTITUDE HIGH FOREST (*Kamuŋga Geni*), 4,500'–6,000'

The entire area above a line ranging from 5,000' to 5,500' is under unbroken high forest. Both the structure and composition of this association are easier to observe than in the lower altitude remnants. A forest census was undertaken at Tendopeŋ, altitude 5,000', on a plot 200'x17'. The survey is summarized in Table 13. Because of the difficulties in securing adequate botanical samples from the large trees, most of the components of the A stratum remain unidentified.

Table 13. Survey of High Forest at Tendopeŋ
(Altitude 5,000′; Plot 3,325 sq. ft.; 200′ x 17′)

"A" Stratum

Native name	Spec. no.	*Cir- cumf.	Lowest branch (est.)	Native cate- gory	Identifi- cation	Com- ments
dukumpina	256	6′2″	50′	apuŋ		
munduka	93	7′3″	60′	apuŋ	Dilleniaceae, Dillenia sp.	
yaŋgra		7′	70′	apuŋ		buttress
dumbi		3′	60′	apuŋ		roots
yimboka		5′6″	70′	apuŋ		buttress roots
yimuŋger		2′5″	60′	apuŋ		
dupai	381	5′6″	40′	apuŋ	Lauraceae, Litsea sp.	
miñiŋgambo	334	3′	50′	apuŋ	Rubiaceae, sp.	
yendek	286	6′	60′	apuŋ		buttress roots

Total "A" Stratum: 9 trees

"B" Stratum

Native name	Spec. no.	*Cir- cumf.	Lowest branch (est.)	Native cate- gory	Identifi- cation	Com- ments
rama	143	3′	25′	apuŋ	Urticaceae sp.	
tondomane	76/84	1′8″	15′	apuŋ	Theaceae, Ternstroemia sp.	
ger	365	3′	25′	apuŋ	Euphorbiaceae Codiaeum variegatum (L)	
kina	223	2′6″	15′	apuŋ		

Total "B" Stratum: 4 trees

"C" Stratum
(circumference over 6″)

Native name	Spec. no.	*Cir- cumf.	Lowest branch (est.)	Native cate- gory	Identifi- cation	Com- ments
dimbi (2 spec.)		8″				
aimam	238	6″	15′	apuŋ	Araliaceae, Boerlagioden- dron sp.	
wombo (2 spec.)		6″	15′	apuŋ		
ameŋgi	152A	6″	15′	apuŋ		
riŋganč (5 spec.)	238	12″	10′	apuŋ	Moraceae, Ficus trachypison	
tandomane	76/84	9″	12′	apuŋ	Theaceae, Ternstoroemia sp.	
dupai	381			apuŋ	Lauraceae, Litsea sp.	
koip	245	6″	20′	apuŋ	Anacardiaceae, Semecarpus, prob. magnificans	
rambai		6″		apuŋ		
da	404/312	6″	8′	apuŋ	Lauraceae, Cryptocarya	

Total "C" Stratum: 16 trees

Table 13 (*continued*)

"D" and "E" Strata

Native name	Spec. no.	*Circumf.	Lowest branch (est.)	Native category	Identification	Comments
1. Other varieties of trees, circumference under 6" (species found in "A," "B," and "C" strata not reported here even if present)						
tamp				apuŋ		
mambruŋ				apuŋ		
2. Shrubs, grasses, vines, etc.						
koriŋgi	109			pikai	*Urticaceae, Elatostema* sp.	ground shrub
anjomar	83			pikai	*Zingiberaceae, Alpinia* sp.	ground shrub
teraipind- pinda	134			bep	*Polypodiaceae, Dennstaedtia* sp.	ground shrub
kabaŋ bep	213			bep	*Cyatheaceae, Cyathea rubiginose*	supported on tree branches, but rooted in ground
doŋgai	137			bep	*Marattiaceae, Angiopteris* sp.	ground shrub
morameka	113/259			gawa	*Piperaceae, ?Piper* sp.	climbing vine
kriŋa	182			gawa	*Pandanaceae, Freycinetia* sp.	climbing vine
gañiŋgai				pikai	*Urticaceae, Elatostema* sp.	ground shrub
mopaka	263			gawa	*?Moraceae, Ficus* sp.	climbing on mundoka (Dillenia) climbing vine
močam	129			pikai	*Araceae, Aglaomena* sp.	ground shrub
tiwaka				gawa		climbing on du- kumpina, climbing vine
terai	134			gawa	*Polypodiaceae, Dennstaedtia* sp.	fern vine, climbing on du- kumpina

Table 13 (*continued*)

Native name	Spec. no.	*Cir- cumf.	Lowest branch (est.)	Native cate- gory	Identifi- cation	Com- ments
kwiop	4/48			bep	*Polypodiaceae, Polypodium* sp.	growing on small rambai tree, a fern vine
yindim				bep		ground shrub
kwiopmai				gawa		climbing fern

* 3′ above ground, or above buttresses.

Other "A" stratum trees noted outside of the survey area included, in addition to many native taxa for which identifications could not be obtained, representatives of at least seven families. These are summarized in Table 14.

Table 14. Identified A Stratum Trees Noted Outside Survey Plot, Tendopeŋ

Family	Genus & species	Native name
Euphorbiaceae	*Macaranga* sp.	konjenipai
Fagaceae	*Quercus* sp.	nuŋ
Lauraceae	*Breilshniedia* sp.	kom
	Cryptocaria sp.	kawit
	Cryptocaria sp.	da
		boko
		gumbiaŋ
Magnoliaceae	*Elmerrillia papuana*	banč
Myrtaceae	*Eugenia* sp.	apeŋ
	Eugenia sp.	nonomba
Winteraceae	*Bubbia* sp.	ruiman

The floristic richness of the "B" and "C" stratum is also hardly illustrated by the census. Elsewhere between 5,000′ and 6,000′ representatives of the *Cunoniaceae, Guttiferae, Leguminosae, Melastomaceae, Myrtaceae, Palmae, Pandanaceae, Podocarpaceae, Rutaceae,* and *Saurauiaceae* families were noted, as well as additional native taxa among the *Euphorbiaceae, Lauraceae, Moraceae,* and *Urticaceae.*

Noted elsewhere in the "D" and "E," or ground, strata were members of the following families: *Balsamiferae, Compositae, Orchidaceae, Polygonaceae, Rubiaceae, Tiliaceae, Violaceae,* and *Umbellaceae,* as well as further representatives of families found on the survey plot.

Among large climbers noted between 5,000′ and 6,000′ were *Anonaceae, Pandanaceae, Rubiaceae,* and *Moraceae,* species. Strangling figs were prominent among the latter. The small climbers included members of the *Convulvulaceae, Ericaceae, Flagellariaceae, Gesneriaceae, Passifloraceae,* and *Rosaceae,* as well as the families found in the survey plot. Ferns, particularly *Asplenium, Lycopodium,* and *Nephrolepsis* are abundant among the epiphytes, as are several native taxa among the *Orchidaceae,* and epiphytic *Araceae* are present. Mosses cover the lower trunk of many "B" and "C" stratum trees and are present in patches on the trunks of the larger trees.

MOSS FOREST (*Kamuŋga Geni*), 6,000′–7,000′

Among the tallest trees in the moss forest are members of the *Lauraceae,* particularly species of *Litsea* and *Cryptocarya,* as well as *Eugenia,* with occasional individuals attaining an estimated height of 100′–125′. In addition to the *Lauraceae* and *Myrtaceae, Guttiferae, Logoniaceae, Melastomaceae,* and *Moraceae* are well represented among the trees. An *Astronia* (*Melastomaceae*) species is particularly abundant. A wild *Musa* sometimes achieves an estimated height of 60′ or 70′, and above 6,500′ two native taxa of *Pandanaceae,* probably separate species of the genus *Pandanus,* become plentiful. Both attain estimated heights of over 80′. *Elatostema* remains abundant on the ground, where representatives of the *Chloranthaceae* and *Marantaceae* families, as well as various ferns, particularly *Dawsonia* and *Polypodium,* are common. Vascular epiphytes and climbers are less common than in the high forest, but epiphytic mosses are much more luxuriant, completely covering the lower trunks of most trees to a depth of an inch or more.

APPENDIX 4

Estimating Yields per Unit Area

In the cases of both taro-yam and sugar-sweet potato gardens, figures are based upon the harvesting records of three gardens. This was necessary because the period of fieldwork, fourteen months, was considerably shorter than the life of any garden, figured from planting to abandonment. Moreover, harvesting records could not be started immediately upon arrival among the Tsembaga: it was necessary first to win the confidence and cooperation of the people. Harvesting records thus began on February 14 and ended on December 14, 1963. There was, therefore, a two-month period of the year for which no records were compiled.

For the first twenty-three weeks of both the taro-yam garden and the sugar-sweet potato garden harvesting figures from the garden of Moramp and Mer at Torpai (3,900'–4,000') were used. This was a mixed garden, resembling taro-yam gardens more closely than sugar-sweet potato gardens. It would have been preferable to use, for the sugar-sweet potato gardens, figures from a true sugar-sweet potato garden but, as has already been mentioned, no true sugar-sweet potato gardens were being made in 1963 because the reduction of the pig herd was imminent. However, the expedient settled upon—that of using the Torpai garden figures for both types of gardens—is not misleading. The two are very similar until the tubers ripen. Some adjustments were made, however. While all of the Torpai harvesting figures were used directly for the taro-yam garden, some of them were halved for the sugar-sweet potato garden computation. These included the figures for *kwiai* (*Setaria palmaefolia*), *ira* (pumpkin), *yibona* (gourd, ? *Lagenaria*), *čeŋmba* (*Rungia klossi*), and miscellaneous greens. It is perhaps the case that a further adjustment should have been made for *pika* (cucumber). In any event, these are low-calorie foods and, with the exception of cucumber, the yields were small. For the period from the twenty-fourth week after planting until the sixty-sixth week, figures are based, for the taro-yam garden, on the

252

garden of Moramp and Mer at Kakopai (3,800′), and, for the sugar-sweet potato garden, on that of Walise and Pambo at Timbikai (4,400′–4,500′). Both of these gardens were planted late in the 1962 planting season, and harvesting records exist from the first extraction of the root crops. The Torpai records also include the first extraction of root crops, so it was possible to fit both the Timbikai and Kakopai records to the Torpai record. It would seem, to put it a little differently, that both Timbikai and Kakopai were planted in late August or early September of 1962, while Torpai was planted in late June of 1963. The nine-week gap thus disappears.

The period from the sixty-seventh week after planting until abandonment is represented, in the case of the taro-yam garden, by the garden of Walise and Pambo at Tipema (4,000′–4,100′), and for the sugar-sweet potato garden by that of Ačimp and Avoi at Unai (4,100′–4,200′). In gardens of this age it is not possible, however, to discover signs indicating the age to within a few weeks, and it may be that nine weeks or more of harvesting figures are lost. The gardens, that is, may have been not sixty-seven but seventy-six or even more weeks of age when records commenced. It is quite clear that they were not under sixty-seven weeks' old when record keeping began because of the great disparity in root crop production in the last month for which records were kept on Kakopai and Timbikai, and the first month for which records were kept on Tipema and Unai. (The per-acre sweet potato yield, for instance, for the last month of Timbikai production was 638 pounds. The first month of Unai records showed a yield of only 158 pounds per acre.) This is not an infallible indication, for sweet potato harvesting drops off quite rapidly in any garden when a younger garden begins to produce in quantity. Unfortunately, the data are not sufficient, because of the nine-week hiatus, to know exactly how rapidly it does decline.

Despite the possibility of the record being short of some weeks of harvesting figures, no adjustments were made. The Unai and Tipema figures were accepted, that is, as if they did in fact represent harvesting between the sixty-seventh and one-hundred-tenth weeks after planting. This has probably resulted in an underestimate of the production for the period. The magnitude of such error, however, in comparison with the total yield of the garden during its entire life cannot be too great.

An additional underestimation results from the fact that I left the field before the gardens were completely abandoned. Some sugar cane and bananas were surely harvested after December 14. Again, the amounts were without doubt insignificant compared to the total harvested during the earlier life of the gardens.

These possible underestimations in regard to the harvesting from gardens over sixty-seven weeks of age are, in a sense, corrective. Both Tipema and Unai are on the government walking track and convenient to later gardens of both Ačimp and Avoi on the one hand, and Walise and Pambo on the other. They were, therefore, during the period after the sixty-seventh week, harvested more intensively and for a longer period than would have been the case had they been in less convenient locations.

Additional errors may have been introduced by some of the adjustment factors employed. These include factors for nonweighed harvesting, percentage of edible portion, and calories per pound of edible portion. All weighing took place at the women's houses. Some food, however, was consumed without being brought home. Bananas, for instance, are a frequent noon-time snack, and often a tuber is thrown on a fire in the garden at mid-day. On some occasions, moreover, an earth-oven is made in the garden and a full meal is taken there.

Most importantly, the "refreshers," sugar and cucumber, are eaten in the garden during the working period. It was my impression that twice as much sugar was consumed away from the women's houses, where weighing took place, as at the houses. This impression is based upon observations made without a scale and may be high.

Finally, some foods, notably bananas, sugar, *pitpit*, and greens, were sometimes brought directly to men's houses for consumption, without having been first weighed.

It will be noted that the factors for nonweighed harvesting differ between the earlier stages and the final stage of the gardens. This is because much of the consumption represented by nonweighed harvesting occurs in the course of work, and little work takes place in old gardens.

The figures for edible portions were worked out by tests in the field. The samples were small, and there are considerable problems involved in working out edible portions. Even within single varieties of single species there is variation between specimens of different sizes, ages, etc. The edible portion factors determined by tests, however, accorded fairly well with figures found in the literature.

Similar problems may be raised concerning the caloric values assigned to the various crops. These, too, vary within single named varieties of different ages, sizes, or origin. Caloric values, like other food values, were taken from a literature in which there is often wide disagreement. Where it was possible, the values adopted were those used in other studies, notably that of Hipsley and Clement (1947) in nearby or similar environments. One of the chief virtues is comparability. Sources for the values are listed in Appendix 9.

All gardens have some idiosyncratic features. The gardens from which yield figures were derived are no exception. Tipema, which represents the sixty-seven to one-hundred-tenth weeks of the taro-yam garden, happened to be totally without *Xanthosoma*, which is generally planted in wet areas at the bottom of slopes. At Tipema, however, the government walking track forms the lower margin of the garden and acts as a kind of drainage ditch, rendering an area that would ordinarily be planted in *Xanthosoma* unsuitable for this crop. It should also be mentioned concerning Tipema that although the amount of *kwiai* present was extraordinary, it may have been further overestimated. Such an overestimation would make little difference in the total caloric figure, however.

It was already mentioned, in respect to the sugar-sweet potato gardens, that cucumber may be overestimated. A further inaccuracy, or inconsistency at least, lies in the banana figures. While it is the case that more bananas are harvested after the sixty-seventh week than before it, the ratio in most cases would not approach the approximately 5.5 to 1 indicated here. With increasing altitude, fewer bananas are planted and maturation is slower. Timbikai, which is about 300' higher than Unai, exemplified this general trend.

APPENDIX 5

Energy Expenditure in Gardening

METHOD

For the purpose of estimating the amount of energy expended in producing an acre of garden, persons of known body weight were observed in the performance of each of the gardening procedures. The amount of time necessary to accomplish the various tasks was recorded. This was converted directly into time per unit area, in the case of garden making. In the case of harvesting it was converted first into time per weight of harvested material. Since yields per unit area were known, it was then possible to convert the time per weight figures into time per unit area figures.

Since the body weights of all persons observed were known, a caloric expenditure per unit of time could be assigned to their efforts in various tasks by reference to *Rates of energy expenditure under varying conditions of activity and body size* (*adults*), a table compiled by Hipsley and Kirk (1965:43) upon the basis of observations and gas exchange measurements made among the Chimbu, a highland New Guinea people. This table summarizes caloric expenditure per minute for persons of various body weights and ages performing twenty-six different tasks.

It could not be assumed, of course, that corresponding procedures of Tsembaga and Chimbu are equally strenuous. Before values from Hipsley's and Kirk's table could be adopted, therefore, evaluations had to be made of the level of effort required in the performance of the various tasks. Such an evaluation was arrived at by counting the number of hand movements per minute and by considering other factors such as the bulk and weight of the materials manipulated. This usually permitted the acceptance of values for particular procedures determined by Hipsley, but in some cases direct adoption was not warranted. Fence making, for example, apparently is not particularly heavy work among the Chimbu, who use much lighter timber than do the Tsembaga. Observation of the

256

procedure among the Tsembaga led me to select Hipsley's and Kirk's values for the heaviest work rather than the value they present for fencing.

PROBLEMS WITH THE METHOD

It may be questioned whether the application to the Tsembaga of figures compiled upon observations of the Chimbu is justified. It may be noted that the Chimbu live and work in a higher, cooler environment than do the Tsembaga. No adjustment has been made for temperature differences, and it may be that the caloric expenditure values assigned to the Tsembaga for various tasks are therefore slightly high.

The Chimbu, moreover, are larger people than the Tsembaga. While Hipsley's and Kirk's figures do include values for body weights within the Tsembaga range, it is possible that some further adjustment would be desirable.

The nutritive statuses, furthermore, of the Chimbu and Tsembaga differ. Venkatachalam (1962:10ff) indicated that the Chimbu suffer more severely from certain dietary deficiencies than do the Tsembaga; these deficiencies may have affected the values that Hipsley and Kirk derived.

Despite these difficulties, the use of values derived from observations made upon another New Guinea population seemed preferable to the use of less detailed tables based upon observations of European populations. It may be suggested, however, that anthropologists who are concerned to estimate energy expenditure should, if at all possible, arrange to have tests made upon the populations with which they are working.

INTER- AND INTRAINDIVIDUAL CONSISTENCY

An additional problem is raised by the possibility that the ranges of performance by various Tsembaga in the several tasks involved in gardening were greater than were reflected by the samples upon which evaluations were based, since samples were small. In the case of fence making, evaluations are based upon observations of only two workers, for example. For other activities the samples were larger, although always of limited size. There are, however, indications that differences in the performances of various actors or single actors at different times were not great. This is most clearly exemplified in the clearing of underbrush, a highly standardized task, since the composition and density of herbaceous undergrowth is similar on most plots in which gardening takes place. The operator removes this material by both uprooting it and by cutting it as close as possible to the surface of the ground with a bushknife. Only on sites on which *kunai* (*Imperata cylindrica*) is prevalent is the procedure different. Because its subsurface structure is rhizomatous, and because the edges of its leaves are razor sharp, no attempt is made to uproot this grass. Where it is plentiful the gardener simply cuts as close to the surface as possible. Such sites are rare, however; on only 6 out of 381 sites examined was *kunai* common. Seven individuals were observed clearing underbrush on three separate days. The results are summarized in Table 15.

Table 15. Clearing Underbrush—Time and Motion Study

Worker's name	Sex	Est. age	Weight in lbs.	Time	No. strokes	Time	No. strokes	Time	No. strokes	Comments
Akis	M	20	88	10:37–10:43	296	11:14–11:20	250	12:14–12:20	248	Only one 3-minute break during period. Next longest break: 15 seconds.
Ačimp	F	50	85	10:55–11:01	244	11:30–11:36	209			No breaks longer than 20 seconds during working period.
Avoi	M	55	94	11:02–11:08	177	11:50–11:56	190			Slower than other workers because of short breaks, and slower strokes.
Meñ	M	28	120	6 min.	233					Longer strokes than any of the others.
Wale	F	35	76	9:53–9:59	246	10:58–11:04	260			No breaks longer than 20 seconds during working period.
Nimini	M	18	96	6 min.	246					
Mer	M	40–45	94	6 min.	316					Stated that he was in a hurry.

Several remarks are in order concerning the results of this limited sampling. First, if the performances of Avoi, who is elderly and frail, and of Mer, who was by his own statement hurrying, are eliminated, the tempo of performance by various actors is quite uniform. Second, the tempo of single actors through time is also quite consistent. It may be mentioned that periods of rest during the course of the work are uncommon, except for a protracted break around mid-day.

In the case of only one of the workers, Wale, was the area cleared actually measured by chain and compass. Over a period of two hours Wale cleared at the rate of 210 square feet per hour. Wale, it may be pointed out, is a very small woman, and the larger, stronger men are able to clear larger areas in the same amount of time. I estimated by eye that Nimini cleared about 250 square feet an hour, and that Meñ, an exceedingly muscular man, was working at about the rate of 300 square feet an hour.

A comparison of the energy performances of Wale, Nimini, and Meñ may be made by referring to the energy expenditure values assigned to various activities by Hipsley in his study of the Chimbu. For an individual of Wale's size, medium-heavy garden work, such as the clearing of underbrush, requires the expenditure of 2.35 calories per minute or 141 calories per hour over basal metabolism. A person of Nimini's size, on the other hand, expends energy at the rate of 2.62 calories per minute, or 157.20 calories per hour. At these rates Wale is expending .67 calories to clear one square foot of underbrush, and if the estimate of 250 square feet per hour in Nimini's case is accurate, he is expending .63 calories per square foot. Meñ expends energy at the rate of 3.28 calories per minute over basal metabolism in this task. If the estimate that 300 square feet are cleared hourly by Meñ is accurate, he is expending .66 calories per square foot.

Harvesting of sweet potatoes shows similar consistency in energy expended per pound of tubers. In a garden about one year of age, Koi, 4′ 5½″ tall and weighing 87 pounds, was timed over a period of 85 minutes. Her work involved about 75 hand movements per minute during the entire harvesting period, and yielded 23 pounds, 2 ounces of tubers. The value assigned her efforts were 1.60 calories per minute, or 5.9 calories per pound of tubers harvested. Ačimp and Walise were also observed in sweet potato harvesting. Their efforts showed slightly poorer results: 6.3 and 6.9 calories expended per pound of sweet potatoes harvested. The tempos at which they worked were similar to that at which Koi worked, but the gardens were somewhat older, fourteen or fifteen months, than the year-old garden in which Koi was observed. Yields were perhaps beginning to fall off slightly. Informants say that in younger gardens return for work is greater, but no figures were obtained, unfortunately, for sweet potato harvesting in gardens under one year in age.

The data are insufficient, but it may be that the evenness of the tempo both through time′ and between individuals represents an approach to some sort of energy optimum in which accomplishment (e.g., square feet of land cleared) is maximized in relation to energy expenditure. A much larger set of observations on persons representing a full range of body sizes would be a worthwhile undertaking. It is possible that such a study would not only yield insights into optimal tempos for particular tasks, but also optimal body sizes for particular tasks or complexes of tasks. It may well be, for example, that the extra energy expended by a 150- or 160-pound man in clearing underbrush would not be matched by additional accomplishment. The caloric expenditure, that is, might rise well above .66 per square foot. This might illuminate a possible selective factor that has generally been ignored in discussions of evolution and might have particular relevance to pygmy populations.

COMPARISON OF CROPS

It may be mentioned that the estimation of the energy expenditure in various procedures involving different crops provides an additional dimension for comparing their desirability to the gardener. For example, the cost of harvesting sweet potatoes, which we take to be 5.9 calories per pound, may be compared to the cost of harvesting *Xanthosoma,* only 1.1 calories per pound. Using a value of 681 calories per pound for sweet potatoes (see Appendix 9) and 658 calories per pound for *Xanthosoma,* the ratio of gross energy yield to energy input in sweet potato harvesting is 116:1, while the ratio of gross energy yield to return in *Xanthosoma* harvesting is 598:1. If corrections are made for the yield of tubers fit for human consumption, the disparity between sweet potatoes and *Xanthosoma* is even greater. Thirty to fifty percent of the sweet potatoes are of small size (under four ounces), which, while edible, are considered unpalatable, being mostly skin. Small *Xanthosoma* tubers, having a thinner skin and a rounder shape, are considered to be quite acceptable.

There are at least thirty-eight named varieties of *Dioscorea* in five different species grown in Tsembaga gardens, and there is a considerable range in the depth at which the tubers mature. The extraction of some types requires that holes three to four feet deep be dug, and even the shallow varieties demand excavations of twelve to eighteen inches for their harvesting. While in some instances fifteen to twenty pounds of tubers may be obtained from a single plant this is rare, and it is clear that in terms of energy expenditure the harvesting of yams is less rewarding than is the harvesting of any other root crop. The figure of ten calories per pound, an estimate, is probably too low. The advantage of the *Dioscorea,* however, aside from their storageability, is just that they do mature at greater depths than do other root crops. Forming a deeplying stratum of edible material that does not impede the development of other more shallow strata, they provide the gardener with the opportunity to increase his per-acre yield. This advantage of *Dioscorea* may be sufficient to offset the costliness of harvesting them.

It may be mentioned that it is not only in harvesting that various crops may have differing energy characteristics. In mixed swiddens of either the taro-yam or sugar-sweet potato types weeds are much more of a problem than they are in the single species stands of *Xanthosoma*, which are planted at the lower, wetter margins of gardens of both kinds. The broad leaves of these plants generally shade out any other species that may attempt to establish themselves in their immediate vicinity. When the size of the energy expenditure in weeding is examined, this difference is seen to be of considerable importance.

ENERGY EXPENDITURE IN VARIOUS TASKS

The clearing of underbrush requires considerably more effort than the clearing of second-growth trees. Before steel was introduced, moreover, the disparity between energy expenditure in these two operations must have been greater, for while stone axes are quite efficient for felling second-growth trees they are poor implements for clearing underbrush. Before the introduction of the bushknife, underbrush was cleared by laying a pole three or four inches in diameter on the ground, pulling the weeds over this pole and chopping them with an ax. The indication is that the bushknife, at least as far as reduction of energy expenditure in gardening is concerned, was a more important introduction than the ax. (The ax is additionally more useful in chopping firewood.)

The amount of energy expended in fencing, about 46 calories per linear foot, goes far to explain why the cultivations of a number of gardeners are clustered, and the cost of transporting foodstuffs from the gardens to the houses provides a strong indication as to why the scattering of gardens as a result of the increasing size of the pig herd is accompanied by a scattering of residences. As noted in Table 5, a reduction of garden-to-house food transportation by 80 percent would improve the energy ratio of sugar-sweet potato gardens from 15.9 to 18.4:1, and that of the taro-yam gardens from 16.5 to 20.1:1. It should be mentioned that it is not only food that is carried from the gardens to the houses but also firewood, for swiddens are the most important sources of this important commodity. (When trees are cut to make a garden some of the logs are split and stacked to dry for fuel. After the abandonment of gardens, pollarded trees are frequently felled for fuel.)

COMPARISON WITH OTHER AREAS

Harris, in the unpublished paper referred to earlier, has assembled estimates of the energy ratios characteristic of several nonmechanized agricultural systems. The Tsembaga ratios, 16.5 to 20.1:1 and 15.9 to 18.4:1, although high, fall within an expected swiddening range. Harris' estimates for swiddening in other areas include Dyak (Borneo) rice swiddens, 10:1, and Tepotzlan (Yucatan) maize swiddens, 13:1 on poor land and 29:1 on good land.

Other agricultural systems may be much more efficient: Harris estimates, on the basis of Fei's (1945) data, that energy ratios in wet rice paddies reach 53.5:1 in Yunan. Harris points out that wet rice agriculture is not always so productive, however. Gerieri (Gambia) swamp rice cultivation shows an energy ratio of 11:1 (Haswell, 1953), which is about the same as the energy ratio (10.7:1) derived for their "savannah hoe cultivation" of other grains. Dyak wet rice cultivation, according to Harris, shows an energy ratio of 14:1.

Furthermore, a direct comparison of Tsembaga and Yunan figures may be misleading. Well over 90 percent of the Tsembaga diet is taken from the swiddens, and the energy expenditure figures presented in Table 5 would include some casual hunting. On the other hand, rice accounts for only 70 to 80 percent of the Yunan diet, and we have no estimate of the efficiency of the processes involved in other aspects of the food quest.

Despite the Yunan estimation, it is possible to say of Tsembaga gardening that although it seems to be characterized by comparatively low yields per unit of area, it shows at the same time comparatively high yields per unit of energy input. This characteristic of Tsembaga swiddening accords well with another of its aspects, i.e., that of disturbing as little as possible the secondary forest community in which the gardening takes place.

High return on energy input may be a characteristic of swiddening in general. Concerning the shifting cultivation of maize by the Amahuaca in eastern Peru, Carneiro says, "All in all, then, Amahuaca shifting cultivation is, in spite of its rudimentary form, thoroughly capable of producing the food abundantly, reliably, and with relatively little expenditure of labor" (Carneiro, 1964:18). Concerning Hanunoo dry rice cultivation, Conklin (1957:152) suggests an adjusted value of 2.5 kilograms of unhusked rice (caloric value 3,600 calories/kg.) as the return per man hour of labor. He notes, "This rough estimate compares favorably with labor cost figures for rice production under the best conditions elsewhere in the tropics." Both Carneiro's and Conklin's statements are, admittedly, based upon only partial quantification of the relevant variables, but both are sophisticated and experienced fieldworkers.

APPENDIX 6

Secondary Growth

Samples of second-growth composition (*riŋgopwai*) were taken by chain transit in six producing gardens between 3,400 and 4,800 feet in altitude. A total of twenty-one arboreal species was noted, with four to ten species in individual gardens. The most common species were *gra* (*Dodonaea viscosa*), specimens of which were in total the most numerous, but which were represented in only four out of six of the gardens, and *pokai* (*Alphitonia iacana*), somewhat less numerous than *gra* but appearing in all gardens. Also common was *gapni* (*Homolanthus* sp.), which appeared in five out of six gardens and was almost as numerous as *pokai*. These three species accounted for 43 percent of the sample, which included 117 specimens. Table 16 summarizes the composition of the sample. At least eight of these trees, *kobenum, kamakai, ganč, gonwant, gum, noŋ, riŋganč*, and *yiŋgra*, also occur in the primary forest.

There are some differences between gardens in the composition of the arboreal component of their early fallow associations, but it is not possible for me to state to what extent these differences are a function of altitude or of other factors, such as local edaphic conditions, proximity to virgin forest, or length of the previous fallow. Figures in Table 16 should not be taken to indicate differences in the prevalence of trees in the various gardens; there are differences, but they are not reflected in the sample.

The speed with which individual trees grow, and the prevalence of trees on the plot varies, roughly, inversely with altitude. More second-growth trees appear on lower altitude gardens and grow faster than in the higher altitude gardens, although this correlation is sometimes masked by local conditions. In one garden at 3,600 feet not included in the sample, the average height of second-growth trees was estimated, less than eighteen months after planting, to be twelve to fourteen feet, and they

Table 16. Trees Appearing in Tsembaga Gardens prior to Their Abandonment

Family	Genus & species	Native name	Porakump 3,400'	Tipema 4,000'	Tapipe 4,100'	Unai 4,400'	Timbikai 4,500'	Bokandipe 4,800'	Total
Cunoniaceae	Caldcluvia sp.	bokanč					2		2
Cyatheaceae	Cyathea angiensis	yimunt		3				6	9
Euphorbiaceae	Homolanthus sp.	gapni	1	2	7	1	1		12
Fagaceae	Quercus sp.	noŋ						1	1
Guttiferae	Garcinia sp.	gum						1	1
Melastomaceae	Melastoma malabathricum	wopkai		2			1		3
Moraceae	Ficus puncens	kobenum					3	2	5
	Ficus trachypison	ringanč				1			1
Rhamnaceae	Alphitonia iacana	pokai	3	1	2	3	4	2	15
Rubiaceae	sp.	ganč		2	1				3
Sapindaceae	Dodonaea viscosa	gra	6			1	3	12	22
Saurauiaceae	Saurauia sp.	goŋgo		3			1		4
Solanaceae	Solanum sp.	gon		3				7	10
Sterculiaceae	Colona scabra	kamkai		2	1			2	5
Ulmaceae	Gironniera sp.	penda				1	1	2	4
	sp.	dima		2					2
Urticaceae	Procris sp.	pentapent			2				2
Verbenaceae	Geunsia farinosa	gonwanč						1	1
Unidentified		beknan		2					2
"		mopo					1	2	3
"		yaŋgra	1		5		3		9
Total specimens in sample			11	22	19	9	29	26	116
Total named types represented			4	10	7	5	10	10	21

were close enough together for their crowns to have almost formed a continuous canopy. This garden, except for some bananas that remained to be harvested, had been abandoned between fourteen and sixteen months after planting. It seems probable that it was the density of the secondary growth that forced this early abandonment. Secondary growth in the higher altitude gardens seems to achieve somewhat less height and considerably less density in similar lengths of time. It is perhaps for this reason that they usually remain in production longer; sugar and *pitpit*, as well as bananas, are taken in some cases more than twenty-four months after planting in gardens between 4,500 and 5,000 feet in altitude.

While the development of the arboreal component of the secondary growth may be a direct function of altitudinal differences with attendant variations in temperature and edaphic conditions, it might also be a result of the difference in planting patterns at different altitudes. In the higher altitude gardens there is heavier planting in sweet potato. The presence of sweet potato is said to inhibit the growth of weeds, and it may inhibit the growth of young trees as well. Moreover, the techniques for harvesting sweet potato may result in the accidental removal of young trees.

The floristic composition of the herbaceous component of the second growth previous to the abandonment of the gardens shows about the same richness but somewhat less variation among gardens than the arboreal component. The composition of the sample collected by the same chain transits is summarized in Table 17.

The sampling technique is less likely to reveal uncommon herbaceous types than arboreal types, and the overall floristic composition of the herbaceous component of early secondary growth must be richer than the

Table 17. Herbs Appearing in Tsembaga Gardens prior to Their Abandonment

Family	Genus & species	Native name	Porakump 3,400'	Tipema 4,000'	Tapipe 4,100'	Unai 4,400'	Timbikai 4,500'	Bokandipe 4,800'	Total
Balsaminaceae	Impatiens platypelia	korambe		1				1	2
Compositae	Blumea balsamifera	kwirañ	1	25	10	19	16	13	84
	Microglossa pyrofilia	ringop gaua		1					1
Cyperaceae	Scleria sp.	riai	1		4		1	1	7
Gramineae	Coix lachrimajobi	kongun	1	1	12		18	2	34
	Imperata cylindrica	korndo	1	2	1	1		4	9
	Isachne myosotis	pingo	1					10	11
	Ischaemum digitatum	bombak				1	1	3	5
	Paspalum conjugatum	tamo		4	7		4		15
	Phragmites karka	yamboč					2		2
	Polytoca aerophyla	wandama						8	8
	Setaria palmaefolia	korami	3	8	12	4		1	28
Orchidaceae	sp.	tiokum	1		1				2
Rosaceae	Rubus moluccanus	kurkur					1	2	3
Ferns	Cyclosorus ?truncatus	aruk		3			3		6
	Diplazium sp.	rangilopa					1		1
	Nephrolepsis schlechteri	nomapunt-mai			1				1
	Pteris sp.	bor		10			12		22
	Pteris sp.	kembor	6	2	1	2			11
Total specimens in sample			15	58	50	43	54	32	252
Total named types represented			8	11	10	8	8	7	19

sample reveals. The predominant species, however, are certainly represented. Three types that did not show up should be mentioned. These are *ambek* (*Solanum nigrum*), *mañump* (*Cyathea* sp.), and *kaŋgup* (*Cyathea* sp.). *Ambek* appears very early in newly burned gardens and, being edible, is harvested. *Mañump,* an edible fern appearing in gardens below 4,000 feet, is also harvested. *Kaŋgup,* also an edible tree fern, appears in gardens as well as *riŋgopwai* above 400 feet, is also allowed to mature, and is eventually harvested. *Kaŋgup* and *mañump* are protected, particularly when they appear in pandanus groves.

Edible mushrooms of several named varieties may also be considered to be part of the fallow, appearing on rotting logs and stumps of the cut *duk mi.*

Kunai (*Imperata cylindrica*), a notorious pest, is relatively rare in the sample. Prevalence of this grass on a site indicates deflection from a succession leading to an arboreal climax to a succession leading to a stable grassy disclimax, which it dominates. Its rarity in Tsembaga gardens indicates that such a disclimax is not being induced on the sites sampled. Less precise observations made on other gardens indicates that what is true for the sample is true for Tsembaga gardens generally.

The floristic richness of the *riŋgopwai* association increases rapidly with age. A survey of an area of several acres at 4,800 feet, part of which had been planted three and a half, and part four and a half, years previously, showed 118 native named types, most of which represented species. All the arboreal species present were probably reported, but it is possible that a good many less obvious herbaceous species were not.

The arboreal component of this association consisted of at least thirty-six named native types in thirty-two genera and twenty-two families. At least eighteen of these types are also found in the virgin forest; it thus seems that at an early age secondary growth already begins to bear a floristic resemblance to the virgin forest characteristic of its altitude. A contrasting survey at lower altitudes of sites that had lain fallow for a similar length of time was not conducted, however. The composition of the arboreal component of this association is presented in Table 18. Many of the trees on this site were twenty feet high, and diameters estimated at three to four inches were the rule. They were scattered over the area, their crowns not touching. This site was close to the settlement, however, and it is likely that the formation of a canopy was being suppressed by pigs, who in their rooting continually destroyed the seedlings appearing in the spaces between the well-established specimens.

A census of trees on an 11,010-square-foot site at an altitude of 4,200 feet, which had last been cultivated twenty to twenty-five years earlier

Table 18. Arboreal Component, Secondary Growth (Pra and Gerki,
4,800'–5,000', Two to Three Years after Abandonment)

Family	Genus & species	Native name
Dilleniaceae	*Dillenia* sp.	munduka
Ebenaceae	*Diospyros* sp.	wonom
Ericaceae	*Rhododendron macregorii*	mer
Euphorbiaceae	*Breynia* sp.	nonmanč
	Glochidion sp.	mbanmban
	Homolanthus sp.	gapni
	Macaranga sp.	apapa
	Mallotus sp.	goŋgenaga
	Phyllanthus sp.	yuarundo
Fagaceae	*Quercus* sp.	noŋ
Guttiferae	*Garcinia* sp.	gum
Leguminosae	*Desmodium sequax*	koraindindiye
Moraceae	*Ficus* sp.	baŋgambai
	Ficus sp.	danje
Myrtaceae	*Cleistanthus* sp.	timbi
	?*Decaspermum necrophyllus*	jijimbint
	Octamyrtus durmanni	
	Eugenia sp.	aŋkunung
	Eugenia sp.	tandapa
Palmae	*Licuala* sp.	morapmai
Podocarpaceae	*Podocarpus* sp.	minjaun
Rubiaceae	*Mussaenda pondosa*	goimbambo
	Psychotria sp.	yuaroro
Sapindaceae	*Dodonaea viscosa*	gra
	Mischocondon sp.	birpi
Saurauiaceae	*Saurauia* sp.	rokunt
Solanaceae	*Lycianthes* sp.	kapaŋ
	Solanum sp.	gon
Theaceae	*Ternstroemia* sp.	tondamane
Thymelaeaceae	*Phaleria nisidae*	pukna
Ulmaceae	*Gironniera* sp.	penta
Urticaceae	?*Leucosyke* sp.	naŋgrek
	Maoutia sp.	noŋgamba
	Procris sp.	pent pent
Verbenaceae	*Geunsia farinosa*	gonwant
Unidentified		kumpnai

Total tree species represented: 35

and which was about to be cultivated again, is summarized in Table 19. This association seemed less varied than the three- to four-year-old association discussed above. Only twenty-six native named types were noted. Resemblance to virgin forest, however, seemed to have increased; at least eighteen of the twenty-six are also found in the *geni*.

The large number of the tree fern *yimunt* (*Cyathea angiensis*) is unusual. Single species stands of *yimunt*, or associations approaching single species stands, are regarded by the Tsembaga as indicative of poor soil. The gardeners, however, informed me that the soil was good on this site, and soil sampling showed no special deficiency. There are indications that at an earlier stage in the fallow development on this site, *Cyathea* shared dominance with the quick-growing types *gra* (*Dodoneae viscosa*) and

Table 19. Census of Trees, Twenty- to Twenty-Five-Year-Old Second Growth
(Tipema, Altitude 4,200'; Plot 11,010 Square Feet)

Family	Genus & species	Native name	No. spec. above 6" circumf.	Largest spec. circumf. at 3'	Largest spec. height (est. feet)
	Specimens 6" circumferences or larger				
Casuarinaceae	Casuarina papuana	ndumi	4	3'	60–70
Cunoniaceae	Caldcluvia	bokanč	2	1'6"	30
Cyatheaceae	Cyathea angiensis	yimunt	54	1'8"	25
Ebenaceae	Diospyros sp.	wonum	4	1'5"	30
Euphorbiaceae	Homolanthus sp.	gapni	1	1'4"	25
	Mallotus sp.	gimbint	2	9"	20
Moraceae	Ficus puncens	kobenum	4	7"	25
	Ficus trachypison	riŋganč	6	1'	20
Myrtaceae	Eugenia sp.	tandapa	1	6"	12
Ochnaceae	Schuurmansia meningsii	arare	1	1'3"	20
Rhamnaceae	Alphitonia iacana	pokai	3	2'6"	50
Rubiaceae	Psychotria sp.	burai	1	4"	20
Sapindaceae	Dodonaea viscosa	gra	4	1'	35
Saurauiaceae	Saurauia sp.	gaŋgo	15	2'6"	35
Solanaceae	Solanum sp.	gon	2	2'	35
Urticaceae	Missiessya sp.	yamo	5	1'3"	25
		rama	2	10"	20
Unidentified		mopo	4	2'6"	35
"		kariŋanč	1	3'1"	50
"		marmar	1	7"	15

Total specimens 6" circumference or larger: 117

Other named types present, under 6" circumference

Melastomaceae	Melastoma malabathricum	wopkai
Moraceae	Ficus calopilinia	muruŋga
	Ficus wassa	kundua
Unidentified		dukumpina
"		punt
"		raŋgan

Total named tree types: 26

pokai (*Alphitonia iacana*), which were, at the time of the census, quite
obviously being suppressed. Two of the four *gra* present were moribund.

The structure of this twenty- to twenty-five-year-old secondary forest
differed markedly from the structure of the three- to four-year-old association. The sizes of individual specimens are indicated in Table 19. The
crowns of the larger trees formed an unbroken canopy over the entire
area, so that the ground layer of shrubs, grasses, and creeping vines was,
except for an occasional sunbeam, in shade.

A further idea of the association is perhaps conveyed by the density of trees over six inches in circumference: there were ninety-four square feet per specimen. This seems typical. In intervening spaces, in addition to the sapling types listed in Table 19, rather large *yikon* (*Piper* sp.) bushes, or shrubs, were present on the site. Density of undergrowth was not, however, sufficient to impede rather extended visibility five to six feet above the ground.

APPENDIX 7

Commonly Propagated Plants

Table 20. Commonly Propagated Plants, Tsembaga

Family	Genus & species	Native name	Life form	Use	Where planted
Acanthaceae	*Graptophyllum* sp.	yenJim	bush	landscaping	at houses and raku
Anacardiaceae	*Mangifera indica*	wowi	tree	food (fruit)	wora
Araucariaceae	*Araucaria hunsteinii*	yuk	tree	house protection	At houses and raku
Cruciferae	*Roripa*[a] *Nasturtium aquaticum*	gonbi	herb	food (leaves)	shallow stream beds
Euphorbiaceae	*Aleurites moluccana*	kaba	tree	food (nuts)	close to houses in wora
	Codiaeum variegatum	ger	bush	boundary mark	on boundaries
Gnetaceae	*Gnetum gnemon*	ambiam	tree	food (leaves)	wora
Gramineae	*Bambusa forbesii*	kinjen	reed	roofing (leaves)	kamuŋga-wora amaŋ & wora
	Bambusa sp.	muŋ[b]	bamboo	building	near houses
Leguminosae	*Erythrina* sp.	yaur	tree	food (leaves)	near houses
Liliaceae	*Cordyline fruticosa*	rumbim[c]	small tree	boundary marker and ritual	boundaries, raku, houses
Moraceae	*Ficus wassa*	beka (kundua)	tree	food (leaves, fruit), fiber, pith	wora
	Artocarpus sp.	mokoi	tree	Food (fruit)	below 3,800'
Myrtaceae	*Cleistanthus* sp.	timbi	tree	ritual	near wora raku
Palmae	sp.	bina	tree	bows, arrows, spears	wora
Thymelaeaceae	*Phaleria* sp.	pukna	tree	fiber, pith	near houses
Urticaceae	*Oreocnida* sp.	rumen	bush	forms hedge	house, raku, boundaries
Zingiberaceae	*Amomum* cf. *polycarpum*	gunuma	reed	ritual, food (fruit)	boundaries, houses, raku
Unidentified		tup kalom	bush	dye, red	near houses
"		tup ruŋgi	bush	dye, black	near houses

[a] European watercress introduced ca. 1957.
[b] Many named types, probably species.
[c] Many named types, horticultural varieties.

270

APPENDIX 8

Nondomesticated Resources

The following lists of nondomesticated materials used by the Tsembaga cannot be regarded as exhaustive. Each item is listed in the association in which it is most commonly, although not in all cases exclusively, found. Each is followed by one or more code letters indicating the use or uses to which it is put by the Tsembaga; a key to these code letters follows Table 25.

Tentative bird identifications were made by Dr. Ralph Bulmer, and they may be found in Rappaport (1966). The native categories *ma* and *koi* have been glossed, for convenience, as marsupials and rats, respectively. These equivalences are only approximate, for the former may include giant rats while the latter may include small marsupials. It would be more accurate to define *ma* as wild mammals, excluding pigs and bats, over 4 or 5 inches high when standing on all fours, while *koi* are mammals under this size.

Table 21. Nondomesticated Resources Most Commonly Found in the Kamuŋga Geni Association (Primary Forest, 5,000′–7,000′)

Life form	Family	Genus & species	Native name	Uses*
		FLORA		
TREES	*Anacardiaceae*	*Semecarpus ?magnificans*	kuip	M
		?Pentaspadon or *Rhus* sp.	kariŋanč	TFn
	Cunoniaceae	*Caldcluvia* sp.	bokanč	B
	Euphorbiaceae	*Macaranga* sp.	konjenpai	Fl
				(smoked)
		Codiaeum variegatum	ger	R
	Fagaceae	*Quercus* sp.	nuŋ	B
	Guttiferae	*Garcinia* sp.	gun	R
		Garcinia sp.	tandapa	T
	Lauraceae	*Breilschmiedia* sp.	kom	RFl
		Cryptocarya sp.	kawit	RD
		Cryptocarya sp.	da	R
		Litsea sp.	dapai	RO
		?	krim	DTS

271

Table 21 (*continued*)

Life form	Family	Genus & species	Native name	Uses*
TREES cont.	*Lauraceae*	?	boko	R
		?	gumbiaŋ	R
	Leguminosae	*Albizzia* sp.	kanam	RT
	Loganiaceae	*Fagraea racemosa*	borumoi	S
	Melastomaceae	*Astronia* sp.	kukair	RS
	Moraceae	*Ficus calopilina*	muruŋ	XM
		Ficus dammaropsis	timnai	Ff
		Ficus trachypison	ringanč	BS
		Ficus sp.	gimbondum	XS
	Myrtaceae	*Eugenia* sp.	nonomba	RD
		Eugenia sp.	apeŋ	TD
		Decaspermum sp.	dam nene	B
	Palmae	*Calamus* sp.	kumbaka	T
		?	kumur	BSFs
	Pandanaceae	*Freycinetia* sp.	koraiŋga	T
		Pandanus sp.	buk	T
		Pandanus sp.	pima	BFf
		Pandanus sp.	taba	Ff
		Pandanus sp.	tumbama	BT
	Rubiaceae	?	ganč	R
		?	miñiŋgambo	M
	Rutaceae	?	konjup	RFl
	Theaceae	*Ternstroemia* sp.	tondomane	B
	Ulmaceae	?	dima	T
	Urticaceae	?	rama	Fl
	Winteraceae	*Bubbia* sp.	ruimam	D
	Unidentified		aimeŋga	MD
	"		ameŋgi	T
	"		air	T
	"		koro	B
	"		muŋr	RS
	"		gambo	TM
	"		nokopač	M
	"		nombon	X
	"		tiŋgia	T
SHRUBS & HERBS	*Chloranthaceae*	*Chloranthus* sp.	korap	RFl
			korap muŋa	
	Cyatheaceae	*Cyathea* sp.	noŋgam	D
	Gesneriaceae	*Cyrtandra* sp.	welenče	RFl
	Gramineae	*Bambusa* sp.	koa	TD
	Marantaceae	*Phrynium* sp.	miŋgin	BS
	Marattiaceae	*Angiopteris* sp.	doŋgai	R
	Palmae	?	mandiŋga	BS
	Piperaceae	*Piper* sp.	kere kere	R
		Piper sp.	čerap	S
	Pittosporaceae	*Pittosporum undulatum*	ambuŋgai	M
	Rutaceae	*Evodia anisodora*	tumbup	A
	Tiliaceae	*Microcos* sp.	ninkmai	Fl
	Urticaceae	*Elatostema* sp.	gañiŋgai	RM
	Zingiberaceae	*Alpinia* sp.	bañaŋgoi	RDS
		Alpinia sp.	puplaka	BS
	Unidentified		kopeŋga	XFl
	"		piŋgo	Fl
	"		morno	M
	"		gonbi	Fl
	"		puŋ	M
	"		tokmai	O
	"		kwipo	
	"		nink amp	RFl

Table 21 (*continued*)

Life form	Family	Genus & species	Native name	Uses*
VINES	*Cucurbitaceae*		gambroŋgin	T
			yibona	FlT
	Ericaceae	*Dimorphanthera* sp.	ayuk	BS
	Gesneriaceae	*Aeschynanthus* sp.	koramp	BOS
			andika	
	Monimiaceae	*Palmeria* sp.	kep ndim·	Fl
	Pandanaceae	*Freycinetia* sp.	kriŋa	XS
		Freycinetia sp.	kwiŋgaka	O
	Piperaceae	*Piper* sp.	morameka	RFl
	Urticaceae	*Elatostema* sp.	ap	M
			čembamai	
		Pipturus sp.	deraka	RS
EPIPHYTES	*Cyatheaceae*	*Dawsonia* sp.	ka rawambo	O
	Lycopodiaceae	*Lycopodium* sp.	ap diŋgambe	R
	Orchidaceae	*Dendrobium* sp.	kanjkai	O
	Polypodiaceae	*Polypodium* sp.	kwiop	Fl

BIRDS (kabaŋ)
At least 19 native taxa, 18 of which are eaten, 12 of which are valuable for feathers. Most important are:

Greater Sickle-Bill	karanč	WF
Six Plumed Bird of Paradise	kiawoi	WF
Princess Stephanie Bird of Paradise	kombom	WF
Gardener Bower Bird	kombek	WF
Haryopsis sp.	binan	WF
Cassowary	kombri or yoŋge	WFT
King of Saxony Bird of Paradise	nomapunt	WF
Magnificent Bird of Paradise	pieŋmai	WF
Superb Bird of Paradise	yenandiok	WF

FUNGI (bai)
At least 8 native taxa, all unidentified, all used for food.

FAUNA

MARSUPIALS (ma): At least 16 native taxa, all unidentified, used for food, ornamentation, fiber, hides; some are wealth items.

RATS (koi): At least 6 native taxa, all used as food by women and children.

INSECT LARVAE (čuma): One native taxon, found in stumps, highly prized food.

* See notes to Table 25 for key to abbreviations.

Table 22. Nondomesticated Resources Most Commonly Found in the Tsembaga
Wora Geni Association (Primary Forest, 2,200'–4,000')

Life form	Family	Genus & species	Native name	Uses*
		FLORA		
TREES	Anacardiaceae	Mangifera sp.	wowi	Ff
		Spondius dulcis	aipan	R
	Araucariaceae	Araucaria hunsteinii	juk	T
	Casuarinaceae	Casuarina papuana	jimi	ASB
		Casuarina sp.	kepir	ASB
	Euphorbiacene	Aleurites moluccana	kaba	Fn
	Flacourtiaceae	Pangium edule	topia	R
	Leguminosae	Erythrina sp.	yaur	Fl
	Magnoliaceae	Elmerrillia papuana	banč	R
	Pandanaceae	Pandanus sp.	miyom	B
	Sapindaceae	Planchonella sp.	aŋa	A
	Vitaceae	Leea sp.	bebon	B
SHRUBS	Amaryllidaceae	Crinum sp.	yimane	T

FAUNA

BIRDS (kabaŋ)
At least 7 native taxa, all of which are eaten. The feathers of 4 are used as adornment,
but only 2 are considered valuable. These are:

		Cacatua galerita	akaka	FW
		Lesser Bird of Paradise	yambai	FW

MARSUPIALS (ma): At least 6 native taxa, all unidentified, used for food, hides, fiber,
ornamentation, and wealth objects.

RATS (koi): At least 1 native taxon, used as food for women and children.

SNAKES (noma): At least 2 native taxa, used for food.

LIZARDS (tum): At least 1 native taxon, used for food and hide.

* See notes to Table 25 for key to abbreviations.

Table 23. Nondomesticated Resources Most Commonly Found in Tsembaga
Ringopwai (Secondary Growth) Associations

Life form	Family	Genus & species	Native name	Uses*
		FLORA		
TREES	Cyatheaceae	Cyathea angiensis	yimunt	Fl
		Cyathea, new species	kaŋgup	Fl
	Ebenaceae	Diospyros sp.	wonum	M
	Euphorbiaceae	Breynia sp.	non manč	R
		Phyllanthus sp.	dikambo	B
			jimbonk	RM
	Melastomaceae	Melastoma malabathricum	wop kai	X
	Moraceae	Ficus sp.	danje	T
	Palmae	Licuala sp.	moropmai	T
	Rhamnaceae	Alphitonia iacana	pokai	BM
	Sapindaceae	Dodonaea viscosa	gra	B

Table 23 (*continued*)

Life form	Family	Genus & species	Native name	Uses*
TREES *cont.*		*Mischocodon* sp.	birpi	B
	Saurauiaceae	*Saurauia* sp.	rokunt	B
	Solanaceae	*Lycianthes* sp.	kapaŋ	R
		Solanum sp.	gon	RM
	Ulmaceae	*Gironniera* sp.	penta	B
	Urticaceae	*Missiessya* sp.	yamo	FlSM
	Verbenaceae	*Geunsia farinosa* Bl.	gonwant	M
	Unidentified		yent	B
	"		raŋgan	T
	"		kop	X
	"		mar mar	B
HERBS & **SHRUBS**	*Acanthaceae*	*Rungia klossi*	tok mai čeŋmba	Fl
	Araceae	*Aglaonema* sp.	močam	RD
		Alocasia sp.	gump	S
	Commelinaceae	*Commelina* sp.	komerik	Fl
	Compositae	*Bidens pilosa*	womemuk	MO
		Blumea sp.	gumbandi	M
	Cyatheaceae	*Cyathea rubiginosa*	kabaŋ bep	Fl
	Gramineae	*Bambusa forbesii*	kinjen	B
		Coix lachrymajobi	koŋgun	OA
		Imperata cylindrica	korndo	B
		Miscanthus floridulus	ripa	T
		Phragmites karka:	yamboč	M
		Setaria palmaefolia	korami	Fs
	Orchidaceae	?*Calanthe* sp.	korndo tiokum	SR
		Spathoglottis sp.	korndo tiokum	SR
	Piperaceae	*Piper* sp.	yikun	RD
	Polypodiaceae	*Dennstaedtia* sp.	terai	Fl
	Urticaceae	sp.	nent	M
	Zingiberaceae	*Costus* sp.	monomp	B
		Riedelia sp.	yenjim	M
		Cyclosorus sp.	aruk	Fl
		Diplazium sp.	raŋgilopa	Fl
	Unidentified		rum rena	Fl
VINES	*Asclepiadaceae*	*Hoya* sp.	koiwundo	SB
	Gesneriaceae	*Aeschynanthus* sp.	yimbuŋk	SB
	Liliaceae	*Smilax* sp.	gum biogun	T
	Melastomaceae	*Medinella* sp.	aikumbindi	B
	Moraceae	*Ficus* sp.	mopakai	SB
	Pandanaceae	*Freycenetia* sp.	kwiŋgaka	O
	Passifloraceae	*Adenis* sp.	akar	SB

FUNGI (bai): At least 7 native taxa used as food.

FAUNA

SNAKES (noma): At least 4 native taxa, all used for food, one for hide (python).

INSECTS (baŋ): At least 8 native taxa, 7 used for food, 1 for medicine, 1 for ornament.

* See notes to Table 25 for key to abbreviations.

Table 24. Nondomesticated Resources Most Commonly Found in Streams
and on Stream Banks in Tsembaga Territory

Life form	Family	Genus & species	Native name	Uses*
		FLORA		
TREES	*Myrtaceae*	*Cleistanthus* sp.	timbi	R
	Unidentified		pima kumbent	R
BUSHES,	*Moraceae*	*Ficus andenosperma*	anjai	Fl
SHRUBS,	*Myrtaceae*	*Eugenia* sp.	druo	R
HERBS	*Urticaceae*	*Laportea* sp.	čenaŋ gumiŋga	Fl

FAUNA

MARSUPIALS (ma): At least 3 native taxa, used for food.

BIRDS (kabaŋ): At least 3 native taxa used for food.

FROGS (kamp): Many taxa, used for food by women and children.

CRABS (korapa): One native taxon, used for food.

FISH: Two native taxa, *kobe* (eel), and *tuoi* (catfish), both eaten; *kobe* also used in rituals.

* See notes to Table 25 for key to abbreviations.

Table 25. Nondomesticated Resources Commonly Found in Two or More
Associations in Tsembaga Territory

Life form	Family	Genus & species	Native name	Uses*
		FLORA		
TREES	*Araliaceae*	*Boerlagiodendron* sp.	aimam	B
	Dilleniaceae	*Dillenia* sp.	munduka	SB
	Euphorbiaceae	*Homolanthus* sp.	tup kalom	X
	Leguminosae	*Desmodium sequax*	korai jnjie	O
	Meliaceae	*Chisocheton* sp.	birpi	Fn
	Moraceae	*Ficus puncens*	kobenum	Flf
		Ficus wassa	beka	XFlf
	Myrtaceae	*Descapermum necrophyllus*	jinjimbint	R
	Thymelaceaceae	*Phalerium nisidai*	pukna	X
	Urticaceae	*Maoutia* sp.	noŋgamba	X
		Oreocnida sp.	rumem	B
	Unidentified		membra	B
	"		dukumpna	Flf
	"		pia	B
	"		punt	B
HERBS &	*Gramineae*	*Bambusa* sp.	waia	BT
SHRUBS	*Lycopodiaceae*	*Dimorphanthera* sp.	koropi mai	M
	Zingiberaceae	*Alpina* sp.	anjomar	S
			gaunai	M
	Unidentified		mi muŋga	M

Table 25 (*continued*)

Life form	Family	Genus & species	Native name	Uses*
VINES	*Convolvulaceae*	*Lepistemon urceolatum*	apop	SB
	Cucurbitaceae	?*Trichosanthes* sp.	jen	Ff
	Flagellariaceae	*Flagellaria indica*	goŋ	SB
	Polypodaceae	*Dicranopteris pinearis*	mombo	B
	Zingiberaceae	?*Alpinia* sp.	čawaka	SB
	Unidentified		mundunt	SB

FAUNA

BIRDS (kabaŋ): At least 40 native taxa, used for food, ornamentation, and wealth objects.

MARSUPIALS (ma): At least 3 native taxa, used for food, fiber, ornamentation, and wealth objects.

RATS (koi): At least 1 taxon, used as food by women and children.

WILD PIG (konj): 1 taxon, used as food.

SNAKES (noma): At least 2 taxa used for food.

* Uses of Plants and Animals:

A. Agronomic—Used to protect other plants, or to improve their yields; plants that are sometimes planted to improve the associations that develop on abandoned gardens; and indicator plants (plants whose achievement of a particular stage of maturation or a particular stage in a reproduction cycle serves as a signal to undertake one or another subsistence activity).

B. Building Materials—Used in the construction of quasi-permanent structures, usually houses and fences.

D. Dress—Used without processing as part of the costume; usually leaves used as coverings for buttocks.

F Food—Only materials customarily ingested by humans. It does not include materials habitually consumed by livestock and wild animals but not human beings. In the case of plant foods, the part of the plant used is designated by a small letter: (f) fruit; (l) leaf; (n) nut; (r) root; (s) stem.

M. Medicinal, Hygienic, Cosmetic—Used in any procedure "magical," "religious," or empirical, the aim of which is to cure an existing physical disability. Also included are any materials expended in procedures that produce or maintain personal cleanliness, and materials which are used as cosmetics.

O. Ornamentation—Worn on the person as adornment, but do not, like cosmetics, lose their physical properties after a single wearing.

R. Ritual—Used in rituals with the exception of those included in category M.

S. Supplies—Used once, then discarded, e.g., leaves for temporary packages, vines to tie firewood, leaves used in earth ovens. Items included in categories B, D, F, and M are excepted.

T. Technological—Used to make tools, weapons, or containers that are not discarded after being used once.

W. Wealth Objects—May be exchanged for steel tools, shell objects and, in former times, stone axes (most importantly feathers and furs).

X. Important for their fibers or dyestuffs, which are used in the manufacture of bark cloth, net bags, loin cloths, etc.

APPENDIX 9

Diet

MEASUREMENT OF THE NUTRITIVE VALUE
OF TSEMBAGA INTAKE DERIVED FROM PLANTS

Fruits and vegetables comprise approximately 99 percent, by weight, of the usual daily Tsembaga intake.

Total Intake, by Weight, of the Tomegai

All vegetable foodstuffs brought home to the four hearths of the Tomegai clan were weighed daily, by named variety, from February 14, 1963, to December 14, 1963. For the purpose of estimating intake the figures from March 11 to November 8, a period during which both the pig and human populations were relatively stable, form the basis of the estimate.

From the gross weights brought home, two deductions were made. First, the harvester was asked to set aside the ration for pigs. The weight of that ration was subtracted from the gross weight, leaving the weight available for human consumption. Second, a factor for waste in preparation was subtracted from the remaining amount. The values assigned to waste are in the case of each item based upon tests in the field. The figures remaining after the two deductions indicate total weights of edible portions brought to the houses.

To these figures are added values for the consumption of vegetable foods away from the house. These values are based upon observations of people eating on the paths, in the bush, and in the gardens. The resulting figures are taken to be total weight of edible portion available for human consumption.

The procedures for obtaining this final figure may be summarized in the following equation:

(Gross weight brought home + estimated weight consumed away from home) − (pig ration + waste) = total weight of edible portion available for consumption by humans.

These figures are tabulated in columns 1–5 of Table 26.

It may be that some of the difficulties in deriving quantities of edible portion available for human consumption are apparent. In common with the attempt to estimate garden yields, there is the problem of estimating the weights of foodstuffs that were consumed without having first been brought to the houses. Values were assigned on the basis of observations made without the benefit of scales. The quantities consumed away from the houses are not large in any event, and it is therefore not likely that estimation resulted in an error of more than one or two percent except in the cases of sugar cane and cucumbers, where error could have been greater.

The values assigned to the pig ration reflect the weight of foodstuffs explicitly set aside for them. However, women were frequently observed feeding the pigs tidbits from the portion set aside for humans. No deductions were made from the human portion for these morsels. The daily human ration is therefore represented as slightly higher, in comparison to the ration set aside for pigs, than it actually is.

The percentage values assigned to waste were based upon a limited number of tests in each case, and the amount of waste varies with the age, freshness, size, etc., of specimens, even within particular varieties of the same species. The values I assigned on the basis of tests do, however, approximate standard values found in the literature.

The Value of Food Ingested

Nutritive values derived from the literature were assigned to each item. Wherever possible, values used by other New Guinea workers were adopted to facilitate comparability. In most cases these workers adopted values derived from samples taken from the general area in which they worked. Other things being equal, it seemed methodologically preferable to accept values derived from the analyses of New Guinea specimens rather than values taken from specimens grown elsewhere. In some instances the values used may be high. The caloric value for sweet potato, for instance, derived from Hipsley and Clements (1947), is 681 per pound of edible portion. Other authorities record considerably lower figures. It is upon the basis of Hipsley's and Clements' values, however, that the Chimbu, Busama, Kaiapat, Patep, and Kavataria diets were evaluated, and the adoption of the same values, so far as possible, facili-

Table 26. Total Intake of the Tomegai Clan

	1	2	3	4	5	6	7	8	9	10
Crop	Total weighed, in lbs.	Ration for pigs, in lbs.	Available for humans, in lbs.	Edible portion factors, in %	Edible portions for humans, in lbs.	Calories/lb. edible portions	Authority*	Calories, human intake	% Protein edible portion	Authority*
Roots										
Sweet potato	9,944.50	5,554.22	4,390.28	80	3,512.23	681	3	2,391,828.63	.9–1.7	5
Xanthosoma	1,505.50	14.50	1,491.00	80	1,192.80	658	3	784,862.40	1.4–1.9	5
Colocasia	3,834.75		3,834.75	85	3,159.54	658	3	2,078,977.32	1.4–1.9	5
Manioc	1,349.25	1,106.39	242.86	80	194.29	595	3	115,602.55	.7–1.2	5
Yams	1,942.50		1,942.50	85	1,641.60	486	3	652,017.68	1.9–2.0	5
Total roots								6,023,288.58		
Trees										
Banana	1,682.50	54.90	1,627.60	70	1,139.32	427	3	486,489.64	1.1	3
Artocarpus	105.50		105.50	50	52.75	295	1	15,561.25	1.0	1
Marita	861.50		861.50	43	370.45	762	7	282,282.90	3.7	7
Total trees								784,333.79		
Misc. Garden										
Corn	8.50		8.50	29	2.47	463	6	1,143.61	3.7	6
Peas and beans	4.75		4.75	95	4.51	440	3	1,984.40	8.1	3
Pumpkin	234.25	33.26	200.99	68	136.67	200	3	27,334.00	1.5	3
Gourd	13.75		13.75	68	9.35	154	1	1,439.90	1.3	1
Total misc. garden								31,901.91		
Leaves										
Hibiscus	1,373.75		1,373.75	95	1,305.06	136	3	177,488.16	5.7	2
Rungia klossi	316.75		316.75	95	300.91	136	3	40,923.76	3.8	2
Sweet potato leaves	138.25		138.25	95	131.34	218	5	28,632.12	3.6	5
Assorted others	244.50		244.50	95	232.28	136	3	31,590.08	3.8	2
Total leaves								278,634.12		
Grasses and Inflorescences										
Pitpit-dičiŋ variety	1,142.00		1,142.00	40	456.80	104	4	47,507.20	4.1	2
Pitpit-dičiŋ, trimmed	124.75		124.75	95	118.51	104	4	12,325.04	4.1	2
Pitpit, all other var.	816.25		816.25	60	489.75	104	4	50,854.00	4.1	2
Pitpit, all other var. trimmed	61.75		61.75	95	58.66	104	4	6,100.64	4.1	2
Setaria	692.75		692.75	17	117.77	101	8	11,994.75	1.4	8
Setaria, trimmed	61.75		61.75	95	58.66	101	8	5,924.90	1.4	8
Total grasses and inflor.								134,706.53		
Refreshers										
Sugar cane	3,368.00	249.50	3,118.50	30	935.55	263	3	246,049.65	.4	3
Cucumbers	216.50	10.80	205.70	95	195.42	50	3	9,771.00	.6	3
Total refreshers								255,820.65		
Totals, all sources								7,508,685.58		

* Authorities:
(1) FAO Nutritional Study No. 11.
(2) Hamilton, 1955.
(3) Hipsley and Clements, 1947.
(4) Hitchcock, N. 1962.
(5) Massal and Barrau, 1956.

(6) Osmund and Wilson.
(7) Peters, 1958.
(8) Wenkam, K., Department of nutrition, University of Hawaii, personal communication.

(16 Persons, 13 Pigs; March 11–November 8, 1963)

11 Protein ingested by humans, minimum lbs.	12 Protein ingested by humans, maximum lbs.	13 Factors for additional intake, in %	14 Total estimated caloric intake	15 Total estimated Protein intake, minimum lbs.	16 Total estimated Protein intake, maximum lbs.	17 Fat, in %	18 Authority *	19 Total fat intake, in lbs.	20 Calcium, mgm./lb.	21 Authority *	22 Total calcium intake, mgm.
31.61	59.71	5	2,511,420.06	33.19	62.70	.3	5	10.53	68	3	2,188.16
16.70	22.66	5	824,105.52	17.54	23.79	.2	5	2.39	177	3	2,029.84
44.23	60.03	5	2,182,926.19	46.44	63.03	.2	5	6.32	177	3	5,591.43
1.36	2.33	5	121,382.68	1.43	2.45	.3	5	.58	114	3	221.16
25.49	26.83	5	684,618.56	26.76	28.17				45	5	738.45
12.53	12.53	20	583,787.57	15.04	15.04	.5	1	5.70	36	3	410.04
.53	.53		15,561.25	.53	.53	.6	1	.32	168	1	87.36
13.71	13.71	25	289,339.97	17.14	17.14	14.0	3	5.19			
.91	.91	5	1,150.79	.96	.96	4.3	1	1.06	32	1	.64
.37	.37		1,984.40	.36	.36	3.9	3	1.76	136	6	5.44
2.05	2.05		27,334.00	2.05	2.05				91	3	23.76
.11	.11		1,439.90	.12	.12	.2	1	.02	54	1	4.86
74.38	74.38	2	181,037.92	75.87	75.87	.3	4	1.92	1,685	4	21,989.25
11.43	11.43	2	41,542.24	11.66	11.66	.3	4	.90	1,685	4	5,055.00
4.73	4.73	2	29,204.76	4.82	4.82	.7	5	.92	340	5	445.40
8.83	8.83	2	31,921.89	9.01	9.01	.3	4	.70	1,685	4	3,909.20
18.73	18.73	2	48,457.34	19.10	19.10	.2	3	.91	95	3	433.20
4.86	4.86	2	12,471.54	4.96	4.96	.2	3	.14	95	3	112.10
20.08	20.08	2	51,871.08	20.48	20.48	.2	3	.98	95	3	464.55
2.41	2.41	2	6,222.65	2.46	2.46	.2	3	.12	95	3	51.50
1.65	1.65	2	7,808.15	1.68	1.68	.6	8	.71	95	8	111.15
.72	.72	2	3,889.16	.73	.73	.6	8	.35	95	8	51.50
3.74	3.74	200	738,148.95	11.22	11.22				45	3	420.75
1.17	1.17	50	14,656.50	1.36	1.36				104		202.80
302.33	354.50		8,412,483.06	324.91	379.69			41.52			44,547.54

tates comparisons within Australian New Guinea. It may be, however, that these values should be adjusted in any comparison with nutritional data collected in other parts of the world.

Nutritional values are summarized in columns 6, 9, 17, 20 of Table 26. The sources from whom the figures were adopted appear in adjacent columns.

Nutritional Values of Individual Intakes

The sample for which quantitative consumption data were collected consisted of sixteen persons for a period of 246 days. Not all sixteen were present every day, and on some occasions visitors were fed; therefore a record was kept of who ate at each hearth every day. The persons who were fed fell into a number of different age and sex categories, each of which had a different intake. The problem of assigning values to the intake of each age-sex category theoretically can be solved simply: one merely measures the quantities served to persons of each category. Among the Maring such a procedure was not practical. It would have required first that the observer be on hand with a portion scale while the food was being consumed, and left-overs may be eaten late at night or early in the morning, when tubers may also be cooked for later consumption as between-meal snacks. Unless the observer takes up more or less permanent residence next to the larder of a single household, some of this consumption is bound to escape his attention.

As an alternative, ratios for the quantity of intake of persons in the various age and sex categories were devised. These were based upon suggested caloric allowances published by Venkatachalam (1962:10), following Langley (1947:134). The daily caloric allowances listed here are proposed by Venkatachalam and Langley for the categories included in the sample:

Adult males	2,500
Adult females	2,100
Adolescent females	2,050
Children 5–10 years	1,300
Children 3–5 years	1,200
Children 1 year	850

The ratio of these values was assumed to reflect the comparative ingestion of persons in the various age-sex categories. An adult female, for instance, was assumed to eat 21/25 as much as an adult male. A child five to ten years of age was assumed to eat 13/25 as much as an adult male, and so on. The problems of such a procedure are clearly understood. It is no doubt the case that actual practice deviates from ideal apportionment patterns. This procedure is adopted as the lesser of the possible evils: I believe greater error would have resulted from an attempt to estimate the comparative sizes of actual portions.

The suggested caloric values were divided by 100; the resultant figures may be referred to as "trophic units." An adult male represents twenty-five trophic units, an adult female twenty-one, etc. These were then multiplied by the number of consumer days in each category, yielding the number of trophic unit days in each, and a total of trophic unit days for the entire sample was taken. The total values of the several nutrients were then divided by the total number of trophic unit days to arrive at a trophic unit day value for each nutrient. From this, the daily intake of each nutrient for each category of persons was derived.

COMPARISON OF TSEMBAGA AND OTHER NEW GUINEA DIETS

Table 27 compares the Tsembaga diet to that of five other New Guinea groups. The figures published for Busuma, Kaiapit, Patep, and Kavataria

Table 27. Comparative Values of Six New Guinea Diets

Place	Source	Daily calories	Daily protein, in grams			Daily calcium, in grams	Total daily intake, in grams
			Veg.	Animal	Total		
Busama	Hipsley and Clements, 1947	1,223	14.4	4.7	19.1	.5	794
Kaiapit	Hipsley and Clements, 1947	1,609	21.7	3.1	24.8	.6	1,013
Patep	Hipsley and Clements, 1947	1,904	22.3	2.1	24.4	.6	1,387
Kavataria	Hipsley and Clements, 1947	1,600	22.4	18.4	41.3	.3	1,256
Chimbu	Venkatachalam, 1962	1,930	20.8	?	20.8 +		1,627
Tsembaga, minimum			34.7	?	34.7 +		
Tsembaga, maximum		2,015	46.8	?	46.8 +	1.2	2,287

are total per capita figures. No breakdown by age or sex categories is provided. It was therefore necessary to determine overall per capita figures for the intake of various nutrients by Tsembaga. The usefulness of such figures is limited to purposes of comparison. For purposes of evaluation, separate figures by age and sex category are preferable.

The information summarized in Table 27 suggests the marked superiority of the Tsembaga diet over those of the other groups. The differences between the Tsembaga and several of the other groups are so large, however, that they are suspect. The size of the disparities becomes increasingly apparent when gross intake is compared. Langley reports Busama intake to be 794 grams per day (1947:112–15). Tsembaga intake was almost three times as great. Langley states that there was a food shortage at Busama at the time of the survey, but no mention is made of a food shortage at Kaiapit, where the reported daily intake was only 1,013 grams, less than half that of the Tsembaga.

The methods employed by the New Guinea Food Survey expedition in 1947 are not made fully explicit, so it is impossible to judge whether different procedures led to different results. My belief is, nevertheless, that figures for Busama, Kaiapit, Patep, and Kavataria, which were derived from a limited number of visits to houses at mealtimes, do not adequately represent per capita consumption in those communities. With the exception of Patep, they seem much too low.

The Chimbu figure lends support to the Tsembaga figure. Much of the difference in the weights of Tsembaga and Chimbu intakes lies in the availability to the Tsembaga of greater amounts of nonstarch vegetables. It is in this difference that the qualitative as well as quantitative superiority of Tsembaga diet over Chimbu lies. Apparently absent from the diet of the latter are some of the leaves that constitute the most important source of both protein and calcium for the Tsembaga. It is probably altitudinal limitations that deprive the Chimbu of these valuable greens.

APPENDIX 10

Carrying Capacity

CARRYING CAPACITY FORMULA

Carneiro's formula for carrying capacity is the one used here.

$$(1) \qquad P = \frac{\dfrac{T}{R+Y} \times Y}{A}$$

Where:

P = The population which may be supported.

T = Total arable land.

R = Length of fallow in years.

Y = Length of cropping period in years.

A = The area of cultivated land required to provide the "average individual" with the amount of food he ordinarily derives from cultivated plants per year.

THE VALUES OF VARIABLES T AND R

The total area of arable land is not easy to determine in terrain as rugged as that occupied by the Tsembaga. The difference between orthographic and surface areas is substantial, due to both general and localized sloping. My calculation is that Tsembaga territory comprises, in total, 2,033 acres by orthographic measurements made on an aerial photograph. The total territory may be divided into a number of areas in terms of altitude, past use, vegetation cover, and agricultural potential. These discriminations are summarized in Table 28.

The 100 ± acres estimated to be arable in the Jimi Valley and the 200 ± acres estimated to be arable in the high altitude virgin forest in the Simbai Valley were not measured. These figures represent estimates, based upon walks through the areas, of the comparative size of areas un-

Table 28. Tsembaga Territory, Arable and Nonarable Land

Area	Total acreage	Arable	Nonarable
High-altitude high forest, Jimi Valley	343	100 ±	243
High-altitude high forest, Simbai Valley	602	200 ±	402
Secondary forest (gardened areas), Simbai Valley	1,019	864	150
Low-altitude forest remnants	28		28
Grassland	41		41
Totals	2,033	1,164	864

der high forest and nonarable moss forest. The border between these areas is indistinct. The area under high forest in the Simbai Valley seems never to have been gardened, and no gardening has been undertaken by Tsembaga in the Jimi Valley area for many years.

The figure in Table 28 for grassland includes only the one extensive area noted in Chapter 3. Allowance has been made for other, smaller grassy areas in the figure for nonarable land within the secondary forest. Similarly, the figure for low-altitude forest includes only areas of 3 to 4 acres or more. Smaller patches, like the smaller grassy areas, are included in the figure for nonarable land within the secondary forest. This latter figure is an estimate that allows for stream beds, rocky areas, gullies, and slopes over 43°, as well as for the small grassy areas and small patches of forest. The figure of 150 acres is probably conservative.

The areas tabulated above are orthographic areas. The terrain, however, is very rugged. The general slope in the areas that can be gardened is about 20°. This increases surface over planimetric area by a factor of 16.15:15. The intricate dissection of the terrain by streams and spurs projecting from the mountain wall further complicates the surface and increases its area, but there is no means for judging by how much. It will be assumed here that slopes in other directions approximate the general slope. Surface area will thus be taken as $16.15^2:15^2$, or 116.48 percent of orthographic area. Arable surface is summarized in Table 29.

Table 29. Arable Land Area Corrected for Slope, Tsembaga Territory

Location and association	Acreage
Simbai Valley secondary forest and gardens	1,002
Simbai Valley high forest	235
Jimi Valley high forest	116
Economic population density, total arable area:	97 p.s.m.
Economic population density, secondary forest and gardens:	124 p.s.m.

It is not the case, however, that all areas are equally productive. In an earlier section it was shown that the sweet potato gardens that are planted at higher altitudes in the secondary forest produce only 92.6 percent as many calories (4,418,215) in the twelve months of maximal production as do the taro-yam gardens planted at lower altitudes. An adjustment must be made for this difference. Again, however, a distinct boundary between the two zones cannot be drawn, for the region between 4,000 and 4,400 feet altitude is transitional. The lower zone will be said to consist of 650 acres and the upper, slightly less productive, areas 352.

It is reasonable to expect that gardens that might be cut in the high-altitude virgin forest, would, in the long run, show even lower productivity than those in the upper portion of the secondary forest. It will be assumed here that the diminishment in productivity would be of an order similar to that between the lower two zones. Arable land in the virgin forest will be regarded as 92.6 percent as productive as land in the upper portion of the secondary forest. Differences in lengths of fallow, as well as differences in yields, must also be considered. In an earlier section a value of fifteen years was adopted for the lower secondary forest zone and twenty-five years for the upper secondary forest zone. It is reasonable to expect that fallows on gardens cut in the virgin forest between 5,200 and 6,000 feet would be even longer. A figure of thirty-five years will be assumed here.

The three land classes that have been distinguished, differing both in productivity and length of fallow, are summarized in Table 30. These

Table 30. Tsembaga Arable Land Classes

Class	Acres	Productivity	Frequency of use
I	650	1.000	15 years 1.000
II	352	.926	25 years .600
III	351	.857	35 years .430

productivity and frequency of use factors permit the areas included in the three classes to be reduced to equivalent figures. Areas in Classes II and III, that is, may be expressed in terms of equivalent amounts of Class I land.

THE VALUE OF VARIABLE A

The value for A, the amount of land required for the "average individual," is a function of the age-sex composition of the particular population under study. The figure used here is based upon the age-sex composition of the Tsembaga in 1963. If there were changes in the propor-

288

Appendix 10

tions of persons in the various age-sex categories, each of which have different trophic requirements, there would be a change in the value of A.

Values for Variable A, Pig Population at Minimum

Actual measurements, based upon chain and compass mapping, are available for total acreage in production when the pig population was at a maximum. The areas of the gardens of the Tomegai clan are also available for 1963, when the herd was reduced to a minimum. These and other figures permit the determination of variable A for the Tsembaga when their pig herd was at a minimum in three ways. All three calculations will be made here as a check upon each other.

(A) The total annual caloric requirements of the entire population, with the pig herd at a minimum, may be divided by the annual per-acre yields of taro-yam gardens. The production of taro-yam gardens, rather than sugar-sweet potato gardens, may be taken because, as it has already been mentioned, virtually no separate sugar-sweet potato gardens are planted when the pig herd is at its minimum. Actual weighings have demonstrated that 85 percent of the total caloric yield of the taro-yam gardens is harvested during one twelve-month period. It is this figure, 4,418,215 calories, which is, accordingly, used in this calculation.

Total Tsembaga consumption is presented in Table 31. The number of

Table 31. Total Caloric Requirements, All Tsembaga

Age	Sex	Trophic units	Daily per capita intake (cal.)	Number of persons in category	Total daily consumption of category (cal.)
Over 50	male	20	2,060	8	16,480
	female	16	1,648	12	19,776
21–49	male	25	2,575	49	126,175
	female	21	2,163	40	86,520
15–20	male	29	2,987	11	32,857
	female	20.5	2,112	7	14,784
10–15	male	22	2,266	15	33,990
	female	21	2,163	8	17,304
5–10	male-female	15	1,339	25	33,475
0–5	male-female	10	1,030	29	29,870

Total daily consumption: 411,231 cal.
Total annual consumption: 150,089,315 cal.
Total trophic units: 4,042

trophic units represented by categories not included within the Tomegai clan, from whom all consumption data were gathered, are derived from Langley (1947:134).

The amount of acreage (Gs) that must be put into production annually to fulfill Tsembaga trophic requirements may be solved for by the following simple equation:

(2)
$$Gs = \frac{Ct - Co}{Ca}$$

Where:

Ct = Total caloric requirements, Tsembaga.
Co = Calories available from old gardens (15% of total).
Ca = Caloric yield per acre, taro-yam gardens, 24–76 weeks after planting.

$$Gs = \frac{150,089,315 - 22,513,389}{4,418,215}$$

A value may now be assigned variable A through solution of the following equation:

(3)
$$A = \frac{Gs}{P}$$

Where:

P = Total Tsembaga population (204 persons).

$$A = \frac{28.87}{204}$$

A = .142 acres.

(B) The acreage per "trophic unit" placed in production by the Tomegai clan in 1963 may be calculated from the total area they placed in production in 1963 by solution of the following equation:

(4)
$$Ua = \frac{Gn}{U}$$

Where:

Ua = Acreage per trophic unit.
Gn = Acreage put into production by the Tomegai, 1963 (3.07 acres).
U = Total trophic units, Tomegai clan (313).

$$Ua = \frac{3.07}{313}$$

Ua = .0098 acres

If the acreage per trophic unit is then multiplied by the total trophic units of all the Tsembaga, a figure for minimal required acreage is obtained.

(5) $4042 \times .0098 = 39.61$ acres

$$A = \frac{39.61}{204}$$

$A = .194$ acres

(C) Another calculation may be made by extending a comparison of the acreages placed in production by the Tomegai in 1962 and 1963 to the acreage of all of the Tsembaga.

The following areas are known by measurement:
Gl = Total acreage put into production, 1962.
Gt = Acreage put into production by Tomegai, 1962.
Gn = Acreage put into production by Tomegai, 1963.

To solve for total acreage put into production in 1963 (Gs), the following ratio may be used:

(6) $Gl:Gs = Gt:Gn$

Correction must be made for the differences in the ratios of sugar-sweet potato gardens to taro-yam gardens in the two years. This may be accomplished by using the factor that converts Class II to Class I to land.

Tomegai gardens, 1962 (actual measurement)
Area in acres, sugar-sweet potato gardens:
2.56 corrected: 2.37
Area in acres, taro-yam gardens   2.27
Total acreage corrected: 4.64

Tomegai gardens, 1963 (actual measurement)
Area in acres, sugar-sweet potato gardens:
.19 corrected: .18
Area in acres, taro-yam gardens: 2.89
Total acreage corrected: 3.07

All Tsembaga gardens, 1962 (actual measurement)
Area in acres, sugar-sweet potato gardens:
19.34 corrected: 17.91
Area in acres, taro-yam gardens: 27.84
Total corrected: 45.75

Values are now available for solution of ratio (6).

(6) $45.75 : Gs = 4.64 : 3.07$

$\qquad$ Gs = 30.27

(7) $A = \dfrac{30.27}{204}$

$$A = .148 \text{ acres}$$

The discrepancy between calculations 1 and 2 is .052 acres per person, in aggregate 10.74 acres, or approximately 27%. Discrepancies of this magnitude are, perhaps, to be expected when values rest in part upon measurements undertaken in terrain as broken as that occupied by the Tsembaga and upon the extension of measurements of intake, themselves subject to some imprecision. It is probable, however, that this discrepancy has its basis not so much in errors in measurement as in actual differences in gardening practice. Calculation C bears out this interpretation. It will be noted that the Tomegai clan comprises 313 "trophic units," 7.77% of the total of 4,042 "trophic units" for the entire Tsembaga. In 1962, however, Tomegai gardens comprised 4.55 acres (corrected) or 9.94% of the total of 45.75 acres (corrected) put into production by all Tsembaga. The discrepancy between 7.77% and 9.94%, approximately 22%, corresponds closely to the discrepancy between calculations B and C, and may cancel it. It may be, that is, that the Tomegai regularly put larger-than-average amounts of land into cultivation, or at least did so in 1963 as well as 1962. This would not affect the reliability of derivation C, nor would the reliability of derivation A be affected unless it could be shown that the Tomegai eat more than other Tsembaga, and that there has therefore been an error made in extending Tomegai trophic requirements to the entire local population. There is no reason to believe this. Tomegai adult males are slightly below (approximately 3 kg) the average weight of all Tsembaga adult males, and the average weight of Tomegai adult females falls almost exactly on the average for the Tsembaga adult females as a whole. Moreover, the Tomegai do not seem to be either more or less active than other Tsembaga.

Their greater-than-average acreage in cultivation in 1962 cannot be explained, secondly, by the possession of a greater-than-average number of pigs by the Tomegai, since this was not the case. The ratio of pigs (of 120- to 150-pound size) to people for all the Tsembaga in 1962 was 83:1. The ratio of Tomegai pigs to Tomegai was .81:1.

Another explanation might have to do with land quality. There is no reason to believe, however, and considerable reason to reject, the notion that Tomegai gardens were on poorer-than-average land in 1962 or, as a rule, at other times.

Two explanations may be suggested. First, Tomegai male gardeners included six men making all their gardens and one man making half his gardens with the four Tomegai women and the one Tomegai adolescent girl (whose gardening activities may be counted as half that of an adult woman). This ratio of 6.5 male gardeners to 4.5 female gardeners exceeds the average, which is approximately 6.7:5.7. It is likely that with more males engaged in clearing, more acreage will be put into production.

Second, the discrepancy may be random. It is not likely that any group of ten or eleven gardeners will put into production the same amount of acreage as any other group of similar size, even within the same local population. The Tomegai may be particularly industrious (although it didn't seem so) or it may be that the measurements were taken in years when their acreage under production exceeded the average because of such considerations as the configuration of the land on the sites they were gardening. I believe the latter to be most likely.

It is probable that errors in measurement, sampling error, and differences in actual practice have all contributed to the discrepancy between calculations 1 and 2. The indication is, however, that a value of .194 for variable A is too high, and that more realistic values are derived in the two other calculations. Both extremes, however, will be used in further calculations.

Value for Variable A, Pig Population at Maximum

Since actual measurements were made of the total area put into production when the pig population was at its maximum, no estimate need be made. The amount, 47.18 acres, has already been introduced in previous calculations, where an adjustment to reduce it to its Class I equivalent, 45.75 acres, was made.

The formula solving for variable A may now be applied for acreage per capita under production when the pig population is at maximum.

(8) $$A = \frac{45.75}{204}$$

$$A = .224 \text{ acres}$$

ESTIMATION OF CARRYING CAPACITY FOR HUMANS

Values for all variables are now provided, enabling us to solve for the maximum number of human beings that could be supported on Tsembaga territory by using formula (1).

Carrying Capacity of Secondary Forest Areas

Separate calculations will be made for the maximum number of people who could be supported on areas either under cultivation or under secondary forest at the time of fieldwork when (1) the pig population is at minimum, (defined as the ratio pigs : people = .29:1, pigs averaging 60 to 75 pounds) and (2) when the pig population is at maximum, (defined as the ratio pigs : people = .83:1, pigs averaging 120 to 150 pounds).

CARRYING CAPACITY, PIG POPULATION AT MINIMUM

Three values for variable A were derived; calculations will be made using all three.

(1)
$$P = \frac{\dfrac{T}{R + Y} \times Y}{A}$$

$$P = \frac{\dfrac{T \text{ class I} + (T \text{ class II} \times .926 \times .6)}{(R + Y)} \times Y}{A}$$

a) A = .142 acres

$$P = \frac{\dfrac{650 + (352 \times .926 \times .6)}{14 + 1} \times 1}{.142}$$

$$P = \frac{\dfrac{846}{15}}{.142}$$

$$P = \frac{56.40}{.142}$$

$$P = 397 \text{ persons}$$

b) A = .148 acres

$$P = \frac{56.40}{.148}$$

$$P = 383 \text{ persons}$$

c) A = .194 acres

$$P = \frac{56.40}{.194}$$

$$P = 290 \text{ persons}$$

CARRYING CAPACITY, PIG POPULATION AT MAXIMUM

Only one value for variable A will be used, since it was obtained by actual measurements.

$$P = \frac{\frac{T}{R+Y} \times Y}{A}$$

$$P = \frac{56.40}{.224}$$

$$P = 251 \text{ persons}$$

Carrying Capacity, Land under High Forest

Estimates will be made for (1) pig population at minimum and (2) pig population at maximum.

CARRYING CAPACITY, PIG POPULATION AT MINIMUM

(1) $$P = \frac{\frac{T \text{ class III}}{R+Y} \times Y}{A}$$

$$P = \frac{\frac{351 \times .857 \times .43}{14 + 1} \times 1}{A}$$

a) A = .142 acres

$$P = \frac{\frac{129}{15}}{.146}$$

$$P = 60 \text{ persons}$$

b) A = .194 persons

$$P = \frac{\frac{129}{15}}{.194}$$

$$P = 44 \text{ persons}$$

CARRYING CAPACITY, PIG POPULATION AT MAXIMUM

$$A = .224 \text{ acres}$$

$$P = \frac{\frac{129}{15}}{.224}$$

$$P = 38 \text{ persons}$$

ESTIMATION OF CARRYING CAPACITY FOR PIGS

As in the case of the human population, estimates will be made separately for (1) areas under cultivation and secondary forest during the fieldwork period, and (2) areas under high forest but which were deemed to be arable. Domestic food requirements only are considered. No attempt was made to estimate the requirements of the animals for grazing land.

Carrying Capacity for Pigs, Land under Cultivation and Secondary Forest

Two methods are used as a check upon each other: (1) the number of pigs that could be supported beyond the maximum of 1962 is computed and added to the maximum, and (2) the number of pigs that could be supported above the minimum is added to the minimum.

COMPUTING CARRYING CAPACITY FOR PIGS, BY INCREMENT
TO MAXIMUM POPULATION

The following formula (9) may be used:

(9) $$Pp = Nm + Na$$

Where:

Pp = The carrying capacity for pigs, holding human population constant (204 persons distributed in age-sex categories as in Table 1).

Nm = Maximum herd size, as censused (169 pigs, average size 3.8, or 120 to 150 pounds).

Na = Additional pigs, which may be supported without shortening fallows or bringing virgin forest into production. Na may be solved for by the following equation:

(10) $$Na = \frac{T - Gl}{K}$$

T = Total Class I or Class I-equivalent land which may be put into cultivation annually without shortening fallows or bringing virgin forest into production.

$$T = \frac{\text{T Class I} + (\text{T Class II} \times .926 \times .6)}{R + Y} \times Y.$$

Gl = Total acreage of Class I or Class I-equivalent land put into production when the pig population was at maximum size. Values have been assigned by actual measurements of all gardens in 1962.

K = Amount of land required to feed each 120- to 150-pound pig in excess of those included in the minimum pig population. K has been assigned a value of .15 acres (see Chapter 3, p. 62).

These equivalents may now replace unknowns in formula (9).

$$Pp = Nm + Na$$

$$Pp = Nm + \frac{T - Gl}{K}$$

$$Pp = Nm +$$

$$\frac{\dfrac{\text{T Class I} + (\text{T Class II} \times .926 \times .6) \times Y - [\text{G Class I} + (\text{G Class II} \times .926)]}{(R + Y)}}{K}$$

$$Pp = 169 + \frac{\dfrac{650 + (352 \times .926)}{(14 + 1)} \times 1 - (27.84 + 17.91)}{.15}$$

$$Pp = 169 + \frac{56.40 - 45.75}{.15}$$

$$Pp = 169 + 71$$

$$Pp = 240 \text{ pigs averaging 120 to 150 pounds}$$

COMPUTING CARRYING CAPACITY FOR PIGS BY INCREMENT
TO THE MINIMUM POPULATION

The following formula is used:

(11) $$Pp = \frac{Ns}{2} + Nb$$

Where:

Pp = The carrying capacity for pigs of an average size of 120 to 150 pounds, holding human population constant (204 persons distributed in age-sex categories in Table 1).

Ns = The number of pigs, averaging 60 to 75 pounds comprising the minimum pig herd (Nov. 1963).

2 = A correcting factor, converting average size of animals when pig population is minimum (60 to 75 lbs.) to average size when pig population is maximum (120 to 150 lbs.).

Nb = The number of additional pigs of size 120 to 150 pounds which may be supported without shortening fallows or bringing virgin forest into production. Nb may be solved for by the following equation:

(12) $$Nb = \frac{T - Gs}{K}.$$

Where:

T and K have the same values as in formula (10). Gs represents total acreage of Class I or Class I-equivalent land under production when the pig population was at a minimum. Three values have already been derived for Gs. Calculations will be made using the two extremes: 28.87 and 39.61 acres.

a) Value of Gs = 39.61 acres

$$Pp = \frac{Ns}{2} + \frac{T - Gs}{K}$$

$$Pp = \frac{60}{2} + \frac{56.40 - 39.61}{.15}$$

Pp = 142 pigs averaging 120 to 150 pounds.

b) Value of Gs = 28.87 acres

$$Pp = \frac{60}{2} + \frac{56.40 - 28.87}{.15}$$

Pp = 214 pigs averaging 120 to 150 pounds

Carrying Capacity for Pigs, Land under High Forest

Only formula (11) will be used. Adjustment must be made, however, in the value of Ns. This adjustment is accomplished by solving the following ratio for X.

(13) $Gl:Gh = Ns:X$

   Where:

   Gl = The maximum amount of Class I and Class II land that could be put under production at one time without shortening fallows. This has already been determined (see p. 293) to be 56.40 acres.

   Gh = The maximum amount of Class III land that could be put under production at one time allowing a 35-year fallow. This has already been determined to be 8.6 acres.

   Ns = The number of pigs, averaging 60 to 75 pounds, comprising the minimum pig herd (Nov. 1963). This number, by census, was determined to be 60.

   $56.40:8.6 = 60:X$

   $X = 9.1$

Values may now be provided for all variables in formula

(11) $$Pp = \frac{Ns}{2} + Nb$$

                              $$Pp = \frac{9.1}{2} + \frac{8.6}{.15}$$

   Pp = 62 pigs averaging 120 to 150 pounds.

EPILOGUE, 1984

OUTLINE OF CONTENTS

INTRODUCTION

Clarification, the criticism of some critiques, and the conservation of what I think worth saving form one of the purposes of this epilogue. I have already responded to certain critics in earlier publications and shall incorporate portions of those earlier discussions into this more extended one because they are crucial to it. I will enlarge upon those earlier rejoinders here and will discuss a wider range of issues and respond to a larger number of critics than did they. I apologize to those serious critics whose comments I have not addressed. Despite the length of this epilogue it could not be comprehensive.

The second general reason for this epilogue is really the more important of the two. It is to carry forward, if I can, discussion of some of the important issues raised by critics or entailed in responses to their critiques. Some of these issues, having been framed in terms of this ethnography's particulars, require ethnographically particular rejoinders, but it is with the general issues and not ethnographic particulars that I am concerned, and it is in terms of general issues that this epilogue is organized.

I shall make no attempt to correct or update ethnography in this epilogue. Such corrections will be published with the results of my visit to the Tsembaga from October 1981 to August 1982. Since my first visit to the area in 1962–63 (which coincided with the research of A. P. Vayda, Cherry Lowman-Vayda, Ann Rappaport, and Allison and Marek Jablanko), four anthropologists (Georgeda Buchbinder, Christopher Healy, Edward Li Puma, and Neal McLean) have worked among the Maring, as have three geographers (William Clarke, Har-

ley Manner, and John Street), and one student of comparative law
(Robin MacKenzie). Although there have been some differences in
interpretations, no important ethnographic disagreements have yet
appeared among us.

The logic by which this epilogue is organized may not be immediately apparent. I begin with issues of a very general nature, issues
surrounding the character of ecological approaches in anthropology
generally, and proceed to matters of a more detailed nature, some
methodological and technical. There is a concurrent movement from
consideration of synchronic functional formulations to adaptive systemic accounts. At the end, in the last two sections, there is a return
to issues of great generality.

In more detail, the discussion in section 1, which is a response to
the charge that ecological approaches in anthropology represent a form
of vulgar materialism, leads to, in section 2, the distinction between
economic and ecological formulations. This discussion is based upon
some modern readings of Heraclitus. Section 3 considers the relationship between native understandings and ecological principles, and
leads, in section 4, to discussions of "ecology fetishism" and of whether
ecological formulations are explanations or "problematics." Section 5
deals with the relationship between cognized and operational models.
Sections 6 through 9 address aspects of functionalism that I believe
to have been misunderstood. Section 6 is concerned with function
and description, section 7 with criteria for assessing the functional or
adaptive characteristics, not of items or elements included in systems, but of systems as wholes. Section 8 explores differences between formal and final causal formulations, often fallaciously lumped
as "functional." Section 9 considers systemic analysis as a reform of
functional formulations and examines some of the problems of systemic formulations. These include metrical problems, and problems
of some of the quantitative data published in *Pigs for the Ancestors*
are discussed. (Because of its specialized nature, criticism of the nutritional aspects of the book are not dealt with in the body of the
epilogue but in appendix 11.) Section 10 focuses on units of analysis,
sections 11 and 12 on the concept of negative feedback and its place
in *Pigs for the Ancestors*. Section 13 offers an abbreviated account of
a formulation of adaptation that I have described in greater detail

elsewhere. Section 14 deals with a larger issue raised by earlier discussion of the relationship between native and analytic models—the
vying claims of subjective and objective perspectives in anthropological study. Section 15 is concerned with possibilities for the development of more comprehensive "structures of understanding" than any
currently in favor.

Given the variety of issues and criticism that I attempt to address,
and what may be an idiosyncratic and possibly inconsistent way of
addressing them, most readers are sure to find something in this epilogue with which they will disagree. I myself surely will, no doubt
soon after the epilogue is bound with the original text. This is only
one moment in the ongoing process by which we formulate our understanding of ourselves and the systems in which we live.

SECTION 1

Ecology as Vulgar Materialism

It is useful to begin with the characterization of "the ecological anthropology of Vayda, Rappaport and others" as a form of "vulgar materialism" (Friedman, 1974:444). If the term *vulgar materialism* were nothing more than pejorative there would be no need to take note of it. Responding to it does, however, offer an opportunity to address in general terms the relationship of social forms to technologies and environments and to begin to contrast ecological and economic formulations. *Vulgar materialism* does have a technical meaning that Friedman gives as follows:

> Vulgar materialism, mechanical materialism, and economism are terms which refer to a simplistic kind of materialism, rejected by Marx, which envisages social forms as mere epiphenomena of technologies and environments, either by direct causation or by some economic rationality which makes institutions the product of social optimisation. This approach has made its appearance in the form of what Sahlins has called the "new materialism" (1969:30): neofunctional ecology and cultural materialism, both of which are embedded in the functionalist-empiricist ideology which has characterised most of American social science. [1974:456–57]

Two aspects of this definition or characterization bear comment. First, there is the matter of "social forms as mere epiphenomena of technologies and environments." What seems to be implied by use of the term *epiphenomena* here is that social forms are caused by, or emerge out of (perhaps as some sort of by-product), the interactions of environments and technologies. If this is a criterion of vulgar materialism then *Pigs for the Ancestors* is not vulgarly materialistic because it does not attempt to account for the emergence of the social forms with which it is concerned, except, perhaps, in a few sentences (p. 231, above) taking note of strong similarities among the ritual practices of different Highlands people and suggesting that the variations among them may be the result of "differences in the ecological circumstances of various populations." This brief suggestion followed an earlier article by Vayda and me (1967) in which we (also briefly) suggested that cultures generate (in accordance with their own constraints) ranges of forms from among which environments select in a manner that may be generally similar to the ways in which natural selection operates upon populations of organisms. I grant that this formulation was vague, that it was hardly original, and that it does not constitute an adequate account of the relationship of culture to environment, particularly of the mutually causal and constraining processes that characterize the evolution or "emergence" of human social forms, anthropocentric ecosystems, and even humanity itself. I simply assert here that it is an account that does not take social forms to be mere epiphenomena of technologies and environments. It is an account to which, I believe, most ecologically oriented anthropologists would subscribe, although few of them would take it to be an adequate characterization of sociocultural evolution. It was not offered as such. Most ecological anthropologists would also recognize the importance of dialectical processes internal to societies in the transformation of social forms. It is worth noting that Friedman accompanies his criticism with a rather similar proposal—that environments, as it were, select from among the range of possible transformations of structures those that do in fact occur. It does not seem to me that there are fundamental differences between his suggestion, which he offers as an insight emerging new from the conjunction of structuralism and Marxism, and ours, which followed from a much older evolutionary tradition. His emphasis upon structural transformation, inexplicit in our formulation, is a useful explication, but no more than that, inasmuch as structural transformation is an entailment of any evolutionary sequence. If there is no transformation there is no evolution.

I am led here to a second point in Friedman's criticism. He also considers to be vulgarly materialist a view which would take as causal an economic rationality, making institutions the products of social optimization. The charge is difficult to deal with because of the vagueness of the terms. *Rationality* implies, if it does not entail, consciousness, purpose, and deliberateness. *Economic rationality* implies that consciousness and deliberateness are put to the task of weighing alternatives with respect to differences in the advantages they may be expected to confer upon those who have the opportunity to select among them. The goals of economic rationality, it is generally assumed, are highly specific and it is also usually assumed that the aim of economic rationality is to maximize these specifics, whatever they may be. Economic rationality is in its nature competitive and individualistic.

Pigs for the Ancestors did, of course, consider behavior that may aptly be described as economic. Individual choices are made with respect to the disposal of pigs; women, I suppose, assess the degrees to which their backs ache against the goals of their husbands; people must be concerned with trade-offs between the work of pig raising and the trouble following garden invasions on the one hand, and the satisfaction of their allies with the pork they are given on the other, and so on. Whether these and other considerations are weighed rationally is not a matter which need concern us. One of the main points of the analysis, however, was that the Maring ritual regulation is surely not to be understood as an outcome of the economistic behavior of individuals or as compatible with the economic goals of individuals in all particulars, contrary to criticisms of Bennett (1976:185–86, 206) and Bergmann (1975:7). Indeed, the Maring ritual cycle stands against or constrains the economic and political goals of individuals and even of corporate groups. In some instances it induces them to behave in ways which do the opposite of maximizing their positions vis-à-vis others. This argument seems to me to be implicit throughout *Pigs for the Ancestors*, but was made explicit in at least one passage (p. 239), and has been argued at length elsewhere (Kelly and Rappaport, 1975).

I have argued that ritual regulation among the Maring is generally consonant with the imperatives of social groups and ecosystems. A charge of *ecological* rationality might have been more apposite (were it not for the fact that Maring understandings of nature are not encoded in explicitly ecological terms). "Ecological rationality" (which may be observed in some individuals) is not simply an extension of economic rationality into the environmental domain. It incorporates the principles of persistence of systems in which individual actors participate and upon which their continued existence is contingent. As such it *contradicts* a rationality which is concerned with the maximization of the immediate and individual interests of separate actors vis-à-vis those systems.

SECTION 2

Economism, Ecologism, and Logos

It is especially important to emphasize the contrast between economic and ecological rationality in light of the assertion of their kinship by Marshall Sahlins (1976b:84ff.). Sahlins takes both to be varieties of "practical reason" and claims that their invocation in anthropological attempts at understanding divests the objects studied of their distinctively cultural qualities. Both, he argues "exchange . . . meaningful content for functional truth" (p. 88), a form of transaction constituting "vulgar Marxism" in Sartre's usage. This critique, which is not Sahlins's alone, is perhaps the most influential to have been brought to bear upon ecological formulations. It is one which has contributed to the unhappy polarization of the field into "materialist" versus "interpretive" or "symbolic" camps, a matter to which we shall return. In the last section I suggested that economic rationality is actor-oriented whereas ecological logic is not. We must pursue the implications of this contrast.

As I see the matter the relationship of economic rationality to ecological logic is similar to, or even a contemporary expression of, the relationship of *idia phronesis* to *logos* in the thought of Heraclitus (or what is known of it; Heraclitus survives only in fragments preserved in the works of later writers; see Kirk, 1954).

I associate ecological order with the term *logos* which, by Heraclitus's time, had come to denote the "rational relation of things to one another" and had already acquired "the general sense of order or measure" (Kleinknecht, 1967:78). The term *order* implies a unification of some sort and, according to Heidegger (1959:127f.), the "to-getherness" of all "things that are" is fundamental to Heraclitus's con-ception, as holism is to ecological thought. In his reading of Fragment 114, Heidegger characterizes this "togetherness" in extreme terms: "the original unifying unity of what tends apart." In his summary discussion of Fragments 1, 2, 50, and 114 G. S. Kirk (1954:32) agrees. "The chief content of the *Logos* is that all things are one." Heidegger observes that permanence and endurance are also fundamental to the logos as it was conceived by the philosopher remembered best for the dictum "Everything flows." Kleinknecht concurs: "It is the tran-scendent and lasting order in which eternal flux occurs" (1967:81). In the centuries following Heraclitus *logos* became ever more explicitly "a term for the ordered and teleologically orientated nature of the world. . . . The principle which creates the world, i.e. which orders and constitutes it. . . . The world is a grand unfolding of the *logos*" (Kleinknecht, 1967:81f.).

Logos also possesses the quality of *alethia* which, etymologically, denotes "non-concealment" (Bultmann, 1967:238) but is generally glossed as "truth"—not so much the truth that some statements pos-sess by virtue of their correspondence to existing states of affairs, but the simple fact of those states of affairs themselves: not the truth of words but of things, that which may "disclose itself as it really is . . . the full or real state of affairs to be maintained against different state-ments." Its opposites are *pseudos*, "deception," and *doxa*, the latter, according to Bultmann, being understood as "appearance" or "mere opinion." As the "truth of things" the notion of *alethia* was closely related to *physis* which Kirk, after considerable discussion, renders "the real constitution of a thing, or of things severally" (1954:230).

Logos, in sum, in the thought of Heraclitus and his followers, des-ignated the principle through which the cosmos is generated, or-dered, unified, and maintained, or even the ordered, unified, evolv-ing cosmos itself. Despite the meanings adhering to the term in later, especially Christian, thought, *logos* in Heraclitus signifies "neither meaning nor word nor doctrine" (Heidegger, 1959:128), but an order binding together a world that includes meanings and those for whom they are meaningful. Contemporary ecological thought also conceives a unified nature within which humanity not only has a place but within

which the meanings manufactured by humans may have ordering—
and disordering—power.

By Heraclitus's time it was thought that "the same *logos* constitutes
the being of both cosmos and man." The logos is, therefore, the common principle making possible "understanding between man and the
world and also between men" (Kleinknecht, 1967:81). Later it becomes explicit that "the particular logos of man . . . is part of the
general logos . . . which achieves awareness in man" (1967:85). As
such it is "not taken to be something which is merely grasped theoretically. It claims a man. It determines his true life and conduct.
The logos is thus the norm" (1967:81).

Although the logos is an ordering of nature it is clear that *as such*
it possesses an irreducible social component. It "constitutes the norm,"
and it assimilates those who follow it into "a great cosmos," thereby
binding them to each other (Kleinknecht, 1967:85). It also may be
shared. Kirk (1954:32) writes: "The *logos* according to which all things
came to be is 'common' in two senses: it is universal and it is equally
apprehensible to all." In later centuries the logos comes to be regarded as "the basic fact in all life in society" and as such is "the
decisive point in the politics of Socrates and Plato" (Kleinknecht,
1967:83).

The general conception of *logos* developing in Heraclitus's time
and in ensuing centuries was of a unified natural order constituted on
the one hand by processes—climatic, tectonic, and biotic—over which
humanity exercises no control and, on the other hand, by human
thought and action producing social constructions in dynamic, fluctuating, tense and even violent harmony with the rest of the cosmos.
The holism of this formulation, stripped of its possible mysticism, is
also characteristic of what I take to be ecological thought.

In the Heraclitean conception humanity has a unique and awful
responsibility for the realization of logos. It is in humanity and, as far
as humanity knows, in humanity alone that logos reaches consciousness. Humanity, therefore, is the only way the world has to think
about itself. To "follow the logos" is to think *as part* of the world on
behalf of the world as a whole.

But, according to Heraclitus, those who follow the logos are few.

First, although the logos is not beyond the reach of human intelligence it is not available to casual observation. Its harmony lies concealed beneath—or above—the world's apparent conflicts, disorders, and tensions and can only be revealed through effort or work in the sense, according to Heidegger (1959:191), of *ergon*, "the creation that discloses the truth of something that is present" (he offers as examples the work of the word in thought and poetry, the work of stone in temple and statue, the work of the *polis*, to which may be added the work of ritual or liturgy, a term, incidentally, derived from *laos ergon*, the "work of the people").

For another thing, humans are likely to be misled by other forms of thought: ". . . it is necessary to follow the common [universal, apprehensible to all, shared] but although the Logos is common the many live as though they had a private understanding" (Kirk, 1954:57).

This disparaging allusion to private understanding expresses a radical distinction in Heraclitus between "human wisdom which is the same kind as the divine" and "other forms of cleverness." Human wisdom "is of greater importance . . . because only by possessing it can man adequately assimilate himself to the ordered world of which he is a part" (Kirk, 1954:385). Other forms of cleverness constitute "private understanding." Lodged in the ordinary consciousnesses of distinct individuals and growing out of the knowledge of separation from others that is the common sense of individual consciousness, private understanding throws between logos and its comprehension the barriers of *pseudos*, *doxa*, and *idia phronesis*. As appearance, *doxa* may generate misinterpretation; as opinion, it harbors the possibility of error and error's defense. Deception, error, and misinterpretation may generate the conception and establishment of orders that violate logos, orders that cannot be maintained without damage to the world. The most important substantive problem to be addressed by an ecologically oriented anthropology may well be disparities between natural order and human understanding.

Doxa is extremely difficult—arguably impossible—to avoid, for, as Heraclitus knew (Kirk 1954:65), even the assertion of logos, in its opposition to other assertions, can itself be taken to be no more than *doxa*.

Idia phronesis is "practical wisdom," "individual prudence," "the logic of private advantage,"* the thought of the individual who, in his separation, is concerned to maximize his position vis-à-vis others. The similarity or even identity of *idia phronesis* and economic rationality is patent. To follow the logos is to think and act as part of the world for the sake of the world, but to be guided by *idia phronesis* is to think and act against the world. To follow the logos is to strengthen the world's unity; to act in accordance with *idia phronesis* may be to undo the world. For the world is first broken and then dissolved by the apotheosis of self-interest, ever more destructive as special interests ramify with the elaboration of the division of labor, as technology becomes increasingly powerful, as money penetrates into ever more areas of life, and as knowledge itself is fragmented. The state of the world stands in evidence. If economic rationality and ecological logic are both forms of practical reason as Sahlins would have it, they are very different forms with very different material, social, and moral consequences. The contrast between them, moreover, has implications for the use of individual decision-making models in ecological anthropology, a matter to which we shall return in section 10.

*These glosses were suggested by Keith Hart.

SECTION 3

Ecological Principles and Native Understandings

That the conceptions represented in the Maring ritual cycle are consonant with ecological principle constituted an important part of the interpretation offered in *Pigs for the Ancestors*. It is a shortcoming of the book that the accord between the religious logic of this liturgical order and ecosystemic and other requirements was not accounted for, a shortcoming to which several critics have called attention. Burnham, for instance, commenting on a later work, observes, "Rappaport is simply telling us that, at least among primitive societies, we can trust in the ecological wisdom of the actors" (1979:198).

I am not in a position to account historically for the consonance of the understandings encoded in the Maring liturgical order or of the actions it ordains with Maring ecosystemic requirements. In a response to James G. Peoples's sociobiological reinterpretation of the cycle (1982:304) I did elaborate a little upon the suggestion made in *Pigs for the Ancestors* (p. 231), to which I have already alluded, that the Maring liturgical order and its understandings may be one of a family of cognate forms, widespread in the Central Highlands, possibly including the Chimbu *Bugla Gende* (Brookfield and Brown, 1963), the Metlpa *Moka* (Strathern, 1971), the Enga *Te* (Meggitt, 1965) as well as the liturgical orders of the Siane (Salisbury, 1965), the Kuma (Reay, 1959), the Daribi (Wagner, 1972), and others. I further suggested (1982) that they could have become differentiated through a process of adaptive radiation, their structures, functions, contents, and cosmologies being differently transformed in response to differing environmental circumstances. I do not pretend that such a gen-

313

eral and schematic proposal constitutes an adequate response to the request for a particular account; I offer it as no more than a suggestion for a line of investigation. There is, nevertheless, more to say not only about the Maring case in particular, but about the relationship between native understanding and ecological principles generally.

LOGOS, LITURGY, AND SANCTITY

Much of the "ecological wisdom" of which Burnham speaks is, among the Maring, part of a corpus of mundane knowledge developed pragmatically by generations of gardeners. As such it is not mysterious. General governance of production is, however, encoded in the ritual cycle and something should be said here about ritual's special capacities in this regard. I suggested in *Pigs for the Ancestors* (p. 236) and elaborated the suggestion in later publications (1971c, 1971d, 1979d, 1979e) that in the absence of discrete authorities in whom power is vested, compliance to conventions may be secured by sanctifying them. Sanctity is a "functional equivalent" of power (that is, people may comply with authorities for a number of reasons; the authority may be powerful or persuasive or sanctified). I have further argued (1979c) that sanctity, which I have defined as "the quality of unquestionableness imputed by congregations to postulates in their nature absolutely unfalsifiable and objectively unverifiable," is a product of the *form which is* ritual. To encode conventions in a ritual cycle is ipso facto to sanctify them—to ascribe legitimacy to them. Because ritual's antiquity is beyond doubt and because its performance does not necessarily require the presence or even existence of discrete human authorities, it is plausible to propose that ritual constituted humanity's primordial means for establishing convention, and thus that it is the primordial basis by which humans established and maintained order within and between their own groups and between their own groups and their environments (see Rappaport, 1971b, 1979a, 1979b).

In section 2 I proposed a resemblance, association, or even identity between a broadly conceived ecological order and the notion of *logos* as it seems to have been conceived by Heraclitus. Now I would add that there is an obvious affinity between *logos* and liturgy. I have defined ritual as *the performance of more or less invariant sequences*

of formal acts and utterances not encoded by the performers
(1979d:175). I have argued (1979d) that rituals, or liturgical orders,
establish (i.e., enunciate *and* accept) *logoi;* for, by definition, in performing a ritual the participant conforms to, which is to say "follows,"
its order. In its performance the order that it encodes—the set of
conventions it ordains—is realized (i.e., made real). More than that:
it is given life and voice by the breath and bodies of the performers.
Participants become parts of the orders in which they participate. It
hardly does justice to the relationship of participants to the conventions represented in the orders in which they participate to say that
they accept them as sacred or sanctified, for in becoming parts of the
orders they realize they become *unified* with them. I have already
proposed that the essence of sanctity is unquestionableness, a generalized quality which subsumes more specific ones: truthfulness,
propriety, morality, and, of course, legitimacy. Whether or not participants abide by the conventional rules sanctified in rituals in which
they themselves perform, the rules are binding for them. For performers, noncompliance is not simply a neutral failure to conform. It
is violation or infraction of sanctified terms which they, having accepted, are obligated to honor. Breach of such obligations constitutes
sacrilege. To cite terms used by Kleinknecht in reference to the ancient Greek concept of *logos,* the relationship of the performer to the
conventions he enlivens in the performance of a ritual is not one of
mere "theoretical understanding." The order of which he becomes a
part "claims" the performer. Its claims are always moral and sometimes legal and emotional as well.

THE ADAPTIVENESS OF SANCTIFIED UNDERSTANDINGS

It follows from such an account that the relationship of participants
to the conventional understandings and rules organized in liturgical
orders is different from the relationship of moderns to secular cognized models composed of scientific and practical knowledge organized by preference and notions of advantage (economic rationality).
Whereas the latter would seem relativistic, pragmatic, and flexible
the former would seem—if invariance is the essence of ritual form,
and sanctity the essence of the conventions it represents—absolute

and inflexible. As such it would be incapable of the sort of adaptiveness by which I would account for the development of the particulars of the Maring ritual cycle. It is undoubtedly the case that liturgical orders have sometimes resisted transformations felt to be urgently needed by their congregations and, possibly, judged to be crucial by objective criteria as well. The position of the Catholic church on birth control in the face of widespread defiance, defection, and challenges to the very bases of its authority stands as a possible example. I have argued elsewhere, however, that although liturgical orders are subject to such difficulties, such vexations do not arise out of sanctification itself. They are the consequences, rather, of disorderings in relations of sanctity, particularly in the relationship between the specificity of a rule and the degree of sanctity ascribed to it. "Oversanctification," imputing great sanctity to rules of high specificity, reduces the flexibility of a system (see Rappaport, 1971d, 1976, 1978b, 1978a, 1979a).

I have suggested, exemplifying with understandings encoded in Maring rituals, that the "cognized models" organized in liturgy are not mere heaps or collections of rules and doctrines but are sets of understandings hierarchically ordered along a number of dimensions, including sanctity and mutability, and that adaptiveness is intrinsic to such a hierarchy (1979b). I can give no more than a brief account of this discussion here.

At the apogee of the hierarchy of understandings encoded in Maring liturgy stand postulates concerning the existence of spirits. Ultimately sacred, these understandings are usually devoid of empirical referents and are virtually accepted as unquestionable, immutable, and in some sense eternal. At the second level cosmological structure is elaborated in a set of axioms by or through which the spirits postulated at the highest level are associated with elements and relations of the material and social world in a set of abstract structural oppositions that apply to both: as the red spirits are hot, hard, dry, and strong, so are men; as the spirits of the low ground are cold, soft, wet, and fertile, so are women. These relations are given concreteness and specificity in yet a third level of understandings constituted of rules and taboos concerning actions appropriate or inappropriate in terms of the cosmological structure represented in the axioms of the second level. These rules, this is to say, realize or substantiate in behavior the abstractions of cosmological structure expressed axiomatically. It may be that this level consists of two or more sublevels distinguished by different degrees of specificity versus generality, rules of "higher order" being more general. A fourth level of understandings appearing in Maring ritual is composed of indications of material and social conditions prevailing in the everyday world. These indications are expressed in rituals (which they may have, in fact, triggered) where they are translated into cosmological terms (e.g., a parasitic number of pigs becomes "enough pigs to repay the ancestors") and serve to stimulate action (bring rules into play) in such terms. Secular knowledge of the everyday world constitutes a fifth level of understanding that, for the most part, remains external to ritual. It is at this level that classification seems to be most highly elaborated and it is here that pragmatic expertise is developed: knowledge of gardening, pig husbandry, hunting, gathering, and so on.

Whereas the postulates that stand at the apogee are ultimately sacred and thus immutable, the understandings of lower levels are not sacred themselves, but merely sanctified through association with the ultimately sacred. As such they are more or less open to change. (In his review of my book *Ecology, Meaning and Religion*, Fabian [1982] seriously misunderstood the distinction between ultimately sacred and merely sanctified.) Cosmological axioms, for instance, which among the Maring impose a binary distinction upon the things of the world, while highly resistant to fundamental changes, could be modified or elaborated through additions to or changes in the elements constituting its sets of opposing qualities, or through its application to new elements in the everyday world. Such changes in cosmological axioms could be accomplished without challenge to ultimate sacred postulates. Similarly, the rules for realizing cosmological axioms in behavior can change without any change whatsoever in the cosmological axioms to which they give substance. A rule change was reported in *Pigs for the Ancestors*. In that instance the high order rule, or principle, that ancestors must be repaid for their help in the last round of warfare before new hostilities could be initiated, was retained while the lower order rule specifying just how the obligation was to be fulfilled was modified. This change took place, I believe, in response to changes in historical and demographic circumstances. The lower levels of understanding are more immediately sensitive to changes in mundane circumstances than are the understandings of higher order rationalizing them and, presumably, of the highest order from which their sanctity flows. Mundane knowledge, a fifth level external to ritual, is pragmatic, empirical, unsanctified, and as open to change among the Maring as it is among members of fully modern societies. The hierarchy of understandings comprising the cognized models organized by liturgy is, thus, one of sanctity, mutability, concreteness, and specificity. They also have temporal characteristics, running from the putatively eternal qualities of ultimate sacred postulates to the ever-fluctuating values of indicators of contemporary conditions. In these continua of sanctity and the other qualities I have noted lies adaptive capacity—the ability of a system both to maintain its continuity and to transform itself in response to changes in its surrounding conditions, a matter to which we shall return in section 13.

Despite the adaptiveness which I claim for properly functioning liturgical orders and the cognized models they organize and preserve I do not claim that ritual cycles or other forms of liturgical order will necessarily represent *logos* in either Heraclitus's sense or mine (should they be different). The conventions encoded in liturgical orders are seldom if ever explicitly cognizant of ecological principles as Western science would state them and need not be in harmony with such principles. It is even to be expected that the understandings of religions making universalist claims, divorced as they are likely to be from the particulars of any ecosystem, will violate ecological principles. Although liturgy sanctifies whatever conventions it encodes and the performance of ritual ordains compliance with these conventions, there is no guarantee that those conventions will be in harmony with ecological principles. The degree to which they are or are not is in large measure contingent upon factors external to the liturgical orders in which they are represented.

THE ENVIRONMENT OF UNDERSTANDING IN TRIBAL SOCIETIES

I have already stated that I did not and could not provide a historical account of how "ecological wisdom" came to be enshrined in the Maring ritual cycle (*Pigs for the Ancestors* was, after all, an *ethnog-*

raphy based upon events occurring during the field period and upon the memories of informants living at that time). Given, however, the particulars of Maring life, especially its mode of subsistence, we might expect, and certainly should not be surprised, that environmental as well as social and political relations are represented, regulated and transformed in the course of their liturgical order's performance, or that the operations of the cycle are compatible with ecological principles.

It is surely the case that some tribal societies have seriously degraded the environments upon which they depend and it may be that many others have not done so only because their population densities have been low (Clarke, 1982:301) and their technologies have lacked power (although we should keep in mind that much damage can be done with nothing more than axes and fire). Nevertheless it does not seem to be invoking some lost wisdom of "primitives" to propose that the relationships of members of tribal societies to their environments is such as to encourage ecologically sound thought and practice. Of especial—and obvious—importance is a rudimentary division of labor with the household being the primary unit of production (see Sahlins, 1972). In horticultural societies virtually everyone is directly engaged in plant cultivation and in such situations practices that are ecologically sound come close to coinciding with the practices that constitute sound husbandry. Signs of environmental degradation are likely to be apparent quickly to those who can do something about them and, moreover, are often motivated to do so, knowing that degradation is likely to require increased investment of labor for equivalent returns (as, for instance, in the intensification of effort when bush is replaced by grass in the successions following the abandonment of swiddens [Boserup, 1965; Clarke, 1966]). It is not always possible for people to ameliorate such trends, of course. Among swiddeners they are often an effect of fallow periods being shortened as a consequence of population growth; some Jimi Valley Maring have already seen major portions of their forests replaced by grass. Clarke (1982:301) is certainly correct in proposing that the ritual cycle would not protect the Tsembaga or other Maring from similar degradation should their population densities become sufficiently high. I have implied as much in *Pigs for the Ancestors* (p. 82n).

Other factors also tend to favor a close relationship between, if not coincidence of, the thought and practice of tribal husbandry and ecological principle. For one thing, production is generally for use and exchange rather than for profit, and the forces tending to increase yields to produce surpluses are limited and weak (see Sahlins, 1972, especially chapters 2 and 3). For another thing, although relations in tribal societies are no less, and perhaps even more, vexed by conflicts of interest than in other societies, to the extent that they are internally relatively undifferentiated they are free of conflicts between *special* interests that could become especially destructive.

That some tribal peoples—the Maring among them—seem to have some awareness of the cyclical and reticulate nature of ecosystemic processes follows from direct and comprehensive participation in those processes. (For instance, the Maring association of fertility and death is grounded in an awareness that new plant growth is encouraged by the decay of dead vegetation.) Such awareness may be especially well developed among tribal plant cultivators who must manage the delicate ecosystems upon which they rely, who are, in other words, the dominant species in anthropocentric ecosystems, the species setting the conditions that encourage or discourage the presence of other species.

CONSCIOUSNESS, REGULATION, AND DECISION MAKING

We are led here to questions concerning the degree to which consciousness of ecosystemic and perhaps other material factors enter into Maring regulatory operations, and to what extent they are deliberate or purposeful. John Bennett (1976) has been particularly concerned with this matter.

> Roy Rappaport proposes the existence of control mechanisms operating through ritual observances . . . in relatively isolated tribal groups, but whether these observations function as controls serendipitously or whether the group developed them in order to obtain control is not known. Nor is it clear whether the members of the society are aware of the ecological control functions of the ritual. [p. 62]

"Control," Bennett notes, "is not always, if ever, automatic; frequently, the system must be cognitively objectified and arbitrarily modified, or at least an attempt must be made to do so." Later he asserts that

> Rappaport does not seem to have seriously considered the nature of information flow in human societies, or to realize that overt decision making is a part—perhaps the most important part—in feedback processes in human affairs. He seems to want to keep his regulatory processes at some covert level below·the interplay of human discourse and action behavior and resist acknowledgement that direct methods keep the whole thing going most of the time. [p. 206]

I shall deal with regulation more fully in a later section. The matter of main concern here is the actors' consciousness of the effects of their actions and my failure to take purposeful decision making into account in what seems to be, after all, a very mundane activity.

> Does Rappaport mean to imply that the very practical problem of depredative pigs has to be solved by indirect ritual communications? . . . At best it does not appear to be a very efficient process. [p. 206]

The questions raised by Bennett are important. I probably did not emphasize sufficiently the role of conscious, pragmatic decision making in the affairs of the Maring (see section 10). It did not occur to me that they would not be noticed by readers in the course of the account even if they remained, in part, implicit. As far as actual subsistence practice is concerned pragmatic decisions are, of course, consciously and deliberately made with respect to gardening, silviculture, pig husbandry and hunting. Nowhere in the text is there any suggestion that it is otherwise. The Maring are brilliant and pragmatic gardeners and they spend a great deal of time, effort, and thought on the acquisition and care of pigs.

The account I offered also allowed for conscious decisions with respect to the disposal of pigs. When the Maring reached a consensus that the number of pigs was sufficient to repay ancestors a *kaiko* was staged and the pig herd reduced. The decision to hold a *kaiko* was grounded in empirical considerations—the burdens of a large pig population—and the response was rational, having the effect *among other things* (which were also reported above) of reducing the pig herd. Although the *kaiko's* constituent rituals followed each other in fixed order, and although each required the killing of some pigs, participants were required to make decisions not only concerning the disposal of those pigs (which ones to kill where and when, to be dedicated to which ancestor, cuts of pork to be given to which kinsmen, etc.) but concerning other matters as well: when, precisely, to hold particular rituals, whom to invite to the *kaiko* and in what order, the order in which men's names were to be sung out at the *puve*, where to plant boundary stakes in some instances, and so on. Some time after a *kaiko's* conclusion decisions were also made concerning the reinitiation of hostilities.

In sum, there was a great deal of room for conscious decision making in Maring subsistence practice, ritual activity, and social and political relations, and the account provided in *Pigs for the Ancestors* does not suggest otherwise. The ritual cycle did not operate automatically. What it did do, among other things, was to set the terms by which decisions of certain sorts were to be made or, to put it differently, it was the locus of assumptions concerning the world's nature with respect to which decisions were made. Such assumptions are, in many or even most cultures, outside of the awareness of the actors. It may be argued that their representation in ritual brings them more fully into the light of consciousness than is usually the case. These assumptions are represented in a set of rituals which "cognitively objectifies" the world in terms that include spirits, animals, plants and, of course, humans—both local performers and others. Moreover, human actors consciously modify the conventions governing the system from time to time, as they did when they expanded the rules stipulating acceptable ways to repay ancestors. This modification was hardly arbitrary, however. It may have been motivated by changed demographic circumstances and it conformed to the general logic of the system being modified.

The ritual cycle did specify, in a rather rigid way, actions (which I claimed to be regulatory) to be taken under certain stipulated circumstances. I called attention to the relative inflexibility of this aspect of the Maring liturgical order in comparing it to the governance of Polynesian chiefs (pp. 220ff.) noting, however, that "it is their very inflexibility that makes it possible for ritual cycles to regulate relationships between autonomous local groups, particularly in respect to warfare" (p. 223).

This matter leads to another difficulty in Bennett's critique, possibly flowing from a misunderstanding on his part concerning the cycle. He speaks as if the account I offered proposed that the *purpose* of the cycle is simply to regulate the pig population. The last citation suggests this, as does the following:

> There are, of course, less theoretically conceived explanations for the New Guinea behavior vis a vis swine that do not depend on animal analogies in human behavior nor on demonstrations of states of subtle ecosystemic balance in ritual behavior and natural phenomena. These . . . people appear to have a familiar livestock management problem: raising swine in unconfined spaces on natural forage. . . .
>
> People who raise pigs in the open thus have a recurrent problem: for different reasons at different times, the cost of raising pigs exceeds the gain. . . . One can visualize what Vayda, Leeds, and Smith (1961) have already described: consultations among Melanesian men on the need for control of pig populations. But other solutions could easily occur. . . . There almost certainly was more than one alternative, and the precise role of ritual in this situation must have been a variable, not a constant. [pp. 185–86]

It is difficult to follow Bennett's thought here. If he is saying that the ritual cycle is merely a way of regulating a pig population, a culturally particular way of dealing with "a familiar problem in livestock management," he is ethnographically in error. It also governs the frequency of warfare, distributes local pork widely (both, by the way, effects obvious to the participants), and so on. If, on the other hand, he is arguing that the ritual cycle is too elaborate to be accounted for by the need to regulate pigs, an argument more in accord, I believe, with his general preference for consciousness and choice, against whom is he inveighing? I not only agree, but insist that there would be better ways to deal with a surfeit of swine if that were all there were to it. I observed in the original work that "more sensitive system regulation, such as that found in Polynesia, might avoid the wide fluctuations in the value of variables noted in the Maring area (e.g., in the size of pig herds and the amounts of land in cultivation)" (p. 223). But the ritual cycle was not merely regulating pig demography. It was regulating it in a particular sort of way, a way which contributed to the governance of relations between groups, as I pointed out: "It must be emphasized, however, that in the Maring case the fluctuations themselves are of great value, for they are critically important in the regulation of intergroup relations" (p. 223).

One further point concerning consciousness, mystification, and purpose leads us back to the matter of *logos* versus *idia phronesis*, ecological principle versus economic rationality. Such effects of the cycle as the establishment of sanctified truces, the reduction of pig herds and consequently of gardens in production, and the social benefits of distributing local pork throughout the region were recognized by the participants. The general purpose of the ritual cycle, however, was cosmic and virtually explicit: to mend a world rent by warfare. This grand purpose, also recognized by some if not most of the participants, subsumed the effects just mentioned: they contributed to, or were aspects of, the world's reintegration, along with such others as the abrogation of taboos.

Now the actions ordained by such a purpose do not always coincide with what a materially maximizing theory of self-interest would suggest. Abiding by *rumbim* truces is probably not to the immediate material advantage of large, land-short groups surrounded by weaker neighbors (p. 239). Feeding pigs for years until the sacrifices required in the *kaiko* rather than killing, consuming, and replacing them when they reach full growth is not what we would generally regard as rational economic behavior.

The ritual cycle, like many human conventions, is not an economizing mechanism in a simple individualistic, material sense. On the contrary, it stands opposed to the particularistic or selfish economizing behavior of individuals or small groups. This may be a general characteristic of ritual regulation in egalitarian societies, but be this as it may, we may be reminded here of Bergson's characterization of religion as "society's defense against the dissolvant power of human intelligence."

COMPLEMENTARITY IN PAPUAN AND
ECOLOGICAL THOUGHT

The coincidence or compatibility of the cognized models of some New Guinea and possibly other tribal peoples with ecological principle was addressed by Roy Wagner (1977) in a remarkable essay too complex to summarize here. He argues that environment becomes "a kind of pan-biotic 'superculture,' an organic 'ecumene,' in which all the differentiated tribes, clans, and nations [i.e., species] have a part to play" (p. 397). As such it is a "moral collectivity" and as such it comes to "approximate the semiotic orientation that is manifest in the world views of tribal peoples, including those of the Papuan area" (p. 397).

Drawing upon his own work among the Daribi (Wagner, 1972) and alluding to Siane cosmology (Salisbury, 1965) as well as considering the Maring cosmology, Wagner argues that for Papuans the essence of "what we are disposed to call 'humanity' " is "social relationship." This is "the very ground of being" but is not a property distinctive of our species. It pervades the world generally. Social relationship among the beings inhabiting this world recognizes the differences among them and is founded upon an assumption of complementarity intrinsic to differentiation.

It is . . . by differentiating the various beings in an appropriate manner, that man precipitates . . . a beneficent relational flow. . . . Ritual life is a task of sustaining and renewing the differentiations between man and the other sorts of beings. . . .

The discretion and ritual solicitude with which these personified aspects of man's physical surroundings are approached is strongly suggestive of the ecologist's attitude toward organisms other than man, in deference to the needs and qualities of the environment. [pp. 397–98]

Wagner concludes that among the Maring and other Papuans

man himself, in his ideal of "humanness," embodies and expresses the sum total of the relational flow among the complementary beings of the world, much as man's life is realized [among the Maring] in temporal-spatial movements between the adjacent spaces of *wora* [low ground] and *kamungga* [high ground]. The Tsembaga term for this moral totality is *nomane* which can be used in the sense of "the moral soul" . . . [but also] in that of "tradition." Humanity is a totality or completeness, a relation that is precipitated and evoked by the differentiation of ritual and the surrounding world. [p. 399]

In a forthcoming work I propose that the Maring concept of *nomane* resembles the Heraclitean *logos* and take it to be an instance of the many *logoi* implicit in the world's liturgical orders.

THE ENVIRONMENT OF UNDERSTANDING IN MODERN SOCIETIES

Although their roles as ecological dominants may sometimes force an awareness of ecosystemic reticulations and circularities upon the consciousnesses or into the symbolic structures of tribal cultivators, ecological dominance itself obviously does not guarantee such awareness, let alone the institution of environmentally conservative practices. Modern industrial societies are, after all, both ecologically dominant and environmentally destructive. It is of interest in this regard that in nonanthropocentric ecosystems the dominant species are usually plants—oaks and hickories, say, in a temperate forest—or sessile animals, like the corals in reef communities. Such creatures fill the dominant role simply by standing there (Rappaport, 1970a). In contrast, however, humans must behave more or less continuously to fulfill that role, and there seems to be nothing in their individual natures to prevent them from acting erroneously, selfishly, destructively, or neglectfully. Their activities, moreover, are especially vulnerable to disruption. Anthropocentric ecosystems are relatively unstable not only because the cultivated species of which they are composed are relatively few and relatively helpless (often requiring constant protection and nurturance if they are to survive), but also because the instability inherent in both the nature of their membership and the simplicity of their structures is magnified by the unreliability of their dominants (1970a, 1970b). Their vulnerability to disruption may increase in the course of social evolution as a concomitant of increasing interdependence among ever more specialized sectors of society and ever more specialized geographic regions. Be this as it may, the circumstances of life in modern industrial societies do not encourage ecological awareness.

In such societies highly ramified divisions of labor free the productive activities of most people from direct engagement with the natural environment and even those who are directly engaged are likely to be highly specialized. Few, if any, have direct experience of nature's reticulations or circles. Each individual is directly acquainted with no more than a portion of such a web or an arc on such a circle. Conceptions at once holistic and naturalistic are likely to be lost from general consciousness, to be rediscovered if at all by such sciences as ecology.

The cognitive effects of an increasingly specialized division of labor are abetted by another concomitant of social evolution. With the scale of human societies expanding to, in some instances, continental proportions there is an inversion in the relationship between society and ecosystem. Whereas autonomous groups in tribal societies generally participate in what may be regarded as single ecosystems, nation-states are likely to encompass many such systems. As a portion of a society's territory a forest, for example, may no longer be conceived as an all-embracing ecosystem, "Mother and Father to us all" as the Ituri pygmys would have it (Turnbull, 1962), or a crucial link in the circle of fertility and death as it is to the Maring. It is likely to be degraded to the status of commodity, a "natural resource" or "raw material" to be exploited by members of a superordinate socioeconomic system operating in terms of a logic in which ecological principles have no place of their own, entering only as terms pointing to certain costs which, more likely than not, are ignored.

We are led to the place of such sciences as ecology, anthropology, and other holistic disciplines in such societies. Holistic though they may be they undoubtedly owe their very existence to the specialization (or fragmentation) of knowledge which characterizes modern scholarship and upon which its enormous advances are founded. As such they are imprisoned in a paradox or contradiction. Despite their holism they are, in the organization of knowledge, specialized fields institutionalized in relatively obscure academic disciplines where they are isolated from the conduct of everyday affairs. Whether or not their findings and perspectives are "accurate," "true," "correct," or "adaptive" is almost beside the point because they are powerless. They do not constitute the paradigms by which contemporary societies or their members generally formulate their relationships to the worlds—physical, biotic, and social—by which they are surrounded and upon which they depend. The paradigm dominating humanity's interaction with nature is not ecological. It is economic. *Idia phronesis* is misrepresented and even apotheosized as *logos* in the understandings engendered by formal economics. That which stood against the "dissolvant power" of economic rationality is itself dissolved.

The development of all-purpose money has cognitive effects relating to the usurpation of *logos*'s place by *idia phronesis* and to consequent ecosystemic degradation. Ecosystems are usually composed of large numbers of *distinctive* components in relationships of complex interdependence. Their distinctiveness, as Wagner emphasizes (1977), is recognized by Papuans and protected by their rituals. But the application of a common monetary metric to dissimilar things has a troublesome semantic consequence. It reduces their *qualitative distinctiveness* to the status of mere *quantitative difference*. With money serving as a predominant ground for evaluation at the same time that it represents wealth, evaluation becomes little more than what is called "the bottom line," the result of operations of addition and subtraction into which intrinsically nonmetrical considerations may be forced by the specious objectivity of cost-benefit analysis. Ecological distinctions (not to mention those between correct and erroneous, good and bad, right and wrong, perhaps even true and false) are dissolved by the logic of more and less. Information in the technical sense is based upon distinctions and thus the world's information is reduced. Although information alone does not constitute meaning it is one of meaning's constituents (Rappaport, 1979b:126f.), and thus a world in which arithmetic is regnant becomes less meaningful even as it is ecologically degraded.

As money may erase distinctions between things which are contemporary so it may deform longer-term temporal processes. Devices like depreciation rates, and depletion allowances subordinate such matters as sustaining yields and conserving ecosystemic constituents to a monetary logic that permits and in some instances encourages the narrowly defined short-run interests of the few to take precedence over the general long-run interests of the many or the whole.

I do recognize the facilitating role that all-purpose money has played in production and exchange. Its appearance was indispensable to the full development of the division of labor in complex societies. As such, its appearance in the ancient Near East must be regarded as a milestone in sociocultural evolution. But evolutionary advances, even fundamental advances like the advent of money and elaborations in the division of labor, set new problems as they solve older ones, new problems that may not manifest themselves fully for centuries or even millennia.

When monetary logic is associated with production for gain, not only is ecological awareness obscured but the likelihood of ecosystemic degradation is increased. This likelihood is further increased in industrial societies, societies in which production is expanded to meet the voracious appetites of machinery for such substances as coal and petroleum. Given the centrality of industry to the economics of such societies there is an inversion of the relationship between humans and the tools they invent. Whereas in early industrialized societies machines may be regarded as extensions of humanity (Catton, 1978), in the mature industrial societies humans become extensions of machines. The means of production become the mode of production. The process of production—ultimately the operation of machinery—becomes an end in itself. The product becomes, in effect, a by-product or even waste product of the industrial metabolism. In such circumstances it is not that the narrowly defined and short-run interests of those powerful men we take to own industry come to prevail. It is that the requirements of the industrial metabolism—the interests of machines themselves, machines that even powerful men serve—come to prevail. Needless to say, the interests of machines and organisms do not coincide. It is in accordance with the logic of economic systems dominated by the interests of industry to tear the tops off complex congeries of ecosystems like West Virginia to get at one simple substance, coal. It is further in accord with that logic to weaken legislation requiring restoration of the land after it has been strip-mined.

The circumstances of industrialized societies are not, then, such as to enhance ecological awareness or to give ecological formulations authoritative status in the conduct of social affairs generally or in the governance of environmental relations more particularly. It may be that conditions prevailing in the very societies in which a self-conscious ecology developed make it difficult not only for us to formulate our own relationships to our environments in ecological terms, but also for us to conceive how the understandings encoded in the socially dominant cognized models of tribal peoples could possibly come to be compatible with ecological principles.

Ecological formulations of environmental relations are both well-developed and empirically grounded in modern societies, but are nevertheless relatively powerless. In contrast, environmental relations are understood in supernatural terms by Maring and some other tribal peoples in New Guinea, and such understandings are governing. I have argued elsewhere (1971b, 1979b) that there may be no simple, direct relationship between the amount of testable empirical knowledge encoded in a people's general understandings of the world and the ecological appropriateness of the behavior elicited by those understandings. It is not certain that the representations of nature provided to us by an empirical science will better elicit behavior likely to enhance survival than will images of a world inhabited by spirits to whom respect is due.

I have not asserted in *Pigs for the Ancestors* or anywhere else that social and cultural forms and the relations among them always and everywhere somehow absorb ecosystemic imperatives and institute ecologically sound practices. Such is not the case in industrialized societies or, for that matter, among all tribal peoples. I have argued in a number of publications (especially 1970a, 1971d, 1972, 1976a, 1978b, 1979a) that sociocultural forms and ecosystemic considerations often are, are likely to be, indeed may inevitably come to be, at odds. I have further argued that difficulties become greater as sociocultural evolution proceeds. This is not the enunciation of a Rousseauian credo nor a plea for the conduct of human affairs in the naive terms of what Bennett (1976:181) has called "ecosystemicism." It is simply a recognition that every evolutionary advance is likely to pose new problems as it ameliorates older ones and that some problems are intrinsic to increasing social and technological complexity and scale.

SECTION 4

Ecology Fetishism, Ecological Explanation, and an Ecological Problematic

I am led here to a related indictment, that of what Sahlins calls "ecology fetishism." It is, he says, associated with a

> materialism [which] allows itself to ignore the distinctive quality of human action as meaningfully organized—that it may proceed to organize meaning as an instrumental mystification of natural reason. Its "empiricism" then consists in the radical practice of the idea that nothing is in fact what it appears, i.e., culturally, but is translated instead into natural coordinates or consequences. The result is a kind of "ecology fetishism" whereby corn, beans and squash become an unbalanced diet, . . . ritual pig slaughter and distribution to affines a mode of remaining within "the limits of carrying capacity," the social order "a population of organisms." [1976a:298]

We are well warned by Sahlins to guard against simplistic equations of meaning with "instrumental mystifications of natural reason." Some of the interpretations in *Pigs for the Ancestors*—particularly in matters relating to food consumption—may have been little more than that. The most glaring example is probably the discussion of salt consumption in wartime (pp. 135ff.), but other instances can surely be found in *Pigs for the Ancestors* and in other ecologically oriented works by other authors. I will, nevertheless, suggest that Sahlins's discussion, both in the work cited and in *Culture and Practical Reason* (1976b:87ff.) is not clarifying and in some respects is misleading.

We will return in section 10 to the alleged reduction of social orders
to populations of organisms.

THE MEANINGFUL, THE OBJECTIVE, AND
"NATURAL REASON"

More needs to be said about ecology fetishism and "natural reason," the scientific mystification of the cultural as no more than a
disguise for the "natural." An instance, Sahlins claims, is provided by
the observation that corn, beans, and squash provide an unbalanced
diet. I disagree. To observe that the nutrition provided by the famous
New World plant trinity is inadequate is, assuming it to be correct,
simply to report an "objective fact," that is, one belonging to a domain constituted by empirical observation, including appropriate
quantitative techniques. Such a statement taken alone surely does
"ignore the distinctive quality of human life as meaningfully organized." Just as surely it does not provide an instance of "meaning as
instrumental mystification of natural reason" simply because it doesn't
say anything about meaning at all, nor does it even imply any pre-
scriptions whatsoever as to how meaning is to be construed. Because
it is devoid of any report, description, or interpretation of the meaning of the corn, bean, and squash trinity to those who "think it" as
well as eat it, the statement falls short of constituting an adequate
ethnographic account. If, however, what is meant by an adequate
ethnographic account is one which provides an accurate and more or
less general account of conditions prevailing among a group of people
during a particular period in its history, then a report, description, or
interpretation of the meanings of corn, beans, and squash to those
whose diet as well as thought is constituted by these plants is, in the
absence of any consideration of their nutritional value, also inadequate.

It should not be, but apparently is, necessary to note that ethogra-
phies are not composed of single statements. That a statement is, in
itself, inadequate as an account of, let us say, corn, beans, and squash
in the lives of a people cannot possibly mean that it does not make an
important or crucial contribution to what might qualify as an adequate account. Concern with the objective factors in part composing

a group's condition, it should hardly be necessary to note, does not constitute treating them as objects or animals.

Having cleared away some underbrush we can get to Sahlins's main point concerning ecology fetishism, a critique which was not so much a response to *Pigs for the Ancestors* as to a statement I made in a later essay, as the following passage from *Culture and Practical Reason* (1976b:87) makes clear:

> The new ecological functionalism demonstrates that the effect of Malinowski's resolution of cultural content to biological function, particularly the symbolic to the instrumental, is a final solution to the culture problem. For it becomes explicit that culture does not warrant any special understanding, that is, as distinct from a biological explanation. In this event culture disappears.
>
> As in Malinowski's functionalism this process depends upon the theoretical appropriation of cultural qualities to organic effects: a translation that not only dissolves the cultural specifications but allows them to reappear in more scientific (i.e., quantifiable) form. Rappaport explains: . . . .

Sahlins then cites a programmatic statement from my essay "Nature, Culture, and Ecological Anthropology" (1971b):

> *While the questions are asked about cultural phenomena, they are answered in terms of the effects of culturally informed behavior and biological systems: organisms, populations and ecosystems.* The distinctive characteristic of ecological anthropology is not simply that it takes environmental factors into consideration in its attempts to elucidate cultural phenomena, but that it gives biological meaning to the key terms—adaptation, homeostasis, adequate functioning, survival—of its formulations. [p. 243, italics in original]

The merits of this critique must be recognized. The emphasis put upon organic and ecological functions in explanations of cultural phenomena was too great in early formulations of what Sahlins calls the "new ecology," including that developed in *Pigs for the Ancestors*. There was a tendency to strip cultural phenomena of their distinctiveness as such and to grant to the possibly adaptive roles of some cultural forms a comprehensive significance approaching explanatory sufficiency. The explanatory power of the general ecological formulation was, in short, exaggerated. However, societies or cultures do not shape and reshape themselves in vacuums, nor are they the only source of the world's or their own forms. Adaptation to environment does have a place in the ways in which cultures and societies organize themselves. We shall consider this matter in later sections. A further qualification of the criticism is to be registered here. Ecologically oriented anthropologists have generally focused quite directly on the environmental relations of human groups. Few would have denied that answers to many questions lie beyond the grasp of ecological or adaptive formulations. After completing the analysis reported in *Pigs for the Ancestors*, I realized that it told me nothing about ritual per se or, for that matter, why regulatory functions I attributed to the Maring ritual cycle in particular were embedded in a ritual. The path from ritual in Maring environmental and political relations led me first to questions concerning sanctity and sanctification and from there to a concern with ritual's internal structure. I have devoted most of the past few years to this aspect of ritual, an aspect to the elucidation of which ecological principles have little if anything to contribute. It has not occurred to me, however, that ecological or adaptive principles are of no use because they do not illuminate ritual's dark interiors nor, conversely, that the principles in terms of which I have tried to understand ritual's internal logic are to be discarded because they do not illuminate ritual's external relations. The contrasting formulations deal with different aspects of reality and are properly complementary rather than alternative.

ECOLOGY AS EXPLANATION OR PROBLEMATIC

The nature of the general ecological formulation proposed by Vayda and me (1967), which I attempted to apply in *Pigs for the Ancestors* and to elaborate in other essays (1969, 1971b), was ambiguous. It was not clear whether it was meant to be an explanatory paradigm—one through which a population's social order, or culture, or aspects of them, could be accounted for—or whether it was a perspective from which problems could be defined. Although the distinction is not sharp—the concept of adaptation as a process brings them rather close together—they are far from identical. In some ways they are, in fact, antithetical. Elements of both were expressed and were meant to be expressed in "Nature, Culture, and Ecological Anthropology" (the essay against which Sahlins reacted so strongly). Not only was the formulation ambiguous. The formulator was ambivalent.

I have already agreed that the explanatory power of the formulations was more limited than I and others had supposed and need say no more about the matter here. The problems posed by the formulation as "problematic" are in large measure implicit in the passage from "Nature, Culture, and Ecological Anthropology" cited by Sahlins and recalled above. In more general terms they are the substantive problems becoming apparent when humans are viewed as organisms in ecosystems. Whereas a "purely explanatory" use of the ecological formulation might attempt to account for cultural forms in terms of their adaptiveness the use of the formulation as a problematic proposes that the adaptiveness of those forms is always open to question.

I should stress that the ecological formulation as problematic does not, *contra* Sahlins (1976b:x), understand "custom" to be mere "fetishized utility." The *very problem* is that it is not. Nor does it deny that "the distinctive quality of man [is] not that he must live in a material world, [a] circumstance he shares with all organisms, but that he does so according to a meaningful scheme of his own devising, in which capacity mankind is unique" (Sahlins, 1976b:viii). It insists that this is so, but demurs from important elements in the continuation of Sahlins's declaration:

> It therefore takes as the decisive quality of this culture—as giving each mode of life the properties that characterize it—not that this culture must conform to material constraints but that it does so according to a definite symbolic schema which is never the only one possible. Hence it is culture which constitutes utility.

Cultures and the societies governed in their terms surely proceed in accordance with definite and particular symbolic schemes. It does not follow, however, that they "must *conform* to material constraints" in terms of these schemes. Such schemes may be capable of leading their followers into *violation* of the material limits of the systems in which they are set. The utilities that cultures constitute and sometimes maintain for long periods of time may contradict organic and ecosystemic requirements. It is surely true that the "distinctive quality of man" is that he lives in the material world according to meaningful schemes of his own devising. It is also true that this distinctive quality has set for man distinctive problems that cannot be fully grasped without viewing humans as organisms in environments. What seems to me distinctive of humanity is that it lives in terms of meanings it itself must construct but it is not fully constituted by those meanings, nor is the world in which it lives. Humanity no whit less than any other species is a product of organic evolution. The makers of meaning are organisms living in and absolutely dependent upon ecological processes, processes constituted not by meanings but by natural law. We are a species that lives in terms of meanings in a physical world devoid of intrinsic meaning but subject to causal law. The meanings humans construct (including our understandings of causal law) not only do not establish those laws but are in considerable degree ignorant of them. We are, furthermore, only loosely constrained by our circumstances from constructing meanings that do not conform to law or, for that matter, even to organic need. We are not, this is to say, debarred from the construction of self-destructive or even world-destructive follies. To content ourselves with the statement, "Culture constitutes utility," and let that be the end of the matter is to banish into irrelevance one of the fundamental problems if not *the* fundamental problem distinctive of what is called "the human condition."

If we are concerned with a species that is, as it were, caught between law and meaning, neither of which can be reduced to the other, then an anthropology which takes culture to be fully constitutive of human life is as inadequate as one which takes noncultural nature to be so. Radical separation of the two enterprises that have proceeded in anthropology from its earliest days—the one objective, inspired by the biological sciences and seeking laws and causes, the other subjective, inspired by linguistics and the humanities and seeking meaning—is a profound error, for the relationship between them in all its difficulty, ambiguity, and tension is a reflection of the nature of the species that is our subject.

SECTION 5

Further Discussion of Cognized Models

To deal with the relationship between *natural* law and *cultural* meaning as they interact in the affairs of human groups I have proposed (1963, 1968, 1971) that it is necessary for ethnographers to prepare two models of their subject matter and then to integrate them. One of these models is an attempt to describe the ecological system through empirical operations, basic to which are metrical procedures: weighing, counting, measuring such elements as soil constituents, rainfall, harvests, herds of livestock, individual consumption, acreage in production, human population size, and so on. I have labeled this model the "operational model." I will return to problems of operational models in later sections.

The second class, which I have called "cognized models," attempts to describe people's knowledge and beliefs concerning their environments. Conklin (1957), Frake (1962), Berlin, Breedlove, and Raven (1974), and other ethnoscientists have made important contributions to ethnographic formalization of cognized models of a different sort, but the taxonomic formulation which has informed much of their activity cannot in itself represent native understandings of systemic interactions among elements in their environments and between themselves and those elements.

The account of Maring understandings of the environment offered in *Pigs for the Ancestors* was not, in essence, taxonomic although it included taxonomic elements. It did attempt to illuminate relationships among components of the environment (including spirits), but it fell far short of formal description. The term *cognized model* does not appear until the conclusion (p. 237). A somewhat more formal account of Maring understandings was presented in "Nature, Culture, and Ecological Anthropology" (1971b), where it was accompanied by an elaborate diagram which, with slight modification, is reproduced here. A later and fuller discussion of the structure and nature of cognized models in general appears in "On Cognized Models" (1979b). I have already cited that essay (see section 3) particularly with respect to the hierarchical structure of the cognized model organized by the Maring liturgical order and perhaps liturgical orders generally. I have also touched upon differences in the environments of understandings in tribal and modern societies, the relationship between forms of understanding and power and the semantic consequences of money. All of these matters are discussed more fully in the 1979 essay. Orders of meaning, the "illocutionary" or "performative" force of cognized models, the social loci of knowledge, comparative redundancy, the naturalization of the conventional, and a number of other issues are also treated there.

INADEQUACIES IN THE EARLIER FORMULATIONS

Certain inadequacies of earlier formulations considered in "On Cognized Models" should be noted here, however.

Few if any societies break the world into the more or less distinct systems distinguished by Western categories. As we have seen (Wagner, 1977), not all Papuans distinguish environment from social relations. Among the Maring ecological, political, and social relations are not separately conceived and their governance not only follows a common set of principles but is integrated by the ritual cycle. Moreover, the principles and understandings that account for the structure and state of the world and invest the world and actions taken within it with meaning are not confined to the particular material and social relations regulated. They include as well metaphysical abstractions of great generality. If analysts' representations of the cognized models in accordance with which actions in the environment are undertaken were restricted to folk accounts of ecosystemic elements, little more than folk taxonomies and gardening or hunting lore would be included in them. The elements of which actors understand their environments to be composed and their understandings of how these

elements are processually related should be represented in the larger metaphysical, moral, and epistemic contexts which, as far as the actors are concerned, give them value and significance. In other words, they should not be alienated from other processes—social, political, or spiritual—from which they are not separated in the actors' minds. As Frithjof Bergmann (1975) has observed, although it may be that the Maring liturgical order regulates social, political, and ecosystemic relations, the Maring liturgical order and possibly liturgical orders generally seem far richer in understandings and meanings than such governance requires. This proposes that the cycle's regulatory operations cannot account for all aspects of the cycle, a proposal in full accord with the discussion thus far. Of more interest here is that it also implies a more reciprocal relationship than was explicitly recognized in *Pigs for the Ancestors* between the governing liturgical order and the processes and relations governed. As the ritual cycle *guides* and *regulates* those processes so do they *substantiate* the understandings guiding them and *support* the institutions within which those understandings have their locus. As the liturgical order may contribute to the persistence of the material relations it governs so do those material relations contribute to the persistence of the order represented in the liturgy. To put this a little differently, inasmuch as the values and meanings encoded in the liturgical order—or in whatever regulatory institutions a society possesses—are dominant it is to their persistence that regulation or governance is explicitly addressed. Values and meanings organize the teleology of the systems in which they occur. It is neither objectively identified organic well-being nor ecosystemic integrity but culturally constructed value and meaning that the cybernetics of human social systems tend, in the first instance, to preserve. The relationship of these culturally constructed meanings and values to organic well-being and ecosystemic integrity is the central problem for ecological anthropology.

THE RELATIONSHIP BETWEEN COGNIZED AND OPERATIONAL MODELS

This aspect of the cybernetics of sociocultural systems and of the relationship between cognized and operational models was in fact tacitly recognized and given methodological expression near the conclusion of *Pigs for the Ancestors*: . . . *"what is the relationship between the reference values or ranges of values of the cognized model and the goal ranges of the operational model?"* (p. 241). Despite the emphasis which should have accrued to this question by virtue of its position in the book, an emphasis reinforced by italics, it has been generally ignored. It merits some attention.

First, to hark back to section 4, if reference values, which lie in the domain of meaning, and goal ranges, which lie in the domain of natural law, can differ, a possibility made explicit in this passage, then it is apparent that the approach to understandings proposed in *Pigs for the Ancestors* was not simply "an instrumental mystification of natural reason." If I seem to be belaboring a point already sufficiently made I do so because Sahlins is not alone in entertaining such a misunderstanding. It also seems to be lodged within ecological anthropology itself. In a recent review article Orlove (1980:242) states that in "neofunctionalist" ecological anthropology, a category to which he assigns me, "Values and preferences are explained by being reduced to the ecological functions they serve."

Second, the passage also makes a clear if implicit distinction between economic considerations, which are among those represented in culturally constituted reference values, and ecological factors, which constitute goal ranges.

A third point follows from the second. I have stipulated that the assignment of limits to goal ranges is to be made by reference to considerations distinct from the values at which the relevant variable (e.g., numbers of pigs) are in fact equilibrated. This stipulation is necessary if another common failing of functional or systemic formulations, namely that they fall into tautology, is to be avoided. If the level at which a variable is in fact equilibrated is taken ipso facto to represent an equilibrium or homeostatic value, or goal range, for that variable, there is, ipso facto, tautology. However, if it is defined by reference to independent criteria tautology is avoided. Reference values (the values with respect to which equilibration or regulation takes place) and goal ranges (the ranges of values defining "homeostasis," "adequate functioning," "survival," etc.) *must* be established independently.

A fourth general point may be implicit in the label "operational model" but needs to be made explicit. I call the model of relationships among significant material variables constructed by the analyst (independent of the understandings of the actors) the "operational model" because it should be constructed in accordance with explicit empirical operations stipulated by appropriate methodological canons. The attempt is to provide a description of natural processes. Analysts are thus implicitly claiming for themselves a knowledge of nature that may not be available to the actors, but the label *operational model* tacitly recognizes that the model is not of nature itself. It is a function of operations whose relationship to the processes being represented is always open to question. Other operational models of the same portion of the world can always be constructed through different operations related to the "nature" being represented through different rules of reference. The procedure is open to a cultural relativistic critique, of course: operations stipulated by a scientific method and undertaken in accordance with a scientific theory are simply following the folk understandings of Western society and do not represent nature any more accurately than does any tribe's understanding of its environment. I regard such an extreme relativism wrong-headed but will not argue it here. I will simply note that the operational model is an attempt to represent nature in the terms of Western science.

A fifth general point is implicit in both the third and the fourth. If reference values and goal ranges are established independently it is possible to discover instances in which reference values fall outside of goal ranges. Such a condition, I have suggested (1979a) could possibly be taken to indicate dysfunction under stable conditions. The possibility that reference values may violate goal ranges was raised in the last pages of *Pigs for the Ancestors* in a discussion of the relationship between cognized and operational models. It was further suggested in that discussion (p. 241) that "if cognized models are important components of control mechanisms their consideration in evolutionary as well as functional studies is warranted," and the questions of the varying abilities of cognized models to modify themselves was raised.

A last general point should be made here. It would be an error to argue that culturally constructed values and understandings and the social institutions representing and reproducing them—liturgical orders, chiefs, motherlands—are maladaptive, dysfunctional, or oppressive because they demand contributions of treasure, sweat, and sometimes blood from those who accept them. No meaning comes free of charge and there may even be a direct relationship between a meaning's cost and its power. Nevertheless, the costs of some meanings may be too high. Sustaining them may be to perpetuate misery or even to endanger the societies accepting them or the ecosystems upon which they depend. In contradiction of the doctrine of cultural relativism it may be asserted that some of the understandings that societies construct for themselves are false because they lead those for whom they are meaningful to act in ways so at variance with the natural constitution of the world as to make damage to it and to themselves inevitable. The lawful order of nature—through which the organic processes underlying understanding and convention evolved—continues to provide criteria by which the appropriateness of understandings and conventions can be assessed. Such criteria suggest to us, for example, that the conventional orders of industrialized capitalism, which must expand to remain stable, are maladaptive because they must sooner or later degrade the finite ecosystemic processes over which they exercise dominion but upon which they depend.

It nevertheless must be recognized (as I have in "On Cognized Models" [1979b] and elsewhere) that the assessment of cognized models and the reference values they incorporate in terms of their ecological and biological effects is fraught with difficulties.

First, problems beset the use of biological criteria themselves. For one thing, legitimate candidates for inclusion are innumerable. For another, despite their apparently substantial nature the significance of their values is often ambiguous (for example, how much protein does a child of a certain age and body size require?); Slobodkin and Rapoport (1974) have gone so far as to say that it may not even be possible to specify any particular features of biological structure or operation that will always and everywhere abet the persistence of the systems in which they occur. Moreover, selection pressure can be construed in some instances at least as pressure on the goal ranges of physiological variables: when selection pressure is strong the ranges of some individuals will be exceeded. Second, the complexity of living systems is of such an order that their responses to perturbations may be counterintuitive or have counterintuitive consequences. It is therefore difficult to predict the organic or ecosystemic effects of many actions. Finally, the metrical difficulties of establishing values for such things as diet are serious, a matter to which we shall return in this epilogue but which is also treated in appendix 11.

These problems do not call into question the validity of a concern with the organic and ecosystemic consequences of actions elicited by cognized models. They do call into question the *procedure* of invoking *specific* quantified biological standards as criteria for the adequacy of cognized models.

The rejection of such criteria might seem to leave the notion of the adaptiveness of cognized models so vague as to be meaningless but arguments concerning the structure of meaning and understanding advanced in "On Cognized Models" (see especially pp. 116–26, 128–31, 137–43) save us from exchanging specious precision for pious vacuity. Implicit in these arguments is the proposal that it is possible to stipulate formal *orderings* of understandings that preserve understanding, meaning, and meaningfulness and that, in preserving these, preserve other living processes as well. Such a suggestion is less mysterious than it may at first appear. The proposal, in short, is that disorderings of hierarchical relations among understandings differing in the qualities of sanctity, authority, mutability, temporality, contingency, specificity, concreteness, and logical type lead not only to the disruption of understanding and the subversion of meaning but, by disrupting orderly regulatory operations, to the disruption of social and ecosystemic processes as well. To put this in the converse, if hierarchical relations among understandings remain orderly and if action conforms to such an orderly structure of understandings, then biological and ecosystemic processes are likely to be preserved.*

*The argument upon which the proposal is based follows a lead advanced by Bateson in his profound but generally unappreciated essay, "The Role of Somatic Change in Evolution" (1963). I have elaborated it in several essays (1976b, 1978b, 1979a) and outlined some of its features in section 13 of this epilogue.

SECTION 6

Function and Description

In the first sentence of its first paragraph I declared *Pigs for the Ancestors* to be a functional study; much of the criticism of it has focused upon its functionalist character (see, for example, Ellen, 1982; Friedman, 1974; Jorgensen, 1972:328ff.; Orlove, 1980). The approach that it exemplified, which Vayda and I had espoused in an essay published the year before *Pigs for the Ancestors* appeared (Vayda and Rappaport, 1967), was soon labeled "the new ecology" to distinguish it from the older "cultural ecology" formulated by Julian Steward (1955). The "new ecology" thus came to be identified with the "new functionalism," a term used by Friedman not so much to distinguish it from but to relate it to the "old functionalism," the difference between the two being that "the field of application has changed to show the rationality of institutions with respect to their environments rather than to other elements in the society" (1974:457).

The matter is difficult and complex. For one thing I do not wish to defend the ill-defined corpus of doctrines the term *functionalism* denotes from criticism with which I myself have agreed in print (1968, 1971b; Vayda and Rappaport, 1967). Moreover, critics of *Pigs for the Ancestors* have generally ignored the fact that the study upon which it was based was guided by criticisms of functionalism, rather than functional doctrine per se. This is, I think, implicit throughout the book, although it was made explicit on only one occasion in the text (p. 230). (Vayda also discusses the issue in his foreward to the volume.)

Following Murphy (1970), Friedman notes two related difficulties

345

associated with the concept of function, and he asserts that they continue to plague the "new ecology."

   a. In its more modest form, it dissolves into pure description.
The function of the stomach is to digest food; the function of
ritual pig slaughter is to regulate pig populations—i.e., the function of x is to do what it does. The word here is totally superfluous and adds no information unless we assume some metaphysical notion of purpose implied in the following.
   b. By extension to the teleological meaning, "function" becomes "adaptive function." Here we are still dealing with our
first definition, "the function of x is to do what it does," but now
the "what it does" is not an observed datum, and we are left with
what is basically a description of imaginary relations, where the
"function" is assumed rather than demonstrated. [1974:457]

I agree that the term *function* adds nothing to statements that simply describe the immediate result or product of the operation of some
system, structure, or process. In the analysis of any particular case
the term "function" should be reserved for the designation of the
contribution made by components of defined systems to the unitary
character or maintenance of those systems. It was so used in *Pigs for
the Ancestors*, both explicitly and implicitly.

Although I agree that functional assertions and simple descriptions
should not be confused, description is in itself worthwhile. The first
duty of an ethnographer is to report as thoroughly and accurately as
he or she can. If the ethnographer does not also provide an "explanation," others may be able to do so. There is more to be said in favor
of description, however, than that it reports that which may eventually be explained. "What is being done" by an organ or an institution
is not always as patent as Friedman's parodic examples might suggest.
While men have always had a kind of commonsense awareness of
what the stomach, heart, and eyes "do," they have not always had
such an awareness of either the outputs of, say, the pancreas, the
thyroid, and the vermiform appendix, or of the place of these outputs
in the maintenance of the organisms of which they are part. Discourse concerning these matters, whether or not it is in some narrow
sense explanatory (Hempel [1959] and Nagel [1961] agree that it may

be), is not superfluous, and discoveries concerning them are, of course, highly informative. We should beware of confusing explanation with informativeness, or understanding (see Bergmann, 1975).

It is not the case, however, that analyses generally designated "functional" or "systemic" are always actually concerned with "what *x* does." They may be at least as concerned with how systems work as with what they do, and may even take the latter for granted. Men "knew" that the stomach digested food long before they knew how, but elucidation of the ways in which various organic structures and substances join together in the complex processes of anabolism and catabolism is, obviously, enormously informative, and important as well. Similarly, to leave Friedman's organic example for a cultural one, we might say, for example, that anthropology has known since Durkheim's time that rituals establish or enhance solidarity among those joining in their performance. Indeed, an awareness of this has no doubt been part of general common sense since time immemorial. Yet we have much to learn about just *how* ritual creates this solidarity.

In sum, whether or not they are "explanatory" (and if properly formulated and appropriately applied they are so), statements of "what it does" and "how it does it" may well be among the most informative, important, and interesting that can be made concerning an organ, an institution, or a convention. To put this a little differently, among the most informative things that can be said about structures or systems, be they organic, social, cultural, or ecological, are statements concerning how they maintain, order, reproduce, and transform themselves. To make such statements concerning structures or systems requires, of course, some elucidation of the parts played by their elements. In *Pigs for the Ancestors* I was concerned not merely with the direct outcome of pig sacrifices, but with the operation of a protracted ritual cycle of which pig sacrifices are a part, and with the place of that cycle in a complex system that included ecosystemic, economic, and political relations.

Friedman seems contemptuous of pure description, but does not indicate what he means by the term. For instance, a statement to the effect that ritual pig slaughters *regulate* pig populations could not be counted as "pure description," if we mean to denote by that phrase accounts of directly observable aspects of events. A sentence stating only that a ritual sacrifice has reduced the number of living pigs would be simply descriptive. The term *regulate*, however, which predicates the sentence that Friedman offers, also and inescapably refers to phenomena *external* to the event being described and, because regulation is not a directly observable datum, it implies or even entails some sort of analytic operation. A similar observation can be made with respect to the term *digest* in the stomach example. When their predicates are spelled out these sentences denote relationships between their subjects and larger structures or systems. Moreover, the relationships denoted by the terms "regulate" and "digest" are supportive or instrumental and properly designated "functional" in the narrowest sense of the term. Digestion is, after all, necessary to the maintenance of life in organisms, regulation to the persistence of living systems of all classes. Thus, even those sentences that Friedman adduces, in virtual parody, as instances of pure description, are better taken as examples of the second class of functional sentences he identifies, a class he summarily dismisses as descriptive of merely "imaginary relations," in which an adaptive function is assumed rather than demonstrated. Friedman provides us with no definition of "adaptation" or "adaptive function," and the imaginary nature of the relations under consideration is asserted as a derogation rather than demonstrated or even discussed (1974:457).

The question of "imaginary" versus "real" relations is, of course, sticky. I would only note that all analytic constructs are, in a sense, "imaginary." To disregard this is to fall into the error of misplaced concreteness. Analytic models should make "facts" intelligible, but such models are not themselves "the facts" nor, for that matter, facts at all except as artifacts of the anthropologist's metaphysics and epistemology. (N.B.: I speak here of elements of *analytic* models, not components of actors' models).

If analytic models are imaginary, then the relationships among their components cannot be other than imaginary. This is not to claim that no "real" relations exist in the world. The more or less unified entities with which anthropologists, ecologists, and, for that matter, all scientists are concerned are made up of parts. Relations among these parts and the units of which they are parts, be they conceived as processes or as things, are not imaginary. Whether or not an analyst gets these relations straight—that is, whether or not these relations are accounted for by his imaginary model—is another matter. Friedman's assertions concerning the imaginary nature of "adaptive functions" do not lead me to abandon my belief that analytic terms like "adaptation" and "adaptive function" correspond to processes occurring in the physical world. It still seems to me too that the systemic and ecological model applied in *Pigs for the Ancestors* so far as it went (and it should not be forgotten in this regard that it subsumed a structural account of the oppositions of Maring religious logic and their mediation, in accordance with which regulatory activities were performed), provided a reasonable account of the Maring materials. Others may disagree and are free to offer alternative accounts. I am, in fact, pleased that the description provided in this book has been adequate to serve as the basis for understandings of the Maring materials different from mine (see, for example, Friedman, 1974, and Peoples, 1982).

SECTION 7

Ecology and the Rationality of Systems

Functional formulations often identify what Friedman has called the "rationality of elements" while ignoring the "rationality" or "irrationality" of the systems of which they are parts. I agree with this charge and would extend it to systemic accounts as well. As Vayda has observed, "a concern with how extant systems operate by no means commits the analyst to the proposition that no other systems could operate better" (1968:x); Harris (1966) has also been explicit about this. I believe Friedman errs, however, in asserting that this is a "deadly weakness of functionalism" if he means (1) that it is intrinsic to the logic of functional (or systemic) analyses, or (2) that it is peculiar to such analyses.

The weakness of which Friedman speaks is not peculiar to functionalism per se. It is, rather, intrinsic to the doctrine of cultural relativism with which functional formulations have often been associated. To obviate the problem, we need supracultural criteria by which to assess both the operations of particular systems and the effects of their operations. Ecological theory and general systems theory (the latter being concerned, among other things, with the *structure* of self-regulating and self-organizing, i.e. adaptive, processes) provide such criteria. What Friedman means by the "rationality" of systems, and at least what I mean by the adaptiveness of systems as well as of elements, may be assessed with respect to their organic and ecosystemic consequences and the extent to which their structures are self-regulating and self-organizing, the extent, that is, to which they can continue to respond to stresses through reversible changes in their states or irreversible changes in their structures.

Although ecological theory and the theory of adaptive structure do provide criteria by which the operation of systems may be assessed, I do not claim that they *alone* provide such criteria. Over half a century ago, for instance, Sapir suggested that cultures may be judged "genuine" or "spurious" in terms of their internal consistency and the opportunities they provide to individuals for personal realization (1924). The application of one such set of criteria does not preclude the simultaneous application of others, and I raise no objection in principle to the application of standards, such as those that Sapir suggested, to sociocultural systems generally, if they are derived from an explicit theory and if some sort of objective import can be given to their key terms. Such standards are further strengthened by claims to empirical testability; but even if their terms cannot be given hard objective meaning they may have a subjective or intuitive validity that should not be dismissed even though great caution is required when subjectivity and intuition are put in the service of evaluation.

A variety of supracultural criteria might, then, be put to the task of assessing sociocultural systems. Of these, ecological, biological, and adaptive criteria are indispensable for several reasons. Relating as they do to matters of survival, they are, in a crucial sense, fundamental.

Furthermore, ecological criteria and biological criteria in general enjoy a high degree of objectivity. Ecological criteria are material, often amenable to quantification, and viable limits for ecological and biological variables can at least theoretically be established (but see section 9 of this essay for a discussion of the difficulties). Adaptive criteria are structural and quasi-logical. Systems which are characterized by, or defined by, adaptive processes, a class that includes all living systems (organisms, populations, and ecosystems), seem to be, and probably must be, organized both hierarchically and cybernetically. While much work remains to be done on the conceptualization of the adaptive processes and on complex adaptive organization, it does already seem possible to specify some of the structural features requisite to systems if orderly adaptive processes are to continue within them (see section 13 below; Bateson, 1963; Pattee, 1973; Piaget, 1971;

Rappaport, 1978b, 1979a; Simon, 1969; Slobodkin and Rapoport, 1974).
*If these structural features can be identified, then disorderings of
them can be recognized and taken, prima facie, to be maladaptive.*

Finally, and most problematic, ecological, biological, and adaptive
theories, including as they do in their formulations such units as organisms and associations of organisms, are not only commensurable with theories pertaining to all of life, but may also provide a
framework within which some criteria drawn from other substantive
theories could be organized and related to each other in an orderly
fashion. Even psychological and humanistic criteria might be accommodated. For instance, adaptive structures are in their nature self-
regulated. Adequate regulation requires that regulators contain informational variety equivalent to the variety manifested in the phenomena to be regulated. The fact that humans play regulatory roles in
sociocultural and ecological systems argues against their narrow specialization, a matter that troubled Sapir long ago. Let me reiterate,
however, that I do not claim that ecological, biological, and adaptive
criteria have exclusive rights to the assessment of social systems or
that they can order or dominate all other criteria. They surely cannot
subsume all of the humanistic concerns that properly reside in humans and that should not be discounted because they are intangible.

To summarize, the implication of the argument presented in this
section is that the "new ecology" is not the same as the old functionalism because when "the field of application has changed to show the
rationality of institutions with respect to environments," and, I would
add, to organic and adaptive considerations as well, a fundamental
change has taken place. The inclusion of these factors provides a ground
for assessing what Friedman calls "the rationality of systems" as well
as the rationality of their elements.

SECTION 8

Fallacy, Final Cause, and Formal Cause

In an introduction to a group of essays including my "Flow of Energy in an Agricultural Society" (1971a), Jorgensen (1972:328f.) took the opportunity to level another traditional criticism of functionalism against the Maring study. Following Brown (1963) and Hempel (1959) he noted that functional formulations suffer from the fallacy of "affirming phenomena that arise as a consequence of the premise" (1972:328). This criticism, which has virtually been accorded the status of an eternal verity, requires discussion not only with respect to its applicability to the Maring but, much more importantly, with respect to its general validity.

It is surely invalid to claim, as some functional analyses may, that an "item" or "trait" is present in a system because the system functions adequately if and only if a certain condition is met and the "item" meets the condition. Only in instances in which the item present and only that item could meet the condition, it is said, can a functional statement account for the item's presence. Such functional indispensability is at least empirically difficult and possibly logically impossible to demonstrate. This criticism was proposed before the turn of the century by Durkheim (1938:90) and as strong as it is it may not be strong enough. It could be argued that even if an item were shown to be functionally indispensable at a particular time and place the problem of its origin would remain unaddressed.

This criticism seems to me to be off the mark with respect to *Pigs for the Ancestors*. It is true, as I have already noted, that in a brief passage (p. 231) I suggested that the Maring ritual cycle might be a local variation of a generalized highland form and that the peculiar characteristics of the local variation might be accounted for by local environmental conditions. This is not a simple functional proposal, but an adaptive one, for it implies adaptive radiation. Be this as it may, the aim of the book was not to account for either the presence or the origin of the ritual cycle, and it was not asserted that the regulatory functions ascribed to the cycle could not be fulfilled by other mechanisms. The ritual cycle was taken as a given, and the aim of the book was simply to elucidate its place in the operation of a particular system during a particular period in its history.

FUNCTIONS, ORIGINS, AND THE PERSISTENCE OF CONVENTION

The validity of such a limited enterprise has, however, recently been called into question by James Peoples, using *Pigs for the Ancestors* as his case in point. Consideration of his argument will prepare the way for criticism of the general doctrine with which we are most importantly concerned. Peoples states:

> Most social scientific theories departing from the proposition that behaviors exist because of their advantages assume that the issue of how the behaviors originated and evolved to their observed state is . . . "lost in history." . . . However, whenever we learn of a complex of behaviors such as the Maring ritual cycle, and read that they persist because they maintain a system by their regulatory functions, we are justified in wondering how such complicated mechanisms could have originated in the first place . . . [and] how they could have persisted in competition with a multitude of easily invented functional equivalents. Those who adopt the functionalist perspective often attempt to avoid the difficult problem of origins by limiting their . . . analysis . . . [to] how behaviors "work" thus claiming that the question of why [those] behaviors exist . . . is a separate issue (Vayda and Rappaport 1968). . . . Certainly, it is one thing to show how, given that the ritual cycle is now widespread among the Maring, they derive benefits from it; given that at its origin some groups lacked

it, those groups that did possess it gained an advantage so that it spread. . . . Yet unless at its origin it yielded some advantage to its practitioners it is difficult to imagine how it could have developed its observed form and spread. . . . It might well be advantageous for the Maring to possess a ritual cycle (or its functional equivalent). . . . But unless there is some evolutionary process through which they can evolve such a mechanism, this adaptive benefit will not be realized. The important conclusion is that it is only legitimate to separate the analysis of functional workings from the problem of origins if a plausible model of origins and evolution can be constructed that is consistent with the functionalist hypothesis. Therefore the student of function cannot legitimately side-step the origins issue. [1982:294–95]

Peoples raises important questions concerning the origin and propagation of conventions such as the Maring ritual cycle. I do not, however, agree that accounts of origins are requisite to elucidations of the ways in which the conventions operate in the systems of which they are parts. His claim, if elevated to the status of a general principle, would invalidate the descriptions physiologists provide of the workings of organs unless they could account for their evolution, and closer to home, would do in much of ethnography as well. I may, of course, be construing Peoples's assertion (that it is "only legitimate to separate the analysis of functional workings from the problem of origins if a plausible model of origins and evolution can be constructed that is consistent with the functionalist hypothesis") more rigorously than he meant it to be taken. In the absence of historical evidence it may be that some sort of abstract account or even a statement of general principles would satisfy the condition of plausibility for a "model of origins and evolution." If such is the case my few sentences concerning adaptive radiation might qualify. I take the Maring ritual cycle and the cosmology associated with it to be one of a family of cognate forms widespread in the New Guinea highlands, a family which may ultimately include the Enga *Te*, the Melpa *Moka*, and the *Chimbu Bugla Gende*. It is plausible that the structure, functions, and contents of these cycles became differentiated as a response to differences in environmental conditions, demographic vicissitudes, and historical circumstances. Recent modifications of the Maring ritual cycle in response to the imposition of the *Pax Australiensis*, the introduction of Christianity, and incorporation into a national system (noted during my last visit to Tsembaga in 1981–82 and to be reported in later publications) indicate how adaptive such conventions may be.

Peoples wonders not only how mechanisms as complicated as the Maring ritual cycle originated but "how they could have persisted in competition with a multitude of easily invented functional equivalents." I would ask what "easily invented functional equivalents" might be in the Maring case. Chiefs? A council of elders drawn from all local groups? A bicameral legislature? A priesthood? A moment's reflection suggests that all of these functional equivalents are implausible or unfeasible. It is easier to conceive of a *logical* category of functional equivalents than to make an *empirical* or even plausible case for the emergence of particular equivalents in particular cases. Evolution, biological as well as cultural, is a matter of *bricolage*. Populations of organisms and cultures respond to perturbation—adapt—with what they have on hand and it is fruitless to argue the *logical* possibility of innumerable equivalents in the face of empirical limitations imposed upon any evolving system by what it has on hand at a particular moment in its history.

I outline what I take to be the properties of adaptive systems—systems which can modify or reorganize themselves in response to perturbations originating in their environments or themselves—in section 13 and at greater length in several essays already cited. In another essay (1979e) I have discussed the adaptive characteristics of ritual, a matter touched upon in an earlier section of this essay. Suffice it to note here that, *contra* Peoples, I do not take the Maring ritual cycle to be a very complex mechanism. It requires no special personnel, its information-processing capacities are very limited, its operation is only occasional, and it requires no obedience to commands of living persons (see pp. 220–23). In contrast to most other regulatory mechanisms ritual cycles can govern some of the interactions of large numbers of people in the absence of powerful or even discrete authorities. They thus may be established under conditions in which discrete authorities could not be supported. I have therefore proposed (1971d, 1979d, 1979e) that ritual may be the primordial mechanism of governance among humans.

My phrase "the establishment of ritual cycles" may be misleading. Although individual rituals may sometimes be invented they usually include elements of older liturgies, and whole liturgical orders (like the Maring cycle) seldom if ever are created ex nihilo. They are modifications of existing liturgical orders. To find the "absolute origins" of any liturgical order it would probably be necessary to go back to the origins of religion—which I believe to have coincided with the emergence of language (Rappaport, 1971d, 1976b, 1979e). Moments commemorated as the inauguration of new liturgical orders are likely to be no more than the moments when connections to older orders were deliberately severed. In sum, liturgical orders do not originate in the same way that consciously invented social regulatory mechanisms like the American Constitution do. They not only have persisted since primordial times but are understood to have done so. Therein lies part of the ground of the sanctity that provides the basis of their authority.

FINAL CAUSE, FORMAL CAUSE, AND THE FALLACY OF CROSSED EXPLICATION

Our discussion of "easily invented" functional equivalents suggests that the general criticism of functional formulations raised at the beginning of this section (that they affirm their consequents) is itself open to criticism. Because the dictum is virtually taken to be self-evidently true it is worth discussing some of its difficulties.

First, it is surely true that functional statements alone cannot account for origin or presence, but they may form indispensable components of more elaborate formulations that can. Although "items" other than those present could conceivably fulfill indispensable functions, given the limited cultural materials (structural, ideological, technical, social, political, or whatever) usually available at any particular time and place, only the item or form present, or a limited range of them, could have emerged. It might be supposed, for instance, that a king or bicameral parliament could have done everything that the Maring ritual cycle was doing but given the cultural materials available a ritual cycle, and neither kings nor parliaments, did, in fact, emerge.

To use Aristotelian terminology, neither final nor efficient nor material cause is alone sufficient to account for presence or origin, but taken together they may be. Environmental changes are of the class of processes that can qualify as efficient causes, as are internal perturbations, inducing systems to respond (change their states or structures) within the constraints of their previously existing constitutions (material cause) in such a way as to perpetuate themselves (final cause, or what is ordinarily meant by "function").

Aristotle proposed a fourth type of cause, namely formal cause. I take this to refer to the entailment of operations of particular sorts by the formal characteristics of structures. Some confusion has resulted from the conflation of formal and final causal accounts under the label "functional." Raymond Kelly and I (1975) have attempted to clarify some of the issues; I shall take this opportunity to elaborate our earlier discussion.

In its most common usage the term *function* implies final cause, a functional formulation being one seeking to explain or elucidate an item in a system by specifying its contribution to the survival, persistence, or "adequate functioning" of that system. Although functional formulations are often improperly constructed, and although their proper limits have often been violated, this concept of function, particularly when expressed in the rigorous terms of an empirically based systemic analysis and informed by a substantive theory, does, I believe, have a legitimate place in the social sciences. That it may be impossible to demonstrate the functional indispensability of particular items does not vitiate the value of the final causal conception of function. It must be understood, however, that final causal accounts are properly only system-specific. For instance, that a ritual cycle regulates the social, political, and ecological relationships of the Maring people such that the frequency of warfare, the intensity of land use, and the divisive effects of internal quarreling among the members of local groups are all kept within viable limits does not mean that forms or structures that we would recognize as *ritual* perform similar functions anywhere else in the world. The specification of a particular form or item (e.g., ritual) does not entail the specification of its *particular* contribution to any system in which it appears. Conversely, the specification of a particular *function* in a particular system does not entail the form of the mechanism fulfilling it. This autonomy of form and of function is sometimes considered to be lethal to the notion of function as an explanatory concept. In fact, it simply proposes the limitations of final causal statements.

We may turn to the other form of argument which is sometimes labeled "functional," but which differs importantly from final causal formulations. In fact, it is formal causal, and as such virtually the inverse of the final causal type. Its aim is not to elucidate the contribution that some "item" or "component" or "form" makes to the system of which it is a part, but to elucidate what *follows from,* or is *entailed by* or *intrinsic to,* a particular form or *structure.*

A formal causal account is certainly not limited to cybernetic mechanisms but is nicely illustrated by them. The term *cybernetic* denotes a structure or form of a particular sort, that of the closed causal loop. Intrinsic to, or entailed by, the operation of a simple cybernetic structure is "negative feedback," such that deviations of the states of loop components from reference values initiate processes tending to return those states to their reference values. (We needn't go into the matter of "positive feedback" or "deviation amplification" here.)

A number of observations are in order. First, because cybernetic structure entails regulation, wherever the structure is observed the state of some variable is being equilibrated at or around some reference value. In contrast to simple final causal accounts, which are properly only system-specific, *formal causal accounts are universalist.*

Second, formal causal accounts are properly applied only to structures, that is, to phenomena that may be formally described in terms of enduring *internal* relations among their components. Cybernetic structure is a proper object of such formulations, but the class of such objects is innumerable, certainly including marriage systems and ritual. I have already noted, for instance, that elsewhere I have defined ritual as the performance of more or less invariant sequences of formal acts and utterances not encoded by the performers (1979d). This definition, specifying as it does a number of features and relations among them, designates a structure; I have argued that this structure

entails social contract, morality, a paradigm of creation, a concept of
the sacred and a notion of the divine.

Third, if particular entailments are intrinsic to a particular structure and only to that structure (e.g., to the cybernetic structure, or
to the structure which is ritual), it may be argued that those structures are without equivalents. I have so argued for ritual, and a similar argument could be made for cybernetic structure (see Piaget,
1971:15). If the unique entailments of a particular structure are crucial to the persistence or survival of systems in general then it may
be said that that structure is not only without equivalents but indispensable. This may account for the ubiquitous occurrence of such
structures as the ritual form.

Fourth, this argument would seem to contradict the dictum that
function cannot account for presence because of the impossibility of
demonstrating the indispensability of even those items performing
indispensable functions. It seems to propose that there is an aspect
or class of phenomena, namely structure or structures, for which claims
of functional uniqueness and indispensability can, in fact, be made.
The contradiction, however, is more apparent than real because the
entailments of structure are not properly regarded as functions in the
final causal sense. What is entailed by a structure does not *in itself*
constitute a *specific* contribution to the maintenance of any *particular*
system in which it appears. The proposition that a cybernetic mechanism equilibrates the state of a variable around some reference value
may sound like a final causal statement. It is not, however, because
it alone does not take account of the relationship of the reference
value to the persistence or survival of any particular system. We could,
for instance, set a thermostat to maintain a temperature that would
kill us. Similarly, the proposition that the *structure* of ritual is such
as to invest the *contents* of ritual with morality does not in itself take
into account the relationship of the particular practices or conceptions
invested with morality to the persistence or adequate functioning of
any of the particular systems of which they are parts. The assertion,
then, that ritual makes its contents moral is not adequate as a final
causal statement.

Fifth, recognition that that which is intrinsic to a structure is not
ipso facto final causal does not deny significance to it. It is not vacuous

to claim that morality and social contract are intrinsic to the structure of ritual. Statements concerning entailments are not simple functional statements in the final causal sense, but statements of another order. It could be said, I suppose, that formal causal formulations are metafunctional, or perhaps it would be better to say that they are statements concerning metafunctions. That is, they are not properly attempts to stipulate the contribution that a form or structure makes to the persistence of any particular system in which it occurs, but to identify what is *intrinsic* to that form or structure that makes it suitable to fulfill the range of specific functions its instances do fulfill in the diversity of systems in which they occur.

In summary, I have noted two contrasting types of account, one final-causal and system-specific, the other formal-causal and universalist. The two have not been sufficiently distinguished in anthropological thought (both often being called "functional"), and the error for which Kelly (Kelly and Rappaport, 1975) coined the label "the fallacy of crossed explicanda" has sometimes followed from this confusion. This fallacy, which might be regarded as an error in logical typing (Bateson, 1972) occurs when final causal statements are offered in instances in which formal causal statements are appropriate and vice versa. For example, to state that it is *in the nature* of ritual to regulate ecological and political relations in the way that I attempted to demonstrate it did for the Maring would be to make a formal causal assertion where final causal statements are appropriate. Such an assertion would tend to trivialize ritual and would also be false on empirical grounds. We can cite innumerable instances in which ritual has nothing whatever to do with political or ecological relations.

Conversely, an attempt to account, let us say, for the division of labor in nineteenth-century France by invoking Durkheim's assertion that organic solidarity is intrinsic to the division of labor, as a final causal statement ("the division of labor in nineteenth-century France enhanced the organic solidarity of French society"), to make, that is, a final causal assertion where a formal causal one might be appropriate, would not be so much wrong as banal, vacuous, and thus inadequate (see Bergmann, 1975).

SECTION 9

Systemic Analysis

We do well to remember that when Brown (1963), Collins (1965), Hempel (1959), and Nagel (1961) exposed problems besetting functionalism, they did not propose to do away with the concept of function, which they took to have a valid place in the social sciences. They were simply attempting to specify the proper limits of functional statements and to purge functional analyses of the faults that often or even usually vitiate them.

These philosophers argued that there are several related reasons for the frequent failure of functional analyses. Among them are the following:

1. Functional statements are frequently untestable because their key terms lack empirical import (e.g., there is often a failure to provide objective criteria for such terms as "adequate functioning").

2. The entities to which functional assertions refer are frequently not specified with sufficient precision to permit rigorous analysis (including the empirical definition of key terms).

3. The entities to which functional statements refer are not always proper objects of such statements.

4. There is often a failure to make explicit the hypotheses of self-regulation implicit in functional formulations or to identify mechanisms of self-regulation precisely.

These criticisms, which seem to me to have been justified, added up to a call for the replacement of vague *functional* formulations by more rigorous *systemic* constructions. That Hempel (whom I am mainly following here) made no sharp distinction between the two may have constituted a tacit recognition on his part that the latter may be regarded as a reform of the former. Be this as it may, *Pigs for the Ancestors*, written with this general critique of functional analysis in mind, was an attempt at systemic analysis, an analysis in which units are clearly specified, the goal ranges and reference values of key variables are given objective import, and regulatory mechanisms are identified.

1. The units to which the book's functional* assertions in the main referred were specific and concrete: organisms, self-defined groups of organisms (such as local populations), and ecosystems. Procedures for identifying these units were made explicit when it seemed necessary to do so and the selection of these rather than other units for analysis was argued on the grounds that (a) they correspond to units in biological theory generally, including ecological theory; (b) they are units recognized by the Maring themselves—individuals, clans, sub-clans, clan clusters, local groups, local territories, and Maring society; and (c) they correspond to units recognized in social theory. Whether or not these units are proper objects of functional or adaptive formulations is another matter. Their recognition as discrete by the Maring and their commensurability with units in social and ecological theory suggests that they are and I took them to be so. There is, however, no consensus on these matters and we shall return to the matter of units in section 10.

2. Hypotheses of self-regulation were made explicit (in terms which were admittedly insufficiently precise) in the introduction and the mechanisms through which self-regulation was effected were identified in the course of the work, it being argued that they resided mainly in the ritual cycle.

*I would now prefer to use the term *adaptive* rather than *functional*. Simple functional formulations are no more than final causal, but adaptive formulations also include material causal and, of course, efficient causal factors as well. I take ecological and systemic formulations to be, at least implicitly, adaptive rather than merely functional, although I have myself to blame for labeling *Pigs for the Ancestors* a functional study.

3. An attempt was made to give empirical import to such key terms
as "adequate functioning" by translating them into more specific
terms (carrying capacities for pigs and people, fulfillment of nutritional requirements, length of fallow, warfare frequencies, etc.)
and an attempt was also made to determine the current states
of relevant variables through a range of quantitative procedures:
censusing, weighing, counting, surveying.

That *Pigs for the Ancestors* failed to meet the rigorous requirements of systemic analysis in all respects must be freely admitted.
We shall return to these failures shortly. It is important to point out
first that systems analysis has problems of its own. (For an interesting
discussion of these problems see Bennett, 1976, especially chapters
3 and 4.)

PROBLEMS IN SYSTEMIC ANALYSIS

Systemic analysis makes no prescription concerning the variables
to be included in the analytic system. Their selection is a product of
hypotheses concerning interrelations among the phenomena under
investigation. While the rigorous specification of systems ameliorates
the vagueness that often vitiates looser functional formulations, it increases the danger that crucial components or aspects of the natural
or cultural system being represented will be omitted. Since systemic
analyses, like looser functional formulations, are concerned to elucidate the ways in which order is maintained in systems that naturally
tend toward disorder or entropy, it may be—although it is not logically entailed that this should be so—that there is a tendency to ignore the disorderly and to include only the orderly, even though the
notion of self-regulation, virtually intrinsic to the notion of system,
implies response to *perturbation*. Nevertheless, by "giving himself
the system," so to speak, the maintenance of which he takes it to be
his task to elucidate, the analyst may affirm whatever assumptions
concerning harmony and orderliness he entertained at the outset
without fear of overthrow. The dilemma is, simply, that the abstrac-
tion necessary to derive analytically tractable systems from the complexity of nature and culture puts systemic formulations in danger of

becoming unreal or unfalsifiable. This, of course, is not very different from the difficulties besetting all of science. The point here is that this difficulty is *exacerbated* by increased rigor, more specifically, by increasingly rigorous canons of specification. The problem is not hopeless, of course. Systemic analyses do not usually take place in contexts devoid of substantive theories. Such theories usually include references to units that can be taken to be the systems forming the object of investigation, and also are likely to include criteria for establishing the goal ranges of the variables which they specify as crucial to systemic persistence. Ecology provides one such body of theory, discriminating discrete units on several levels of inclusiveness, many of which are directly available to observation (e.g., organisms), and some of which correspond to self-defining and self-bounding entities (e.g., Maring local populations). For the analyst to take such units as the object of his investigation is to go far toward avoiding the problems implicit in "giving himself the system," but this remains an ever-present danger.

INADEQUACIES OF *PIGS FOR THE ANCESTORS* AS A SYSTEMIC ANALYSIS

Much has been written about how and why *Pigs for the Ancestors* did not live up to the stern requirements of systemic analysis. The propriety of the units selected for analysis has been attacked for one thing, and for another my assertions of self-regulation have been questioned. I will deal with these matters in later sections. First I must deal with more fundamental problems, problems concerning the empirical values of key variables and relations among them. I myself called attention to some metrical and conceptual difficulties in the text. Yet I believe that some of the critiques in this regard not only are off the mark but they distract us from meaningful issues. Bennett, for instance, writes:

Rappaport's study was the best documented piece of research in cultural anthropology at the time of its publication: its ten appendices provide an unmatched assemblage of data on climate, agricultural output, flora, and energy expenditure for the community and its environs. However, these data are not systematically tied into the interpretive analysis of how ritual and other behaviors serve as automatic regulatory mechanisms, that is, the study is not a rigorous, quantitatively based documentation of the ecophysiological causes of human behavioral responses to needs. It is, despite its rich data background, fundamentally an analogic operation, in which ecosystemic complexities and a generalized impression of ecological causation are plausibly suggested but never worked out in detail. That is, Rappaport followed the protocol but not the analytic operations of the natural-ecological approach. [1976:181]

I shall deal with the charge that the analysis was "fundamentally an analogic operation" in section 10. Here I am concerned with Bennett's assertion that "these data are not systematically tied into the interpretive analysis." Nowhere in Bennett's critique does he substantiate this assertion or make it sufficiently specific to understand what he might take to be an adequate integration of data with interpretation. It is of course true that not all of the data assembled in the appendices were incorporated in the analysis. There was, with respect to the interpretation, a surplus of data. Data are, after all, collected prior to analysis and when the bulk of them were collected I had no glimmering of the system later delineated in the analysis. Should the data not required by the analysis have been discarded previous to publication? I think not. These data were entered into appendices not only because, as Bennett notes, they provided background but because they might prove useful to others for whatever ends they might wish to put them: for the enrichment of the analysis offered by me, for the construction of alternatives, for purposes altogether extraneous to my own.

Having agreed that the appendices include data that were not tied into the interpretation I will now claim that much of the quantitative data *did* enter into the analysis. Garden production, acreage in production, energy expenditure, amounts consumed by pigs, and the values of other variables entered into the analysis. Even such things as lists of virgin forest species figured indirectly. Their presence in successions following the abandonment of gardens was taken to indicate that successions had not been deflected from a movement toward a climax association.

I might also note here that it would be hard to imagine how Shantzis and Behrens (1973) and more recently Samuels (1983) could, independently of me, have constructed computer models of the system described in the book if the relevant quantitative data were not integrated into that system. (I hasten to note that Samuels' interpretation does not agree with mine.) I may also call attention here to the diagram on page 339, which represents the relationships analyzed in the book.

I am not clear upon what ground Bennett made his assertion. It may rest upon certain misunderstandings of the interpretation I have offered. I have already noted his misunderstandings concerning the degree to which the regulatory operation of the cycle is automatic and with respect to the place of the regulation of pig populations in the total analysis. He also follows McArthur (1974, 1977) in mistaking what I proposed to be the significance of pork distribution and consumption at the *kaiko* itself (see section 10). It may be, however, that his charge represents a demand for more precision and rigor than I supplied. In the absence of specifications by him of what would constitute adequacy in this regard, I cannot say. Nevertheless, an important·question is raised here. What level of precision is required? What constitutes adequate demonstration in anthropology? Canons can be so sternly set as to be, for all practical purposes, impossible to satisfy. This problem is not confined to the social sciences, of course.

Let us turn now to more substantive difficulties and shortcomings. First, there is the problem of providing empirical import for such key terms as "adequate functioning," "survival," "homeostasis," and so on. Although a serious attempt was made to do so in *Pigs for the Ancestors* it must be emphasized that the attempt was only partially successful. The shortcomings of the attempt are themselves instructive, however, for they had the virtue of exposing difficulties of a conceptual as well as metrical nature.

Having defined the units to be considered, an attempt was made to give "homeostasis," or "adequate functioning," empirical import in variable-specific terms. It was conceived, as already noted, in accordance with the strictures of Hempel (1959) and Nagel (1961), as a set of "goal ranges" (i.e., ranges of viability) on variables which, for reasons independent of the mode of operation of the system under consideration, were taken to be crucial to the persistence of that system. Thus, for ecological reasons, carrying capacity and nutritional variables were among those selected. An attempt was made to assign values to them on the basis of observations and measurements.

However, there were lacunae. For instance, upper limits were assigned to the tolerable sizes of pig and human populations but lower limits were not, nor was any value assigned to the tolerable frequency of warfare.

Furthermore, the establishment of goal ranges for some variables is extremely difficult. It is difficult to establish what, for instance, constitutes adequate nutrition, and similar problems beset the determination of other goal ranges entering into the calculation of the more general carrying capacity. Adequate fallow periods, for instance, would be indicated by the attainment of certain values in soil variables but, as Street (1969) has pointed out, the magnitude of measurement errors often exceeds the magnitude of significant changes in values. Even if measurements are precise, or even if such measurement is circumvented by the use of such gross indicators as the presence of climax tree species in successions on abandoned gardens, the time elapsed since the last cultivation may be difficult to ascertain. More fundamental: in a changing world goal ranges may, and do, change. The introduction of a new crop, for instance, may make it possible to support a larger number of people on the same amount of land. The method practiced in this study holds constant more than reality ever does.

Another drawback, related to the last, is that there are metrical problems of great difficulty manifesting themselves in a range of particulars. For instance, voluminous and detailed data were collected on garden yields. All crops brought home for consumption to four households were weighed daily by garden and by named variety (twenty-seven varieties of *Colocasia*, thirty-eight of *Dioscorea*, etc.). Estimates based upon observations were also made of crops consumed in the gardens. Weighings continued for ten months for over twenty gardens. Because these gardens were of different ages it was possible to construct composites for estimating the production of gardens for their entire harvesting lives of over two years. All garden areas were measured by chain and compass and yields were converted to acreage equivalents. I believe that the raw data are excellent. They were collected over a long run, they are very detailed, and they reflect indigenous planting and harvesting practice. However, problems beset conversion of these data into terms comparable to the results of other forms of agriculture and into terms that could be used for nutritional assessment. It was not possible to have my own samples analyzed so I was forced to rely upon published values for calorie and protein content, and published values vary widely. Moreover, although household intake figures were easy to obtain, estimating what proportion of household intake was consumed by each of the residents was extremely difficult. These problems were discussed in chapter 3 and in appendices 4 and 9. (Because of the specialized nature of the criticism of the nutritional data and interpretation I treat it in appendix 11.)

Problems in estimating the amount of energy expended in garden tasks were in a general way similar to those associated with estimating consumption. My observations of gardening tasks were detailed but too few. The main difficulty, however, was that to convert these observations into energetic terms I had to rely upon figures obtained by others using gas-exchange equipment among another population.

Something should be said about the conversion of harvest data into nutritional values and work into energetic terms. As far as harvest data are concerned, raw weight is of comparative use only within species. If one wishes to compare, say, the efficiency or results of swiddening in New Guinea to *padi* in the Philippines it seems to me that a conversion to common metrics is necessary, and, of course, a conversion to calories alone is inadequate. If one wishes to estimate the nutritional values of diets similar conversions are necessary.

All of this seems to me so obvious as to require comment only because some recent discussions have tended to denigrate such calculations, labeling them pejoratively as caloric and protein "obsession" and "nutritional reductionism" (see Brookfield, 1972; Cook, 1973; Ellen, 1982; Little and Morren, 1977:35; Morren, 1977; Vayda and

McCay 1975, 1977). Any data can, of course, be misinterpreted or overinterpreted. The question here is, "What significance is attributed to data converted into terms of calories and proteins?" I do not think that the nutritional aspects of *Pigs for the Ancestors* constituted an instance of caloric or protein "obsession" or "nutritional reductionism" as they are characterized by various authors and summarized by Ellen (1982:47f., 117ff.) It did not (1) represent an attempt to reduce social life "to calories and energy-efficiency computations." (2) It did not deny Scott Cook's truistical declaration (1973:44) that "Man must produce more than calories if calories are to be produced," nor was there any suggestion that economic production can be reduced to the expenditure of calories. (3) There was no claim that "energy balance reflects cultural adaptation." (4) There was no claim that energy capture can serve as a criterion of cultural evolution, a proposition with which I strongly disagree (see Rappaport, 1979a:166). (5) There was no claim that Maring population was limited by calories. There were tentative proposals concerning protein availability, particularly with respect to children and people under stress, but these proposals fell short of claiming protein as a limiting factor. The suggestion (not Ellen's and never direct) that the conversions represented an attempt to dress up ethnography as hard science does not merit a reply.

The fact that the problems attending the collection and processing of harvest and nutritional data were recognized in the book does not dissolve them. Yet as Ellen has said (1982:116), if we recognize our measurements for what they are and use them judiciously they are not devoid of value. Recognition of these difficulties may also lead to methods for circumventing or minimizing them. It is well to warn against what might be called the "Methodologist's fallacy" here. That it is difficult to establish nutritional requirements, to measure actual intake, and to assess nutritional status does not mean that we can dismiss malnutrition as a real problem. That carrying capacity might defy precise specification and that it might change does not mean that environmental degradation doesn't occur or that overexploitation is never a problem. The real problems of the real world cannot be ignored because they strain our methods.

Units and Their Implications

I have noted that the units figuring in the analysis offered in *Pigs for the Ancestors* were selected because they were recognized and named by the Maring themselves and thus could claim a "natural validity," a validity distinct from the analysis, and because they could, with no slight to their special characteristics, be regarded as instances of units appearing in both ecological theory (organisms, populations, and ecosystems) and social theory (individual actors, descent groups, local groups, territories, societies).

The selection of units for any particular analysis is, of course, only in part a function of the theory that informs it. It is also a function of the problem at hand, in both its details and its magnitude. Although the participation of populations in ecosystems is assumed in a classic form of ecology, populations and ecosystems may not always be useful or even feasible units of analysis. We might assume, for instance, that the territory and citizenry of China constitute a population in an ecosystem, but their use as units would permit only the grossest forms of analysis. That I used certain units in *Pigs for the Ancestors* should not be taken to mean that I advocate that they are universally appropriate. Other units, whose connection to those appearing in theory are less direct than in the Maring case, may often be more feasible or useful.

My advocacy of an ecology in which populations and ecosystems appear as theoretical entities does not constitute an assertion that no other approach is valid. Vayda and McCay (1975), among others, have proposed that it is fruitful to focus upon the responses of individuals and groups to perturbations in their environments, noting that such a focus does not require the discrimination of populations or ecosystems. I not only have nothing against such an approach, which is adaptive rather than strictly ecological, but have myself written upon it (1971d, 1978b, 1979a) and will discuss it later in this epilogue. It seems to me, however, that such an approach is not necessarily in competition with the ecosystemic formulation represented in *Pigs for the Ancestors*. The two are complementary. Lately, however, the propriety of units appearing in *Pigs for the Ancestors* has come under attack on theoretical grounds. Some anthropologists have questioned the very existence of ecosystems and McCay and others have questioned the validity of analyses focusing upon groups, proposing that the behavior of individuals coping with problems should be our central concern.

We shall now turn to the analytic units discriminated in *Pigs for the Ancestors*, first noting a stipulation of Brown's (1963:110) concerning functional statements generally which holds within more rigorous systemic analyses as well. Functional statements, he asserts, hold only with respect to systems of a certain type, namely those that are "self-persisting." Nagel (1961) agrees, stating that functional statements are appropriate in connection with systems incorporating "self-regulating mechanisms." Brown proposes that a system can be taken to be self-persisting if it includes self-regulatory devices or mechanisms. The question of self-regulation is, thus, closely related to the matter of appropriate units of analysis.

ECOSYSTEMS

In the conclusion of this book, I defined an ecosystem as "a demarcated portion of the biosphere that includes living organisms and non-living substances interacting to produce a systemic exchange of materials among the living components and between the living components and the nonliving substances" (p. 225). It may be asked whether or not such a unit falls into the class of self-persisting systems defined by Brown. Some anthropologists think that they do not. Friedman, for instance, has written, "An eco-system is not organized as such. It is the result of the mutual and usually partial adaptation of populations each of which has laws of functioning that are internally determined" (1974:466). Vayda and McCay (1975:229ff.) are in rather close agreement. Citing Colinvaux's (1973:549) remark that "nowhere can we find discrete ecosystems, let alone ecosystems with the self-organizing properties implied by the concept of climax," they assert that "the ecosystem is an analytic, not a biological entity." They propose that "interactions observed in complex ecosystems need not be regarded as expressing self-organizing properties of the systems themselves; instead they can be understood as the consequences of the various and variable adaptive strategies of individual organisms living together in restricted spaces." (While Friedman favors the "social formation" as an analytic unit, Vayda and McCay assign priority to the individual organism because natural selection operates on individuals.)

I regard all of this as rather muddled. The distinction that Vayda and McCay make between the analytic and biological seems to me to be a mistaken one. It is surely the case that there are few, if any, ecosystems less inclusive than the solar system that are hermetically sealed to flows of matter, energy, and information across their borders. Their boundaries must, therefore, be specified analytically, as must those of social formations or, for that matter, social units of any sort. The question of the criteria used to discriminate ecosystems from the continuity of natural phenomena is, of course, strategic, and I have discussed it elsewhere (1969, 1971a), proposing that in some instances it is useful to see a single population participating in more than one ecosystem, while in others two or more human populations may be taken to be participating in a single ecosystem. In *Pigs for the Ancestors* the criterion for establishing the boundaries of local ecosystems in what was a continuous biotic association, it is important to note, was human territoriality. The Maring are horticulturalists and, as such, ecological dominants. They set the conditions encouraging or discouraging the presence of other species, and they attempt to construct anthropocentric ecosystems within areas in which the engagement of humans in interspecies exchanges is conventionally regulated. Maring local groups are regulating the ecosystems within which they participate, or, to put it in the converse, the domain of the regulatory operations of a local group in this instance defines an ecosystem. Because a Maring local group is a component of the ecosystem which it regulates (and upon the perpetuation of which its own persistence is contingent) the ecosystem is by definition self-regulating.

It might be argued that self-regulatory properties are peculiar to anthropocentric ecosystems. I think this is not the case. Self-regulating mechanisms, I believe, inhere in ecosystems *qua* ecosystems *as well as* in their constituent populations. That there are self-regulating mechanisms at one level of organization does not mean that there are none at others. Every population in every ecosystem *must* have "internally determined laws of functioning" of its own, but this does not mean that there are not self-regulating mechanisms emerging out of relations between and among populations—as is the case of the mutual regulation of predator and prey populations. Ecosystemic self-regulation may be a product of dynamic interaction among a number of species none of whom exercises central control or is even dominant in a less active way. Such diffuse regulation is not unfamiliar to us; it animates, at least conceptually, the "perfect market" of economic mythology.

Ecosystems do seem to be self-regulated, then, and they show other indications of being "organized as such." For one thing they possess well-known structural characteristics. Regardless of what their constituent species may be, ecological systems are roughly cyclical with respect to material flow and pyramidal with respect to the productivity, energy flux, and regulation of constituent populations. They also seem to possess "self-organizing" properties. They transform themselves in response to changes in external conditions, sometimes by replacing all their constituent species with populations of other species, sometimes by the mutual adaptation of their constituent species. (I am not sure what Friedman means when he asserts that these adaptations are only "partial." Biological adaptation cannot create ex nihilo. It can do no more than transform what is present. As such, adaptation can never be more than partial in some sense. Nevertheless, some astounding relationships—e.g., between termites and the *Myxotricha paradoxa* living in their guts—have evolved, relationships of such intricacy and intimacy that the term *coevolution* has been used to refer to the mutual causal processes through which they have emerged.)

Although ecosystems include species that have come together accidentally, forming relationships that are, at the outset, only crudely articulated, the constitutions of such systems are likely to become increasingly elaborate and coercive through time. Many ecologists continue to believe that ecosystemic successions, unless they are arrested or deflected, exhibit holistic tendencies, and that these tendencies are similar in systems very different in species composition (see Odum, 1969; Margalef, 1968). Under more or less stable conditions, it is proposed, the number of species of which ecosystems are composed increases, perhaps to some maximum; the species present become increasingly specialized and an increasing proportion of them is composed of large, longer-lived, slower-breeding organisms. The system as a whole requires less and less energy flux per unit of standing biomass to sustain itself, but productivity per unit of area increases. Material and energy pathways proliferate, as do regulatory mechanisms. Systemic redundancy thus offsets the loss of systemic stability that might otherwise be a concomitant of the increasing specialization of the species present. Colinvaux (1973, especially chapters 6 and 40) has argued that successional properties have been oversimplified and their commonalities exaggerated, but even he does not dismiss them. The adjudication of this argument must be left to biological ecologists. Whatever the outcome of their debate may be, however, there are sufficient grounds for taking ecosystems to be organized as such and to be members of the class of "self-persistent" systems, although differing from other classes of such systems in important respects, including relative coherence, relative autonomy of their subsystems, and sharpness of boundaries.

ECOSYSTEMS AND INTERLEVEL CONTRADICTION

A statement of Robert Murphy's could, nevertheless, be taken to be an argument against using the ecosystem as an object of functional or systemic statements even though the organized status of such systems is granted.

Higher order phenomena arrange lower order phenomena to their purposes, though they may not change their properties. Corre-

spondingly, human social systems reach out and embrace ecosystems rather than the reverse proposition, and culture reor-
ders nature and makes appendages of the parts of it that are
relevant to the human situation. [1970:169]

The only qualification I would voice with respect to this statement
is that it may not apply to hunting and gathering populations. With
food production—or at least with plant cultivation—men become
ecological dominants, setting the conditions encouraging or discouraging the presence of populations of other species. The burden of
regulating anthropocentric ecosystems rests largely upon the humans
dominating them. That humans attempt to put nature to their own
purposes (i.e., to regulate ecosystems in accordance with what they
take to be their self-interest) is true, but this is hardly the end of the
matter. We want to know how this is done; what the purposes and
understanding of the actors may be; to what degree these purposes
are themselves constituted, coerced, or constrained by environmental characteristics; the degree to which they conform to, or are even
explicitly concerned with or informed by, an awareness of the requirements of ecosystemic perpetuation and, of course, whether actions guided by such purposes are compatible with ecosystemic requisites or ecologically degrading or destructive. I have argued that
Tsembaga practice was at the least compatible with the perpetuation
of their ecosystem. Earlier in this epilogue I suggested that such compatibility may not be unusual in societies of small, highly self-suffi-
cient preindustrial food cultivators, all of whose full members are engaged in gardening, but I also made clear that I do not take it always
to prevail even among such peoples.

Cultivation demands that complex climax communities of plants
and animals be replaced by simpler communities composed of smaller
numbers of species selected by humans according to criteria of apparent usefulness, and arranged by them in limited numbers of short
food chains of which the humans themselves strive to be the termi-
nus. Such communities are likely to be less stable than the climax
communities they replace. The relatively degraded nature of anthropocentric ecosystems is in part a function of their simplicity (but for
recent questioning of the diversity–stability hypothesis see Becker-

man, 1983; Hames, 1983), in part a function of the nature of their constituent species: often poorly adapted to local conditions, often helpless, frequently unable even to reproduce without some assistance. And humans are poor dominants. It is interesting to note that dominants—the species setting the conditions that encourage or discourage the presence of others—in nonanthropocentric ecosystems are almost always plants, like oak trees in temperate forests, or animals resembling plants, like corals in reef-lagoon communities. They are well suited to their role, for their mere nonpurposive existence fulfills well the needs of their associated species. Humans, on the other hand, must maintain their dominance through behavior. Because their behavior is less reliable than the simple existence of oak trees, because they are capable of acting selfishly and maliciously, because they often act in ignorance, because they can make mistakes, and because their purposes may not coincide with the needs of the systems which they dominate, humans set conditions that tend toward instability (Rappaport, 1970a, 1970b).

To insist upon the self-regulating, self-organizing characteristics of ecosystems is not to claim that only ecosystems are organized. Well-defined social units and individual organisms are also constituted systems with "laws of functioning that are internally determined." Observing that ecosystems are constituted does not deny to the organisms and populations of organisms (including human groups) participating in them their relative autonomy. Conversely, recognizing the relative autonomy of a social unit does not deny the organization of the ecosystem of which it is a part, any more than recognizing the relative autonomy of individuals denies the organization of the social units of which individuals are always members. A refusal to recognize the organization of more inclusive systems is tantamount to arguing for the absolute autonomy of systems—at one or another level of inclusiveness—operating in larger fields which are not systematic, or systematic only in a derivative sense. (Laissez-faire capitalists, for instance, would claim that individuals or corporations are properly autonomous, operating within a larger economic field that has systemic qualities, e.g., "the hidden hand," only as a byproduct of the interaction of its autonomous constituents.) The complexity of the world does not warrant such a view even for analytic heuristic purposes.

We must recognize that more inclusive entities are indeed organized systems, made up of components that are themselves relatively autonomous. Ecosystems, for instance, include populations which are, in turn, composed of individuals. While it may be, as systems theory proposes, that *generally* similar principles organize systems at various levels of inclusiveness, important differences in their more *specific* "laws of functioning" should be recognized.

A difference to which little attention has been given is that of the differential degrees of coherence that systems of different classes both require and can tolerate. By "relative coherence" I refer to the degree to which changes in one component of a system effect changes in other components of the system. A fully coherent system is one in which any change in any component results in an immediate and proportional change in all other components. As no living system could be totally incoherent, neither could any living system be fully coherent, for disruptions anywhere would immediately spread everywhere. Perhaps because their functioning depends upon fine, quick, and continual coordination of parts, organisms are, and must be, more coherent than social systems. Conversely, the degree of coherence continually required by organisms would probably be intolerable for social systems (which may attain levels of coherence comparable to that of organisms only in extraordinary circumstances, such as rituals, for relatively brief periods). Ecosystems are probably less coherent than social systems, at least human social systems (perhaps because orderly relations within ecosystems depend more on increasing redundancy than upon coordination). Their low degree of coherence may well be in large part responsible for our frequent failure to recognize their systemic characteristics.

It is obvious that the maintenance of systems and the purposes of their relatively autonomous components do not always coincide. Humans can surely do violence to the structure and function of the ecosystems that they come to dominate, just as certain subsystems of societies, such as industries, can do violence to the social entities that they come to dominate. Although such violation is not unexampled among tribal peoples, I have already suggested that its likelihood is increased and its effects extended and intensified by increased differentiation of society, by alienating or at least separating the economic rationality of individuals from direct ecological imperatives, by production for gain rather than use, and by industrialization.

The imperatives of individual existence often bring individuals into conflict with the social systems of which they are members; the cultural imperatives of social systems may lead to actions at variance with ecological principles. Contradiction between constituted systems on various levels of inclusiveness—between individuals and societies, between societies and ecosystems—are inevitable. Sahlins (1969) and Friedman (1974) err, I think, in taking ecological or adaptive formulations to be "innocent of a concern for contradiction." Elsewhere (1970b, 1978b, 1979a) I have discussed maladaptation in structural terms, proposing that it is to be understood as, or as resulting from, among other things, interlevel contradiction. Indeed, it seems to me that it is Friedman's argument, not adaptive and ecological formulations, that is analytically innocent of a concern for interlevel contradiction. He is right in insisting upon the relative autonomy of certain social entities, yet he denies organization or even reality to the systems that include the systems he recognizes. But if reality or organization is denied to ecological systems how is it possible to discover contradictions between them and the entities participating in them? We may not only miss much of explanatory importance but also much of what is problematic or even poignant or tragic in the human condition. The impoverishment of the perspective is increased if relevance is also denied to the relative autonomy of the individuals composing the social entities with which Friedman is concerned. It should not be forgotten that one of the perennial concerns of human thought about the human condition is with the problems congregating in the relationship between individuals and the societies of which they are members, problems which are conceptually summarized in such phrases as "the problem of freedom"—or of happiness, duty, honor, authenticity, ambition, responsibility, obligation, or ethics. Even granting the systemic nature of ecosystems, the question remains, however, whether or not ecosystems are properly thought of as units of analysis. There are difficulties in establishing their boundaries, and, more generally, their ultracomplexity leads to problems in comprehending interactions among their constituents. I do not believe that any natural ecosystem has ever been anything like

fully modeled. The accounts or descriptions of ecosystems which ecological anthropologists may produce, even in cooperation with specialists, are the merest sketches. We can do little more than outline
the general structure of such systems, try to measure a few important
interactions, and attempt to locate the species with which we are
concerned in the web. In practice, it seems, we may not be far from
Steward's (1955) "significant environment."

That ecosystems are complex beyond realistic possibilities of comprehensive modeling does not distinguish them radically from other
entities with which we deal and which we take to be units of analysis:
organisms, social groups, social formations, populations, cultures.
Moran (1983) proposes that the ecosystem is conceptually important
even if it presents difficulties as a unit of analysis. (He adds the matter
of variable scale to the problems of boundary and complexity.) I agree.
If the ecosystemic concept is abandoned we are faced with a choice.
We either find some other way of representing the systemic character
of surrounding nature or we confine ourselves to the study of decon-
textualized interactions between humans as individuals or groups on
the one hand and one or a very few nonhuman elements in their
surroundings on the other. To the extent that ecology is defined by a
commitment to a holistic view of nature the latter choice is not ecological but anti-ecological.

ECOLOGICAL POPULATIONS

The analytic use of populations as environed units distinguishes
what others have called "the new ecology" most clearly from the "cultural ecology" of Julian Steward (1955), in which cultures are taken
to be the environed units. The choice has attracted considerable criticism. Sahlins, for instance, has declared that in the "translation of a
'social order' into a 'population of organisms' . . . everything that is
distinctively cultural about the object has been allowed to escape"
(1976b:298). This is, in my view, a misunderstanding and because this
misunderstanding persists it is well to make clear some of the considerations that entered into the analytic choice of the population two
decades ago.

First, difficulties are entailed by the use of cultures or their parts (e.g., Steward's "culture core") as environed units in ecological analyses, and when cultures are combined with an ecosystemic concept of the environment these difficulties are increased. Such a choice is the result of a rather subtle methodological or even logical confusion, a confusion between an explicandum on the one hand and, on the other, the primary units of analysis, the major components of analytic or descriptive models, the elements seen to stand in relation to each other in the system under study.

This confusion is easy to fall into, and it is understandable that anthropologists interested in the formative effects of environments on cultures would take cultures, or parts of cultures, to be their primary units of analysis. The conception of culture as an order of phenomena distinct from the psychological, biological, and inorganic has been one of anthropology's important contributions to Western thought. Inasmuch as cultural phenomena may be distinguished from other phenomena and inasmuch as culture, however it is understood, is what most cultural anthropologists wish to elucidate, cultures or their constituents have seemed obvious choices for referent units in ecological as well as other anthropological formulations. Indeed, such a choice seems almost inevitable, considering that culture is conceived by many anthropologists not only to be ontologically distinct from biological, psychological, and inorganic phenomena, but processually independent of them as well. Culture, it is said, "obeys laws of its own," laws distinct from those governing organic and inorganic processes.

At the same time that cultural ecology took cultures, distinct from the organisms bearing them, to be interacting with environments, it borrowed the concept of ecosystem from general ecology. In the resulting formulation, cultures simply interact with ecosystems. But cultures and ecosystems are not directly commensurable. An ecosystem is a system of matter and energy transactions among unlike populations or organisms and between them and the nonliving substances by which they are surrounded. Culture is the category of phenomena distinguished from others by its contingency upon symbols. The incommensurability of ecosystems and cultures becomes clear when one considers the analogy implicit in the notion of cultures (independent of, or at least conceptually separated from,

culture-bearing organisms) interacting with other components of ecological systems:

CULTURE : ECOSYSTEM : : ANIMAL POPULATION : ECOSYSTEM

It is ironic that the choice of cultures as primary units of analysis in
cultural-ecological formulations aimed to protect the uniqueness of
culture against the degrading power of ecological principles, but it
has the opposite effect, for the processual equivalence of cultures and
animal populations is logically entailed by it. The analogy not only
implies that they have similar requirements which must be fulfilled
in similar ways and that they are similarly limited by environmental
constraints, but also that cultures, far from obeying laws of their own,
are directly subject to the same laws as those governing animal populations. No cultural ecologist (in the strict sense) has ever taken such
a position, of course, and, I am sure, none ever intended to do so. It
is nevertheless intrinsic to the eclectic conjunction of incommensur-
able and incongruent terms that characterizes the cultural-ecological
conception. Eclectic formulations bring together the disparate terms
they subsume only by violating some or all of them. In the case at
hand the violence is wreaked upon the notion of culture, for it, or
some of its aspects, such as the social order, may be conflated with
biological phenomena.
    This problem is illustrated by difficulties experienced by Marshall
Sahlins in *Social Stratification in Polynesia*. It was his thesis that certain differences in the social orders of Polynesian societies, in particular differences in social stratification, were to be accounted for by
differences in productivity. In societies such as those of pre-contact
Polynesia, the term *productivity* must refer to the yields of horticulture and fishing. Lacking direct production data, Sahlins attempted
to estimate the comparative productivity of the societies in question
by comparing the size of the largest networks through which garden,
grove, and fishing yields were distributed in each society, making the
assumption that the larger the network and the more frequently it
operated, the greater the surplus and therefore the higher the productivity. The relationship between surplus and productivity is problematic, however, and there is no reason to believe, prima facie, that

a society of a certain size organized into a single distributive network produces more per capita than a smaller society, or more than one of the same size organized into a number of smaller networks. Moreover, if the scope of the distributive prerogatives vested in chiefs is an aspect of stratification, and if stratification is to be accounted for by productivity, to read productivity from the size of redistributive networks brings the argument perilously close to circularity.

The dubiety of a long inferential chain and the dangers of circularity can be avoided however. Productivity in an ecological sense is understood as the amount of biomass or energy produced per unit of area per unit of time. The horticultural productivity of societies can thus be compared in such terms as tons per acre per year. In the absence of harvest and landing data indices may or must be used, but the size of redistributive networks is not an appropriate one. In relatively undifferentiated nonindustrial societies like those of Polynesia, however, in which production is for use rather than for gain, and in which populations are closely related genetically and possess similar arrays of tools, it is reasonable to infer comparative productivity, or production, from a comparison of the densities of the populations supported by that production. Such a comparison indicates that there was probably no correlation between social stratification and productivity, in aboriginal Polynesia. But the point I wish to make here is that I believe Sahlins's difficulties have followed from a failure to distinguish an aspect of social orders—the size of redistributive networks—from a biological characteristic of populations, namely their densities.

We may recall here Bennett's charge, cited in an earlier section, that the analysis developed in *Pigs for the Ancestors* was, in its use of a general ecological paradigm, "merely an analogic operation." Bennett is mistaken. The analysis represented a deliberate, self-conscious attempt to replace the inappropriate and deforming analogy underlying "cultural ecology" (an analogy which takes human cultures and animal populations to be equivalents) with a homology. As such it represented an attempt to replace a mode of analysis which is merely eclectic with one which is appropriately synthetic. Synthetic formulations, in contrast to those which are merely eclectic, subsume the subject matter of what had previously been separate realms of discourse under terms of sufficient generality to accommodate both without distortion. They do not ignore or deny distinctions but employ terms of sufficiently high logical type to encompass seemingly disparate phenomena as more or less distinct members of subclasses of a common class.

The first step in moving toward any synthesis is to find terms expressing commonalities. In the case of the place of humans in ecosystemic processes, rather than attending only to that which distinguishes the human species from other species, synthesis *begins* with what is common to all of them and *then* proceeds to whatever may distinguish them. We thus begin with the simple observation that the human species is, after all, a species among species and that, as such, humanity's relations with its physical and biotic environments are, like those of other animals, continuous, indissoluble, and necessary. It follows that it is not only possible but proper to take populations of the human species to be environed units in ecological formulations.

In this book and elsewhere I have defined *ecological population* as an aggregate of organisms sharing distinctive means for maintaining a common set of material relations with the other components of the ecosystem in which they together participate. An ecosystem, as we have already noted, is the total of ecological populations and nonliving substances bound together in material exchanges in a demarcated portion of the biosphere. The terms *ecosystem* and *human population*, taken in the ecological sense (and not, for instance, in the sense of a simple census count in a polity of some sort) are fully commensurable and congruent.

But what of culture? Is its uniqueness ignored, violated, degraded, or reduced by the synthesis represented in this general form of ecological anthropology? I think not. For purposes of ecological accounts, accounts which are concerned (possibly among other things) with the relations of humans with their environments, cultures or their constituents can be included among the properties of populations.

In this view cultures are not analogous to animal populations, but constitute the major and most distinctive means by which human populations maintain common sets of material relations with other components of the ecosystems in which they participate. Culture, in other words, is central to the adaptive characteristics of the species; cultures, in turn, are central to the adaptations of the many more or less distinctive populations into which the species is organized.

If the concept of culture as adaptation is the truth it is not the whole truth. While it would be hard to imagine the emergence of culture out of a precultural substrate as other than a strongly-selected-for innovation in the adaptive process itself, it would be equally difficult to argue that, having emerged, culture has remained nothing more than an adaptive apparatus in the service of the organic processes of a particular species. Once emerged, cultures both developed needs of their own and established the goals, values, and purposes of humans. It becomes no longer clear whether culture is a symbolic means to organic ends or organisms living means to cultural ends, for humans come to serve and preserve their cultures as much as, or even more than, their cultures serve and preserve them.

Ecological populations, as I have defined them, are units engaged in material exchanges with other, ecologically dissimilar, populations and with nonliving substances in their environments. I have noted that cultures, having emerged, develop needs distinct from the organic needs of their populations. In the course of human history the requirements of their cultural constituents have been responsible for an ever-increasing proportion of the total demands made by human populations upon their environments, and there has also been a shift in the components of the environment directly affected. Energy consumption serves as one indicator. Among the Tsembaga it stands at 2,000–3,000 K per capita per day, plus whatever is supplied by wood burned as fuel. A recent estimate for the United States placed energy consumption at 230,000 K per capita per day (E. Cook, 1971). Needless to say, an overwhelming proportion of the excess in American over Maring energy flux is consumed by machines. Correlated with this trend is a shift from activities that mainly affect other species, primarily plants, to activities that directly affect the substrate, such as industrialized agriculture and the extraction of coal, petroleum, and ores. Whereas the effects of relatively small-scale exploitation of living species are likely to be transitory, since living species generally are able to regenerate themselves, large-scale alterations of the nonliving substrate are likely to be permanently damaging.

This account proposes that a culture's own requisites, and the values, purposes, and goals which it ordains, may come to be at odds with the organic needs of the humans striving to live by and fulfill them, and may also violate the ecosystems in which they are fulfilled. That the cultural properties of human populations may be inimical to their organic characteristics is as inherent to the view expressed here as is the recognition that aspects of cultures are properly regarded as central to the adaptations of their bearers. The contradiction, perhaps inevitable, between the cultural and the biological is, in my view, among the most fundamental problems to be addressed by an ecologically aware anthropology.

I have referred to the cultural properties of human populations. Without some elucidation the vagueness of this usage can only hide problems. In its simplest sense a property is something possessed. The term also denotes characteristic traits or peculiarities of an entity or class; and in logic a property is a predictable feature common and peculiar to a class, necessarily predicated of its essence without being part of that essence (*American Heritage Dictionary*, 1979). In its relationship to an essential humanity, cultures conform to all of these definitions. There are no human populations that do not possess a culture, nor does any culture exist independent of some population or populations of humans. It seems commonsensical, on the other hand, to take organic characteristics to be not so much properties of human populations but their very essence. Nevertheless, it may be as reasonable to conceive of human populations as possessing organic as well as cultural properties. There is, at any rate, a real sense in which human organisms are possessed by the cultures prevailing in the populations of which they are members.

That the cultural and organic properties of humanity are mutually dependent needs no discussion. It may, however, be worth noting that their relationship is not symmetrical. Although no group or assemblage of human organisms could survive physically in the absence of culture it is not the case that any *paticular* convention or set of conventions is indispensable to that survival. In contrast, the persistence of all cultural properties is contingent upon their realization by living humans. Cultures do not, as is sometimes said, "develop lives of their own." They can "live" only in the lives of those whose thought and action they form. Organic processes and cultural order are bound together in human life and its evolution.

That the realization of culture is contingent upon the lives of organisms does not mean that all of culture is to be accounted for in ecological or adaptive terms. Such theories cannot, by themselves, constitute a general theory or explanation of culture, although it may be that some anthropologists, including me (Rappaport 1971b; Vayda and Rappaport, 1967), have come close to trying to make them do so from time to time. The perspectives of ecology, adaptation, and evolution do, however, have a contribution to make to a general understanding of culture and to understandings of particular cultures.

It does not seem to me, in sum, that any violation of culture's unique characteristics is entailed, nor its magnitude diminished, when cultures are taken to be properties of populations. The social order is not thereby reduced to the status of the organic, as Sahlins (1967a:298) has charged. Indeed, the organic characteristics of human populations are more clearly distinguished from the cultural conventions ordering those populations than they are in the cultural ecology of Steward or the early Sahlins. To distinguish is not to separate, of course. In this view the cultural and organic properties of populations are neither inappropriately conflated nor radically separated. The attempt is to find terms commensurable with all of nature while giving full consideration to the uniqueness of human life.

Although anthropologists like to think of themselves as especially free from ethnocentrism, they have traditionally been concerned with those aspects of existence that are unique to humans. Anthropology is, in short, anthropocentric and it would be surprising if it weren't. But by focusing upon those aspects of human existence that are unique to humanity we tend to ignore other aspects that, although not unique to human life, are nonetheless parts of it. Such a stance may lead us to separate ourselves from, or even oppose ourselves to, the rest of nature in our daily lives and public affairs, with the unhappy consequences we see developing in the environment around us.

There is also a conceptual effect which requires comment. In our formal attempts to understand our relation to the rest of the world we are encouraged to seek special explanations, explanations which, founded upon assumptions of uniqueness, can cover only one, or at best a narrow range, of cases, and we are dissuaded from attempts to understand cultural phenomena in terms of principles that apply to other species as well. Whether such general principles have much to contribute to our understanding of culture or the human condition is discussed further in the final section of this epilogue. Here it may be suggested that formulations that illuminate similarities rather than emphasize differences have a proper place in our epistemologies, not always as alternatives to more special explanations but as complements to them. It may even be proposed that the exposure of similarities among phenomena such as organisms, populations, or even living systems generally precedes adequate understanding of the differences among them. Unless similarities are recognized and understood the magnitude and significance of differences cannot be comprehended. What to a more general perspective appear to be variations on a common theme may seem to a narrower perspective to be enormous differences of kind.

It seems to me, in sum, that the use of the human population in ecological analyses preserves a view of humanity as part of nature at the same time that it recognizes the uniqueness conferred upon the species by culture. As such it preserves the terms defining the condition of a creature that can live only in terms of meanings, largely culturally constituted, in a world to which law is intrinsic but meaning is not.

LOCAL AND REGIONAL POPULATIONS

I will turn now to a more or less common criticism of *Pigs for the Ancestors* put by Roy Ellen in the following way:

> Rappaport's analysis is based upon an assumption that the Tsembaga represent a closed spatial and temporal system, at least as far as the variables which he discusses are concerned. He had to assume that the Tsembaga and Maring are relatively isolated and constitute a population in dynamic balance with its environment. The data clearly suggest that his assumptions are not valid. [1982:185–186]

I find this criticism mystifying. Although I argued that the identification of local groups as ecological populations is appropriate to the analysis of localized interspecific trophic exchanges among the Maring, I *did not* argue that such transactions exhaust the exchange relationships of any Maring local group. *All* local groups of tribal people, with the possible exception of a few isolated on remote islands or in the deep reaches of the Arctic, engage in exchanges with other human groups living in other localities. The materials exchanged may include foodstuffs, but trade goods, valuables, personnel, and such services as ritual support, military reinforcement, and hospitality in times of emergency are often more important. Moreover, territory may be reallocated from time to time among the local groups occupying a region through such processes as warfare, migration, and alliance formation. Such extralocal relations were not slighted in *Pigs for the Ancestors*. They were, in fact, crucial to the account presented, occupying a chapter of their own, figuring prominently in the chapter on the ritual cycle, and receiving considerable attention in the final chapter.

Although I adduced evidence to show that the Tsembaga alone derive subsistence from their territory and almost only from their territory, and although I claimed that a similar degree of local trophic self-sufficiency is general among the Maring, my account *did not* indicate and *certainly* did not assume that Maring local groups are "relatively isolated" from each other nor that the Maring as a whole are isolated from other peoples in the general area. (I may also note in passing that I did not *assume* that either the Tsembaga or the Maring are in dynamic equilibrium with the environment. I did adduce some evidence, largely floristic, that led me to *conclude* (correctly or incorrectly) that the Tsembaga were not degrading their environment. I said nothing about other Maring local groups in this respect. See Manner [1981] for an account of Kauwasi territory.) In sum, it seems to me that the charge that "Rappaport's analysis is based upon the assumption that the Tsembaga represent a closed spatial and temporal system" is simply incorrect. The assumptions first attributed to me and then proclaimed invalid were not in fact mine.

I did argue in the conclusion of *Pigs for the Ancestors* and elsewhere (1969, 1971b) that "the concept of the ecosystem [and of the ecological population] which provides a convenient frame or model for the analysis of trophic exchanges between ecologically dissimilar [i.e., occupying different niches] populations occupying single localities can accommodate only by the introduction of analogy nontrophic . . . exchanges between ecologically similar populations occupying separate localities" (p. 225, above). To deal with transactions of the latter sort I suggested that we recognize that local groups (and by implication the separate subgroups and individuals composing them) not only participate as ecological populations in local ecosystems but also constitute elements or components of regional systems. Among tribal peoples ecosystems are likely to be more or less localized systems of interspecies exchanges with trophic exchanges being the most important class of transactions taking place in them. Regional systems are more dispersed systems of intraspecies exchanges with the most important transactions likely to be exchanges of personnel, information, and services of various sorts, as well as trade goods and valuables.

Ecosystems and regional systems can *usually* be distinguished among tribal peoples by differences in the degrees to which they are spatially limited. Local territorial groups and the territories they claim can often be taken to constitute ecosystems. The aggregate of local groups interacting in an area may constitute a regional system. Such clarity does not always prevail, however, because territoriality is not always strongly developed among tribal peoples and is often weakly developed or nonexistent among hunters and gatherers. Even in instances in which particular local groups are associated with particular areas as, for instance, among bushmen bands (Lee, 1976; Yellen, 1976) individuals are able to move from one group to another with great ease. In such cases I have suggested (1971b:250) that the ecological population may have to be taken to include all the bands living in the region, and the region as a whole the ecosystem. Observations and measurements performed on one or several local groups can then be used as statistical samples of the environmental relations of the entire population. The local group, this is to say, is in such cases a *sample*, and *not* an analytic *object* in its own right (see Arensberg, 1961).

There are grounds for distinguishing ecosystems and regional systems, grounds which are, in fact, more fundamental than simple local concentration versus regional dispersion. First, there is the matter of the relationships among constituent units. Ecosystems are composed of more or less continuous interactions among ecologically dissimilar populations, that is, populations, usually of different species, occupying distinctive positions in networks of trophic exchanges. Regional systems are composed of interactions among ecologically similar populations, that is, distinct populations of the same species occupying similar or equivalent ecological niches. Maring local groups constitute units in both (local) ecosystems and a wider regional system.

Ecosystems and regional systems are "about" different things. Ecosystems are systems of matter and energy exchanges among unlike species. These exchanges are, in the main, trophic and the system is "concerned with" sustenance. The transactions typical of regional systems are, in contrast, mainly nontrophic. Food may, of course, figure in regional exchanges (often symbolically), but exchanges of personnel, valuables, trade goods, services, and information are frequently of greater material importance. The system is "about" population dispersion, defense, aggression, non-food necessities, luxuries and valuables, reproduction, social relations, and ritual. It is economic, social, political, and religious in nature.

Third, the formal characteristics of the exchanges are different in the two sorts of systems. The trophic exchanges defining ecosystems are two-party exchanges in which the material exchanged is one of the parties—one eats the other. The exchanges defining regional systems are also exchanges between two parties, but the objects exchanged, be they material goods, information, services, or men or women given in marriage, are separate from the exchanging parties. Exchanges in the regional system are intrinsically social in nature— they are between similar parties that, as a rule, survive the exchange and usually benefit from it in one way or another. (Warfare is an exception.) Ecosystemic exchanges, in contrast, do not seem intrinsically social. They are between dissimilar parties, one of which usually does not survive the exchange. It is, however, no less striking because well known that ecosystemic exchanges are, despite their intrinsically antisocial nature, often viewed in social terms. Marsupials, for instance, are taken by the Maring to be "the pigs of the Red

Spirits" and we may recall here Wagner's (1977) discussion of Melanesian conceptions of humanity.

Although the discrimination of an ecological system and a regional system was sufficient for the relatively simple situation prevailing in the Simbai Valley between 1962 and 1964 I recognized (p. 227n) that more complex situations might require more elaborate discriminations.

Another point is to be made here. It is useful to discriminate between ecosystems and regional systems even in instances in which the two are geographically and demographically coextensive because such a discrimination focuses attention on the manner in which the discriminated systems are articulated. Articulation between unlike processes is not to be taken for granted. Questions concerning the matter include the extent to which events in one system affect events in the other (whether ecosystemic processes are buffered against economic processes, for instance, or whether one system is continuously, sporadically, or periodically responsive to occurrences in the other, and so on). Regional and ecosystemic relations are articulated through local organization and local ritual cycles which, in *Pigs for the Ancestors,* were taken to be outcomes of participating in ecosystemic processes on the one hand and regional relations on the other.

I have also suggested, not only in *Pigs for the Ancestors* (p. 229), but elsewhere (1971c), that focusing upon the ways in which distinct systems are articulated may enlarge our understanding of particular institutions. I proposed, for example, that Maring ritual operates as a binary transducer, "translating," as it were, changes in the state of one system into information meaningful in the terms of another. I have further argued more recently that this capacity of ritual has wider application than the articulation of ecosystemic and regional systems, being manifested most generally in the articulation of private psychophysical processes to public social systems (1979d:187f.).

I have labeled the aggregate of local groups that together comprise regional systems "regional populations." As I noted in the conclusion of *Pigs for the Ancestors,* regional populations may resemble or even be identical with other associations identified by anthropologists and other scientists—the populations of demographers, the breeding populations of geneticists, the societies of sociologists and anthropol-

ogists (which I would define as associations of organisms whose interactions are governed by common sets of conventions). Like these units
the boundaries of regional systems are typically vague or clinal rather
than sharp. I have also suggested that whereas regional populations
persist indefinitely, the local groups which are their constituents are
more or less ephemeral (see Lowman-Vayda, 1980).

SOCIAL FACTORS

The charge that I assumed the Tsembaga to be more isolated than
is the case is related to the general criticism that insufficient weight
was given to social factors in *Pigs for the Ancestors*. This criticism
does have some merit. Biological and ecological considerations were
emphasized largely because they were relatively novel and social considerations were not. To say that undue emphasis was given to certain
factors is not to say insufficient weight was given to others, however.
Emphasis is rhetorical, "weight" an analytic matter. The rhetorical
emphasis may have distracted readers from social elements that did,
in fact, figure in the analysis. It may still be that some social considerations were undervalued, but critics seem to have missed some of
the social elements that I took to be integral to the argument.

A common criticism has focused upon the dynamics of the pig population, specifically, that I did not consider sufficiently the motives
for raising pigs or the strategies for disposing of them. I did emphasize that the *number* of pigs taken to be "sufficient to repay the ancestors" was not determined by social obligations, but was an outcome
of local processes. More precisely, it was a number that was sufficiently burdensome or troublesome to a large enough proportion of
the locals to effect a consensus. No critic has effectively challenged
this attempt to account for the size of the pig population at the time
of the *kaiko*. My further proposal that the number of pigs at the time
of their sacrifice is likely to be below the carrying capacity of the
territory for pigs is much more controversial and has, in fact, been
effectively criticized (see section 11 of this epilogue).

Although my emphasis was on the size of the pig population and
its relationship to carrying capacity, the account did make clear, I
believe, that the *kaiko*, which provides the occasions for sacrifice of

large numbers of pigs, is social, political, and religious in nature. This is to say that the pigs killed in its course are put to social, political, and religious ends. There has been some misunderstanding of this, particularly on the part of McArthur (1974, 1977), who has been followed in this by Bennett (see section 9). McArthur understood the general argument to propose (1) that the consumption of pork is confined to periods of stress when the consumption of high-quality protein is especially valuable, and (2) that the *kaiko*, when much pork is consumed, is such a time of stress. This is *not* the argument. I argued that (1) limiting the consumption of pork outside of festivals and warfare to contexts in which psychological stress is likely makes best possible nutritional use of the limited pork available to the Tsembaga; (2) the number of pigs born and growing to maturity is likely to exceed the number required for sacrifices in connection with stressful events, and thus the pig population will grow; (3) sooner or later this "surplus" of pigs will become burdensome; and (4) the burden is reduced by sacrifices during the *kaiko*, when the pigs accumulated are dedicated to social, political, and religious ends. The nutritional aspects of this argument are taken up in appendix 11.

Two points, although implicit, should have been made more explicit in the book. First, the ability to stage a *kaiko* demonstrates a local group's capacity to defend itself successfully, to flourish ecologically (as indicated by the growth of the pig population), and to fulfill its obligations to its allies and ancestors through presentations of pork. Such a demonstration is prerequisite to full and unimpeded participation by a local group in the regional system. There is, consequently, an alternation, so to speak, between the periods when *rumbim* is in the ground, during which the attention and efforts of local groups are focused upon local processes, and the periods following *kaiko* and culminating in war when attention and effort focuses more on regional relations. The second point to be stressed is that, although the reservation of pork for consumption during periods of stress may be of nutritional value, it is clear that the disposition of pigs is not to be accounted for in nutritional terms. I did not claim extraordinary importance for the nutritional value of the pork consumed during *kaiko*. McArthur (1977:124) has said that I have failed to recognize how wasteful Maring practices are, proposing that "pigs are a source of prestige as well as protein."

Rather than condemning these practices as wasteful I would prefer to see the use of livestock and its slaughter in the governance of political relations as costly in nutritional terms. If the growth of the pig population is to be regarded as an index of the ecological and economic competence requisite to political actions of certain sorts (notably the initiation of warfare) by local groups as wholes, then decisions concerning the disposition of pigs are taken out of individual hands and nutritional ends are tempered by or even subordinated to the governance of regional relations. The governance of intergroup relations and the acquisition of prestige are not mutually exclusive, of course, but McArthur is simply mistaken in her assertion (1974:119) that competition for either prestige or for "power to determine matters of policy" is a particularly prominent feature of Maring life.

Ellen (1982:184) has also noted that Lowman-Vayda (1971) has reported that the Kauwasi Maring kill more pigs for affinal prestations than they do for misfortune or warfare in nonfestival years, the implication being that this contradicts my understanding of Tsembaga practice. I must call attention to the fact that I published the same information (in the form of a personal communication from Lowman-Vayda) in *Pigs for the Ancestors* (p. 82) where I accounted for differences between Tsembaga and Kauwasi practice in terms of major differences in their horticulture (note 4, page 82).

Another common criticism has been that I have not given sufficient weight to the role of big men in the management of affairs, particularly in the initiation of warfare and the *kaiko*. I did discuss big men in chapter 2, where I also discussed the ways in which groups forge decisions, but perhaps I did not make myself clear. I will, therefore, reiterate my observations, reinforced by a recent visit, that the Tsembaga had no big men in the classic sense during my visit in 1962–63. There were no individuals who by virtue of their economic positions could command or coerce the performances of subordinates or who competed in giving gifts or feasts; there were no reservoirs of potential supporters to be attracted or lost. There were, and are, as I stated in chapter 2, men who are called "big men" (*yu yundoi, yu maiwai*).

Big men on the average had more pigs, pear shells, and wives than other men, but were not remarkably wealthy. Their influence was not grounded in wealth, but in valor, intelligence, and articulateness. Their opinions, which they could usually express forcefully and colorfully, were respected. Big men, it is said, "have talk." Given the fact that a group's decisions are reached through the "talk becoming one" big men do, of course, influence the decisions of local groups. What I have said is that the decisions reached by groups, whether or not they are strongly influenced by particular men (as, I suppose, they usually are) are circumscribed by the conventions of the ritual cycle (see pp. 220ff.).

INDIVIDUALS—THEIR DECISIONS, THEIR ACTIONS

Since the publication of *Pigs for the Ancestors* increased emphasis has been given in ecological formulations to individuals and their decisions and actions (Ellen, 1982; McCay, 1978; Orlove, 1980; Vayda and McCay, 1975). This trend is not confined to ecological anthropology, but is a more or less special manifestation of a movement in the field generally. Ortner (1984) notes that "For the past few years there has been growing interest in analysis focused through one or another of a bundle of interrelated terms: practice, praxis, action, interaction, activity, experience, performance. A second and closely related bundle of terms focuses on the doer of all that doing: agent, actor, person, self, individual, subject." She further suggests that this trend promises to be the most salient characteristic of the anthropology of the eighties. The development is to be given a qualified welcome. Earlier analyses in ecological anthropology, reflecting a general deficiency in cultural and social anthropology, did not pay sufficient attention to the purposes motivating individual actions, actions which, when aggregated, constitute group events; nor did they pay sufficient attention to behavioral variations among individuals, to differences in the understandings of the world entertained by individuals, to individuals as adaptive units, or to conflicts between individual actors or between individuals and the groups to which they belong.

Pigs for the Ancestors has been faulted on these grounds, and, like most analyses of its time, it was open to these criticisms. It is worth noting, however, that the book was centrally concerned with ritual, secondarily with warfare, two of the most highly integrated forms of social activity undertaken by humans. In ritual and war the purposes of individuals are more comprehensively aggregated, their concerns more rigorously subordinated, their actions more tightly coordinated than in other sorts of human enterprise. In no other situations do groups act more as groups and less as aggregates of autonomous individuals than they do in the performance of rituals, and warfare is characterized by the enunciation of common purposes, high degrees of coordination, and frequent replacement of self-interest by self-sacrifice. Preparation for rituals commemorating warfare occupied most of the time and thought of most people during the fourteen months that I lived among the Tsembaga. Ritual is a mode of action conforming more closely than any other to "ideal structure" and that is what I saw. I did give a great deal of attention in *Pigs for the Ancestors* and in subsequent publications (especially 1971b, 1979b, and sections 3 and 5 above) to the "cognized model"—the shared understandings underlying individual understandings, choices, and actions—but not to those individual understandings, choices and actions themselves. The analysis would have been richer had I done so.

Although the development of what is being called "practice theory" may ameliorate deficiencies now apparent in earlier anthropological accounts, some questions concerning it must be raised. Many of these questions are asked and discussed more fully in Ortner's essay.

First, it may be asked what the choices and actions of individuals are meant to account for in anthropological analyses. Human choices and actions, it is hardly necessary to say, are informed by understandings which are culturally constituted. Most of these understandings have an assumed or explicit public core, a core of understandings upon or around which there is general agreement. Individual variations are expressed in details or, more importantly, in differences among the conclusions that different individuals may derive from what they take to be the same sets of facts or differences in the strategies employed by individuals standing in varying relationships to the same facts. Accounts of events should, of course, take into consideration the individual variations that are implicated in precipitating them. An adequate account of the occurrence of the *kaiko* would, for instance, have attended to the details of consensus formation. Consideration of such matters may show significant processual differences between events of different sorts. For instance, the decision of a local group to begin its *kaiko* comes out of a more or less protracted process of consensus formation that must, eventually, enlist the support of a preponderance of the membership. In contrast, the decision to go to war, a decision binding upon a corporate group, can be preempted by any individual or small group of individuals who take it upon themselves to avenge the death of a kinsman by killing a member of another group. (Situations in which corporations are held hostage by individuals are not limited to tribal societies. In Northern Ireland the most carefully laid arrangements for peace are vulnerable to veto by any single Catholic or Protestant who owns a gun or can scrape together the makings of a bomb.)

Of more interest and importance than the extent to which individual actions and decisions account for events is the extent to which they can account for conventions and institutions and for changes in them. To put this differently, to what extent may practice account for structure and changes in it? An older anthropology which took action to be largely the enactment of culturally prescribed rules would have replied "very little." More recently, however, interest in the ways in which practice may modify or transform social and cultural forms has grown. I have made some suggestions bearing upon this issue, concerning the ways in which cognized models may be transformed in response to changing historical conditions (1979b) and the ways in which individual decisions to participate or not to participate in rituals may result in the maintenance or transformation of social structures (1971c, 1971d, 1978a, 1979e).

The increased concern with practice which seems widespread in contemporary anthropology generally recognizes the existence of sociocultural structures, systems, or formations with properties distinct from the individuals realizing them. The novelty, such as it is, is that the relationship between social process and individual action is now taken to be a "problematic" in its own right. It is now being seen in more reciprocal or mutually formative terms than it had been, but outside of ecological anthropology and sociobiology there has not been any attempt to reduce social phenomena to aggregated individual behavior. Herein lies what may be rather special about developments in sociobiology and the current in ecological anthropology influenced by sociobiology. Whereas the roots of the "practice movement" in anthropology generally lie squarely within traditions which take group phenomena to be central (see Ortner, 1984) the theoretical ground of the new concern in ecological anthropology lies, at least in large part, in evolutionary biology and in formal economics. Orlove (1980:248) has written that the recent emphasis on decision-making models in ecological anthropology "corresponds to recent developments in biological ecology, with its stress on natural selection at the level of individual organisms as a principle which organizes populations and communities." In more particular terms it represents an attempt to make anthropological formulations compatible with the general rejection in biology of group selection as a process figuring significantly in organic evolution.

Earlier anthropologies erred in undervaluing action, individual or otherwise, which they were inclined to dismiss as little more than the enactment of culturally encoded patterns for behavior—the mere realization of cultural and social forms in practice. In contrast, implicit in what Orlove calls "processual ecology" is a tendency to take social and cultural forms to be little more than the sums of decisions made by individuals acting in terms of their own self-interest. To put this in slightly different terms, in accounting for conventions—publicly accepted understandings, rules, and practices—explanatory priority is given to the advantages they confer upon those *individuals* accepting them. Calculi of advantage are formalized in "microeconomic models [which] resemble economic models of choice making," (Orlove, 1980:247)although "satisficing,""minimaxing,""optimizing,"and "hierarchies of strategies" may in some instances replace simple maximizing. That which is maximized, optimized, or whatever can be organic—either physiological or genetic, with inclusive fitness being the measure of the latter—or straightforwardly economic or political, being measured in wealth or power.

Although it may be that neglect of the individual in particular and practice in general required rectification it seems to me that the correction entailed in such a program is in danger of becoming excessive, not simply replacing one error with another, but replacing neglect of the individual with something even more serious, the dissolution of the social as such. There are several more particular points to be made in this regard.

First, on the face of it at least, conventions do not necessarily aid and abet individuals in their competition against each other or against their environments. More typically, in fact, they constrain the actions of individuals in their dealings with others. It can, of course, be argued that some individuals or groups are always more favored by prevailing conventions than are others, that such inequities are inevitable, and that competition for control of the apparatus for reproducing and transforming convention animates many societies. Nevertheless, to account for convention (or, if you prefer, culture) in general in such terms leads to a notion of explanation as nothing more than exposé, a concept of culture as nothing more than a set of species-specific modes of social domination.

The second point is related to the first. It may be that, given any set of conventions, people will behave in accordance with what they take to be their own interests. This hypothesis concerning the *behavioral* propensities of individuals does not, however, account for the particular cultural forms or conventions prevailing in any society. It proposes what people will do *given* the existence of *any* such forms. The hypotheses of humans as maximizers of individual advantage or as maximizers of inclusive fitness are behavioral hypotheses devoid of any specific cultural content, and cannot account for that content.

A third related point is that the hypothesis that individuals will behave in terms of what they perceive to be their self-interest does not account for what they perceive those interests to be. Even if individuals' perceptions of self-interest are more or less idiosyncratic formulations of universal, general, and natural "maximizing" or "optimizing" proclivities, it can hardly be doubted that culturally particular definitions of that self-interest intervene.

Fourth, it follows that if concepts of self-interest are culturally formulated, then self-interest can be defined in terms which are at variance from, or even contradictory to, the immediate material advantage of the living individual or the long-term advantage of his or her genotype. The use of language even makes it possible to define individual advantages in ways which separate it from personal survival:

the reward of a valorous death in battle is Valhalla, of an inglorious death in bed, Hel. Individuals can easily be led to sacrifice themselves in terms of "their own best interests." History is generous in bestowing examples upon us. Attempts to account for all these cases in terms of the increased reproductive success of the hero's brothers and sisters seem to me pathetic. We may conclude, I think, that whatever may be the case among other species the use of language, which makes possible such conceptions as honor, morality, altruism, honesty, valor, righteousness, prestige, gods, heaven, and hell, makes group selection important among humans. By *group selection* I mean selection for and perpetuation of conventions enhancing the persistence of groups, even though these conventions can be disadvantageous to those individuals whose actions accord most closely with them.

Fifth, the subordination of the properties of groups to the interest of individuals in adaptive formulations is unwarranted by observation. If adaptation is a process of response to perturbations adaptive units may be defined by unitary response to such disturbances. Response to perturbation is not a property exclusive to individual organisms, but inheres in groups at virtually all levels of inclusiveness: families, sub-clans, clans, local populations, and even states. In dismissing the adaptive properties that may inhere in any particular level there is not only a risk of misconceiving the structure of adaptive processes as wholes, but also of missing both deformations of that structure and interlevel conflicts in adaptive processes.

Sixth, Orlove himself notes (1980:248) that "actor-based models have tended to treat environmental variables as part of a relatively static set of external constraints to which individuals respond and adapt. . . . They have thus omitted some of the concerns of ecological anthropology." I would go further. There is a danger here, particularly when the assumption of an ecosystem is abandoned, that environmental variables will be construed as little more than a set of natural resources and natural hazards, raw commodities or goods on the one hand, and dangers, potential liabilities, and "bads" on the other. Ecological anthropology is in danger of being replaced by environmental economics. Economic activity entails valuation: decisions are made, presumably to apply scarce resources to differentially graded ends.

Microeconomic models, which "resemble economic models of choice making" (Orlove, 1980:247), models that have been developed in societies with money and markets, may be inappropriate for the representation of such values. Cost-benefit analysis that transforms distinctions between unlike things into mere quantitative differences by reducing all things to a common metric is, I think, especially inappropriate for understanding choices in societies without money.

Reliance upon actor-based models alone does not merely omit some of ecological anthropology's concerns. It ignores what I take to be its most fundamental problem. We are concerned with a species that lives in terms of meanings in a universe devoid of meaning but subject to law. The relationship of actions formulated in terms of meaning to the systems constituted by natural law within which they occur is, in my view, the essential problematic of ecological anthropology. It is missed by approaches which focus upon actors and ignore or deny the systemic character of an encompassing nature.

I earlier suggested that this problematic not only describes the human condition but provides a set of supracultural criteria in terms of which human actions can be assessed. It could be argued that the social sciences have no right to make assessments and that the general approach is ideological. If we are going to address contemporary problems we are, of course, going to make assessments and we may as well make them upon explicit grounds. Assessment is, I suppose, in some degree ideological, even when the attempt is to assess the adaptiveness of understandings, conventions, and actions in terms which are as objective as possible.

We may note here that theory in anthropology, and perhaps more generally in the social sciences, seems to be rather sensitive to events in the larger society. As the ecosystemically oriented ecological anthropology of the early 1970s may have been responsive to the ecology movement, so may the more recent actor-oriented perspective in anthropology be an expression of the "new individualism" of the late 1970s, an individualism encouraged by the exhaustion of liberalism and the rise of neoconservatism in politics and expressed more generally in what Christopher Lasch (1978) calls "The New Narcissism." Recent trends in ecological anthropology are no less subject to the ideological fashions prevailing in the society at large than were earlier ones.

I have noted a series of units, ranging in inclusiveness from the individual to the ecosystem, that figure in ecological concept and method as they have developed in anthropology. Moran (1983), following prevailing thought in general ecology, has reminded us that ecosystems themselves can be discriminated at many levels, from small systems occupying only portions of the territories of local groups to the biosphere. If this is the case human aggregations of various magnitudes of inclusiveness, up to the human species as a whole, may, under certain circumstances, be regarded as ecological populations. The important point here, however, is that attention to units at one level does not preclude the existence or significance of those at others. This would not need to be asserted were it not for the fact that some modes of analysis have ignored individual choices and actions, others would dissolve the social as no more than the aggregation of individual behavior, and some have denied the existence or significance of ecosystems. The banishment of any one of these levels—the individual, the social, the ecological—from our analyses is a very serious mistake, conferring upon us no benefits and costing us dearly.

SECTION 11

Negative Feedback

We have continually touched upon the matter of regulation, and may now deal with another of the important criticisms of functionalism raised by Hempel, namely that the self-regulatory mechanisms implicit in functional formulations are not made explicit. I claim that *Pigs for the Ancestors* met this criterion adequately. The self-regulatory processes inhering in the ritual cycle of the Tsembaga were described in narrative form in sufficient detail to make possible its computer modeling without requests from the modelers for additional data (Shantzis and Behrens, 1973; Samuels 1982). In a later work (Rappaport, 1971c), the Tsembaga system, including its regulatory mechanisms, was represented diagrammatically. This diagram, with minor modifications, is reproduced on page 339. Friedman (1974), however, has taken issue with my analysis of ritual regulation, arguing that I have misused the general concept of negative feedback. Although he is mistaken in his assessment of my use of the concept he does expose a serious logical error in my argument. The issue is a complicated one but it is worth discussing in detail.

Friedman's first point is a general one. He defines negative feedback systems as "systems in which certain variables are kept within certain crucial limits by the operation of other variables which are *dependent functions of those limits*" (1974:459; italics in original), and says that he fails "to see that the environment limit is involved at all [in the Tsembaga case], since . . . the [ritual] cycle is triggered way below carrying capacity, and other groups probably come closer to that limit" (1974:460). Later he elucidates his argument with the fol-

404

lowing analogy: "If a thermostat is set for 75 degrees, but the furnace which it regulates breaks down at 65 degrees every time, then we cannot speak of negative feedback" (1974:460).

We disagree on the nature of negative feedback. Negative feedback is simply a process in which deviations from *reference values* initiate operations tending to return the state of the deviating variable to its reference value. The relationship of reference values to *goal ranges* (what Friedman probably means by "limits," i.e., the possible range of viable or homeostatic states) is a separate question, and a very important one, as I stressed in the closing pages of the Maring book (see p. 241, above). In a discussion of the relationship between cognized and operational models I called attention to problems that may develop in cybernetic operation itself.

> First, what is the relationship between signs and the processes they are taken to indicate? Is it the case, for instance, that such processes as environmental degradation are detected (indicated by signs) early, or only when they are well advanced? Second, to what extent do reference values, which are likely to reflect people's wants rather than their needs, correspond to the actual material requirements of the local population, the ecosystem, or the regional population? *In other words, what is the relationship between the reference value or ranges of values of the cognized model and the goal ranges of the operational model?* [1978:240–41; italics in original]

I did not make explicit that the "wants" referred to in this passage are culturally determined, a product of ideology, ambition, social relations, or social structure. I simply took that for granted and assumed that anyone who read the book would also take it for granted. It may be that I should have discussed more fully the possible sociocultural factors that entered into the reference value for pig herd size. I argued that although the slain pigs were put to culturally determined ends, the reference value itself is a reflection of a local population's tolerance for the labor requirements of pigs or the disruptive capacity of pigs. The more important point I wish to reiterate here is that the reference values upon which negative feedback operation is equilibrated *may lie outside of independently specified goal ranges*. To paraphrase Friedman's thermostat analogy, we could set a thermostat at 40° and sit around shivering, or at 110° and collapse from heat prostration. More to the point, our own society offers a large number of instances of economically conceived reference values, which are of course culturally determined, being maintained *outside* of environmental and physiological goal ranges. I think we can say that this is "dysfunctional" or "maladaptive" even if the economic system is working well for the time being (which, of course, it isn't). This is to say that *negative feedback need not be homeostatic.* (For a fuller discussion see Rappaport, 1979c.)

This leads us to the logical error that Friedman has exposed. He notes that "while it is valid to *describe* [italics in original] the ritual cycle as operating to keep the pig population below a certain level, it is incorrect to claim that it is a *homeostat* [italics added] when no relation has been shown to exist between the limit and the triggering of the cycle" (1974:460). His point is correct, and it does rightly point to a deficiency in *Pigs for the Ancestors.* I showed no intrinsic relationship between women's labor and carrying capacity, and there may not be any. I did argue, however, that in more densely populated areas the depredations of pigs, rather than their labor requirements, may trigger *kaikos* (pp. 16off.; see also pp. 70 and 116). I further argued that the frequency of garden invasions by pigs is density-dependent and as such may be related, in a rough way, to environmental limits. To use terms that I was not aware of at the time, what was implied was multi-phasic regulation (Vayda, 1974), in which at low densities women's labor is operative while at high densities environmental considerations predominate.

Friedman relegates his discussion of garden invasions by pigs to a footnote in which he seems to dismiss the possible relationship of density dependence to environmental limits (and in which he also makes an ethnographic error—conflicts concerning pigs are not generated in "the nuclear phase of a pulsating settlement pattern" [1974:467 n.18] but throughout the dispersal which they in part motivate). Yet, admittedly, my own argument concerning the density-dependent nature of pig-caused conflict and the relationship of this density dependence to environmental limits was not supported by sufficient data. Moreover, I did not, in accordance with the strictures of Hempel, specify the range of conditions (e.g., the human demographic range) under which the regulatory mechanism of the ritual cycle would keep pig herd size within environmental capacity. My case, then, for asserting that the regulatory operation of the ritual cycle is homeostatic was incomplete, to say the least.

It is worth noting, as I did in the first edition of this book (p. 163), that the problem under discussion here is not necessarily one of analysis. It is certainly the case that maximal pig population size among the Tsembaga was equilibrated well below environmental limits, but this may not be unusual. It does not amount to an acceptance of Wynne-Edwards' argument (1962) for the ubiquitous nature of group selection to note that he and others have argued that populations of many species are maintained at levels well below carrying capacity (i.e., environmental limits) by such endogenous factors as crowding stress; it is not always clear how or even if such factors or the processes generating them relate to environmental limits.

SECTION 12

Ritual: Regulated or Regulating?

Friedman raises one other problem concerning Maring regulation that remains to be discussed.

> The principal limit of the system as it is described by Rappaport is the point at which physical strain on women builds up. Since it is they who are burdened with the task of feeding and managing the pigs, they are the first to feel the diminishing returns on increased labour. All the evidence he presents indicates that it is this strain in the system which triggers the cycle. Yet his own "explanation" appears to turn the whole thing upside down since he assumes that it is the ritual cycle which regulates labour and not the converse. [1974:459–60]

Friedman is correct in his reading of the ethnography when he notes that it is "the strain" of too many pigs that triggers the *kaiko*. I tried very hard to argue that very point, and the attempt to use it in criticism of the analysis suggests to me a misunderstanding of cybernetic operation. The very same point could be made concerning thermostats, which, I am sure, Friedman will admit to the class of cybernetic regulators. It is a rise in room temperature, an outcome of the furnace's operation, that triggers the regulatory reaction of the thermostat, namely to turn off the furnace. Similarly, it is the increase in pig population to intolerable limits, as indicated by complaints concerning labor and conflicts resulting from porcine depredations, that triggers the regulatory reaction of the ritual cycle, namely the *kaiko*,

408

which "turns off" the pigs. If the ritual cycle is not a regulatory mechanism, neither is the thermostat.

We note in these examples that cybernetic or negative feedback regulation takes the form of a closed loop: it has a circular causal structure. A change in the value of a variable itself initiates a process that either limits further change or returns the value to its former level. The basic difficulty in Friedman's argument seems to be that it attempts to impose a notion of linear causality upon a system which is in its nature circular. The linear assumption is implicit in the view that *either* the *kaiko or* the labor is causal.

Granting the circular structure of cybernetic systems, one still might ask why it should be said that the ritual cycle regulates pig demography, warfare frequency, etc., and not that they regulate the ritual cycle. The same question may be asked about the regulatory relationship of the thermostat and the furnace.

The self-regulatory operations of all systems are, of course, contingent upon the dynamic interaction of these systems' components, and in some systems discrete regulators are not to be distinguished. Nevertheless, there surely are grounds for taking thermostats and Maring ritual cycles to be regulators. The Maring ritual cycle includes a set of standard corrective responses to deviations in the values of variables external to itself, for instance, the labor of which Friedman speaks. One basis for saying that the ritual cycle regulates labor and not vice versa is the fact that "amount of labor" is not a regulatory response, but rather a variable which may deviate from a reference value or goal range (thus requiring regulation). It is important to make clear, however, that the ritual cycle is not simply a set of corrective responses, for it is also the locus of the conventions in accordance with which those corrective responses are undertaken and conducted. It embodies a set of instructions for a communal corrective program. Thermostats, analogously, also contain instructions, albeit rather simple ones. The regulator is that component of a circular causal system which contains the instructions in accordance with which the system operates. In the sorts of systems exemplified by the Tsembaga and their relations with other species and groups, the regulator is the dominant information-processing component in systems of matter and energy transactions. The information processed is culturally encoded. It is founded upon cultural perceptions of natural processes which may, of course, be "objectively" inaccurate and which are also likely to be shaped by social factors. The difficulties and burdens of swine husbandry notwithstanding, the conventions affecting it and the ritual cycle could have been different. Pigs could have been agisted, and additional contexts for sacrificing them could have been designated.

THE RITUAL MODE OF PRODUCTION

It may be possible to add another justification to those already offered for taking the ritual cycle to be regulator rather than regulated, although this may be little more than a translation of the preceding argument into other terms. The ritual cycle constitutes, or at least codifies, the relations of production of Maring society. To use Friedman's definition,

> relations of production are those *social relations* which dominate (i.e., determine the economic rationality of) the material process of production in given techno-ecological conditions. . . . More specifically they determine . . . the use to be made of the environment . . . the division of productive labour . . . [and] the forms of appropriation and distribution. [1974:446]

The ritual cycle is a sacred structure within which productive and reproductive activities (ecological, biological, and social) proceed, and in terms of which social, political, and ecological relations are defined and given meaning. It thus may be suggested that ritual regulation comprises a mode of production commensurable with feudalism, capitalism, and oriental despotism. Because the operation of ritually regulated societies does not entail social stratification or even ranking, ritual itself may constitute a very old or even primordial mode of production.

SECTION 13

Transformation

Questions of time and transformation remain to be discussed. *Pigs for the Ancestors* was an ethnography sharing with most other ethnographies grounding in relatively brief fieldwork. I was resident with the Tsembaga for fourteen months—hardly enough time to observe much structural change or to recognize it if it were occurring. Furthermore, my observations concentrated upon what was mainly occupying the thought and activity of the Tsembaga during my visit, namely the performance of rituals. Ritual is, of course, among the most conservative of human activities. In the nature of things, therefore, the analysis was concerned with the mechanisms of maintenance rather than change. It was clear that epochal changes were about to occur—peace had been imposed by the Australian administration—but little if any structural transformation had so far resulted from *Pax Australiensis*. The criticism that *Pigs for the Ancestors* ignores change seems to me inappropriate. It has been said, however, that the book exemplifies an approach that will not or cannot deal with change. Diener and Robkin, for instance, assert that Vayda and I express "interest only in 'how systems function' " and that this constitutes a "retreat from evolution" (1978:493). Burnham, after a brief and misleading characterization of a discussion of adaptation written by me (1977; see also 1971d, 1976b, 1978b, 1979a), states that "the scheme of analysis is clearly incapable of dealing with social change" (1979:198), an assertion repeated by Brown (1979:236) in the same volume.

Although simple functional formulations may be well suited to the consideration of changes in the states of systems they are, I agree, ill-equipped to deal with structural change and may impose specious assumptions of stasis upon dynamic realities. As Ellen has recently noted, however, there is "nothing in the basic tenets of systems theory or in the study of systems and their operation which is inimical to a consideration of change" (1982:195). I have in several essays made some tentative suggestions concerning processes of adaptation that seem to be compatible with the use of the term in anthropology and biology and that do deal with structural change in systemic terms.

The term *adaptation* is generally associated with the term *environment* and thus with ecological formulations. It is certainly the case that adaptive processes are manifested or realized only in particular environments, social, cultural or physical. Nevertheless a *general* theory of adaptation is not so much concerned with the particulars of any environment as it is with those structural characteristics of systems which make it possible for them to transform themselves in response to environmental fluctuation, change, or opportunity. Adaptive formulations thus have ecological implications but are not properly subsumed under the category of ecological formulations. It also should be clear that they are neither simple functional formulations because they are concerned with structural transformations nor are they simply models of change because they are as concerned with the persistence of systems as with changes in them. In fact, the distinction between maintenance and change, "diachrony and synchrony," dissolves in the dynamics of adaptive processes. Adaptive formulations, moreover, are formal as well as final causal, emphasizing not only the goals and effects of processes but the *structure* of those processes as well. Indeed, the concept of adaptation is fundamentally structural (in the sense expressed, but hardly originated, by Piaget [1971]) because adaptive operation has certain structural entailments or, to put it differently, orderly adaptive operation is contingent upon the prevalence of certain relationships among the components of the systems in which it occurs. This is to say that beneath specific and categorical differences adaptive systems are organized by a generally similar architecture, or possess generally similar structures. This is not immediately apparent and is rather complex. Those interested in fuller accounts may consult the more detailed discussions cited above.

ADAPTATION

I have in the past taken the term *adaptation* to refer to the processes through which living systems maintain homeostasis in the face of perturbations resulting from both short-term environmental fluctuations and long-term nonreversing environmental changes. Adaptive processes involve both reversible changes in systemic states and less reversible or irreversible changes in systemic structure. Several features of this definition require comment or revision.

First, I include within the category *living systems* not only individual organisms but associations of organisms of various sorts. Any association that can be shown to respond on occasion as a unit to perturbations qualifies. It seems clear that social units do so respond. It is possible that ecosystems do as well but this is, as I have already noted, debatable.

The application of a common set of concepts to individuals and organized associations of organisms, some of which are culturally governed, may attract charges of organic analogizing. Such a criticism would be, I think, misplaced. To recognize a similarity among systems of different classes does not deny their differences. I have suggested (1979a:152f.) that differences among systems in their relative autonomy, in the degrees of coherence they require and can tolerate, and, I would add here, in their abilities to expand and contract are closely related to differences in the specific ways in which they respond to perturbation. That adaptive processes inhere in systems at various levels of inclusiveness and that the included systems enjoy varying degrees of relative autonomy suggests that the responses of included and including systems may be at odds. I have already remarked in other contexts that interlevel contradictions are inevitable.

Second, relatively autonomous adaptive systems as such do not have special goals, purposes, or functions. They cannot be defined, as can the specialized subsystems which are their parts, by some special product (like petroleum or pituitrin) or by some special activity (e.g., the heart or the I.R.S.). The ultimate goal or purpose of adaptive systems is properly so low in specificity as to seem a non-goal. It is simply to persist. As Slobodkin (1968) put it in a discussion of the difficulty of applying game theory to evolution, they are "players of the existential game," a game that is peculiar in that the only reward for successful play is to be allowed to continue to play, a game in which the phrase "cashing in your chips" is a euphemism for losing. Individual humans and societies may, of course, mystify such goals (or non-goals) while maintaining their low specificity (e.g., "It is the goal of society to serve God"), but to set for themselves enduring goals as specific as those appropriate for their [specialized] subsystems is likely to reduce their chances of staying in the existential game by reducing their flexibility. Central to adaptation is the maintenance of systemic flexibility, the maintenance of an ability to keep responding homeostatically to perturbations the magnitude and nature of which usually cannot be predicted given the world's complexity.

Third, the term *environment* is meant to embrace cultural and social as well as physical and biotic phenomena. The units adapting to their environments may include individuals, social groups or formations of some sort, and, possibly, ecosystems (which may respond as systemic wholes to large-scale, long-range changes such as those of climate). To the extent that anthropology is a social science it may be expected to be centrally concerned with social groups or formations.

A revision or addendum is required here. The definition upon which I have relied locates the sources of perturbation to which adaptive processes respond in the environments of adapting units—that is to say, external to them. Perturbations may, however, be internal in origin. Social units are, quite possibly, more continually and more seriously perturbed by the actions and inactions of their constituent members and special purpose subsystems than they are by environmental change. Adaptive response is response to perturbation be it internal or external.

Fourth, because the term *homeostasis* seems to generate misunderstanding, it might be well to reword the definition; for instance: "Adaptation refers to the processes through which systems maintain themselves or persist," rather than "through which systems maintain homeostasis." But *homeostasis* does not imply changelessness (see Vayda and McCay, 1975). In an ever-changing world the maintenance of homeostasis requires constant changes of state and, for most systems at least, occasional changes in structure.

Whether or not we use the term *homeostasis* we may note here the deliberate conflation of what are generally taken to be two distinct classes of processes and what generally constitute the foci of two distinct modes of analysis in the social sciences. There are, on the one hand, the processes of self-regulation on which functional analyses focus, and on the other hand, "self-organizing" processes which are the subject matter of evolutionary accounts. The distinction between them has been overdrawn, in my view, because the maintenance ("persistence," "adequate functioning," "survival") of systems in a changing world requires occasional change in their structures as well as constant change in their states. The connecting generalization is what Hockett and Ascher (1964) have called "Romer's Rule," after Alfred S. Romer, the zoologist who first enunciated it in a discussion of the emergence of the amphibia (1954; originally published 1933). The lobe-finned fish, Romer argued, did not come onto dry land to take advantage of its previously unexploited opportunities. Rather, relatively minor modification of their fins and other subsystems made it possible for these creatures to migrate from one drying-up stream or pond to another still containing water during the intermittent droughts presumed to have been frequent during the Devonian period. Such structural changes thus made it possible for them to maintain their general aquatic organization during a period of marked environmental change. In slightly different terms, *self-organizing or evolutionary changes in components of systems are "functions" in the self-regulatory process of the more inclusive and enduring systems of which they are parts.* Structural or evolutionary changes, such as fin to leg, may be *distinguished* from "functional" changes or "systemic adjustments" on some grounds, but they are *not separated* from them in the larger, more inclusive scheme of adaptive processes. Together they form ordered series of responses to perturbations. Several comments are in order before discussing these response sequences.

First, it should be clear that, according to this account, evolutionary change is directed toward the simple persistence of the systems in which it takes place. To put it differently, changes in some parts or subsystems, or in relations among them, make it possible for the rest of the system to persist unchanged. Romer's parable—it may be no more than this—suggests that the most salient question to ask concerning any structural change is, "What does this change maintain unchanged?"

Second, while the goal of an adaptive system, as a player of Slobodkin's existential game, is simply to persist, our account suggests that that which persists is not necessarily any particular feature or component of the adapting system, but simply an organized set of adaptive processes. Even structure may change. It follows that the frequently asked question, "When does a system stop being what it has been and become something else?"—a question that is generally deemed impossible to answer and thus devastating to systemic approaches to evolutionary transformation—is close to nonsensical. There has been, for instance, an unbroken continuity in English society from the days of the heptarchy until today despite enormous changes in both structure and cultural content. In the course of their unbroken successions ecosystems may replace all, or almost all, of their constituent species several times. That we distinguish and name the phases in these successions, just as we may distinguish and name periods in the history of societies, or, for that matter, in the ontogeny of individuals, and that these phases and periods differ in important ways, does not mean that they are discontinuous. Slobodkin and Rapoport (1974) have noted two discrete ways in which distinctive associations of conspecifics can cease to exist, and they have admonished us not to confuse them. On the one hand, there can come a time when no descendants of that association remain alive. At this time we can say that the adaptive processes that it embodied have come to an end; we can further say that the evolutionary process has ended in failure. On the other hand, such an association may apparently cease to exist because its descendants have been so transformed as to warrant being called by a new species name. In this instance the adaptive processes continue and the evolutionary process continues to be successful.

Third, adaptive processes are cybernetic. In response to perturbations corrective programs of some sort are initiated, programs that return deviating variables to their reference values. It is important to make clear, however, that all that is cybernetic does not contribute to the persistence of the systems in which it occurs. Put in the most general informational terms, cybernetic systems attempt to maintain the truth value of propositions about themselves in the face of perturbations tending to falsify them. In systems dominated by humans the propositions so maintained (the society's "highest values," ultimate truths, etc.) may not correspond to or may even contradict the physical and psychic well-being of the individuals who constitute the membership, or even the persistence of the society as a whole. Disorderings in value structure may have severe evolutionary consequences.

RESPONSE SEQUENCES AND STRUCTURAL CHARACTERISTICS

Adaptation is not constituted by isolated responses. Orderly adaptive processes are, rather, organized into sequences of responses, and these sequences *as sequences* have certain interesting structural properties (Bateson, 1963; Frisancho, 1975; Rappaport, 1978b, 1979a; Slobodkin and Rapoport, 1974; Vayda and McCay, 1975). The responses most quickly mobilized are likely to be energetically and behaviorally expensive, but easily and quickly reversible following the cessation of stress. Should a perturbation or stress continue, however, the earlier responses are eventually relieved by slower-acting, less energetically expensive, less easily reversible changes. Responses later in the sequence are likely to be structural (constitutional in social systems, and irreversible somatic change, ultimately genetic change, in organisms and populations of organisms; formally similar sequences can possibly be observed in various psychological processes).

While the earlier responses operate, the system in which they occur may well be deprived of some behavioral flexibility, but the structure of the system remains unchanged. Later responses, although they may be more efficient energetically, and although they do restore some immediate behavioral flexibility to the system, are less easily reversible or even irreversible. Bateson, Slobodkin, and Rapoport have suggested that the *probable* effect of structural change in response to *specific problems* is the reduction of long-term flexibility.

There is likely to be trade-off, then, in adaptive response sequences, of long-term systemic flexibility for immediate efficiency (or other advantage). In an unpredictably changing universe it is good evolutionary strategy, they say, to give up no more systemic flexibility than necessary. The chances for staying in the existential game are better if an evolving system changes neither more nor less than is adequate to deal with the stress it experiences. Structural change in response to particular stresses is likely to increase the specialization of the evolving system as a whole. Increased specialization, in turn, is likely to lead to a narrowing of the range of conditions under which the system can persist. (For a rather similar argument see Sahlins and Service, 1960.)

"Evolutionary wisdom"—the calibration of the magnitude of response to the magnitude and duration of stress—may be intrinsic to the more or less automatic operation and graduated structure of organic response sequences. In human social systems responses are not always or even usually automatic but are under conscious control and their sequences can and do become disordered, a matter to which we shall return. First we need to ask how systems must be constructed if they are to maintain properly graduated order throughout response sequences. The possible structural requirements of adaptive processes have received scant systematic attention in anthropology; my suggestions are exploratory.

First we may note that adaptive systems are always hierarchical in the sense given to the term by Pattee (1973), Piaget (1971), and Simon (1969). This is simply to say that they are relatively autonomous wholes, or integrated entities, made up of parts (which may or may not themselves have high degrees of relative autonomy and which may themselves be made up of parts and so on). The relationship of part to whole is, of course, implicit in the parable of the emerging amphibia. Transformation in one or several subsystems made it possible for the general structure of those organisms to remain unchanged during the initial stage of terrestrial adaptation.

It may be possible to distinguish structural transformations of differing degrees of profundity. "Low-order" transformations, that is, transformations of the internal structure of specific subsystems, may occur frequently, but because complex living systems are, to use Simon's (1969) phrase, "loosely coupled," their effects may be confined to the subsystems in which they occur. High-order transformations, transformations in the structures of more inclusive systems, are rarer, and, of course, their effects are more profound. To speak, simply, of structural transformation is not sufficient, but there are possibilities for identifying transformations of different orders and for considering relations—temporal, causal, and formal—among these transformations.

There is another and less unexceptionable sense in which adaptive structure may be hierarchical. Adaptive systems are, by definition, self-regulating. In response to disturbances of their states they take actions to ameliorate those disturbances. There are several modes of self-regulation (see Rappaport, 1979a:147f.) which combine in the operation of any complex system. The cybernetic mode may be basic, however, and it has a characteristic structure, which is that of a closed circuit. Adaptive processes are not only cybernetic, sequential, and graduated, however. The adaptive organization of any living system could not be simply a collection of more or less distinct circuits. Particular or specific adaptations must be related to each other in more or less orderly ways, and general adaptations, human or otherwise, biological or cultural, may take the form of enormously complex sets of interlocking corrective loops, roughly and generally hierarchically arranged, and including not only mechanisms regulating material variables, but regulators governing relations between regulators, and so on (Kalmus, 1966; Miller, 1965a, 1965b; Pattee, 1973; Rappaport, 1970b, 1971d, 1978b, 1979a; Simon, 1969). Adaptive structures are *structured sets of processes*, and regulatory hierarchies, whether or not they are embodied in particular organs or institutions, are found in all biological and social systems. It is important, however, to issue a caveat here: to say the regulatory structure is hierarchical is *not* to say that it is centralized, nor that it entails social stratification, nor that regulators are always discrete authorities. For instance, among some egalitarian societies, components of regulatory hierarchies are embedded in ritual cycles; in others, in segmentary kinship organization (Brookfield and Brown, 1963; Meggitt, 1962, 1965; Ortiz, 1969; Rappaport, 1968; Sahlins, 1961).

Whereas the adaptive structure of all living systems must share certain fundamental features—hierarchical organization and both self-regulating and self-transforming properties (see Piaget, 1971)—those of different classes surely differ in important respects that may be most significantly related to differences both in their characteristic coherence and in the relative autonomy of their subsystems. There are also, and perhaps related, differences among hierarchies in the extent to which they are organized in accordance with segmentary or sectorial principles (in the former, subsystems at each level are similar, in the latter, differentiated and specialized).

The increasing differentiation, in the course of evolution, of discrete special-purpose subsystems in organisms, societies, and ecosystems has been called "progressive segregation," and it is often accompanied in organisms and social systems, but not ecosystems, by increasing centralization of regulatory operation, or "progressive centralization." In organisms we note the elaboration of central nervous systems, in societies the development of administrative structures. In nonanthropocentric ecosystems at least, regulation seems generally to remain an outcome of dynamic interactions among constituent populations. This contrast between the development of ecological and other systems may rest upon their contrasting bases for order maintenance. The basis of orderliness in ecosystems seems to shift, in the course of their development from "pioneer" to "mature" stages, from a reliance upon the resilience of individual organisms to a reliance upon dynamic interaction among species and upon the increasing redundancy of matter and energy pathways resulting from increased species diversity. These contrasting bases of order maintenance may reflect, as I suggested in section 10, differences in the degrees of coherence that different classes of systems require and can tolerate. Whereas anthropologists traditionally have been concerned with the ways in which the various components of sociocultural systems are bound together—the jargon is "integrated"—they have generally ignored the ways in which the parts and processes of such systems are buffered from each other and each other's disruptions. Organisms are, and in their nature must be, more coherent than social systems, and social systems more coherent than ecosystems. As a rule of thumb, the more inclusive the system, the less coherent it is and must be. The less inclusive the system, the more its internal orderliness and the effectiveness of its activities depends upon the fine coordination of its parts. An organism requires and can tolerate closer coordination of the activities of its parts than societies, and societies more (at least from time to time) than ecosystems. Coordination depends upon centralization, hence progressive centralization in organisms and societies, but not ecosystems.

The relative autonomy of a system is a function of the degree to which the regulatory mechanism upon which its persistence depends are intrinsic to itself. To put it a little differently, "relative autonomy" refers to the extent to which systems are themselves more or less distinct adaptive units. Organs, for instance, have very little autonomy, for they cannot function in the absence of the organisms of which they are parts. Whole organisms have a much higher degree of relative autonomy; they are distinct adaptive units. It should be kept in mind, however, that no system less inclusive than the solar system is absolutely autonomous.

CHARACTERISTICS OF RESPONSE SEQUENCES

Although much conceptual and empirical work needs to be done I have tentatively suggested (Rappaport, 1976a, 1978b, 1979a) that in orderly adaptive systems relations between subsystems and regulators at different levels must be ordered along a number of continua. The simplest and most fundamental of these are entailed by the characteristics of response sequences and include: (1) specificity of goals (from specific "functions" at low levels to general, virtual "non-goals," e.g., persistence, at the highest levels); (2) response time (very fast and continuous operation at low levels, slower response time and discontinuous operation at high levels; (3) reversibility (quickly and easily reversible at low levels, irreversible at highest levels). Other continua that are peculiar to human social systems include (4) sanctity (from absolutely profane at the lowest levels to ultimately sacred at the highest) and (5) regulatory rhetoric (from specific commands at low levels through rules in their nature categorical at middle levels through principle at very high levels to, finally, ultimate sacred postulates. It follows from (4) and (5) that human adaptive systems (6) embody hierarchies of values, with those at lowest levels being "instrumental," those at highest levels "basic" or "fundamental."

In sum, I have suggested that there is a correlation of the dimensions of time, specificity, and reversibility intrinsic to adaptive systems of all classes. In human social systems, these correlations are reflected in differences in the statements that encode regulatory messages. Low-order directives—commands—are generally highly specific both in their concerns and in those to whom they are addressed. They apply typically to particular situations and, being situation-specific, are ephemeral. As compliance fulfills them it dissolves them. Rules, which are typical of middle-range regulation, are categorical rather than situation-specific and are not terminated by single instances of compliance. They are "standing" and endure indefinitely. Principles, characteristic of yet higher order governance, may be understood by those accepting them to reflect enduring or even timeless aspects of morality or nature; and highest-order regulation is often associated with postulates concerning gods and the like, conceived to be altogether outside of time and man's reach. Adaptive structures are constituted by *processes*, experienced by those participating in them as continuously changing in the flux of time, and *components*, understood as immutable and thus not subject to time's vicissitudes. At the heart of evolution and history there is a dynamic relationship between the ever-changing and what is taken to be never-changing. Romer's parable of the amphibia suggests that one of the fundamental questions to ask of any transformation is, "What does this change maintain unchanged?" We may now add that this is not simply an analyst's question. The maintenance of some aspects of systems provides actors with rationales for transforming others.

MALADAPTATION

I have argued that the maintenance of the ability to respond in orderly adaptive fashion depends upon an orderly structure—one in which, regardless of how it is institutionalized, there is correlation of time, specificity, reversibility, sanctity, value, and possibly other dimensions (concreteness, arbitrariness, contingency). It follows that disorderings of such structures—that is, loss of correlation between response time, specificity, reversibility, sanctity, value, duration—will interfere with a system's ability to respond to disturbances. I have suggested that maladaptation should not be confused with stresses or perturbing factors in the environment but should be understood as that which impedes response to stress and perturbation. That is, maladaptation may be conceived as an anomaly or a disordering in the hierarchical and self-regulatory features of adaptive structure.

In other publications (particularly 1976a, 1978b, and 1979a) I have described a number of specific forms of maladaptation and have suggested that many of the innumerable substantive problems with which humanity vexes itself and the world may be outcomes of this limited family of structural disorders. I can only mention and characterize several classes of them briefly here.

1. The simplest and most obvious class of maladaptive forms includes the *cybernetic* disorders:

(a) failure to detect deviation of important variables from reference values;

(b) distortion, impedance, blockage in the transmission of information concerning such deviations to agencies capable of corrective response;

(c) the inability of the agency to "hear" or understand messages transmitted to it; and

(d) the misinterpretation of such messages because reference values are inappropriately set in relation to goal ranges (see section 5 above).

2. Time aberrations are closely related to cybernetic disorders. Just as delay in the reception by responsible agencies of information concerning perturbation may cause difficulties, so may the immediate reception of such information, for this may produce *premature response*. For one thing, many perturbations are self-limiting and don't require responses. More importantly, premature response on the part of high-level agencies can be regarded as an adaptive disorder in its own right, for it may destroy lower-order regulators by continually overriding them. Because the responses of higher-order regulators are likely to be less delicate or reversible than those of a lower order, premature response on the part of high-level agencies is likely to en-

Transformation

tail another adaptive disorder, *overresponse*, response more massive or profound than correction requires. Such responses tend to reduce systemic flexibility and thus commit a system's future more than necessary. Overresponse is probably not possible in strictly biological processes in which adaptive response sequences are ordered not by conscious purpose but by nonconscious somatic and genetic organization. Overresponse may be a pathological product of foresight and imagination, becoming increasingly serious as intelligence comes to control ever more powerful means of effecting its ends.

3. The development of the maladaptive form which I have called *oversegregation* or *overdifferentiation* is associated with increasing social scale. The extreme differentiation of specialized subsystems may be expressed in the division of labor or, perhaps more seriously, it may be expressed geographically as increasingly large regions become increasingly specialized components of a world-embracing economic system. When whole regions are turned into cotton fields or whole countries into banana plantations, the environment is degraded as economic self-sufficiency is reduced. With loss of self-sufficiency there is a corresponding loss of local autonomy. Increasingly remote and centralized regulators—operating in terms of increasingly simplified and aggregated variables (like those of economics or *realpolitik*)—do not adequately replace the lost capacity of local systems to govern themselves in their own terms. Economic exploitation, political opression, and ecological degradation are likely outcomes of such a disorder, which may be called *overcentralization*.

4. Another disorder, which may be called *hypercoherence*, is closely related to overdifferentiation and overcentralization. It may, in fact, be a synergistic outcome of these disorders and the cybernetic and temporal difficulties mentioned earlier. The interdependence of the parts of ever more embracing and complex social, political, an economic systems becomes ever tighter as the self-sufficiency of local systems disappears. Coherence reaches dangerous levels as disruptions occurring anywhere spread everywhere with little or no delay.

5. Overdifferentiation and overcentralization are complementary aspects of a more general structural anomaly which may be called the *hierarchical maldistribution of organization*. (The term *organization* is notoriously difficult to define; I take it to refer to complexity and

the means for maintaining order within complexity.) In this disorder. the organization of more inclusive levels seems to be increasing at the expense of organization at local levels. More specifically, organization at the world level is based upon decreasingly organized local, regional, and even national social and ecological systems. It is doubtful that a worldwide system can persist and elaborate itself indefinitely at the expense of its local infrastructures. It may be suggested that the ability of the world system to withstand perturbation would be enhanced by returning to local subsystems some of the autonomy and self-sufficiency they have lost.

6. Another important class of maladaptations has elsewhere (Flannery, 1972; Rappaport, 1971d, 1976a, 1978b, 1979a) been called *usurpation, escalation,* or *overspecification.* I speak here of the tendency of special-purpose subsystems to attempt to dominate the larger, generalized social systems of which they are parts. As they become increasingly powerful their success becomes more likely. Power is not equally distributed throughout highly differentiated "developed" societies but is, rather, concentrated in their industrialized and financial sectors. These sectors come to dominate the agencies charged with regulating them, and the logical end is for the interests of groups of industrial firms, financial institutions, and perhaps related military establishments to be escalated to the status of the larger society's highest general goals, values, or regulatory principles. ("The business of America is business"; "What's good for General Motors is good for America.") No matter how benign or public-spirited such interests may be, the usurpation of the status of ultimate value by special interest is *always* maladaptive. For a society to commit itself to the *particular* values of one of its subsystems or to the maintenance of conditions favorable to such a subsystem is for it to overspecify or narrow the range of conditions under which it can persist. That is, it reduces its adaptive flexibility. More obviously, with the escalation of the highly specific goals of private concerns or specialized institutions to positions of ultimate value, it becomes increasingly possible for ancient and complex systems, particularly ecological systems, to be disrupted by ever-smaller groups with ever-narrower interests.

7. Another maladaptive form, the *degradation of the sacred,* is a concomitant of usurpation or overspecification. As the specific mate-

rial goals of lower-order systems usurp the places of the general moral postulates of more inclusive social systems, they may lay claim to their sanctity. To use a crude example, if the United States is "one nation under God" and if "the business of America is business," then business is highly sanctified. What is highly sanctified is resistant to change; thus to oversanctify the specific and material is to reduce evolutionary flexibility. (It is of interest that the theologian Paul Tillich (1957) used the term *idolatry* to refer to a similar development, which he characterized as "absolutizing the relative." What he took to be a form of evil we may take to be a form of maladaptation.)

To summarize, maladaptation may be conceived in structural terms. I have made suggestions here concerning some of its forms, but surely there are others. Although schematic, my brief discussion should have made clear that maladaptive disorders and substantive problems are mutually causal. Such substantive problems as economic exploitation and ecological degradation are entailed or generated by deformations of adaptive structure. Conversely, deformations of adaptive structure—maladaptations—may be exacerbated or even generated by substantive developments, particularly but by no means exclusively developments in technology. Be this as it may, social systems may finally become so bound by maladaptations that they can no longer cope with perturbations of either external or internal origin, and can then be corrected only by such radical means as revolution.

I have also implied that the likelihood of adaptive disorders developing as well as the seriousness of their consequences is increased by social stratification, by an increased division of labor, and by high-energy technology. Thus sociocultural evolution itself sets new problems as it ameliorates old ones.

Flannery (1972) took issue with an early formulation of this notion of maladaptation, proposing that structural anomalies themselves could, in fact, stimulate the social transformations constituting sociocultural evolution. I agree. Adaptive disorderings do not necessarily devastate the systems in which they occur and they may sometimes stimulate structural reorganization.

More recent criticism has been less sympathetic to the scheme generally. Burnham (1979:199), citing Holling (1973) and Lewontin

(1969),* argues that relationships between variables may be kept stable without control hierarchies of the sort I propose. Holling's essay is largely concerned to clarify the concepts of resilience and flexibility. My suggestions are concerned with the structure of flexibility or resilience and I see no important disagreements between them and Holling's seminal article. He does not bring hierarchies into his discussion of stability maintenance, but he limits himself to relations between pairs of variables, such as demographic trends in predator and prey populations, whereas my proposals have been concerned with the organization of systems that must deal with the dynamic relations among large numbers of variables at once. Lewontin's essay clarifies and formalizes various concepts of stability. I do not see that my suggestions are at odds with his formulation. A much more serious critique by Jonathan Friedman (1979) appears in the same volume as Burnham's. Friedman notes, among other things, that Prigogine (Prigogine, Allan, and Herman, n.d.; see also Prigogine, 1961, 1980) has demonstrated that "the maintenance of states far from thermodynamic equilibrium is a general phenomenon not limited to living systems" and that their maintenance does not in all cases depend upon internal self-regulatory mechanisms. These "dissipative structures" are maintained by fluxes of energy and we should think not so much in terms of "regulation, maintenance and negative feedback" but of "cycles, structural stability, secular trends, constraints, morphogenesis, limits, crises, 'catastrophe,' etc." (1979:268).

I of course agree that the maintenance of states far from thermodynamic equilibria is not limited to living systems, but is a characteristic of organization generally. All living systems are open, and can persist only by exchanging energy and matter with their environ-

*I cannot help but observe that Burnham's use of citations is strange. For instance, he states, "Rappaport (1977:142, 148–49, 167–68) explicitly identifies the discipline of ecological anthropology as the study of self-persisting systems" (1979:p. 197). I cannot remember *ever* having made such an identification, either implicit or explicit, and certainly did not do so on the pages cited. In fact discussions on most of those pages have nothing to do with the topic of self-perpetuating systems and the term itself does not appear on any of them. I cannot imagine why or on what ground Burnham attributes this identification to me and can only observe that such a misunderstanding or misrepresentation cannot contribute to the clarification of issues.

ments. As such they are a special class of "dissipative structures." Friedman does not deny the existence of cybernetic structures but wishes "only to locate them correctly in reality. . . . While human organisms are indeed cybernetic as individuals social systems are not" (1979:266).

Although I have emphasized self-regulation generally and cybernetic operation specifically I have not meant to imply that all things happening in social systems are to be accounted for in cybernetic terms. The perturbations which I emphasize are not cybernetic. Moreover, I include within the category of cybernetic regulation interactions between relatively autonomous actors in the absence of discrete regulatory agencies—the sort of interactions which Bateson long ago characterized as switches from symmetrical to complementary schismogenesis. This more inclusive view of regulation suggests that recognition of its existence and importance does not deny the importance of limitation, catastrophe, crisis, transformation, and other of the terms that Friedman, following Prigogine, advocates. Some of the terms in the two sets seem, in fact, to be closely related if not identical. Cybernetic or other forms of self-regulation are, I have proposed, among the grounds of structured stability and flexibility in living systems. In sum, there is, I believe, less separating my proposals from Prigogine's than Friedman supposes.

A second point that Friedman raises is that the sociological content of my analysis is insufficient. It has not been fully developed but I do not see that my suggestions are hostile to sociological analysis. Although maladaptations are, in my formulation, deformities in adaptive structure, I have proposed that they stand in a relationship of mutual causality with social problems, particularly problems of inequality and exploitation.

Friedman also takes issue with me on the nature of evolution. He asserts that in my view, "Evolution . . . becomes a well-managed programme instead of the contradictory and violent, even though systematic, process that appears on the surface" (1979:266). This is not my view at all. For any of the relatively autonomous actors subject to the vicissitudes of climate, predators, parasites, and competitors it obviously is not. They are all constantly perturbed or challenged and many or most are eliminated. Whether evolutionary processes appear violent and contradictory or whether they seem harmonious and integrated depends upon the level of organization with which one chooses to fill his horizon. If one takes a stand, as do sociobiologists, among individuals, society is not so much an organized association as it is a field of often violent competition among individuals. If one's view is filled by group phenomena competition among individuals seems softened or may even become invisible as we discern large historical trends. The competition and violence that remain visible to us take place between groups or factions within societies or between societies as wholes. If we move to more inclusive levels, like ecosystems or the biosphere as a whole, the mayhem that is part and parcel of evolutionary processes (although not exhausting them) is again softened as we observe the remarkable accommodations that develop between species and their environments, and the orderly features of ecological successions which move, under some climatic and ecologic conditions, toward an ever-tighter interdependence of the constituent species. Similarly, when we view the evolution of life in general we discern, in the very long run, a movement toward ever more complex organization. The millions of extinctions are softened into increased accommodation, increased differentiation and integration, making possible increases in both the amount of life the world as a whole supports, the complexity of some of the organisms living it, and the amount of consciousness that is engaged in the world's comprehension. That there is harmony and order at one level does not preclude violence and disorder at another. In fact they imply or entail each other as Heraclitus seems to have been saying when he spoke of the *Logos* as an order both underlying and contingent upon the tensions, contradictions, and violence that "appear on the surface."

It should be clear, I think, that the approach I have suggested does not assume a harmony in nature that is only disturbed by human societies, especially our own. Friedman asserts that my suggestions concerning adaptation and evolution present "a blatant case of Rousseauism or ecologism" (1979:263), grounding this charge in my general comparison of ecological felicity as common in tribal societies with ecological destructiveness in contemporary societies. He sees this as an ideological position and a dangerous one at that given that we are living in a period of major crisis (p. 254). I must demur. I do not think it unduly ideological to be especially concerned with the problems confronting one's own society, or to propose that sociocultural evolution sets as well as solves problems or to assert that the problems are of ever-increasing seriousness. When before in human history has it been possible for small groups of men to annihilate the species? When before has the destruction of the atmosphere been a problem? Does not the increasing interdependence of the world's inhabitants set up new possibilities for breakdowns with such consequences as famine? Are these dangers not exacerbated by the simplification of local and regional ecosystems, this simplification itself a result of an increasing economic interdependence consequent to imperialism? To propose that these problems are concomitants of sociocultural evolution hardly qualifies me as a latter-day Rousseau. In fact, the position seems to me less ideological than is the view that sociocultural evolution has been a steady progress onward and upward from savagery.

Friedman asserts that my cure for all of this is ideological in nature. My "political programme," he says, is "consistent with a world view based on control hierarchies dominated by rules, principles, and gods, where there is no conceivable place for socioeconomic structures as such" (1979:264–65). In particular, he attributes to me the view, which I have never espoused, that "we need a new religion" because "we have 'bad' values."

I have, it is true, discussed the adaptive characteristics of sacred and sanctified propositions noting that they are themselves vulnerable to maladaptation (Rappaport, 1971d, 1976a, 1978b, 1979b). Friedman, like Fabian (1982) badly misunderstands my proposals, even adducing arguments in criticism that my formulation not only recognizes but includes. I have, to be sure, discussed the organization of values and the effects of that organization upon adaptive processes. But I have also argued, in this epilogue and elsewhere, that structures of meaning and value may be ordered and disordered by social, economic, and political processes.

There has been much concern over the past two decades about the relationship of anthropology to the peoples constituting its most immediate and obvious subject matter—the few tribal peoples left, peasants, ethnic minorities. Much less thought has been given to anthropology's relationship to the society from which it sprang and which may constitute its less apparent but nevertheless ultimate subject matter. It may be suggested, however, that in its very existence anthropology offers a critique of that society. Criticism implies correction and it may be that the suggestions I have offered concerning the structured nature of maladaptation make a contribution to what might be called a "theory of correction." Conceptualizing the nature of our problems as anomalies of adaptive structure (or in whatever other terms may seem illuminating) does not by itself provide a theory of correction. The term *correction* designates a class of actions, and a theory of correction must be a theory of actions of a certain sort—in my terms, actions to restore adaptiveness to systems atrophied by maladaptations.

Little is known about the characteristics of such action or how to undertake it. Our society, despite its concern with problems and its plethora of designated "problem solvers"—presidents, senators, mayors, social workers—lacks an adequate theory of correction. What is called "problem solving" reifies problems by decontextualizing parts of reality from the matrixes in which they are embedded.

I believe that anthropology does have something to offer to the development of a theory or theories of correction. If this seems presumptuous or dangerous we should keep in mind that social policy is at present informed by views of the world, its ills, and ways to cure its ills provided by other disciplines no better founded and considerably less humane than our own.

SECTION 14

Objective and Subjective Principles in Anthropology

In an essay published some years ago the philosopher Frithjof Bergmann (1975) took the occasion of a critique of *Pigs for the Ancestors*
to mount a more general attack upon scientific approaches to the study
of social and cultural phenomena. Following Monod (1972) he asserts
that "the 'principle of objectivity' represents the one indispensable
foundation upon which 'science' rests" (1975:7). This principle prohibits "subjective" principles of explanation from being "exported,"
that is, applied to natural phenomena. Human activity, however, is
precisely the domain of the subjective,

> in the investigation of cultures or societies, or perhaps of any-
> thing distinctive of man (as opposed to inanimate and animate
> nature) the use of "subjective" principles of explanation clearly
> does not constitute an (improper) "exportation." Man has mo-
> tives and purposes and goals and we have ways of knowing what
> they are. Therefore we confront a choice: we can . . . observe
> the "principle of objectivity" even in these investigations and in
> effect model them after other sciences. The price exacted would
> be much that we genuinely know (which would be excluded be-
> cause both subjective and only subjectively known). . . . Alter-
> natively, we can allow "subjective principles" of explanation and
> . . . pay the price of no longer working in real "science." The
> alternatives are thus between being scientific at the expense of
> knowledge, and gaining knowledge that will no longer form a
> science. [1975:8–9]

432

In light of these difficulties, Bergmann calls for a deep change in the nature of social studies generally: "At the root lies the erroneous assumption that we need a 'science' to know and to understand. What must be disavowed is the epistemology that interpreted the whole of knowledge as analogy to science. Once that epistemology has been discarded the investigation of society can be conceptualized in a new way" (1975:21). In sum, anthropology should stop whoring after the strange gods of physics and openly declare itself a convert to the humanities.

Raymond Kelly and I (1975) have agreed that science is one thing and all of knowledge another, and although science may require obedience to a "principle of objectivity" this is not so for all of knowledge. We have also agreed that in the study of anything distinctive of humanity as a cultural species the use of subjective principles is proper. We believe, however, that the choice Bergmann asks of anthropology—to be either one of the sciences or one of the humanities—is not only unnecessary but mistaken. Anthropology is properly a synthesis of the two. This is not a plea for an easy tolerance of what any and every anthropologist does. What constitutes the proper domains of the subjective on the one hand and the objective on the other is a matter of fundamental importance which remains in some degree ambiguous and even confused. It seems to me certain, however, that clarification will not follow from their radical separation. To choose between subjective and objective principles of elucidation is not only to impoverish our understanding, but also to force us to make the particular set of principles we favor do work for which it is not suited, work properly belonging to the domain of the other. As it is improper to "import" objectivity into the subjective realm, so is it improper to "export" subjectivity into the objective realm. Furthermore, one of the most profound sets of problems with which anthropology should be concerned is that of the relationship of the "subjective domain" (that of goals, motives, purposes, feelings, understandings, misunderstandings, hopes, dreads) to the "objective domain" (of rocks, water, trees, animals, metabolism, endocrine secretion, nutrition, growth, decay, entropy). To choose between objective and subjective principles is to make it impossible from the start to investigate relationships between the domains to which each properly applies, relationships that approximate those between meaning and law, between the conventionally constructed and the naturally constituted. This relationship is distinctive of the human condition.

It is this relationship with which *Pigs for the Ancestors* was centrally concerned. Through both distinguishing and relating subjective cognized and objective operational models it attempted to show purposeful men operating in terms of culturally constituted meanings in a purposeless but lawful natural world. Whereas the strategy was, I think, proper, I will freely admit that the attempt was flawed. Some of the "objective" data were inadequate and some meanings were missed, misunderstood, or, possibly, infected by what Sahlins (1976a: 298) has called "ecology fetishism."

The relationship of meaning to natural processes is hardly a simple one. Meaning is nowhere monolithic. Much of quotidian understanding everywhere is grounded in observations of naturally constituted processes and, through acts of distinction, encoded as "fact" in classifications, either implicit or explicit. Some of these facts are, of course, conventionally established, but concordance is generally high between natural processes and what I have elsewhere called low-order meaning, meaning founded upon distinction (see 1979b:126ff.). Higher-order meanings—the meanings not of distinctions but of similarities underlying distinctions, the meanings of metaphor, symbol, and value—are not grounded directly in observations of nature and are thus relatively free from constraints to conform to it. They are, this is to say, free to organize action in a variety of ways and thus are free to attempt the subordination of natural processes to whatever ends they define—mollifying ancestors, repaying affines, making profits.

I have already suggested that a high concordance between actions organized in terms of higher-order meaning and ecosystemic processes may be common in unstratified and relatively undifferentiated horticultural societies such as that of the Maring. Such concordance may not pertain equally in all domains of such societies, however. For instance, the nutritional soundness of Maring pig husbandry and consumption is probably more dubious than the general ecological soundness of the ritual cycle, probably even more dubious than I cautiously suggested in *Pigs for the Ancestors*. Different conventions, which could have included both agistment and regular slaughter at earlier ages with different rules for distributing pork, might have enhanced the Maring diet significantly. The conventions governing husbandry and slaughter during the period described in the ethnography were, however, central to the maintenance and regulation of social and political relations as well as ecosystemic relations and dietary intake. Meaning and the requisites of the social order were thus served at what might have been significant cost to the health of the organisms whose actions they organized.

It borders on the tautologous to say that meaning is highly valued everywhere because the concept of value is subsumed by the concept of meaning. Be this as it may, humans always and everywhere have been willing to labor, to give treasure, to kill, and even to sacrifice their lives for such meanings as God, Salvation, Fatherland, and Honor. High cost may be prerequisite to deep meaning, and deep meaning may be requisite to the maintenance of social life. It is a vulgar error to consider the costs of meaning—the treasure and labor given to the temple, the bird feathers provided for the chief's cloak, the wounds suffered in defense of gods—to be exploitative simply because those who pay them do not necessarily receive material returns. Too much may sometimes be asked of individuals, however, and populations may be led into decline or extinction by the meanings they entertain.

Of course some meanings are instruments of the survival of the organisms maintaining them, and of course the actions of the selfsame organisms are meaningfully organized in terms of ends that they themselves did not define, that do not emerge naturally out of "natural" or utilitarian considerations, and that may, indeed, be inimical to those who strive toward them. But neither of these two statements by itself provides an adequate account of the relationship of the processes of culturally constituted meaning and natural processes, nor, for that matter, do the two together. What they do delineate is a field for investigation, a set of problems corresponding closely to the characteristics of a species that can only live in terms of meanings it itself must construct surrounded by a nature whose operations it perceives only darkly and through the distorting lenses of its own hopes and ends.

SECTION 15

The Ecology of Explanation

In his general critique of scientific studies of society, Bergmann raises another major objection not only to the systemic account provided in *Pigs for the Ancestors* and other such works, but to the structuralism of Lévi-Strauss as well. He claims that they finally fail because they leave much of what they describe unexplained. The test of a functional account is *"how much* of a given phenomenon the postulated function in the end explains" (1975:3; emphasis in the original). There is in *Pigs for the Ancestors*, he argues, a "gross disproportionality" between the richness of the ethnographic detail and the starkness of the ritual cycle's functions. The functions could have been fulfilled by a less complex instrument and it is not clear what such practices as the prohibition against eating *marita* and *ma* together or terminating the taboo by spitting *marita* seeds into the forest, like countless other practices, have to do with such functions.

The virtues of description for its own sake could once again be raised in defense, of course, but it seemed to Kelly and me that the account of the ritual cycle does not leave readers as completely in the dark about pandanus seeds, marsupial tails, fighting stones, eels, *raua mai*, and other such symbolic phenomena as Bergmann's critique suggested. There was an attempt to indicate, partly through a subsidiary structural analysis made more explicit in later essays (1971b, 1979b), at least some of the ways in which disparate features of Maring culture were interwoven, for example, how the conceptual oppositions between spirits and abstract qualities were related to population trends in pig herds through a ritual cycle. We argued, furthermore, that the relations thus elucidated were not among the phenomena already "richly known" through ordinary experience as members of society, either the Marings' experience or our own. Our common sense would not lead us to expect systemic regulation through an elaborate succession of rituals nor would it lead us from the rituals themselves to their material and social effects. As far as the common sense of the Maring is concerned, it was argued in the conclusion that native understandings must often be at some variance from the actual operations of social systems. This is to claim that knowledge not given to us in other ways was gained through the analysis, although it must be agreed that at the end much remained to be accounted for.

Surely conceptual approaches other than that which dominated the book could have elucidated aspects of ritual that remained untouched by the analysis. It may be asked, however, whether the failure of this or any other analysis to account for all the detailed descriptive material which it presents should be allowed to disqualify, or even demean, what it did accomplish. The most that we can ask of any analysis is that it tell us something that is worth knowing that we otherwise would not know—that it add significantly to our understanding. It would be both mistaken and arrogant to claim for any form of analysis that it explains everything "really important" in the phenomena with which it is concerned. Functional or systemic or structural or symbolic or other sorts of analysis impoverish understanding only when their results are taken to be alternatives to, rather than enlargements of or complements to, knowledge gained through other modes of analysis or through general social experience.

It follows that moving on to other modes of description, analysis, or interpretation, even of the same material, does not indicate a rejection of what has already been done but, simply, a recognition of its limitations. I, for instance, have been led—or pushed—to more recent concerns with the nature of the sacred and the formal characteristics of ritual (see Rappaport, 1979d) by the realization that an ecological and systemic analysis of a ritual cycle says nothing about those aspects of rituals that make them rituals, or about the nature and grounds of sanctity. There never has been, nor will there ever be, a mode of analysis that will tell us everything worth knowing about anything. To persist in demanding the unattainable is unreasonable, but would be more or less harmless if it merely left us in chronic states of disappointment. It does not. It leaves us either with nothing, as we reject everything, or with an undifferentiated everything as we give ourselves too easily to the saving images of the revitalistic movements that, with some regularity, sweep through the discipline promising, if not the keys to the kingdom, the key to the universe—"Culture and Personality" in the thirties, the "New Ethnography" and "Cultural Ecology" in the fifties, "Structuralism" and the "New Ecology" in the sixties, "Structural Marxism," "Sociobiology," and various symbolic schools in the seventies. Those swept up in such movements are inclined either to impoverish understanding by defining "everything worth knowing" as that which can be known through the doctrines to which they are devoted, or to distort understanding by asking more of their theories, methods, or perspectives than they can deliver. Failures resulting from the exportation of sound but limited modes of explanation into unsuitable domains are likely to be mistakenly construed to indicate the bankruptcy of concepts when, in fact, they should be understood as the abuse of those concepts.

To claim that comprehensive understanding, if approachable at all, must be grounded in several modes simultaneously applied may invite a shapeless eclecticism, and as such is not very helpful. If a plurality of explanatory principles are to be invoked effectively they must be related to each other in ordered ways. Questions concerning the proper place of ecological principles, of the notion of function, and of the concepts of system and adaptation in anthropological understanding thus dissolve into the larger question of a general ecology of explanation. There is a need, I think, to elucidate relationships among modes of explanation and explanatory principles.

Matters concerning the structure of comprehensive explanations or accounts are complex and would be better dealt with by philosophers. I may, however, note that we have been touching upon them throughout this epilogue. In the last section, for instance, we considered the relationship of subjective and objective domains, a relationship earlier discussed in sections 3, 4, and 5. The discussion in section 8 of relations among formal, final, efficient and material accounts suggests one obvious way in which ecological explanations fit into a general ecology of explanation. Environmental perturbations can qualify as efficient causes of events in societies or even of changes in the structures of societies. Systems respond to efficient causes within the constraints of their previously existing orders (i.e., structured contents) which, in this terminology, constitute material cause. To claim that the specific characteristics of environments or perturbations in them cannot account for the specific nature of the responses to them—a common complaint—is, first, simply to say that efficient cause is not material cause. (The related complaint that functions do not specify how they are fulfilled in like manner criticizes final cause for not being material cause.) Perhaps more important, the claim, if radically construed, is exaggerated to the point of being misleading or even erroneous. With the possible exception of genetic responses, the characteristics of environments and changes in them do more than stimulate adapting systems to random activity. Problems posed by environments have particular properties that must be accommodated, circumvented, overridden, domesticated, ameliorated, or corrected. While characteristics of or changes in the environment do not determine the specific nature of responses to them, they may establish the general direction or trajectory of those responses more or less stringently and, of course, it is in terms of them that the appropriateness, adequacy, or success of those responses is minimally assessed. That adaptive formulations can seldom provide "uniquely correct answers," as critics have charged, is of course true. Ordered versatility is, after all, the essence of adaptiveness. That the "answers" provided by adaptive formulations are not "uniquely correct" does not mean that they are incorrect or of no account, however.

A related problem bearing upon comprehensive understanding, touched upon earlier, is that of contradiction between the requisites, goals, and effects of the operations of included vs. including systems—organisms, populations of various magnitudes, and ecosystems. Consideration of this general problem, which seems to be one of the most crucial of our time, obviously requires consideration not only of the specific "laws of functioning" of systems at various levels, but of relations between levels. If the relationship of included to including systems is that of part to whole, these hierarchies of interlevel relations may have to possess, as already noted, certain logical and structural characteristics to remain orderly. This suggests that principles of great generality can increase our understanding of some of the detailed characteristics of human social systems.

I will finally note as germane to an ecology of explanation that statements concerning principles of organization may be ordered into explanatory hierarchies. Such principles may be associated with classes of organization of greater or lesser generality, for example, Maring society, human society, single species societies, living systems, information processing systems, physical systems, all systems. (Such hierarchies are different from those of included and including systems alluded to in the last paragraph. Human society, for instance, is a general class which subsumes Maring society as a member. It does not include it as a part in the same way that an organism includes a cell.) Certain phenomena are characteristic of each of these levels and certain laws, regularities, or orders prevail within each of them. For instance, all physical systems are subject to the thermodynamic laws, and all information processing systems to the logic of analogic or digital coding. All living systems are characterized by adaptiveness, all organisms by metabolism, all animals by sentience, all humanity by cultural processes, all Maring by Maring cultural processes. It seems clear that the laws relating to more inclusive classes limit or bound the subclasses they include. For instance, the operation of metabolism conforms to the thermodynamic laws and may, perhaps, be taken to be special cases of them. It also seems that a relationship of contingency between the processes applying to less and more general classes of systems prevails. Metabolism, for example, is a prerequisite of sentience or, to put it in the converse, sentience is contingent upon metabolism. The extent to which functional relations correspond to contingency relations is unclear and may have changed in the course of evolution. Whatever sentience is possessed by, let us say, an earthworm is probably fully in the service of its metabolism and reproduction, but such a simple relation between sense and metabolism is not true of humanity nor even, for that matter, of the higher animals. I have, in other terms, repeatedly spoken of this ambiguity as a source of substantive problems.

The hierarchies that we are considering here are hierarchies of specificity and generality. It follows that goals or requisites of more general categories are given specificity in terms of the specific principles of their individual members. The argument has been made that the more general or inclusive the domain of an explanatory principle the less it is able to account for the particulars of any phenomenon. The laws of gravity, for instance, do not tell us much about culture, cultures, or the human condition. We should not, however, permit an oversimplified dictum to constrain us unduly. It does not seem to me that the principles ordering the phenomena characteristic of, or defining, any level should be allowed to monopolize understanding. Various aspects of a particular phenomenon may be illuminated by reference to the principles of several levels and the resulting account is "thicker," richer, and thus more meaningful than an account that is limited to the explanatory principles of a single level. This seems to be as true of meaning as it is of adaptation. Consider the meanings inhering in the ritual uprooting of *rumbim*.

First, there are the meanings encoded in the particular representations appearing in the ritual—*rumbim, amame,* a special form of oven, particular foodstuffs, the acts of removing the charcoal called *ringi* from men's bodies, of sacrificing pigs, of consuming the contents of the oven, of planting the *rumbim* and the *amame,* and so on. These multivocal representations simplify, symbolize, and "iconify" meanings peculiar to Maring culture—certain spirits, qualities, and social conditions, as well as relations among these and relations of the Maring to them. These meanings, being peculiar to Maring culture, are, of course, to be understood in the terms of Maring culture. That these Maring meanings are represented in the context of a *ritual,* however, leads us out of the level of the particular culture to meanings of a second and more general sort. I have argued elsewhere (1979d) and in this epilogue that certain meanings—social contract, morality, a paradigm of creation, the concept of the sacred, the notion of the divine—inhere in ritual per se. They are entailed by the structure that defines ritual. Ritual, however, is not peculiar to Maring culture. It is a panhuman phenomenon, and it would be a mistake to take its pancultural meanings to be specifically Maring. Moreover, the nature of the "meaningfulness" of the specifically Maring meanings represented in the ritual is different from the meaningfulness of the panhuman ritual form itself.

I have discussed this in detail elsewhere (1979b). Here it must suffice to say that whereas culturally specific representations stand in symbolic and iconic relationships to their culturally specific significations, the meanings peculiar to *ritual* are indexically signaled. Further, the participation (in the ritual) of the sender of ritual messages (who is also their most important receiver) is ipso facto participation in the messages themselves. The meaningfulness of such participation is that of identity, unity, or integration, rather than that of reference or denotation, the form of meaningfulness characterizing the culturally particular meanings by themselves.

There is yet a third level of meaning in ritual: the significance intrinsic to the mere fact of a ritual's performance. In the conclusion of this book and elsewhere (1971d) I have suggested that the mere occurrence of a noncalendrical ritual may be a signal. Since any ritual included in the repertoire of a people can, at any particular time, be in only one of two possible states—occurring or not occurring—occurrence can transmit a binary signal. Although the occurrence of the ritual transmits a "yes/no" signal, it may have been triggered by the achievement or violation of a particular state or range of states of a continuous, "more–less" variable, or even of a complex state or range of states constellated by relationships among a number of such variables. As such, the occurrence of a ritual may be a simple qualitative representation of complex quantitative information or, to put it differently, the occurrence of a ritual may summarize complex analogic information and translate it into the simplest possible digital signal, one for which there is only one alternative. It is of great importance to note that this simple binary characteristic is not peculiar to Maring rituals. In fact, it is not peculiar to ritual. We are speaking here of a much broader phenomenon, a general characteristic of digital information processing.

Our understanding of rituals, then, is increased by appeals to three levels of order. It would have been possible to invoke other levels as well. The point here is that valuable insights concerning detailed aspects of ritual have been vouchsafed to us by the principles governing different levels of order. Of course the general characteristics of ritual and the panhuman meanings they entail do not account for all the symbolic and iconic particularities of Maring, Catholic, or any other ritual. Conversely, the particularities of Maring, Catholic, or any other ritual cannot provide an understanding of why they are represented in ritual and not in some other form. We are led here to a related point. An appeal to more than one level does not simply provide us with several concurrent but more or less autonomous sets of meanings. These sets of meanings are interrelated. For instance, the occurrence of culturally specific representations in ritual contexts sanctifies them and invests them with morality. The performance of a ritual, moreover, entails an acceptance by the performer of an obligation to abide by whatever that ritual encodes. Further implications of the ritual form for what is represented in it are discussed in "The Obvious Aspects of Ritual" and "Sanctity and Lies in Evolution" (Rappaport, 1979d, 1979e). Enough has been said here to indicate that the ritual form is something like a metastatement about the culturally specific meanings it encompasses. I say "something like a metastatement" because rituals possess performative qualities and are not merely statements. The meaningfulness of performatives is not simply the meaningfulness of description, nor even that of evaluation. Performative or "illocutionary" acts or utterances are conventional procedures for bringing into being conventional states of affairs, or even for establishing conventions themselves. As such they are constitutive and their meaningfulness is very different from that of culturally specific representations by themselves. It is a meaningfulness that is, or comes very close to being, causal (see Austin, 1962; Rappaport, 1979d; Searle, 1969).

In sum, our understanding of ritual is not merely enriched by appeals to more than one level of generality. It is, rather, impoverished, incomplete, and inadequate unless we do invoke the meanings of more than one level. The proper citation of the principles of one level does not conflict with the simultaneous citation of those pertaining to other levels. Indeed, to say that the simultaneously invoked principles of the several levels complement each other is inadequate as an expression of the intimacy of their relationship. It would be tempting to say that they complete each other if it were not that our understanding of anything as profound, subtle, various, and ubiquitous as ritual can never be complete: such phenomena forever excite new questions. It should not be forgotten, furthermore, that the scope of that which anthropology seeks to understand is not well or truly represented by any catalogue of the innumerable cultural categories or phenomena, such as ritual or rituals, with which the distinctions of language can provide us. The task of anthropology is not even to be understood as the elucidation of cultures as systems. As Roger Keesing put it a few years ago, we also "want to know how human groups organize and sustain their social life; how biology and experience interact . . . how the nature of that experience shapes personalities; how different— and how similar—are human modes of thought and perception in different times and places; how ways of life change, and what shapes and forms they take in particular setting"(1974:90).

And, I would add, we want to know how cultures come to be at odds with the creatures who bear them and with the ecological systems in which they are set; in what specific forms such contradictions between "nature" and "culture" manifest themselves and whether the difficulties that follow such disorders can be corrected. We also need to understand better how humans may keep from destroying the systems upon which they depend, and themselves as well, when the complexity of those systems exceeds any hope of comprehending them.

APPENDIX 11 (1984)

Nutrition in *Pigs for the Ancestors*

I shall be concerned in this appendix with production and nutrition data presented in *Pigs for the Ancestors* and with some aspects of my interpretation of them. Both have been criticized.

The most comprehensive and detailed criticism of the nutritional aspects of the book has been provided by McArthur. Published originally in the journal *Oceania* in 1974, readers can also find her critique in almost identical form published as chapter 5 in Bayliss-Smith and Feachem (eds.), *Subsistence and Survival: Rural Ecology in the Pacific*, London, 1977. In referring to McArthur's criticisms I shall cite pages in her original publication.

GARDEN PRODUCTION AND
HOUSEHOLD CONSUMPTION

My procedures for collecting the data that served as grounds for estimates of intake are discussed in some detail in the text and in appendix 9. All vegetables brought home to four households were weighed daily. Because I was as interested in garden production as I was in consumption, all foodstuffs were weighed by garden. (At any time all households were harvesting from several gardens differing in age, altitude, crop mix, etc.) Vegetables were weighed daily not only by species, but by named variety. This weighing operation (supplemented by observations in the gardens on food consumed there) served as the basis for both production and consumption estimates.

McArthur takes me to task for not stating who did the daily weighing (1974:93). I doubt that many readers have been troubled by this lacuna, but I may as well take this opportunity to clarify the matter. There were, beside me, two literate and numerate people in Tsembaga in 1962–63—Ann Rappaport, my wife, and my field assistant, Thomas Kavali (who later served for many years as a member of parliament and as minister of lands in the national government). I did the weighing on a great preponderance of days. In my absence either Ann Rappaport or Thomas Kavali did it.

The procedure for estimating food consumed away from the houses was not satisfactory, as I indicated on page 279 above. It was, however, better than guesswork, which was McArthur's characterization (1974:93). I attempted to estimate the size and to count the number of items that I saw consumed in gardens (e.g., one sugar cane, *pa* variety, approximately 2 feet in length, 1½ inches diameter; six cucumbers, 3 to 4 inches in length), and then to weigh comparable amounts on returning home. On a number of occasions I was able to watch particular gardeners for the full day.

McArthur observes that I did not indicate whether I simply added a constant weight for food consumed away from the houses or "if someone checked each day with all or most people in the sample" (1974:93). I did add constants for the consumption of each crop away from the house. These constants appear in column 13 of table 26. I did not, as McArthur suggested I might, persist in checking each day with all or most people in the sample. I found that asking what a person had eaten in the garden during the day irritated some people and amused others; in any event, the answers would not have been useful as consumption data, so I quickly stopped asking. The only foods I knew to be eaten in large amounts away from the houses of the four women during the period March 11–November 8, 1963, were sugar cane and cucumbers. Moderate amounts of bananas and *marita pandanus* were also being consumed elsewhere (the *marita* at men's houses). At times of the year when more corn was available, a larger proportion than indicated of that food was probably consumed in the gardens. All in all, I think that my allowances for foods consumed without being brought home were reasonable. If there were any serious mistakes they were most likely in estimates of sugar cane, a crop whose main nutritional significance is caloric, and calories are not limiting in the Maring diet.

A related shortcoming, which McArthur mentions but does not pursue, is that I assumed that raw food given away by Tomegai gardeners to others before it was brought home was matched by raw foods given to them. This assumption could not have corresponded precisely to the facts, but I have no reason to believe that it did not approximate them.

As McArthur notes I kept no record of wild animal foods consumed. For one thing, such foods most frequently consisted of very small items not brought back to the houses. Women, young children of both sexes, and older girls would eat large insects and mice in the gardens. Boys old enough to be away from their mothers would often wander through the bush in small groups; in the course of their rambles they would sometimes eat nestling birds, small lizards, praying mantises, frogs, and other such game, often shooting them with tiny bows and arrows, then cooking them. My one attempt to estimate how much of such things the boys were eating was a failure. When the boys with whom I was spending the day saw that I was interested in the insects they had captured the occasion became a conscious and systematic bug hunt. I discovered that young boys know a great deal about insects, but not how much of them they ordinarily eat. It could not have been much, for the creatures taken were very small. Rodents trapped in houses in 1981–82, which were much larger than the little boys' prey, seldom weighed more than fifty grams.

Some game was, of course, large enough to be brought home. A taboo on eels prevailed during all but the last few weeks of my stay and few people were hunting or trapping marsupials, so little was taken or consumed. I mentioned wild pig in the text.

I did not attempt to weigh, or otherwise estimate, the amounts of this larger game consumed by the four households because I did not think it worth shaming them to inquire into a matter which I deemed not to make a very important contribution to consumption on most days. (To ask would have been deeply embarrassing to people who had not presented any to me. It did no good to refuse game proffered me because they would have insisted that if I would not eat it myself

I could give it to my assistants.) The flesh eaten on the majority of days ranged from nothing at all to less than one ounce. Later Maring studies have given strong support to my statement that "fruits and vegetables comprise approximately 99 percent by weight of *the usual daily intake of the Tsembaga*" (p. 73; emphasis added). Buchbinder (1973:104), who weighed intakes of a sample of individuals for periods of one to two weeks among the Tuguma, the immediate neighbors of the Tsembaga, found animal food to comprise only .03% of the diet in March and .01% in July. Among the Bomagai-Angoiang, who had a great deal of virgin forest near to hand, she found it to be .2%. Clarke (1971:179) estimates Bomagai-Angoiang daily meat consumption to be higher, but still slightly under 1%. It should be emphasized that these figures, like mine, underrepresent meat in the total diet. What they indicate is the paucity of flesh in usual daily consumption. Rituals, the natural deaths of domestic pigs, luck in the hunt, and festivals provide substantial quantities of meat on rare occasions. On most days, however, there is none.

McArthur questions the method used to account for rations for pigs, which were kept separate from food to be consumed by people. The method itself was explicit: "Records were kept of rations set aside for pigs at the four households . . . for a period of a little over three months. . . . The pig consumption figures were then extended to cover an additional five months. . . ." (p. 59). It did not seem necessary to weigh the pig rations separately for these five months simply because the results had been so consistent. Day-to-day variations disappeared in week-to-week consistency, and a three-month sample seemed adequate. It still does. I chose not to weigh pig and human portions separately for five months simply to speed up, at least a little, the daily task, to reduce by a little bit the degree to which I postponed the women's evening activities and kept one waiting while I weighed the harvest of another.

McArthur further complains that "unfortunately Rappaport does not tell us whether Tsembaga women are accustomed to separating raw food intended for humans and pigs as they did for three months at his request" (1974:94). The crux of the matter is not separation, as into two piles, but selection. Some women are inclined to empty their net bags onto the ground and immediately throw into the pens most of the tubers meant for the pigs. I have seen others, or the same women on other occasions, feed less to the pigs initially, selecting out of an unsorted pile those to be prepared for cooking, leaving the pigs' portion as a residuum. Ordinarily, many or most women probably would have sorted the two categories of tubers without separating them into two distinct piles. What I asked them to do was to put the tubers to be given to the pigs in a separate pile before feeding the animals. Even if the women did not routinely separate the ration for pigs from the ration for humans in the manner asked of them, how else could I have distinguished them? I do not think this step had much, if any, effect upon their criteria for distinguishing tubers for human and animal consumption or upon the actual acts of assortment. The pigs routinely received all tubers below three to four ounces in weight, and heavier tubers that were damaged or so long and thin that their starchy pulp was insubstantial. If, on a particular day, the amount of substandard sweet potatoes was insufficient some better ones would sometimes be given to the pigs. Even large manioc tubers would be fed to the animals: manioc was generally regarded as pig food and, as reported in the text, the pigs got the great bulk of it.

McArthur throws some doubt on the entire weighing procedure in asserting that "it is tedious for any housewife to have an outsider weighing food as she prepares it and the risk of losing her cooperation effectively limits this type of survey to a week or ten days at the most and sometimes as little as a day at a time" (1974:95). I disagree. I was not weighing the food while the women were preparing it, of course, but before they began to do so. My weighing operation was, therefore, much less intrusive than McArthur suggests. Weighing, which took place at each woman's hearth, occupied no more than a few minutes—almost never more than ten—immediately upon the woman's arrival home, or within a quarter of an hour thereafter at most. Weighing became part of the evening routine, a part which the women seemed to find pleasant most of the time. It was a moment to relax and to chat before getting on with the cooking. This may be why the women remained cooperative and good-natured throughout the entire period. I should have noted that they, their husbands, and their grown children were rewarded for their efforts. Each gardener received four shillings per month, an amount they considered handsome, and I also gave them gifts of salt, matches, and face paint sufficient to their needs. (These were items that I exchanged for food with other local people. I accepted no raw vegetables from the households studied, although I sometimes dined at their hearths, a matter which was routinely recorded.)

McArthur suggests that my survey continued for such a long time that it couldn't have been effective, yet on the same page she commends me for its duration—in the course of objecting to the sample. "The duration is excellent, but not the choice of sample. Presumably fifteen of the sixteen are members and wives of the Tomegai clan, and though the members could not demonstrate a common ancestry they believed they were related and therefore they would form a genetic sub-group. Not only that, the Tsembaga population has a higher proportion of children than his sample—approximately nine under the age of 20 for every ten adults, compared to his six. On both points his sample is not representative of the local group" (1974:95).

In the best of all possible worlds one would be able to select a sample that would correspond precisely to the demographic structure of the local group and that would be composed of families which, if not randomly selected, would at least not all be related, as the Tomegai might have thought they were. This is not the best of all possible worlds and I took the *only sample feasible, that is, the sample comprised by my next-door neighbors.* None of the four households was out of eyeshot of my house. In fact, the most distant was little more than fifty feet away. I usually saw the women come home, but in the event I didn't they scarcely had to raise their voices to summon me and my scale. If they had been further away, out of sight and out of hearing, they would have had to send for me and wait for me and there would inevitably have been days missed. This quickly became apparent. Initially, in addition to my survey of the Tomegai, I arranged with a number of other people to mark off 1,000-square-foot plots in their gardens. These areas were to be harvested only in my presence, the harvests serving as samples from which the production of the gardens in which they were located could be estimated. The effort failed dismally. First and most important, the mode of harvesting that the procedure entailed did not correspond to Maring practice, nor could any 1,000-square-foot plot adequately represent the garden in which it was located. Second, I could not always be present when the gardeners wanted to harvest and they therefore harvested from the plots in my absence. I quickly gave up the effort and relied solely upon the Tomegai. The advantages were that I did not need to be present when the crops were harvested, that I was unlikely to miss days, and that I could proceed in a way which minimized their waiting for me. It conserved my time as well as the time of the cooperating gardeners.

As I have already noted, and as was made clear in the book, I was as interested in production as consumption. To get reasonably accurate production figures on swiddens, from which harvesting is daily, it is necessary for the harvesters to conform to their customary practices and for the researcher to weigh harvests daily, ideally throughout the life of the garden (an ideal of which I fell short).

A few days or a week of weighing at a hearth, to be repeated a month or two later, and again a few months after that, might provide some reasonable consumption figures, but would say absolutely nothing about garden production. The procedure that I adopted provided at one and the same time data on (1) production in particular gardens, the size, locations, altitudes and ages of which were known and from which soil samples were taken; (2) seasonal changes in the availability of the various crops planted; and (3) daily consumption aggregated by household. It also could claim the fundamental advantage of being *feasible,* which is more than could be said for a sample that included households further away. Despite McArthur's strictures I do not hesitate to suggest to others that they might find it useful to follow the general outline that I did, that is, using neighboring households for samples and weighing everything brought home every day for as long a period as possible. The methods could have stood a great deal of improvement, but the field is not a laboratory and we cannot expect results in this sort of effort to approach the degree of accuracy considered minimally acceptable in laboratory studies. Such an expectation will result in no field studies at all. Of course we should try to make our field research as good as we can, to improve our methods and to control better for factors that might distort the results of our study. I have never claimed that the data I collected were perfect. I did, and do, claim that they are valuable.

In a discussion of McArthur's critique, Roy Ellen comments:

> But even if we acknowledged the failings of Rappaport and others (among whom I must include myself), there are still very good reasons for anthropologists to collect their own data and for paying some attention to existing data. As with many other fields, data collected in this area by non-specialists may not be as accurate . . . as they might otherwise have been—but they are often the only data that exist. . . . Clearly, there is a need to be enormously careful in choosing samples, selecting methods, and collecting data. But the collection of data always depends upon what is going to be done with them. . . . As in many biological studies, it is more important to focus on a realistic and general model than to be precise. . . . If this is true of physiological work, it must surely also be true in ethnographic work. . . . What is important is to focus on the gross outline structure of energy pathways, control mechanisms, broad relationships and critical ratios of effort and intake according to related social and economic variables. This does not mean that accuracy and careful description are of no consequence. Indeed, it is essential to strive continually for the improvement of field techniques. [1982:116–17]

I cannot object to pleas for more rigorous methods and better data, nor would I deny that the quality of my data could be vastly improved. I nevertheless believe that the quality of the basic data in the area of garden production and *household* consumption—the weights of the various crops harvested and brought to the houses—is relatively high. I have tried to make clear in the original text, in appendices 4, 9, and 10, and now in this appendix, what their shortcomings may be. Taking cognizance of these qualifications and clarifications, students can, I believe, use these data with considerable confidence.

THE PROBLEM OF INDIVIDUAL INTAKE

If the basic consumption data—the weight of crops brought into households—are worthy of considerable confidence, my procedure for assigning portions of the available foodstuffs to the various members of the households is less so. One evening's attempt actually to weigh what each person consumed left me in despair. Although those dining were given individual portions on leaf "plates" everyone also dipped straight into the oven, children ate from the portions of their mothers and fathers, everyone put tubers on the fire individually and then, in as many cases as not, broke morsels from their tubers to give to others. The sheer intrusiveness of inserting the scale between their hands and their mouths, so to speak, was repulsive to me, and it also seemed to me that the attempt was bound to result in deviations from normal consumption. There was, furthermore, no way in which I could sleep in any woman's house, let alone the houses of four of them, to record what they may have snacked upon during the night (and I doubt that very many nutritionists go to such lengths). It was also obviously impossible to follow sixteen people around continually to weigh what they might have eaten away from the house.

To deal with the problem I assigned portions of the total amount of food available to persons in various age and sex categories in ratios derived from suggested caloric allowances published by Venkatachalam (1963) following Langley (1947), both of whom had worked among populations in New Guinea. I reasoned that, whether or not the caloric allowances were realistic, the comparative amounts allowed each category should approximate the comparative amounts they consumed. The procedure, described on pages 282–83, is dubious and I called attention to its fundamental difficulty myself. Be that as it may, on the basis of this procedure I estimated the intakes of members of the various age-sex categories included in the sample. These estimates were reported in table 9 (p. 75).

Georgeda Buchbinder, who made two field trips to the Maring between July 1966 and June 1969, conducted both household and individual consumption studies in nine Maring households, seven among the Tuguma, who are next-door neighbors to the Tsembaga, and two among the Bomagai-Angoiang (1973:98ff.). All food brought home was weighed raw by named variety. Note was made of food intended for pigs, guests, or planting material and these were subtracted from the figures used in the final analysis. Attendance at meals was also recorded "so that individual intakes could be computed in the manner described by Rappaport." In addition, however, Buchbinder also weighed on a portion scale "each individual portion of cooked food eaten by each household member" (p. 99). Each household was under observation for periods of one to two weeks, with two of the Tuguma households restudied after six months.

The Tuguma and Tsembaga are neighbors, allies, and highly intermarried; they "display similar anthropometric characteristics" (Buchbinder, 1973:123). Therefore a comparison of my results with Buchbinder's is important, and is presented in table 32.

Buchbinder states that "because of the fact that actual apportionment studies were done . . . it can safely be assumed that the Tuguma values are more accurate than the Tsembaga ones, and are, in fact, probably typical of both Tuguma and Tsembaga caloric intakes" (1973:124). I generally concur. Disparities between Buchbinder's averages and the values I assigned each category, which are presented in the last column of table 32, may reflect the imprecision of my method. They may also be a function of small sample sizes, however. In any event, our differences are not distressingly large. As her figures give some support to mine so mine support hers, which are also based upon a method that can distort normal consumption.

More significant than disparities between her averages and my estimates is the fact that in all but one of the categories included in the two studies the values I derived lie squarely within the ranges represented in her sample; the sample sizes in the remaining category, 3–5-year-old children, were so small that Buchbinder feels that the difference may not be significant (p. 124). Buchbinder's categories and mine in the 5–10-year-old range are not directly commensurable, but it is nevertheless possible to say that they are not in serious disagreement. The children in my 5–10-year-old category included one boy and one girl, estimated to be 7 or 8 years of age. The figure I allowed for them lies within Buchbinder's ranges for both males and females. Despite the shortcomings of my method, then, the figures that I derived for Tsembaga caloric intake seem to have been realistic.

PROTEIN

As I indicated in the text, I was unable to arrange to have samples of crops grown on Tsembaga territory analyzed for protein, so I was

Table 32. Daily Intake in Calories: Tsembaga (Rappaport) and Tuguma (Buchbinder)

Age-Sex categories	Tsembaga average	Sample size	Tuguma average	Sample size	Tuguma range		Deviation of Tsembaga from Tuguma
					lowest	highest	
Adult males	2575	6	2528	11	1828	3097	+ 1.86%
Adult females	2163	4	2344	9	1463	3017	− 7.72%
Males 10–18		0	1698	7	1440	1824	
Females 10–18	2112	1	1642	5	1011	2291	+28.62%
Children 5–10	1334	2					
Males 5–10			1602	4	1094	2006	− 16.72% [a]
Females 5–10			1401	2	1317	1485	− 4.78% [a]
Children 3–5	1236	2	994	1			+24.34%
Children 0–3	875	1		0			

[a]The Tsembaga figure for children 5–10 is the basis of comparison.

forced to use values appearing in the literature. These appear in column 9 of table 26, pp. 280–81, with the authority from whom they were taken indicated in column 10. Because values varied widely, maximum and minimum percentages of protein content of raw edible portions were presented in column 9, with conversions into pounds of protein available for human consumption provided in columns 11–13, and 15–16.

Two analyses of the protein content of crops grown on Maring territory have been done since the publication of *Pigs for the Ancestors*. First, in the late 1960s, Buchbinder was able to arrange, through the generosity of Dr. Lawrence Malcolm of the Department of Public Health, to have eighty-six tuber samples analyzed. She took them from the territories of six adjacent Maring local groups, running from Tsembaga on the west through the territories of the Tuguma (Mondo), the Kanum-Kaur (Gai), the Kandamdent-Namikai (Nimbra), the Tsengamp-Murimbagai (Tsengamp) and the Fungai-Korama. The samples were collected at approximately similar altitudes, which, although unspecified, must have been a little below 4,000 feet above sea level. The results, which Buchbinder reports in her table 4.4 (p. 110) segregate the samples into three categories: taro, yams, and sweet potato. I summarize Buchbinder's results in table 33. Those interested in greater detail should consult her dissertation (1973:103ff.).

It is immediately apparent that the general averages obtained by Buchbinder all fell outside previously published ranges for New Guinea samples, as did her more particular Tsembaga results. It seems surprising that taro and sweet potato values are below the general range while the yam values are higher. In any event, taro and sweet potatoes are the main constituents of the tuberous portion of the Maring diet—28.8% and 14.0% of the total diet, respectively, according to Buchbinder (1973:104), 25.8% and 21.0% in Tsembaga by my reckoning (see table 8, p. 73). She suggests that "this lower protein value . . . might be enough to make the difference between an adequate diet and one that is deficient in protein" (p. 112).

In 1981 I was able to arrange, through Dr. Peter Heywood, associate director of the Papua New Guinea Institute of Medical Research, to have samples of crops taken for analysis from Tsembaga

Table 33. Protein Content of Root Crops Grown in Various Simbai Maring Locations

Crop	Tsembaga			Simbai: general results					
	Range of % protein values previously published	Sample size	% Protein	Sample size	Average % protein	High % protein	Place	Low % protein	Place
Taro	1.4–1.9	11	.975	47	.95	1.05	Fungai-Korama	.59	Mondo
Yams	1.9–2.0	5	2.040	22	2.32	2.75	Tsengamp	1.90	Fungai-Korama
Sweet potatoes	.9–1.7	5	.750	22	.80	.96	Nimbra	.705	Mondo

Source: Georgeda Buchbinder, 1973.

Table 34. Protein Content of Tsembaga Crops

Protein content (in percentage of raw edible portion)

Common & Latin names	Maring "species"	variety	3900 Grace & Akis	Kakopai 3900 Gau & Apmai	3900 Kap'ka & Yinunk	Jawakai 2400 Grace & Akis	Awerup 3000 Grace & Akis	Nonanungawa 2900 Gau & Apmai	Wimai 2400 Gau & Apmai	Yindokai 4600 War & Pinj	Variety	Species/genus	Range used in 1962–63 estimate
Tubers													
Taro													
Colocasia esculenta	Dong	andambr					.86				.86		
		k'kup					.92				.92		
		alom	1.18*								1.18		
average												.99	1.4–1.9
Chinese taro													
Xanthosoma sagittifolium	Kong		.81			.84			1.21*			.95	1.4–1.9
Sweet potato													
Ipomoea batatas	Ñogai	yamba	1.55*		.94		.83			.68	.92		
		daia					.77	.61		.68	.71		
		aibrup			.69					.51	.51		
average												.81	.9–1.7
Manioc													
Manihot dulcis	Baundi	yipunt	.65				.93	.78			.79	.79	.7–1.2
Yam													
Dioscorea spp.	Tuka			2.32*								1.73	
D. alata & nummularia	Wan	kamban					1.14*						
		apop					1.92				1.92		
		rama					1.44				1.44		
		tamar					.61*				.61		
average (Wan)			1.43								1.43	1.35	
D. bulbifera	Man	kap'ka		1.58								1.58	
average (yams)												1.49	1.9–2.0
Leaves													
Pumpkin leaves (Curcubita pepo)	Ira munga					2.81*			1.46*			2.13	3.8
Sweet potato (Ipomoea batatas)	Ñogai munga	kluo		3.68								3.68	3.6

Food										
Hibiscus (*Hibiscus manihot*)	Cem	gunganaga	4.54	4.26	4.91	4.47			4.54	5.7
Rungia klossi	Čengmba	gore	1.70	1.78		2.19*			1.86	3.8
Tulip (*Gnetum gnemon*)	Tako		6.77*[a]	1.77					2.61	3.8
	Ambiam			2.61					6.77	3.8
Tree fern (*Cyathea* sp.)	Kangup		3.45[b]						3.45	3.8
average (leaves)									3.31	
Grasses & Inflorescences										
Pitpit *Saccharum edule*	Mangap	rumbung			3.69			3.69		
		bewa						4.39		
		kanyang			3.45	3.55		3.50		
		dičing						3.19		
average			4.39*				2.73			
			3.64							4.1
Highland pitpit *Setaria palmaefolia*	Kwiai	kump	.76					.76	3.58	1.4
Sugar cane *Saccharum officinarum*	Bo	ambit'am			.13			.13	.76	
		pa					.12	.12		
		tome					.10	.10		
		kaura			.14		.14	.14	.13	
average									.13	.4
Fruits										
Banana *Musa sapientum*	Yobai	unung		1.50			1.46	1.48		
		bakarai					1.50	1.28		
average					1.05*					
Pumpkin *Curcubita pepo*	Ira		.76						1.38	1.1
									.76	1.5

NOTE: Analysis by Graham Wood, Papua New Guinea Institute of Medical Research. Asterisks indicate that no chemical analysis was done; figures are based on published values.

[a] *Gnetum gnemon* leaves from grove near, but not inside, this garden

[b] *Cyathea* leaves from tree fern stand near, but not inside, this garden

gardens. Accordingly, in June of 1982, Mr. Graham Wood, nutrition-
ist at the Papua New Guinea Institute of Medical Research, spent
two weeks in Tsembaga collecting specimens of important crops from
gardens upon which I was also collecting harvest data. These gardens
were distributed over the range of altitudinal zones, including both
the highest and the lowest on Tsembaga territory. Nineteen of the
samples were collected in the gardens planted at Kakopai in 1981.
This site was the location of the huge *kaiko* garden last planted nineteen years earlier, a garden from which much of the harvest recorded
in *Pigs for the Ancestors* was taken. The results of Mr. Wood's analysis are presented in table 34.

Table 34 speaks for itself. A few points about the data presented
are simply to be emphasized.

First, as in the case of the Buchbinder-Malcolm survey, the protein
contents of Tsembaga *Colocasia, Xanthosoma,* and sweet potato are
well below the range of published values upon which calculations in
Pigs for the Ancestors were based. In contrast to the Buchbinder-
Malcolm figures, the protein contents of yams as well as the other
major tubers are below the published range. Manioc alone stands
inside the range although close to its minimum.

As with the tubers, so with most leaves, inflorescences, sugar cane,
and pumpkin. Only in the cases of bananas, sweet potato leaves, and
Gnetum gnemon leaves do the protein contents of Tsembaga crops
exceed the published values used in the original calculations.

As the most cursory glance at table 34 makes clear, protein content
may vary widely not only within a species, but even within horticultural varieties (see, for instance, the *yamba* variety of sweet potatoes).
There may also be substantial variation within gardens, although this
isn't as clear. Some of the factors affecting the protein content of tubers seem to be highly localized and samples are small. Thus, although
the results of chemical analysis of local specimens are much to be
preferred to published values, they are nevertheless to be accepted
only with caution as representative of the protein content of local
crops generally.

With all these reservations in mind, we may consider recalcula-
tions of total protein consumption by the Tomegai clan for the period
March 11–November 8, 1963, using protein values from the 1982
analysis by the Institute of Medical Research. The new estimates are

presented in table 35. For ease of comparison with the earlier estimates based upon published values (table 26, pp. 280–81) results for certain crops (e.g., leaves) will be aggregated in the same way.

The total of 271.87 pounds now estimated to have been the protein content of foods consumed by the Tomegai is well below the earlier minimum estimate—in fact it is only 83.65% of that amount. It is therefore necessary to reduce proportionately the earlier estimates of protein intake by age and sex categories. At the same time, we may correct the procedure adopted in the original study for allocating to each category the proportion of available food each of its members consumed. The ratios in the text followed those of suggested caloric allowances for various age and sex categories as published by Venkatachalam, following Langley. We may use, instead, ratios based on averages for actual portions served to members of each category in Tuguma, as weighed by Buchbinder and as summarized in table 32 above. Table 36, then, corrects both the protein content of raw foodstuffs and the proportions served within each category.

To summarize, revisions in the protein content of Tsembaga crops and the proportions in which available food was apportioned lead to the conclusion that the protein intake of the Tomegai was significantly lower than originally estimated.

DIETARY ADEQUACY

We may now turn to the question of the nutritional status of the Maring. As I indicated in the text, I was unable to arrange for clinical examinations of the Tsembaga by any qualified person. I therefore based a judgment upon, first, what I took to be the quality of the diet through a comparison of nutrient intakes, as I calculated them, with published standards, and second, upon such observations (explicitly impressionistic) as I had made of people's general appearances (see pp. 77ff.). McArthur takes me to task on both counts and also takes the occasion to consider at some length the "recommendations," "allowances," and "safe levels" published by various agencies and authorities.

Most fundamental are questions concerning the nature of published standards themselves. They are often based upon studies of

Table 35. Total Protein Intake, Tomegai Clan, March 11–November 8, 1963

Crop	Edible portion for humans: lbs. weighed	% Protein IMR Av.	Protein ingested by humans: lbs. weighed portion	Factor for additional intake	Total protein ingested by humans lbs. weighed + estimate	Totals
Roots						
Sweet potato	3512.23	.81	28.44	5	29.86	
Xanthosoma	1192.80	.95	11.33	5	11.90	
Colocasia	3159.54	.99	31.27	5	32.83	
Manioc	194.29	.79	1.53	5	1.61	
Yams	1641.60	1.73	28.39	5	29.80	
Total roots						106.00
Trees						
Banana	1139.32	1.38	15.72	20	18.86	
*Artocarpus**	52.75	1.0	.53		.53	
*Marita**	370.45	3.7	13.71	25	17.14	
Total trees						36.53
Miscellaneous						
Corn*	2.47	3.7	.09	5	.10	
Peas & beans*	4.51	8.1	.37		.37	
Pumpkin	136.67	.76	1.04		1.04	
Gourd*	9.35	1.3	.11		.11	
Total misc.						1.62

Leaves						
Hibiscus	1305.06	4.54	59.25	2	60.44	
Rungia klossi	300.91	1.86	5.60	2	5.71	
Sweet potato leaves	131.34	3.68	4.83	2	4.93	
Other greens[a]	232.28	4.24	9.85	2	10.05	
Total leaves						81.13
Grasses & inflorescences						
Pitpit-dičing	575.31	3.19	18.35	2	18.72	
Pitpit, others	548.41	3.77	20.67	2	21.08	
Setaria	176.43	.76	1.34	2	1.37	
Total grasses & inflorescences						41.17
Refreshers						
Sugar cane	935.55	.13	1.22	200	3.66	
Cucumber*		.6	1.17	50	1.76	
Total refreshers						5.42
Total, all sources						271.87

NOTES: Based upon chemical analysis by Graham Wood, Papua New Guinea Institute of Medical Research, 1982. Asterisks indicate that no chemical analysis was done; figures are based on published values.

[a]Value used is the average of pumpkin leaves, *Cyathea*, *Tako*, and *Gnetum gnemon*.

Table 36. Protein Content of Vegetable Portion of the Tomegai Diet

Category	Sample size	Trophic units[a]	Estimated daily protein consumption[b] grams	Original estimates daily protein intake[c] min. grams	max. grams	Buchbinder Tuguma estimates[d] grams
Adult males	6	25.28	35.64	43.20	58.20	39.20
Adult females	4	23.44	33.05	36.30	48.90	43.40
Males 10–18	0	—	—	—	—	23.50
Females 10–18	1	16.42	23.15	35.40	47.30	27.30
Children 5–10	2	15.02	21.17	22.70	30.30	27.40
Children 3–5	2	9.94	14.01	20.70	28.00	14.40
Children 0–3	1	8.75	12.34	14.70	19.80	—

NOTE: Revised 1984 on the basis of chemical analysis by Graham Wood of the Papua New Guinea Institute of Medical Research and the Tuguma survey of Georgeda Buchbinder.

[a] Revised following Buchbinder.
[b] Revised following Wood and Buchbinder.
[c] See table 9, page 75.
[d] Buchbinder, 1973:120.

well-fed populations differing markedly from those whose diets we are concerned to assess. McArthur also points out that as far as protein requirements or standards for international use are concerned, "the FAO/WHO committees base these on average physiological needs, which are estimates of intakes required to maintain nitrogen balance and normal growth. However, harmful or beneficial effects have not been demonstrated if the amount of protein eaten is far above the probable need. Consequently the committees have tended to err on the generous side. Instead of recommending average figures, as they do for calories, they estimate the mean plus twice the standard deviation, enough to cover practically everybody in the population" (1974: 101). She cites Dubos in this general regard; his observations are worth repeating here:

> Immense numbers of human beings all over the world remain healthy and vigorous on diets that are considered grossly deficient by nutritionists. . . . This paradoxical state of affairs can be explained in part by more efficient use of foodstuffs in underprivileged populations. . . . In addition . . . there are biological adaptations such as the biosynthesis of essential growth factors. . . . Of greater interest and importance probably is the fact that man and animals can develop truly metabolic adaptations to a wide range of nutritional changes, both qualitative and quantitative. [1965:81–82]

I noted (p. 77) that Langley's recommendations were derived from experimental work on Caucasians and that Langley herself pointed to their "wide margin of safety." I therefore suggested that, in the absence of more widespread and pronounced symptoms of protein deficiency, they seemed "unrealistically high," that is, too high to construe as *requirements* for the Maring. This seems to be in accord with McArthur's discussion.

I did not make the same point about the 1964 FAO/WHO requirements, which were much lower for children. McArthur notes that the FAO/WHO standards were changed in 1973 to what are called "safe" levels of protein intake: "These are intended to exceed the actual physiological need of all but a small minority of people. Rappaport seems to have taken as his standards the average protein 'requirements' suggested by the 1965 FAO/WHO committee, but for children over ten years and for adults these now exceed the most recently suggested 'safe' levels" (1974:101–02). Her generally objurgatory tone suggests that I am somehow at fault for failing to consider in an account published in 1968 changes in standards published in 1973. Leaving aside the validity of her remarks as criticism the general warning is well taken: not only may standards change; expert opinion on the *very nature* of standards may change.

In fact, in a passage that McArthur cites, the 1973 FAO/WHO report includes its own warning about the use of a protein standard: "The safe level of protein intake can . . . be used to obtain preliminary information on the adequacy of the protein intake of individuals as well as groups of persons, but should never be used as the sole basis for the evaluation of nutritional status. For the latter purpose other criteria, such as clinical and biological examinations, are also needed" (FAO/WHO, 1973:11).

I was aware of this, and I acknowledged that "a clinical assessment of the nutritive status of the children would have indicated more clearly than the comparison of estimated intakes to standard recommendations whether or not there was sufficient protein in their diets" (p. 77). However, I was not able to have such examinations done. I therefore presented my impressions, such as they were, to augment a dietary evaluation which the FAO/WHO, in a passage cited by McArthur herself, states to have at least preliminary value. I shall note here that these impressions are in line with Heywood's recent characterization of "initial diets (diets previous to the incorporation of Western elements)" in Papua New Guinea generally. Using the percentage of energy derived from protein (PE %) as an index of dietary quality, Heywood states that highland PE percentages were generally lower than those in coastal and riverine regions, and "in all but a few areas the initial PE % was below the estimated requirements" (1981:22).

Two problems besetting the way I attempted to make the case for the marginality (at best) of Maring children's intake may not be sufficiently explicit in McArthur's critique. The first is a statistical matter. I came close to falling into what statisticians call "the ecological fallacy," that is, using aggregated data and standards and averages derived from them (for instance, Langley and FAO/WHO recommendations) to assess the status of individuals. The second problem is a substantive matter. Diet is one thing and nutritional status is another because factors exogenous to the diet enter into the processes affecting the nutritional status of any individual. Some of these factors are environmental (e.g., air temperature); activity level is also, of course, important, as is infection. (For a general discussion on the subject see the National Academy of Sciences' *Proceedings of a Workshop: Impact of Infection on the Nutritional Status of the Host,* 1977.) It is doubtful, to say the least, that nutritional status can ever be reliably determined without examination of individuals' physical conditions. This is not to say, however, that it is useless to estimate nutrient contents of diets, even on an aggregated basis and assessing them by comparison with the published recommendations of such authorities as the expert committees impaneled by FAO/WHO. If the diet seems to meet or exceed whatever the standard or safe level may be, but the nutritional condition of the population, or some segment of it, seems poor, we are obviously led to ask why.

It is well established that infection and injury increase protein and caloric requirements. Hornstein, in his introduction to the National Academy of Sciences' *Proceedings* (1977), notes two "key nutrition-related health problems" in less developed countries. There is, first, "the inefficient use of food energy and nutrients, owing to widespread infections which impede intestinal absorption of nutrients and fevers which increase body metabolism and accelerate caloric and protein use." The second key problem, poor "health delivery capability" contributes to the first (1977:1204). Whereas Dubos observed that immense numbers of people seem to thrive on diets well below FAO/WHO recommendations, the problem of the Maring seemed just the opposite: they seemed not to thrive on what appeared to be—at least in comparison with the diets of other New Guinea populations—a rather decent intake. (Recalculation of the apportionment of household food intakes among consumers of various age and sex categories and analysis of the protein content of various crops have required reevaluation as discussed earlier in this appendix, but at the time the diet appeared to be comparatively good. Now it seems less so.)

A first question, of course, is whether my impressions of the nutritional status of the Tsembaga approximated reality. I suggested that children in particular were, as it were, barely getting by, as far as protein was concerned, but I saw no signs of gross malnutrition—nothing that I recognized as marasmus or kwashiorkor.

It is in a sense presumptuous to say that Buchbinder's work in the Simbai Valley in the late 1960s and early 1970s generally supports my impressions; her work on nutritional status was so much more detailed, systematic, and rigorous than mine. With the help of Dr. John Stanhope, an epidemiologist from the Public Health Department of the Territory of Papua and New Guinea, she undertook a clinical examination of virtually the entire Simbai Maring population. A large number of blood samples were collected for hemoglobin and haptoglobin analysis, and Buchbinder did an anthropometric survey of the entire population. The results of her work are presented in her unpublished dissertation (Columbia, 1973) and in a number of articles (Buchbinder, 1976, 1977; Buchbinder and Clark, 1971). Here I can do no more than summarize a few of her more salient results. She found certain health problems to be widespread in the area. These included protein-calorie malnutrition, malaria, severe symptoms of iodine deficiency, and respiratory infections. Signs and symptoms of protein deficiency included relatively high incidences of liver enlargement and enlargement of the parotids (which, she notes [1973:150], some but by no means all workers take to be, simply, an adaptation to high starch intake). She also believes the diminutive size of Maring adults to be in some degree a result of stunting from malnutrition. Evidence of protein deficiency among children included hair signs, depigmentation, edema, and muscle wasting. She also saw five cases of frank kwashiorkor, one in Tsembaga, two in Tuguma, and two in Gai immediately to the east of the Tuguma (1973:150). Twenty-two percent of the 0–5-year-olds in Tsembaga and 23.5% of those in Tuguma showed signs of protein-calorie malnutrition in 1968 (1977:118). These figures do not include all of those whose growth seemed retarded. She observes that growth retardation, which is considered by Jelliffe (1966) to be "the first sign of protein-calorie malnutrition," is common. Judging by a number of criteria (1973:152ff.), she suggests that "it is likely that the Simbai Maring, and particularly those in the northwest, are among the most slowly growing people in the world. There is enough evidence to suggest that at least a large component of their short stature is due to nutritional stunting as a result of protein and iodine deficiency" (1973:214ff.).

A word concerning the iodine deficiency that she observed, but I did not, is necessary. It is certainly possible that some symptoms of iodine deficiency escaped my untrained eye, but I don't think frank goiter or widespread cretinism would have. Be this as it may, severe symptoms of iodine deficiency were prevalent in the late 1960s. Buchbinder (1976) takes it to have been in large measure a result of the use of noniodized commercial salt, a practice introduced soon after my departure from the field which prevailed for a few years before being corrected.

The appearance of severe iodine deficiency symptoms among the Simbai Maring between 1964 and 1968 may have contributed to a more general deterioration in health during that period. This possibility gets some support from the continuation of the general population decline that seemed to have commenced well before I arrived in 1962. According to Buchbinder, the decline proceeded at a rate between − .8 and − .9 per annum from 1963 to 1968, possibly accelerating toward the end of that period. Among the Tuguma, who numbered 255 in August 1966, forty-three died by May 1969, including nine of the twelve children born (1977:121). "Most deaths resulted from an acute respiratory infection, most probably influenza followed by pneumonia, and the course of the illness was extremely rapid. Most of those who died of this infection did so within 24–48 hours after the onset of symptoms (1977:121f.). She believes that death rate would have been higher had she not been there to administer antibiotics and to help people to the aid post.

Addressing the problem of "why the Maring appear to be suffering more from protein malnutrition than some highlands populations, like the Chimbo and Enga who have diets lower in protein," Buchbinder argues that there is a synergism among protein deficiency, iodine deficiency, malaria, and respiratory infections (1973:214ff.). To put this a little differently, what would have been adequate protein intake for healthy individuals was inadequate for people suffering from both chronic and acute infections and from other deficiencies. In the presence of such stresses, symptoms of protein deficiency develop where otherwise they would not. Having developed, protein deficiency weakens resistance to further infection. To put this yet another way, infection, fever, and injury as well increase protein requirements.

If, during the period of my fieldwork, iodine deficiency were contributing less, or not at all, to the deadly synergism of which Buchbinder speaks, then protein deficiency may not have been quite as serious a problem then as it was later. If infections of foreign origin, such as the respiratory diseases that Buchbinder found to be so lethal, were even less prevalent in precontact times the protein content of the diet would have been yet more adequate in those days. It may be that my characterization of the protein content of the Tsembaga diet as "marginal" made it seem better than it was. I did not, at any rate, mean to suggest that the nutritional status was very good when I was there; it was probably even worse than I took it to be. In general, however, there is a high degree of agreement between my assessment of their nutritional state and the findings of Buchbinder's rigorous examinations of the people themselves.

THE KILLING OF PIGS, THE CONSUMPTION OF PORK, AND INTERGROUP RELATIONS

We may now turn to the place of pork in the Maring diet and social relations. I argued (pp. 78ff.) that in view of "the fact that there is some [protein deficiency] pathology" the contexts in which the Tsembaga consume the limited amounts of domestic pork available to them in *nonfestival years* (p. 84) may be a matter of physiological significance. McArthur misunderstood crucial aspects of my argument and references to her critique by other commentators indicate that they may have followed her into misunderstanding. I shall, therefore, summarize the proposal here.

1. Although misfortunes sometimes do strike pigs directly, and although some are killed in nonfestival as well as festival years for presentation to affines and a few others may be sacrificed during such periods in connection with rituals having nothing to do with misfortune (pp. 155f.), in nonfestival years the sacrifice of significant numbers is demanded for the performance of rituals associated with human misfortune and emergency. Because I was in residence during a festival year this statement stood upon the word of informants.

2. It is plausible that misfortunes and emergencies—in particular illness and injury, but also death and warfare—are occasions of physiological stress. During stress protein-deficient organisms are at greater risk than those not suffering from such deficiencies largely because protein metabolism is accelerated at the same time that its absorption may be impeded and some protein may be lost directly (as from a wound). All of this seemed well established previous to the publication of *Pigs for the Ancestors* (see references cited on pp. 85f.). I do

not now, nor have I ever, claimed expertise in this area, but it does seem to me that recent work has generally corroborated and elaborated the earlier findings. (See the National Academy of Sciences' *Proceedings of a Workshop: Impact of Infection on the Nutritional Status of the Host*, 1977—Keusch, Beisel, Rosenberg et al., Pawanda, Wannemacher, Masoro, Blackburn, Long, and Long et al.)

3. I then argued that "the practice of killing and consuming pigs in connection with emergency and misfortune tends to provide physiological reinforcement when it is needed to those who need it" (p. 87), and thus is an effective way to make use of the limited amounts of pork available. I cited authorities advocating increased protein intake for postoperative patients and for those suffering from infection (pp. 85f.). Again, more recent work seems generally to reinforce that earlier dietary recommendation (see *Proceedings of a Workshop*, especially articles by Bishrian, Long, Blackburn, Waterlow et al., Golden et al., Wilmore et al., Mueller et al., and Feigen) and to elaborate it (for instance, with recommendations for increased requirements subsequent to recovery for "catch-up" growth; see especially Whitehead et al., *Proceedings of a Workshop*).

Although the principle of feeding high-quality protein to those suffering from injury, infection, or sepsis seems well established I did speak with more assurance than was warranted when I proposed that "the contribution of pork to the Tsembaga diet thus seems to be of much greater importance than is indicated by the amounts actually consumed." I qualified this assertion by declaring that "this formulation must remain hypothetical only" until "appropriate physiological tests" are undertaken (p. 87). I also indicated (p. 83n) that precise data on when pigs are actually killed and who eats them were also necessary, but were lacking because I was there at the time of a *kaiko*.

4. Given the practice of killing pigs at times of misfortune or emergency, the amount of time necessary to accumulate enough pigs to repay ancestors and allies for their aid in the last round of warfare is affected by the general well-being of their owners. If they are frequently afflicted the herd will grow slowly or not at all. If they are generally well it will grow rapidly. The Maring recognize this, saying that if a place is "good" it doesn't take many years to accumulate sufficient pigs, but if a place is "bad" it takes longer. Over the long

run, however, the natural increase of the pig population will exceed the ongoing ritual demand, and eventually there will be enough pigs to fulfill debts to ancestors and allies.

5. Although pigs dedicated to ancestors but presented to allies (who are, largely, affines and maternal kin) are obviously being put to social ends, I stated that the number required is not socially stipulated (pp. 153f.). I argued that there are sufficient pigs to repay debts to both the living and the dead when either (a) the labor required to support them becomes too burdensome (pp. 157ff.) or (b) their depredations become intolerable (pp. 160 ff.). Such a herd represents a surplus of animals *over ongoing ritual demands* which are, in significant degree, associated with misfortune. The population dynamics of the pigs, especially the speed with which a "sufficiency" is achieved, is taken by the Maring to be an index of the general well-being, competence, or prosperity of the group. This state has a health component: by and large people are sufficiently healthy for the natural increase of the pig population to exceed ritual demands for pig sacrifices. It has an ecological-agronomic component: gardening and animal husbandry have been sufficiently successful to raise a large number of pigs. Last, but far from least, it has a social, economic, and political component: the local group is capable of meeting its obligations to affines, cognates, and any others who have been its allies and it is thus free to initiate warfare once again.

6. There was no claim, nor did I mean to claim, that the consumption of pigs sacrificed during the *kaiko* ameliorated increases in nutritional deficiencies resulting from stress such as infection, sepsis, injury, death of a near kin, or warfare. I did not and would not claim that the *kaiko* was a time of stress. The pork resulting from the sacrifices during the *kaiko* represented a *surplus, by which was meant an amount over that required for stress-related rituals.* This seemed to me obvious in *Pigs for the Ancestors*, but might have been enunciated more clearly in an earlier article in which I stated that the ritual cycle "distributes local surpluses of pig throughout the regional population in the form of pork, and assures people of high quality protein when they are most in need of it" (1967:29).

That McArthur misunderstood crucial aspects of the argument is clearly indicated when she comments on what she takes to be my hypothesis: "Obviously ritual also dictates the killing of pigs at the year-long activities associated with this festival, and though he does not mention his hypothesis when he describes the resulting distribution of meat, I can see no reason why it should not apply also to this pork" (1974:113). She then proceeds to demonstrate that much of the protein in the pork consumed by the Tsembaga at the *kaiko* was wasted. That is, over 70% would have been deaminated (with the residue simply burnt as energy). I agree. It is probable that much of it was, in that sense, wasted and I never claimed otherwise. I must note, however, that her citation in this connection of Luzbatek's observation of men gorging themselves with ten pounds of pork in a single day is inapposite. The Maring do nothing of the kind.

In sum, my claim was much more limited than McArthur took it to be. I did not claim that *all* pork was eaten when it was most needed, but rather that when pork was most needed the conventions of slaughter and consumption assured its availability. I did not claim that the conventions of pig sacrifice and pork consumption represented the nutritionally best possible use of the limited amount of pork the Maring were capable of raising. It is doubtful that more regular slaughter of the animals at younger ages would have resulted in a significant improvement in the daily diet, but it is possible. This leads to a more important point. I did not claim that the slaughter of pigs and the distribution and consumption of the resulting pork was to be understood only in nutritional terms. That the growth and sacrifice of the pig herd and the distribution of the resulting flesh were central to the regulation of relations between groups is part of the book's main argument. It is obvious, however, that economically and (possibly) nutritionally more "rational" conventions regarding pig sacrifice and pork consumption (such as killing and consuming animals as soon as they reach full growth) would have made it impossible for herd dynamics to play the role that they did in intergroup relations. That some of the protein content of the protein consumed in the form of pork at *kaiko* was wasted (i.e., deaminated) is indisputable, and I never denied this. Such "waste" can, however, be regarded as part of the price of a ritual that, on the one hand, used pig demography in the regulation of intergroup relations and, on the other hand, as I asserted, went far to assure the availability of high-quality protein when needed.

The final question becomes whether or not pork consumption in nonfestival years occurs at times and in ways that provide high-quality protein when people are most in need of it.

Buchbinder (1973:225ff.) has been critical of my argument generally. She argues that from a "strictly biological or nutritional point of view there is no surplus pork among the Maring." She points out that the Tsinginai and Fogaikumpf slaughter pigs one at a time as they become fully grown, and observes that, "from a nutritional as well as an ecological point of view, it would make better sense for the Maring to kill and eat their pigs as they become mature rather than to wait for ceremonial occasions to occur" (p. 226).

I have already indicated what I meant by "surplus," namely excess over ongoing ritual demands, not over nutritional needs. Indeed, my general argument assumed that a good diet would have included much more meat. The question was, given the high value and scarcity of pork, whether killing and consuming pigs on occasions associated with physiological stress was nutritionally more advantageous than eating them as they matured.

Fundamental to the argument, of course, are data concerning consumption patterns in nonfestival years, something which I could not provide but that Buchbinder could. She reports (1973:226ff.) that in the year 1967–68, 184 pigs were consumed by all of the Simbai Maring populations. Of these, forty-seven (25.6%) were killed in connection with human illness, only sixteen being killed for sick females. Of the remainder, she reports that fifteen were killed because they were damaging gardens or appeared likely to do so; twenty-four were killed to celebrate the return of men working on plantations; eighteen were used for affinal payments; eighteen were killed in connection with funerary rites and payments long after death. The remaining sixty-two "were used for a variety of non–stress related purposes; this number included pigs that died of illness or accident. Pigs that die of natural causes may be consumed, usually by women and children" (p. 227). Buchbinder believes that her survey underreports the number of pigs killed in all local communities except Mondo, where she was in residence with the Tuguma, who killed twenty-four pigs, yielding an estimated 1,680 pounds of pork for an average of 7.2 pounds of flesh per capita. This was the second highest among the Simbai groups, being exceeded only by the people at Gunts (Bomagai-Angoiang and Fungai-Korama). She suggests that the large numbers of animals killed at Tuguma might have been in part a function of her presence, for she would sometimes buy fresh pork if it were available, and in part a function of illness. "Mondo was hit most severely by the influenza epidemic in 1968 and a number of pigs were killed in an attempt to appease the angry spirits" (p. 130).

Buchbinder's data do not settle the general argument concerning the value of pork consumption among the Maring in stress-related situations in earlier times. By the time Buchbinder visited the field the patterns for killing and consuming pigs had evidently changed radically. In 1962–63, not a single Maring from the southern wall of the Simbai Valley had returned from work on plantations (indeed, only two Tsembaga had even gone out to work). By 1967–68 the return of workers provided one of the most important occasions for killing pigs. By 1967–68 the *kaiko* associated with the last round of warfare had been completed; with pacification and the coming of Christianity the future of the *kaiko* cycle as an institution was uncertain. This may have had the effect of increasing the number of brideprice payments made during that year. Furthermore, Buchbinder does not tell us just how many of the sixty-two pigs "used for a variety of non–stress related purposes" died of natural causes. My suggestion concerning the *deliberate* killing of animals was not intended to cover such deaths, nor, for that matter, to cover the "execution" of pigs for invading or threatening to invade gardens. If we exclude the fifteen "executed" animals, and a *very* conservatively estimated thirty that may have died of natural causes, then those killed in connection with stress would have been 34% of those deliberately killed by their owners. If (as is more likely) fifty had died natural deaths, 43% of the deliberately killed would have been sacrificed at times of illness. If we also exclude the twenty-four killed upon the return of workers, a use to which *no* pigs were put in 1962–63 or in earlier times, those killed in connection with stress would have been 55% of the total. It also may be that at least some of the eighteen pigs killed for affinal payments in 1967–68 would have lived until the next *kaiko* if people could have looked forward with confidence to such an event's occurrence. In sum, Buchbinder's figures suggest that in 1962–63 and earlier 55–70% of the pigs killed in nonfestival years were killed in circumstances that could have been construed as stress-related.

I surveyed Tsembaga pigs in November 1981 and again during the months of June and July of 1982. During that period thirty-seven pigs, almost all less than three months old, died of natural causes. Most of these were eaten. Forty-one pigs were killed. Of these fourteen were given as affinal payments, twelve remaining within Tsembaga. Three were killed as *acek konč* (taboo pig) in association with these affinal payments (killed and dedicated to the groom's ancestors and consumed by the groom's sub-clan previous to presenting brideprice pigs to the bride's kin). Five were killed for invading gardens or damaging houses, the flesh of one of which was sold to the public. One was killed when a young man left to work on the coast, another to abrogate interdining taboos which would have prevented a young boy whose mother came from Tsevent from staying with the Tuguma while attending school. Another was killed by its owner because it was becoming feral. One pig was killed by its owner in a fit of pique after his wife insulted him (she was very fond of that pig; it was eaten at the men's house and she was denied a portion). A court awarded another, belonging to a young married couple, to compensate the husband's mother who had been insulted by her daughter-in-law.

Of the remaining fourteen pigs killed, eleven were sacrificed in connection with illness, three with death. The number may have been unusually small. There were only three deaths among the Tsembaga during my residence and few of the illnesses suffered were deemed life threatening. The establishment of an aid post in Kinimbong (a little over an hour's walk from Tsembaga) may have had a beneficial effect and I also treated minor infections, dispensed antimalarials, and so forth. (This permitted me to monitor local health.)

The three deceased were an infant, a man in his mid-fifties, and a middle-aged woman. All three died during a two-week period in early March, a time of very heavy rains and much minor respiratory infection. I had left the field for a few days on February 28th, but could not return until March 16th because the rains had closed the local airstrips. The infant and the elderly man, Ar, died during my absence. The woman, Duimba, died the morning after I returned. Another man, gravely ill at the time, survived.

Of the three sacrifices associated with death, two took place at *Gimbai* rituals six weeks or so after the passing of the deceased. They should not, therefore, be associated with whatever stresses afflict those close to the victim at the time of death. The third pig was killed the day after Duimba died. It was given in its entirety to her brother, a Tsengamp man, who took all of the pork back to his own group.

Duimba, an exceptionally strong and apparently healthy woman of about forty, was reported to have become ill on the evening of March 14th, dying on the morning of the 17th. Her symptoms were not respiratory. She was said to have had a high fever and aching head and to have been drowsy or comatose much of the time. Cerebral malaria is a strong possibility. No pigs were killed before she died. Her grief-stricken husband said he had thought she was recovering when she passed away.

Two brothers, Ar and Kumuwai, of the Wendekai sub-clan of the Merkai clan, had become ill a few days earlier. Their symptoms were respiratory. Ar's illness commenced between March 3rd and March 5th. Three pigs were killed for him before he died, on March 8th, 10th, and on the evening of March 11th. He ate none of the latter, and died on the morning of March 12th. Of the earlier two, he ate of the heart, kidneys, kidney fat, lung, and some flesh. I do not know how much he ate. All Merkai and Kwibagai (who live close to the Merkai) received at least a small portion of the pig killed on March 8th (so that all would be kindly disposed to Ar). It was not a very large pig, probably weighing between seventy-five and one hundred pounds. The pigs subsequently killed were largely consumed by Merkai-Wendekai, but there was no rule (contrary to my statement in *Pigs for the Ancestors* on pp. 83f.) restricting the consumption of the flesh to a narrow circle of kin. Kumuwai, Ar's brother, became ill around March 10th. Three pigs were also killed on his account, two while he was still deemed to be gravely ill. Ar's death may have encouraged early sacrifice: the first was killed the day that Ar died, the second on March 14th or 15th. Kumuwai is reported to have eaten internal organs (heart, kidneys, lungs). The last pig was killed on April 1st when it was generally assumed that Kumuwai was on his way to recovery. Kumuwai, with two other Merkai-Wendekai of his generation and his matrilocal sister's son (who lives with him) ate flesh from the head. He himself ate the brain and kidneys. The remaining flesh was distributed in a manner which provided all Merkai and Kwibagai with portions, and the Tomegai also received small amounts of pork from this animal, as did the local evangelist and I.

During his illness, then, Kumuwai had protein in the form of flesh available to him every day. What he consumed consisted in significant part of organ meat. On occasions that I was with him he did not eat a great deal.

Three animals, all small, were killed for the illnesses of three children. In the case of one (a boy of about eighteen months who had not been growing well and who had been subject to coughs and fevers) the child himself ate none of the pork. In the cases of the other two, boys of three and four years of age, the children did have pork to eat for three days, and so did their siblings.

Two animals remain to be accounted for. A medium-sized pig was killed for a woman who suffered an eye infection and a very large animal was sacrificed for a man who was suffering from severe lower-back pain. In both of these instances the animals were killed when the sufferers were clearly on the road to recovery.

What can be said in summary? It seems clear that neither Buchbinder's data nor mine are sufficient either to substantiate or to invalidate the proposal that the conventions of the ritual cycle assure that high-quality protein will be available when it is most needed. A significant proportion of the pigs reported killed by Buchbinder and by me were killed under such circumstances, and I have suggested that both her data and mine indicate that the proportion would have been higher during earlier times and during times when illness is more prevalent.

Much more problematic than the matter of availability is that of the actual patterns of consumption. In no case was it possible for me actually to weigh the amount of flesh eaten by the afflicted person, but the amounts consumed were certainly not large, and may not have always been timely. My belief is that the ritual regulation of pork consumption may have enhanced the diets of the afflicted but that such direct nutritional benefits were rather haphazard and may have been slight. I now think that I put too much emphasis upon possible nutritional advantages of Maring practice in the original formulation.

As Buchbinder and others have argued, it might have been sounder from a strictly nutritional point of view to kill pigs when they became mature than to follow Maring practice (although it also may be that even then pork consumption could not have contributed significantly to the diet on a regular basis). I must reiterate, however, a point clearly made in the book, that Maring sacrificial conventions were part of a ritual cycle regulating intergroup relations as well as consumption. The nutritional consequences must be judged in that context.

Finally, McArthur scolds me for "offering 'solutions' to problems that baffle specialists" and for attempting more than an "individual working alone could successfully carry out" (1974:123). I offered no nutritional solutions, only suggestions and hypotheses. Her stricture against attempting "more than one can successfully carry out" has a chilling effect upon some facets of ecological research, and I believe my efforts, although not fully successful, were more fruitful than her critique was willing to grant. The harvest data are good and adjustments based upon the work of Buchbinder and Wood have improved the consumption data. I do not advocate amateurism but sometimes—often—anthropologists do have to work alone, and sometimes they must try to do things for which they have had little or no training because if they don't do it it won't be done. My reach, as the saying goes, did exceed my grasp—but shouldn't we reach?

BIBLIOGRAPHY FOR THE 1968 EDITION

Albanese, Anthony A., and Louise A. Orto, 1964. The proteins and amino acids, *Modern Nutrition in Health and Disease*, 3d ed. Michael G. Wohl and Robert S. Goodhart, eds. Philadelphia, Lee and Febiger.

Allan, W., 1949. *Studies in African Land Usage in Northern Rhodesia*. Rhodes-Livingstone Papers #15. Livingstone, Northern Rhodesia, The Rhodes-Livingstone Institute.

Allee, W. C., et al., 1949. *Principles of Animal Ecology*. Philadelphia, Saunders.

Andrewartha, H. E., 1961. *Introduction to the Study of Animal Populations*. Chicago, University of Chicago.

Axelrod, A. E., 1964. Nutrition in relation to acquired immunity, *Modern Nutrition in Health and Disease*, 3d ed. Michael G. Wohl and Robert S. Goodhart, eds. Philadelphia, Lee and Febiger.

Bateson, Gregory, 1936. *Naven*. Cambridge, Eng., Cambridge University.

Berg, Clarence, 1948. Protein deficiency and its relationship to nutritional anemia, hypoproteinemia, nutritional edema, and resistance to infection, *Proteins and Amino Acids in Nutrition*. Melville Sahyun, ed. New York, Reinhold.

Bierstadt, Robert, 1950. An analysis of social power, *American Sociological Review*, 15:730–38.

Birdsell, J., 1958. On population structure in generalized hunting and collecting populations, *Evolution*, 12:189–205.

Blest, A. D., 1961. The concept of ritualisation, *Current Problems in Animal Behavior*. W. H. Thorpe and O. L. Zangwill, eds. Cambridge, Eng., Cambridge University.

Brookfield, H. C., 1964. The ecology of highland settlement: some suggestions, *American Anthropologist*, vol. 66, no. 4, part 2, pp. 20–39.

Brookfield, H. C., and Paula Brown, 1958. Chimbu land and society, *Oceania*, 30:1–75.

——— 1963. *Struggle for Land*. Melbourne, Australia, Oxford University.

Bulmer, Ralph, 1960. Political aspects of the Moka ceremonial exchange system among the Kyaka people of the western highlands of New Guinea, *Oceania*, 31:1–13.

———— 1965. The Kyaka of the western highlands, *Gods, Ghosts and Men in Melanesia*. P. Lawrence and M. J. Meggitt, eds. Melbourne, Australia, Oxford University.

Bulmer, Susan and Ralph, 1964. The prehistory of the Australian New Guinea highlands, *American Anthropologist*, vol. 66, no. 4, part 2, pp. 39–76.

Bunzel, Ruth, 1938. The economic organization of primitive peoples, *General Anthropology*. Franz Boas, ed. New York, Heath.

Burkill, Isaac Henry, 1935. *A Dictionary of the Economic Products of the Malay Peninsula*. London, published on behalf of the governments of the Straits Settlements and Federated Malay States by the crown agents for the colonies.

Burton, Benjamin T., ed., 1959. *The Heinz Handbook of Nutrition*. New York, McGraw-Hill.

Carneiro, Robert L., 1956. Slash and burn agriculture: a closer look at its implications for settlement patterns, *Selected Papers of the Fifth International Congress of Anthropological and Ethnological Sciences*. A. F. C. Wallace, ed. Philadelphia.

———— 1964. Shifting cultivation among the Amahuaca of eastern Peru, *Volkerkundliche Abhandlungen*. Band I. Niedersachsisches Landesmuseum Hannover Abteilung fur Volkerkunde.

Chappell, John, 1966. Stone ax factories in the highlands of East New Guinea, *Proceedings of the Prehistoric Society*, 32: 96–121.

Chapple, E. D., and C. S. Coon, 1942, *Principles of Anthropology*. New York, Holt.

Clarke, William, 1966. From extensive to intensive shifting cultivation: A succession from New Guinea, *Ethnology*, 5:347–59.

Clausen, Hjalmar, and Claude Gerwig, 1958. *Pig Breeding, Recording and Progeny Testing in European Countries*. FAO Agricultural Studies #44. Rome, Food and Agriculture Organization of the United Nations.

Collins, Paul, 1965. Functional analyses in the symposium "Man, culture, and animals," *Man, Culture, and Animals*. Anthony Leeds and Andrew P. Vayda, eds. Washington, D. C., American Association for the Advancement of Science 78.

Conklin, H. C., 1957. *Hanunoo Agriculture in the Philippines*. FAO Forestry Development Paper #12. Rome, Food and Agriculture Organization of the United Nations.

———— 1961. The study of shifting cultivation, *Current Anthropology*, 2:27–64.

Cook, S. F., 1946. Human sacrifice and warfare as factors in the demography of pre-colonial Mexico, *Human Biology*, 18:81–100.

Duncan, Otis Dudley, 1961. From social system to ecosystem, *Sociological Inquiry*, 31:140–49.

Durkheim, Emile, 1912. *Les formes élémentaires de la vie religieuse*. Paris, Alcan.

———— 1938. *The Rules of Sociological Method.* 8th ed. Sarah A. Solovay and John H. Mueller, trans. George E. G. Catlin, ed. Glencoe, N.Y., Free Press.
———— 1961. *The Elementary Forms of the Religious Life.* John Ward Swain, trans. New York, Collier.

Elman, Robert, 1951. *Surgical Care. A Practical Physiologic Guide.* New York, Appleton-Century-Crofts.
Etkin, Wm., 1963. Theories of socialization and communication, *Social Behavior and Evolution among the Vertebrates.* Wm. Etkin, ed. Chicago, University of Chicago.

Fei, Hsiao-Kung, 1945. *Earthbound China.* Chicago, University of Chicago.
Firth, Raymond, 1929. *Primitive Economics of the New Zealand Maori.* London, Routledge.
———— 1950. *Primitive Polynesian Economy.* New York, Humanities Press.
Food and Agriculture Organization of the United Nations, 1950. *Calorie Requirements. Report of the Committee on Calorie Requirements.* FAO Nutritional Studies #5. Rome, FAO.
———— 1955. *Protein Requirements.* FAO Nutritional Studies #16 Rome, FAO.
———— 1957. *Calorie Requirements. Report of the Second Committee on Calorie Requirements.* FAO Nutritional Studies #15. Rome, FAO.
———— 1964. *Protein: At the Heart of the World Food Problem.* World Food Problems #5. Rome, FAO.
Frake, Charles O., 1962. Cultural ecology and ethnography, *American Anthropologist, 64:*53–59.
Frank, Lawrence K., 1966. Tactile communication, *Culture and Communication.* Alfred G. Smith, ed. New York, Holt, Rinehart, Winston. Reprinted from *Genetic Psychology Monographs, 56:*209–55.
Freeman, J. D., 1955. *Iban Agriculture. A Report on the Shifting Cultivation of Hill Rice by the Iban of Sarawak.* London, Her Majesty's Stationery Office.
Freud, Sigmund, 1907. Obsessive actions and religious practices, Z. *Religionspsychol.,* vol. I, no. 1, pp. 4–12, trans. in *The Standard Edition of the Complete Psychological Works of Sigmund Freud.* IX. James Strachey, gen. ed. London, Hogarth, 1959.

Glasse, Robert, 1959. Revenge and redress among the Huli: A preliminary account, *Mankind, 5:*273–89.
Gluckman, Max, 1954. *Rituals of Rebellion in Southeast Africa.* The Frazer lecture, 1952. Manchester, Eng., Manchester University.
———— 1962. Les rites de passage. *The Ritual of Social Relations.* Max Gluckman, ed. Manchester, Eng., Manchester University.
Goffman, Erving, 1956. The nature of deference and demeanor, *American Anthropologist, 58:*473–503.
Goldman, Stanford, 1960. Further consideration of cybernetic aspects of ho-

meostasis, *Self-Organizing Systems.* M. C. Yovits and Scott Cameron, eds. New York, Pergamon Press.

Goodenough, Ward, 1955. A problem in Malayo-Polynesian social organization, *American Anthropologist, 57*:71–83.

Hagen, Everett E., 1962. *On the Theory of Social Change.* Homewood, Ill., Dorsey.

Hamilton, L., 1955. Indigenous versus introduced vegetables in the village dietary, *The Papua and New Guinea Agricultural Journal,* 10:54–57.

Harris, Marvin, 1965. The myth of the sacred cow, *Man, Culture, and Animals.* Anthony Leeds and Andrew P. Vayda, eds. Washington, D.C., American Association for the Advancement of Science.

——— n.d. Cultural energy. Unpublished paper.

Haswell, M., *Economics of Agriculture in a Savannah Village.* Colonial Research Studies #8. London, H.M.S.O.

Hatfield, Charlotte, 1954. *Food Composition Tables—Minerals and Vitamins— for International Use.* FAO Nutritional Studies #11. Rome, FAO.

Hawley, Amos, 1944. Ecology and human ecology, *Social Forces,* 22:398–405.

Helm, June, 1962. The ecological approach in anthropology, *The American Journal of Sociology,* 67:630–39.

Hempel, Carl, 1959. The logic of functional analysis, *Symposium on Sociological Theory.* L. Gross, ed. Evanston, Ill., Row, Peterson.

Hendrix, Gertrude, Jacques D. Van Vlack, and William Mitchell, 1966. *Equine-Human Linked Behavior in the Post-natal and Subsequent Care of Highly-Bred Horses.* Paper and film presented to the annual meeting of the American Association for the Advancement of Science, Dec. 26, 1966.

Hinde, R. A., and N. Tinbergen, 1958. The comparative study of species specific behavior, *Behavior and Evolution.* A. Roe and G. G. Simpson, eds. New Haven, Yale University.

Hipsley, E. H., and F. W. Clements, 1947. *Report of the New Guinea Nutrition Survey Expedition.* Canberra, Australia, Department of External Territories.

Hipsley, E. H., and Nancy Kirk, 1965. *Studies of Dietary Intake and the Expenditure of Energy by New Guineans.* South Pacific Commission Technical Paper #147. Noumea, New Caledonia.

Hitchcock, Nancy, 1962. Composition of New Guinea Foodstuffs. Unpublished.

Homans, George C., 1941. Anxiety and ritual: The theories of Malinowski and Radcliffe-Brown, *American Anthropologist, 43*:164–72.

Houssay, Bernardo Alberto, et al., 1955. *Human Physiology,* 2d ed. Juan T. Lewis and Olive T. Lewis, trans. New York, McGraw-Hill.

Izikowitz, Karl Gustav, 1951. *Lamet, Hill Peasants in French Indochina.* Göteborg, Sweden, Etnografiska Museet.

Jay, Phyllis, 1963. The Indian Langur Monkey, *Primate Social Behavior.* Charles H. Southwick, ed. Princeton, Van Nostrand.

Kluckhohn, Clyde, 1944. *Navaho Witchcraft.* Papers of the Peabody Museum of American Archaeology and Ethnology 22, #2. Cambridge, Mass., Harvard University.

Kroeber, A., 1939. *Cultural and Natural Areas of North America.* Berkeley, University of California.

Langley, Doreen, 1947. Part 4, *Report of the New Guinea Nutrition Survey Expedition.* E. H. Hipsley and F. W. Clements, eds. Canberra, Australia, Department of External Territories.

Large, Alfred, and Charles G. Johnson, 1948. Proteins as related to burns, *Proteins and Amino Acids in Nutrition.* Melville Sahyun, ed. New York, Reinhold.

Lawrence, Peter, 1964. *Road Belong Cargo.* Manchester, Eng., Manchester University.

Leach, E. R., 1954. *Political Systems of Highland Burma.* Boston, Beacon.

Linton, Robert, 1955. *The Tree of Culture.* New York, Knopf.

Livingstone, Frank B., 1958. Anthropological implications of sickle cell gene distribution in West Africa, *American Anthropologist,* 60:533–62.

Löffler, Lorenz G., 1960. Bodenbedarf und Ertragsfaktor in Brandrodungsbau, *Tribus,* 9:39–43.

Lund, Charles C., and Stanley M. Levenson, 1948. Protein nutrition in surgical patients, *Proteins and Amino Acids in Nutrition.* Melville Sahyun, ed. New York, Reinhold.

Luzbetak, Louis J., 1954. The socio-religious significance of a New Guinea pig festival, parts I and II, *Anthropological Quarterly,* 2:59–80, 102–28.

Malinowski, Bronislau, 1948. *Magic Science and Religion and Other Essays.* Boston, Beacon.

Massal, E., and Jacques Barrau, 1956. *Food Plants of the South Sea Islands.* South Pacific Commission Technical Paper #94. Noumea, New Caledonia.

Meggitt, M. J., 1958. The Enga of the New Guinea highlands: some preliminary observations, *Oceania,* 28:253–330.

———— 1962. Growth and decline of agnatic descent groups among the Mae Enga of the New Guinea highlands, *Ethnology,* 1:158–67.

———— 1965. *The Lineage System of the Mae Enga of New Guinea.* Edinburgh and London, Oliver and Boyd.

Merton, Robert K., 1949. *Social Theory and Social Structure.* Glencoe, N.Y., Free Press.

Moore, Francis D., 1959. *Metabolic Care of the Surgical Patient.* Philadelphia and London, Saunders.

Moore, Oman Khayyam, 1957. Divination—A new perspective, *American Anthropologist,* 59:64–74.

Miller, Robert J., 1964. Cultures as religious structures, *Symposium on New Approaches to the Study of Religion.* Proceedings of the 1964 annual spring meeting of The American Ethnological Society. June Helm, ed. Seattle, University of Washington.

National Academy of Sciences, 1963. *Evaluation of Protein Quality.* National Research Council Publication 1100. Washington, D.C., NAS-NRC.

Newman, Philip, 1964. Religious belief and ritual in a New Guinea society, *American Anthropologist,* vol. 66, no. 4, part 2, pp. 257–72.

Newton, Kenneth, 1960. Shifting cultivation and crop rotations in the tropics, *Papua and New Guinea Agricultural Journal,* 13:81–118.

Odum, Eugene P., 1959. *Fundamentals of Ecology,* 2d ed. Philadeilphia, Saunders.

Oliver, Douglas, 1955. *A Solomon Island Society; Kinship and Leadership among the Siuai of Bougainville.* Cambridge, Mass., Harvard University.

Oomen, H. A. P. C., 1961. The nutrition situation in western New Guinea, *Journal of Tropical Geography and Medicine,* 13:321–35.

——— 1961. The Papuan child as a survivor, *The Journal of Tropical Pediatrics and African Child Health,* 6:103–21.

Oosterwal, G., 1961. *People of the Tor: A Cultural-Anthropological Study on the Tribes of the Tor Territory.* Assen, Netherlands, Koninklijke Van Gorcum.

Osmund, A., and W. Wilson, 1961. *Tables of Composition of Australian Foods.* Canberra, Australia, Commonwealth Department of Health.

Peters, F. E., 1958. *The Chemical Composition of South Pacific Foods.* South Pacific Commission Technical Paper #115. Noumea, New Caledonia.

Powers, W. T., R. K. Clark, and R. L. McFarland, 1960. A general feedback theory of human behavior, *Perceptual and Motor Skills,* 11:71–88. Reprinted in *Communication and Culture.* Alfred G. Smith, ed. New York, Holt, Rinehart, Winston, 1966.

Radcliffe-Brown, A. R., 1952. Religion and society, *Structure and Function in Primitive Society.* Glencoe, N.Y., Free Press.

Rappaport, Roy A., 1963. Aspects of man's influence upon island ecosystems: alteration and control, *Man's Place in the Island Ecosystem.* F. R. Fosberg, ed. Honolulu, Bishop Museum.

——— 1966. Ritual in the ecology of a New Guinea people. Columbia University, doctoral dissertation.

——— 1967. Ritual regulation of environmental relations among a New Guinea people, *Ethnology,* 6:17–30.

Read, Kenneth, 1952. Nama cult of the central highlands, New Guinea, *Oceania,* 33:1–25.

Reay, Marie, 1959. *The Kuma: Freedom and Conformity in the New Guinea Highlands.* Melbourne, Australia, Melbourne University Press for the Australian National University.

Reik, Theodor, 1962. *Ritual: Four Psychoanalytic Studies.* Douglas Bryan, trans. New York, Grove Press.

Richards, P. W., 1964. *The Tropical Rain Forest. An Ecological Study.* Cambridge, Eng., The University Press.

Robbins, Ross G., 1961. The vegetation of New Guinea, *Australian Territories,* vol. 1, no. 6, pp. 1–12.

――― 1963. The anthropogenic grasslands of New Guinea, *Proceedings of the* UNESCO *Symposium on Humid Tropic Vegetation. Goroka, 1960.* Canberra, Australia, Government Printer.

Ryan, D'arcy, 1959. Clan formation in the Mendi Valley, *Oceania,* 29:257–90.

Sahlins, Marshall David, 1958. *Social Stratification in Polynesia.* Seattle, University of Washington.

――― 1963. Poor man, rich man, big-man, chief: Political types in Melanesia and Polynesia, *Comparative Studies in Society and History,* 5:285–303.

――― 1965. Exchange-value and the diplomacy of primitive trade, *Essays in Economic Anthropology.* Proceedings of the American Ethnological Society. June Helm, ed. Seattle, University of Washington.

Salisbury, Richard F., 1962. Ceremonial economics and political equilibrium, *Actes du VIᵉ Congres International des Science Anthropologiques et Ethnologiques.* I. Paris.

Schwartz, Theodore, 1962. Systems of areal integration: some considerations based on the Admiralty Islands of northern Melanesia, *Anthropological Forum,* 1:56–97.

Simpson, George Gaylord, 1962. Comments on cultural evolution, *Evolution and Man's Progress.* H. Hoagland and R. W. Burhoe, eds. New York, Columbia University.

Stott, D. H., 1962. Cultural and natural checks on population growth, *Culture and the Evolution of Man.* M. F. Ashley Montagu, ed. New York, Oxford University.

Street, John, 1965. Evaluation of the concept of carrying capacity. Unpublished paper, delivered at meeting of Association of Pacific Coast Geographers, Portland, Ore., June 18, 1965.

Tinbergen, N., 1952. The evolution of animal communication—a critical examination of methods, *Symposium of the Zoological Society of London,* 8:1–6.

――― 1963. The evolution of signalling devices, *Social Behavior and Organization among the Vertebrates.* Wm. Etkin, ed. Chicago, University of Chicago.

Vayda, Andrew P., and E. A. Cook, 1964. Structural variability in the Bismarck Mountain cultures of New Guinea: a preliminary report, *Transactions of the New York Academy of Sciences.* ser. II, vol. 26, no. 7, pp. 798–803.

Vayda, Andrew P., Anthony Leeds, and David Smith, 1961. The place of pigs in Melanesian subsistance, *Proceedings of The American Ethnological Society.* Viola E. Garfield, ed. Seattle, University of Washington.

Vayda, Andrew P., and Roy A. Rappaport, 1963. Island cultures, *Man's Place in the Island Ecosystem.* F. R. Fosberg, ed. Honolulu, Bishop Museum.

――― in press. Ecology, cultural and non-cultural, *Introduction to Cultural*

Anthropology: Essays in the Scope and Methods of the Science of Man. James A. Clifton, ed. Boston, Houghton Mifflin.

Venkatachalam, P. S., 1962. *A Study of the Diet, Nutrition and Health of the People of the Chimbu Area.* Monograph #4. Territory of Papua and New Guinea, Department of Public Health.

Waddington, C. H., 1960. Panel three: Man as an organism, *Evolution after Darwin,* vol. III, *Issues in Evolution.* Sol Tax, ed. Chicago, University of Chicago, pp. 171–73.

Wallace, Anthony F. C., 1966. *Religion: An Anthropological View.* New York, Random House.

White, Leslie, 1949. *The Science of Culture.* New York, Farrar Straus.

Wolf, Eric R., 1955. Types of Latin American peasantry: A preliminary discussion, *American Anthropologist,* 57:452–71.

Wurm, Stephan, 1964. Australian New Guinea Highlands languages and the distribution of their typological features, *American Anthropologist,* vol. 66, no. 4, part 2, pp. 77–97.

Wynne-Edwards, V. C., 1962. *Animal Dispersion in Relation to Social Behavior.* Edinburgh and London, Oliver and Boyd.

——— 1965. Self regulating system in populations of animals, *Science, 147:* 1543–47.

Zintel, Harold A., 1964. Nutrition in the care of the surgical patient, *Modern Nutrition in Health and Disease,* 3d ed. Michael G. Wohl and Robert S. Goodhart, eds. Philadelphia, Lee and Febiger.

Zucker, Theodore F., and Lois M. Zucker, 1964. Nutrition and natural resistance to infection, *Modern Nutrition in Health and Disease,* 3d ed. Michael G. Wohl and Robert S. Goodhart, eds. Philadelphia, Lee and Febiger.

SUPPLEMENTARY BIBLIOGRAPHY FOR THE 1984 EDITION

Arensberg, Conrad, 1961. The community as object and sample, *American Anthropologist,* 63:241–64.

Austin, J. L., 1962. *How to Do Things with Words.* Oxford, Oxford University.

Bateson, Gregory, 1963. The role of somatic change in evolution, *Evolution,* 17:529–39. Reprinted in *Steps to an Ecology of Mind.* New York, Ballantine, 1972.

——— 1972. The logical categories of learning and communication, *Steps to an Ecology of Mind.* New York, Ballantine.

Beckerman, Stephan, 1983. Does the swidden ape the jungle? *Human Ecology, 11:1–12.*

Bennett, John, 1976. *The Ecological Transition*. New York, Pergamon Press.

Bergmann, Frithjof, 1975. On the inadequacies of functionalism, *Michigan Discussions in Anthropology*, 1:2–23.

Bergson, Henri, 1935. *The Two Sources of Morality and Religion*. New York, Henry Holt.

Berlin, Brent, D. Breedlove, and P. Raven, 1974. *Principles of Tzeltal Plant Classification: An Introduction to the Botanical Ethnography of a Mayan-speaking People of the Highland Chiapas*. New York, Academic Press.

Boserup, Ester, 1965. *The Conditions of Agricultural Growth; the Economics of Agrarian Change under Population Pressure*. London, Allen and Unwin.

Brookfield, Harold, 1972. Intensification and disintensification in Pacific agriculture: A theoretical approach, *Pacific Viewpoint*, 13:30–48.

Brookfield, H. C., and Paula Brown, 1963. *Struggle for Land*. Melbourne, Australia, Oxford University.

Brown, Paula, 1979. Change and the boundaries of systems in highland New Guinea: The Chimbu, *Social and Ecological Systems*. P. C. Burnham and R. F. Ellen, eds. A.S.A. Monograph #18. London, Academic Press.

Brown, Robert, 1963. *Explanation in Social Science*. Chicago, Aldine.

Buchbinder, Georgeda, 1973. Maring microadaptation: A study of demographic, nutritional, genotypic, and phenotypic variation in a Highland New Guinea population. Ph.D. diss., Columbia University.

—— 1976. Endemic cretinism: A by-product of culture contact, *Nutrition and Anthropology in Action*. T. K. Fitzgerald, ed. Amsterdam, Van Gorcum Press.

—— 1977. Nutritional stress and population decline among the Maring of New Guinea, *Malnutrition, Behavior, and Social Organization*. Lawrence S. Greene, ed. New York, Academic Press.

Buchbinder, G., and P. Clark, 1971. The Maring people of the Bismarck ranges of New Guinea, *Human Biology in Oceania*, 1:121–33.

Bultmann, R., 1967. The Greek and Hellenistic use of *Alethia*, *Theological Dictionary of the New Testament*, vol. 1. Gerhard Kittel, ed. Grand Rapids, William B. Erdmans.

Burnham, Phillip, 1979. Permissive ecology and structural conservatism in Gbaya society, *Social and Ecological Systems*. P. C. Burnham and R. F. Ellen, eds. A.S.A. Monograph #18. London, Academic Press.

Catton, William R., 1978. Carrying capacity, overshoot and the quality of life, *Major Social Issues*. M. Yinger and S. J. Cutler, eds. New York, The Free Press.

Clarke, William, 1966. From extensive to intensive shifting cultivation: A succession from New Guinea, *Ethnology*, 5:347–59.

—— 1971. *People and Place.* Berkeley, University of California.

—— 1982. Comment on James Peoples' "Individual or Group Advantage? A Reinterpretation of the Maring Ritual Cycle," *Current Anthropology,* 23:301.

Colinvaux, P., 1973. *Introduction to Ecology.* New York, John Wiley.

Collins, Paul, 1965. Functional analyses in the symposium "Man, culture, and animals," *Man, Culture, and Animals.* Anthony Leeds and Andrew P. Vayda, eds. Washington, D.C., American Association for the Advancement of Science 78.

Conklin, Harold C., 1957. *Hanunoo Agriculture; A Report on an Integral System of Shifting Cultivation in the Philippines.* FAO Forestry Development Paper #12. Rome, Food and Agricultural Organization of the United Nations.

Cook, Earl, 1971. The flow of energy in an industrial society, *Scientific American,* 225(Sept.):134–44.

Cook, Scott, 1973. Production, ecology, and economic anthropology: notes toward an integrated frame of reference, *Social Science Information,* 12:25–52.

Diener, Paul, and Eugene E. Robkin, 1978. Ecology, evolution, and the search for cultural origins: the question of Islamic pig prohibition, *Current Anthropology,* 19:493–540.

Dubos, René, 1965. *Man Adapting.* New Haven, Yale University.

Durkheim, Emile, 1938. *The Rules of Sociological Method.* 6th ed. George E. G. Catlin, ed. Sarah A. Solovay and John H. Mueller, trans. Glencoe, Ill., Free Press.

Ellen, Roy, 1982. *Environment, Subsistence, and System.* Cambridge, Eng., Cambridge University.

Fabian, Johannes, 1982. On Rappaport's *Ecology, Meaning, and Religion. Current Anthropology,* 23:205–09.

Flannery, Kent, 1972. The cultural evolution of civilizations, *Annual Review of Ecology and Systematics,* 3:399–426.

Food and Agriculture Organization/World Health Organization, 1973. *Energy and Protein Requirements.* WHO Nutrition Meetings Report, Series #52.

Frake, Charles O., 1962. Cultural ecology and ethnography, *American Anthropologist,* 64:53–59.

Friedman, Jonathan, 1974. Marxism, structuralism, and vulgar materialism, *Man,* n.s., 9:444–69.

—— 1979. Hegelian ecology: Between Rousseau and the world spirit, *Social and Ecological System.* P. C. Burnham and Roy Ellen, eds. A.S.A. Monograph #18. London, Academic Press.

Frisancho, Roberto, 1975. Functional adaptation to high altitude hypoxia, *Science*, 187:313–19.

Hames, Raymond, 1983. Monoculture, polyculture, and polyvariety in tropical swidden cultivation, *Human Ecology*, 11:13–34.

Harris, Marvin, 1966. The cultural ecology of India's sacred cattle, *Current Anthropology*, 7:51–60.

Heidegger, Martin, 1959. *An Introduction to Metaphysics*. Ralph Manheim, trans. New Haven, Yale University.

Hempel, Carl, 1959. The logic of functional analysis, *Symposium in Sociological Theory*. Llewelyn Gross, ed. Evanston, Row, Peterson.

Heywood, Peter, 1981. The effect of changing diet on nutritional health in the Pacific. Manuscript prepared for the UNDP/SPC Regional Meeting (Suva) on the effects of urbanization and Western diet on the health of Pacific Island populations.

Hockett, Charles, and Robert Ascher, 1964. The human revolution, *Current Anthropology*, 5:135–68.

Holling, C. S., 1973. Resilience and stability of ecological systems, *Annual Review of Ecology and Systematics*, 4:1–23.

Jelliffe, D. B., 1966. *The Assessment of the Nutritional Status of the Community*. Geneva, WHO Monograph Series #53.

Jorgensen, Joseph, ed., 1972. *Biology and Culture in Modern Perspective*. San Francisco, W. H. Freeman and Co.

Kalmus, Hans, 1966. Control hierarchies, *Regulation and control of living systems*. H. Kalmus, ed. New York, Wiley.

Keesing, Roger, 1974. Theories of culture, *Annual Review of Anthropology*, 3:73–95.

Kelly, Raymond, and Roy A. Rappaport, 1975. Function, generality, and explanatory power: A commentary and response to Bergmann's arguments, *Michigan Discussions in Anthropology*, 1:24–44.

Kirk, G. S., 1954. *Heraclitus, the Cosmic Fragments*. Cambridge, Eng., Cambridge University.

Kleinknecht, H., 1967. The *Logos* in the Greek and Hellenistic world, *Theological Dictionary of the New Testament*, vol. 4. Gerhard Kittel, ed. Grand Rapids, William B. Erdmans.

Lasch, Christopher, 1978. *The Culture of Narcissism: American Life in an Age of Diminishing Expectations*. New York, Norton.

Lee, Richard B., 1976. !Kung spatial organization: An ecological and historical perspective, *Kalahari Hunter-Gatherers, Studies of the !Kung San and Their Neighbors*. R. Lee and I. De Vore, eds. Cambridge, Harvard University.

Lewontin, Richard, 1969. The meaning of stability, *Diversity and Stability in Ecological Systems*. Brookhaven Symposia in Biology, 22:13–24.

Little, M. A. and G. E. B. Morren, 1977. *Ecology, Energetics, and Human Viability*. Dubuque, William Brown.

Lowman-Vayda, Cherry, 1971. Maring big men, *Politics in New Guinea*. R. M. and P. Larence, eds. Nedlands, University of Western Australia.

———— 1980. Environment, society and health: Ecological bases of community growth and decline in the Maring region of Papua New Guinea. Ph. D. diss., Columbia University.

Manner, Harley, 1981. Ecological succession in new and old Swiddens of Montane Papua New Guinea, *Human Ecology*, 9:359–78.

Margalef, Ramon, 1968. *Perspectives in Ecological Theory*. Chicago, University of Chicago.

McArthur, Margaret, 1974. Review of *Pigs for the Ancestors*, *Oceania*, 45:87–123.

———— 1977. Nutritional research in Melanesia: A second look at the Tsembaga, *Subsistence and Survival: Rural Ecology in the Pacific*. T. Bayliss-Smith and R. G. Feachem, eds. London, Academic Press.

McCay, Bonnie, 1978. Systems ecology, people ecology, and the anthropology of fishing communities, *Human Ecology*, 6:397–422.

Meggitt, Mervyn J., 1962. *The Desert People*. Sydney, Angus and Robertson.

———— 1965. *The Lineage System of the Mae/Enga of New Guinea*. Edinburgh and London, Oliver and Boyd.

Miller, James, 1965a. Living systems: Basic concepts, *Behavioral Science*, 10:193–257.

———— 1965b. Living systems: Structure and process, *Behavioral Science*, 10:337–79.

Monod, Jacques, 1972. *Chance and Necessity*. New York, Random House.

Moran, Emilio, 1983. Limitations and advances in ecosystems research, *The Ecosystem Concept in Anthropology*. Emilio Moran, ed. American Association for the Advancement of Science, Selected Symposia Series. In press.

Morren, G. E. B., 1977. From hunting to herding: Pigs and the control of energy in Montane New Guinea, *Subsistence and Survival: Rural Ecology in the Pacific*. T. Bayliss-Smith and R. G. Feachem, eds. London, Academic Press.

Murphy, Robert, 1970. Basin ethnography and ecological theory, *Languages and Cultures of Western North America*. Pocatello, Idaho State University.

Nagel, Ernst, 1961. *The Structure of Science*. New York, Harcourt, Brace and World.

National Academy of Sciences, 1977. *Proceedings of a Workshop: Impact of Infection on Nutritional Status of the Host*. American Journal of Clinical Nutrition, 30:1203–1566.

Odum, Eugene P., 1969. The strategy of ecosystem development, *Science*, 164:262–70.

Orlove, Benjamin, 1980. Ecological anthropology, *Annual Review of Anthropology*, 9:235–73.

Ortiz, Alphonso, 1969. The Tewa World, Space, Time, Being and Becoming in a Pueblo Society. Chicago: Chicago University Press.

Ortner, Sherry, 1984. Theory in anthropology since the sixties, *Comparative Studies in Society and History*, 26 (in press).

Pattee, H. H., ed., 1973. *Hierarchy Theory*. New York, Braziller.

Peoples, James G., 1982. Individual or group advantage? A reinterpretation of the Maring ritual cycle, *Current Anthropology*, 23:291–310.

Piaget, Jean, 1971. *Structuralism*. London, Routledge and Kegan Paul.

Prigogine, I., 1961. *Introduction to the Thermodynamics of Irreversible Processes*. New York, Interscience.

———— 1980. *From Being to Becoming: Time and Complexity in the Physical Sciences*. San Francisco, H. Freeman.

Prigogine, I., P. Allan, and R. Herman, n.d. The evolution of complexity and the laws of nature. Manuscript.

Rappaport, Roy A., 1963. Aspects of man's influence on island ecosystems: Alteration and control, *Man's Place in the Island Ecosystem*. F. R. Fosberg, ed. Honolulu, Bishop Museum.

———— 1968. *Pigs for the Ancestors: Ritual in the Ecology of a New Guinea People*. New Haven, Yale University.

———— 1969. Some suggestions concerning concept and method in ecological anthropology, *Contributions to Anthropology: Ecological Essay*. D. Damas, ed. Ottowa, National Museums of Canada Bulletin #230.

———— 1970a. Purpose, property, and environmental disaster, *Science Looks at Itself*, National Science Teachers Association, eds. New York, Charles Scribner's Sons.

———— 1970b. Sanctity and adaptation, *Io*, 7:46–71. Paper presented at the Wenner-Gren Conference on the Moral and Aesthetic Structure of Human Adaptation, Burg Wartenstein, 1969. Reprinted in *Coevolution*, 1 (Summer) 1977.

———— 1971a. The flow of energy in an agricultural society, *Scientific American*, 225 (Sept.):116–32.

———— 1971b. Nature, culture, and ecological anthropology, *Man, Culture, and Society*, rev. ed. H. Shapiro, ed. New York, Oxford University.

———— 1971c. Ritual, sanctity, and cybernetics, *American Anthropologist*, 73:59–76.

———— 1971d. The sacred in human evolution, *Annual Review of Ecology and Systematics*, 2:23–44.

———— 1972. Forests and the purposes of men, *"Fire in the Environment"* Symposium Proceedings. Forest Service, USDA publication FS–276.

———— 1976a. Adaptation and maladaptation in social systems, *The Ethical Basis of Economic Freedom*. Ivan Hill, ed. Chapel Hill, American Viewpoint.

———— 1976b. Liturgies and lies, *International Yearbook for the Sociology of Religion and Knowledge*, 10:75–104.

———— 1977. Ecology, adaptation, and the ills of functionalism (being, among other things, a response to Jonathan Friedman), *Michigan Discussions in Anthropology*, 2:138–90.

———— 1978a. Adaptation and the structure of ritual, *Human Behavior and Adaptation*. N. Blurton-Jones and V. Reynolds, eds. Society for the Study of Human Biology Symposium No. 18. London, Taylor and Francis.

———— 1978b. Maladaptation in social systems, *Evolution in Social Systems*. J. Friedman and M. Rolands, eds. London, Duckworth.

———— 1979a. Adaptive structure and its disorders, *Ecology, Meaning, and Religion*. Richmond, Calif., North Atlantic Books.

———— 1979b. On cognized models, *Ecology, Meaning, and Religion*. Richmond, Calif., North Atlantic Books.

———— 1979c. Ecology, adaptation, and the ills of functionalism, *Ecology, Meaning, and Religion*. Richmond, Calif., North Atlantic Books.

———— 1979d. The obvious aspects of ritual, *Ecology, Meaning, and Religion*. Richmond, Calif., North Atlantic Books.

———— 1979e. Sanctity and lies in evolution, *Ecology, Meaning, and Religion*. Richmond, Calif., North Atlantic Books.

———— 1982. Comment on James Peoples' "Individual or Group Advantage? A Reinterpretation of the Maring Ritual Cycle," *Current Anthropology*, 23:303–05.

Reay, Marie, 1959. *The Kuma: Freedom and Conformity in the New Guinea Highlands*. Melbourne, Melbourne University Press for Australian National University.

Romer, Alfred S., 1954. *Man and the Vertebrates*. London, Penguin.

Sahlins, Marshall, 1958. *Social Stratification in Polynesia*. Seattle, University of Washington.

———— 1961. *Moala*. Ann Arbor, University of Michigan.

———— 1969. Economic anthropology and anthropological economics, *Social Science Information*, 8:13–33.

———— 1972. *Stone Age Economics*. Chicago, Aldine.

———— 1976a. Comment on A. H. Berger, "Structural and Eclectic Revisions of Marxist Strategy: A Cultural Materialist Critique," *Current Anthropology*, 17:298–300.

———— 1976b. *Culture and Practical Reason*. Chicago, University of Chicago.

Sahlins, Marshall, and Elman Service, eds., 1960. *The Evolution of Culture*. Ann Arbor, University of Michigan.

Salisbury, R. F., 1965. The Siane of the eastern highlands, *Gods, Ghosts, and Men in Melanesia*, P. Lawrence and M. J. Meggitt, eds. Melbourne and New York, Oxford University.

Samuels, Michael, 1983. Popreg I: A simulation of population regulation among the Maring of New Guinea, *Human Ecology*, 10:1–45.

Sapir, Edward, 1924. Culture, genuine and spurious, *American Journal of Sociology*, 29:401–29.

Searle, J. R., 1969. *Speech Acts*. Cambridge, Eng., Cambridge University.

Shantzis, S. B., and W. W. Behrens, 1973. Population control mechanisms in a primitive society, *Toward Global Equilibrium*. D. L. Meadows and M. H. Meadows, eds. Cambridge, Mass., Wright-Allen.

Simon, Herbert, 1969. *The Sciences of the Artificial*. Cambridge, Mass., MIT Press.

Slobodkin, Laurence, 1968. Toward a predictive theory of evolution, *Population Biology and Evolution*. R. C. Lewontin, ed. Syracuse, Syracuse University.

Slobodkin, Laurence, and Anatol Rapoport, 1974. An optimal strategy of evolution, *Quarterly Review of Biology*, 49:181–200.

Steward, Julian, 1955. *The Theory of Culture Change*. Urbana, University of Illinois.

Strathern, Andrew, 1971. *The Rape of Moka: Big Men and Ceremonial Exchange in Mourt Hagen, New Guinea*. Cambridge, Eng., Cambridge University.

Street, John M., 1969. An evaluation of the concept of carrying capacity, *Professional Geographer*, 21, no. 2:104–07.

Tillich, Paul, 1957. *The Dynamics of Faith*. New York, Harper & Row.

Turnbull, Colin, 1962. *The Forest People*. New York, Natural History Press.

Vayda, A. P., 1968. Foreword, *Pigs for the Ancestors*. New Haven, Yale University.

———— 1974. Warfare in ecological perspective, *Annual Review of Ecology and Systematics*, 5:183–93.

Vayda, A. P., A. Leeds, and D. Smith, 1961. The place of pigs in Melanesian subsistence, *Proceedings of the 1961 Annual Spring Meeting of the American Ethnological Society.* Seattle, University of Washington.

Vayda, A. P., and B. McCay, 1975. New directions in ecology and ecological anthropology, *Annual Review of Anthropology*, 4:293–306.

———— 1977. Problems in the identification of environmental problems, *Subsistence and Survival: Rural Ecology in the Pacific.* T. Bayliss-Smith and R. G. Feachem, eds. London, Academic Press.

Vayda, A. P. and R. A. Rappaport, 1967. Ecology, cultural and non-cultural, *Introduction to Cultural Anthropology.* J. Clifton, ed. Boston, Houghton-Mifflin.

Wagner, Roy, 1972. *Habu: The Innovation of Meaning in Daribi Religion.* Chicago, University of Chicago.

———— 1977. Scientific and indigenous Papuan conceptualizations of the innate: a semiotic critique of the ecological perspective, *Subsistence and Survival: Rural Ecology in the Pacific.* T. Bayliss-Smith and R. G. Feachem, eds. London: Academic Press.

Wynne-Edwards, V. C., 1962. *Animal Dispersion in Relation to Social Behaviour.* Edinburgh and London, Oliver and Boyd.

Yellen, John E. 1976. Settlement patterns of the !Kung, *Kalahari Hunter-Gatherers, Studies of the !Kung San and Their Neighbors.* R. Lee and I. De Vore, eds. Cambridge, Harvard University.

INDEX

The index covers the 1968 edition. For topics discussed in the Epilogue, see the outline of contents on pages 299–300.